Arranging the Score

Arranging the Score

Portraits of the Great Arrangers

Gene Lees

CASSELL
London and New York

Cassell
Wellington House
125 Strand
London WC2R 0BB

370 Lexington Avenue
New York
NY 10017-6550

First published 2000 by Cassell by arrangement with Bayou Press Ltd

British Library Cataloguing-in-Publication Data
A catalogue record for this book is available from the British Library.

ISBN 0-304-70488-1 (hardback)

Library of Congress Cataloging-in-Publication Data
Lees, Gene.
    Arranging the score: portraits of the great arrangers / Gene Lees.
        p. cm.
    ISBN 0-304-70488-1 (hb.)
    1. Arrangers (Musicians) —Biography. I. Title.

ML390.L43 1999
781.3′7′0922—dc21
[B]   99-042120

Typeset by Kenneth Burnley, Wirral, Cheshire.
Printed and bound in Great Britain by Biddles Ltd, Guildford and King's Lynn.

Contents

To my great and generous friend,

James Lincoln Collier

Foreword

Since the 1920s, any number of commentators have written about the music that has come to be called jazz. From the beginning, the music and what was written about it have been mired in controversy – black versus white, old versus new, small group versus big band. These were significant issues even in the music's early days, and they remain pertinent today.

The first books and articles on the subject were written by collectors and fans. Few of these writers had musical training, an exception being R. D. Darrell. Later on, attempts at scholarship, mostly European, appeared on various aspects of jazz. The authors' hearts were in the right places, but many of these writings were full of misinformation and half-baked opinions and conclusions. Some of them are still being used as source material for jazz studies, thereby perpetuating mythology and falsehoods. One is that both Bix Beiderbecke and Chet Baker could not read music. Though this has been corrected many times, the untruth continues to appear.

Back in those early days of *Down Beat, Metronome, Melody Maker, Le Jazz Hot*, and other publications that came and went, there was a lot of name-calling, back-biting, and unadulterated silliness. But the music was in the mainstream of popular culture, so the controversy was good for business, sold records and magazines, and generated huge amounts of money for a number of artists. The 1940s and 1950s brought new agendas to writings on jazz, especially after the music ceased to be fodder for the "top ten" music charts. At the same time, a new era of jazz writing, criticism, and scholarship emerged. Such volumes as Rudi Blesh's and Harriet Janis' *They All Played Ragtime*, Leonard Feather's *Inside Bebop*, Nat Shapiro and Nat Hentoff's *Hear Me Talking to Ya*, and Marshall Stearns' *The Story of Jazz* were among the pioneering studies of past and current trends, written by informed enthusiasts who generally did their homework by talking to those who created the music. Perhaps some of the interviews were self-serving, conveying questionable "facts", but the sheer wealth of firsthand information, as well as personnel listings for classic records, were by-products of this era of scholarship.

The 1960s reinforced a feeling that the jazz enthusiast was now part of a decreasing minority, with modality, improvisation without key centers, and "free jazz" confusing the issues. There was still more name-calling and back-biting, which in latter years has taken on a disturbing racial polarity. And yet oral history programs, reissue commitments from record labels, and more studies and biographies continued to clear away many of the mysteries of the music's past while sometimes muddying the waters even more.

It was in the early 1960s that a former newspaper editor and reporter and classical-music critic became suddenly visible in the world of jazz. In 1959, Gene Lees became editor of *Down Beat*, bringing the magazine into a new era and sharply raising the level of literacy. After he left the magazine – at the end of 1961 – his writing began to appear in New York publications, including *Saturday Review, Stereo Review*, and *High Fidelity*, and the audience for his sharp, thought-provoking articles and reviews grew. He knew the people he wrote about – Bill Evans and Gerry Mulligan, for example, were among his closest friends – and they trusted him with information they would not share with any other writer, because they knew he would use what they said respectfully and accurately. Many people will tell you they read his stuff no matter what the subject just for the quality of the writing. He was (and is) often feisty, opinionated, provocative, and stubborn on matters of principle. He loves music of all kinds, not just jazz, and he is intensely loyal to those he respects.

And singers will tell you that he is one of the finest lyricists in the English language. What fewer people know is that he is an outstanding singer, although he rarely does it. If you hear him at the top of his form – and I have heard him that way – he is just about the best there is. When he does an occasional gig somewhere, the room is likely to be full of singers.

One of the things that first drew me to his writing was that he paid attention to arrangers and composers, something few others in the field did, and not only in the field of jazz. He paid attention to the people who wrote in the pop field, such as Nelson Riddle, and movies, the latter including such figures as Hugo Friedhofer, David Raksin, and Henry Mancini.

Arrangers tend to be mystery characters to the public at large. Even music lovers have little insight into the skills necessary to being a professional arranger, how an arrangement is created, the wide latitude in pay scale from a few dollars to a few thousand per arrangement, the lack of copyright coverage, the indignities and tactless behavior of singers, managers, record producers, label owners, and conductors that go with the territory of creating music for hire, the realities of writing quality music and often not being credited or acknowledged for it, and yet the sheer thrill of hearing a piece of music brought to life by skilled musicians before the ink is dry. No one has articulated these ideas with greater understanding and love than Gene Lees.

No one celebrates the people who continue to write for singers and ensembles as much as he does.

This was evident to me when I read his articles in *High Fidelity*. I was a student, and of course fan, in those days, wanting to learn more about arranging and arrangers. Gene was the only one writing about them in a mainstream publication. He discussed Paul Weston, Johnny Mandel, Robert Farnon, Gerry Mulligan, and Hugo Friedhofer, all of whom I wanted to know more about. He wrote about excellent albums that the record labels scarcely promoted at all, such as Patrick Williams' *Threshold*. One of the reasons, I suspect, that he did this is that he knew beyond question far more about classical music than anyone else in the field of jazz and pop journalism.

I bought the albums he discussed, which was not always easy, and I treasured them as he did. He was one of the few writers of prose to show me what pop and jazz music for ensembles could be, instead of where it appeared to be headed. I dug up long-out-of-print recordings of the great arrangers, and gave myself an invaluable education. As a result, I account Gene Lees one of the most important influences in my evolution as a composer, arranger, conductor, and historian.

The essays in the present volume are about arrangers, all of whom are also composers. They appeared first in his publication *Jazzletter*, in which for nearly twenty years he has had the freedom to discuss at whatever length seems appropriate the work of those he respects, and also of the conditions in which they have to work. He is an American treasure, finding the facts, celebrating the best that popular music and jazz have to offer, and helping us continue to explore their riches. One of my heroes, Johnny Mandel (to whom Gene introduced me, incidentally), said it best:

"Most people write of music and musicians like they are fish in an aquarium. Gene is always in there swimming with the rest of us."

JEFFREY SULTANOF

Jeffrey Sultanof has been in music publishing for more than twenty years. He is currently a consultant with Hal Leonard Corporation, where he has edited and produced books on the music of Sonny Rollins, Gil Evans, Gerry Mulligan, and Billy Taylor. He has written arrangements for Lynn Roberts, the Palm Beach Pops Orchestra and, among others, Gene Lees.

1

Introduction

One sunny summer evening when I was about 13, I saw crowds of people pouring into the hockey arena in Niagara Falls, Ontario, Canada. Curious to know what was attracting them, I parked my bicycle behind the arena (in those days one had little fear that one's bicycle would be stolen) and, in the manner of boys of that age, I sneaked in a back exit. What was going on was a big band. I remember watching as dark-skinned musicians in tuxedos assembled on the stage, holding bright shining brass instruments, taking their seats behind music stands. And then a man sat down at the piano and played something and this assemblage hit me with a wall of sound I can still hear in my head, not to mention my heart. I now can even tell you the name of the piece: it was "Take the 'A' Train," it was written by one Billy Strayhorn, the band was that of Duke Ellington, and the year had to be 1941, for that is the copyright date of that piece.

I learned that bands like this came to the arena every Saturday night in the summer, and I went back the following week and heard another of them.

I was overwhelmed by the experience, shaken to my shoes. It was not just the soloists, although I remember the clowning and prancing and trumpet-playing of someone I realized, in much later retrospect, was Ray Nance with Ellington. The next week, I remember, there was a tenor saxophone player who leaned over backwards almost to the stage floor, and that had to have been Joe Thomas with Jimmie Lunceford. With both bands, it was the *totality* of the sound that captivated me, that radiant wall of brass and saxes and what I would learn to call the rhythm section.

I discussed the experience with my Uncle Harry. When I told him about these bands I'd seen, he encouraged my interest and told me I should pay attention as well to someone called Count Basie.

My Uncle Harry – Henry Charles Flatman, born in London, England – was a trombone player and an arranger. He played in Canadian dance bands in the 1920s and 1930s, and I would hear their "remote" broadcasts on the radio. Once one of the bandleaders dedicated a song to me on the air. I am told that I could identify any instrument in the orchestra by its sound by the time I was 3, but that may be merely romantic family lore.

But what held these instruments together in ensemble passages? I even knew the answer to that: people like my Uncle Harry. I remember him sitting at an upright oaken piano with some sort of big board, like a drawing board, propped above the keyboard. He always had a cigarette dangling from his mouth, and one eye would squint to protect itself from the rising tendrils of smoke, while his pencil made small marks on a big paper mounted on that board: score paper, I realized within a few years. He was, I'm sure he explained to me, writing "arrangements" for the band he played in. I seem to recall that he was the first person to tell me the difference between a major and minor chord. Because of him I was always aware that the musicians in a band weren't just making it up, except in the solos. Somebody wrote the passages they played together.

And so from my earliest days I looked on the record labels for the parenthesized names under the song titles to see who wrote a given piece. When the title wasn't that of some popular song and the record was an instrumental, then chances were that the name was that of the man who composed *and* arranged it. Whether I learned their names from the record labels or from *Metronome* or *Down Beat*, I followed with keen interest the work of the arrangers. I became aware of Eddie Durham, whose name was on Glenn Miller's "Sliphorn Jive" which I just loved (he was actually a Basie arranger); Paul Weston and Axel Stordahl who wrote for Tommy Dorsey; Jerry Gray, who wrote "A String of Pearls," and Bill Finegan, who arranged "Little Brown Jug," both for Glenn Miller; and above all Fletcher Henderson, who wrote much of the book (as I would later learn to call it) of the Benny Goodman band. Later, I became aware of Mel Powell's contributions to the Goodman library, such as "Mission to Moscow" and "The Earl," as well as those of Eddie Sauter, including "Benny Rides Again" and "Clarinet a la King." Jimmy Mundy's contributions to that band included "Swingtime in the Rockies" and "Solo Flight," which introduced many listeners to the brilliance of guitarist Charlie Christian. One of the most significant arrangers was Gene Gifford, who wrote "Smoke Rings" and "Casa Loma Stomp" for the Casa Loma Orchestra led by Glen Gray. He was enormously admired by other arrangers, such as Gil Evans, and was an important, if largely unsung, influence.

The better bandleaders always gave credit to their arrangers, whether of "originals" or standards such as "I've Got My Love to Keep Me Warm," and I became aware of Ben Homer and Frank Comstock with Les Brown, and Ralph Burns, Shorty Rogers, and Neal Hefti with Woody Herman, Ray Conniff with the postwar Artie Shaw band ("'S Wonderful" and "Jumpin' on the Merry Go Round" are his charts) and, later, Bill Holman with various bands; Johnny Mandel with Boyd Raeburn, Woody Herman, and others; and then Thad Jones and Gerald Wilson. Some of the arrangers became bandleaders themselves, including Russ Morgan (whose commercial band gave no hint that he had been an important jazz arranger), Larry Clinton, and Les Brown. And of course, there was Duke Ellington, though he was not an arranger who became a bandleader but a bandleader who evolved into an arranger – and one of the most important composers in jazz; some would say *the* most important. One error: I assumed that Duke Ellington wrote everything his band played, only later becoming aware of the enormous role of Billy Strayhorn, who was kept more or less in the background. Strayhorn of course, not Ellington, wrote the band's latter-year theme, "Take the 'A' Train." I was aware very early that someone named Gerry Mulligan – scarcely older than I, although I did not know that then – wrote "Disc Jockey Jump" for Gene Krupa, and someone named Gil Evans did some gorgeous writing for the Claude Thornhill band.

I daresay the arranger I most admired was Sy Oliver. It was many years later that I met him. He wrote the arrangements for an LP Charles Aznavour recorded in English. I wrote most of the English translations and adaptations for that session, and about all I can remember about the date is the awe I felt in shaking the hand of Sy Oliver.

I was captivated by the Tommy Dorsey band of that period. From about 1939 on, I thought it was the hottest band around. I did not then know that Sy Oliver was the reason. He was born Melvin James Oliver in Battle Creek, Michigan, on 17 December 1910. He began as a trumpet player and, like so many arrangers, trained himself, probably by copying down what he heard on records. In 1933, he joined the Jimmie Lunceford band, playing trumpet and writing for it, and it is unquestionable that some of the arrangements I was listening to that night in Niagara Falls were his. Others were surely by Gerald Wilson.

A few years after his death, Sy's widow, Lillian, told me that Lunceford paid Sy poorly and Sy was about to leave the music business, return to school and become a lawyer. He got a call to have a meeting with Tommy Dorsey. Dorsey told him he would pay him 5,000 dollars a year more (a considerable sum in the 1940s) than whatever Lunceford was giving him, pay him well for each individual arrangement as opposed to the $2.50 per chart (including copying) he got from Lunceford, and give him full writing credits and attendant royalties for his work if Sy would join his band. Furthermore, he told Sy that if he would give him a year, he, Tommy, would rebuild the band in whatever way Sy wanted. Sy took the offer, and Tommy rebuilt the band that had in the past been known for "Marie" and "Song of India" and the like. It became the band of Don Lodice, Fred Stulce, Chuck Peterson, Ziggy Elman, Joe Bushkin, and above all Buddy Rich, who gave it the drive

Sy wanted and whom Sy loved. The change was as radical as that in the Woody Herman band from the Band that Plays the Blues to the First Herd of "Caldonia" and "Your Father's Mustache." It became, in essence, the Sy Oliver band led by Tommy Dorsey, and Sy's compositions and charts included "Well Git It!," "Yes Indeed," "Deep River," and, later on (1944) "Opus No. 1," on which Lillian Oliver received royalties until the day she died, and their son Jeff does now.

When I mentioned to Frank Comstock my admiration for Sy Oliver, he said, "I think Sy touched all of us who were arranging in the 1940s and '50s and later." And then he told me something significant.

Frank said that he learned arranging by transcribing Jimmie Lunceford records, which doubtless meant many Sy Oliver charts. Frank's first important professional job was with Sonny Dunham. "And he was known, as I'm sure you're aware, as the white Lunceford," Frank said. The reason, Frank said, was that when Dunham was starting up his band, Lunceford gave him a whole book of his own charts to help him get off the ground. And Frank was hired precisely because he could write in that Lunceford–Oliver manner.

It occurs to me that I must have listened to Frank Comstock charts at the arena in Niagara Falls, for Les Brown's was one of the bands I saw there.

In the various attempts to define jazz, emphasis is usually put on improvisation. Bill Evans once went so far as to say to me that if he heard an Eskimo improvising within his musical system, assuming there was one, he would define that as jazz. It is an answer that will not do.

There are many kinds of music that are based on, or at least rely heavily on, improvisation, including American bluegrass, Spanish flamenco, Greek dance music, Polish polkas, Gypsy string ensembles, Paraguayan harp bands, and Russian balalaika music. They are not jazz. In the early days of the concerto form, the soloist was expected to improvise his cadenzas; and well-trained church organists were expected, indeed required, to be skilled improvisers, up to and including large forms. Gabriel Fauré was organist at La Madeleine. Chopin and Liszt were master improvisers, and the former's impromptus are what the name implies: improvisations that he later set down on paper, there being no tape recorders then. Doubtless he revised them, but equally doubtless they originated in spontaneous inventions. Beethoven was a magnificent improviser, not to mention Bach and Mozart.

Those who like to go into awed rapture at the single-line improvisation of a Stan Getz might well consider the curious career of Alexander Borodin. First of all he was one of the leading Russian scientists of his time, a practicing surgeon *and* chemist, a professor at the St. Petersburg Medico-Surgical Academy. (He took his doctorate on his thesis on the analogy of arsenic acid with phosphoric acid.) Music was never more than a relaxing hobby for him, and his double career raises some interesting questions about our modern theories on left-brain logical thought and right-brain imaging and spatial information processing. Borodin *improvised* his symphonies before writing them down. And if that seems impressive musicianship, consider Glazunov's. Borodin never wrote his Third Symphony down at all: he improvised the first two movements and his friend Glazunov wrote out the first two movements *from memory* in the summer of 1887, a few months after Borodin's death. (He constructed a third movement out of materials left over from other Borodin works, including the opera *Prince Igor*.)

Most of the Borodin Third Symphony, then, is improvised music. I can't imagine that anyone, even Bill Evans (if he were here), would try to call it jazz.

How then are we to define jazz?

The remark "If you have to ask, you ain't never gonna know," attributed to both Louis Armstrong and Fats Waller, is clearly unsatisfactory, though a certain kind of jazz-lover likes to quote it for reasons that remain obscure. You could say that about many kinds of music. It is an evasion of the difficulty of definition.

A simple definition won't cover all the contingencies, and a complex one will prove ponderous and even meaningless. Even if you offer one of those clumsy (and not fully accurate) definitions such as "an American musical form emphasizing improvisation and a characteristic swing and based on African rhythmic and European harmonic and melodic influences," you have come up with something that conveys nothing to a person who has never heard it. Furthermore, the emphasis on improvisation has always been disproportionate. Many outstanding jazz musicians, including Art Tatum and Louis Armstrong, played solos they had worked out and played the same way night after night. Nat Cole's piano in the heads of such hits as "Embraceable You" were carefully worked out and played the same way repeatedly. Bandleaders of the era would tell you their players *had to* play solos exactly as they did on the records: otherwise, some of the audience to a *live* performance would consider itself cheated or, worse, argue that the player wasn't the one who had performed on the record.

If improvisation will not do as the sole defining characteristic of jazz, and if non-improvisation, as in solos by Louis Armstrong and Art Tatum, does not make it *not* jazz, then what does define it?

If it does not cease to be jazz because the soloist sometimes is not improvising, neither does it cease to be jazz because it is written. It would be difficult to argue that what McKinney's Cotton Pickers played wasn't jazz. The multi-instrumentalist and composer Don Redman – who wrote for Fletcher

Henderson's band before Henderson did – became music director of the Cotton Pickers in 1927 and transformed it in a short time from a novelty group into one of the major jazz orchestras. And its emphasis was not so much on soloists as on the writing: Redman's tightly controlled and precise ensemble arranging, beautifully played.

McKinney's Cotton Pickers was based in Detroit, part of the stable of bands operated by the French-born pianist Jean Goldkette: his National Amusement Corporation fielded more than twenty of them, including one under his own name whose personnel included Frank Trumbauer, Bix Beiderbecke, Tommy and Jimmy Dorsey, Joe Venuti, and Spiegle Willcox (who died in 1999 at 96). One of Goldkette's bands, the Orange Blossoms, became the Casa Loma Orchestra, with pioneering writing by Gene Gifford. Artie Shaw has argued that the "swing era" began as a popular musical movement not with Benny Goodman but with the Casa Loma. Also in Detroit, Redman was writing for the Cotton Pickers and Bill Challis for the Goldkette band, both bands influencing throughout America musicians who listened to them on the radio. Gil Evans in Stockton, California, was listening to Gene Gifford's writing on radio "remotes" by the Casa Loma. Even the Isham Jones band of the 1930s was born in Detroit; it was actually organized by Red Norvo. Given all these factors, there is good reason to consider Detroit – awash in money from both the illegal liquor importation from Canada and the expanding automobile industry and willing to spend it freely on entertainment – one of the significant centers of the swing era's development.

But the structural form of the "big band" must be considered the invention of Ferde Grofé, who wrote for the Art Hickman band that was working in San Francisco and almost certainly was influenced by black musicians who had come there from New Orleans. Hickman hired two saxophone players from vaudeville to function as a "choir" in his dance band. The band caused a sensation, and Paul Whiteman was quick to hire Grofé to write for his band, as he was later to hire Bill Challis and various soloists who had been with Goldkette. The band of Paul Specht was also influential, through the new medium of radio broadcasting: its first broadcasts were made as early as 1920. Don Redman for a time worked in the Specht office, and it may well have been the value of his experience there that influenced Fletcher Henderson to hire him. Henderson also hired Bill Challis. Once Henderson got past his classical background and got the hang of this new instrumentation, he became one of the most influential – perhaps, in the larger scale, *the* most influential – writers of the era.

These explorers had no choice but to experiment with the evolving new instrumentation. There was no academic source from which to derive guidance, there were no treatises on the subject. Classical orchestration texts made little, if any, reference to the use of saxophones, particularly saxophones in groups. And these "arrangers" solved the problem, each making his own significant contribution. While Duke Ellington was making far-reaching experiments by mixing colors from the instruments of the dance-band format, the Grofé–Challis–Redman–Henderson–Carter–Oliver axis had the widest influence around the world in the antiphonal use of the "choirs" of the dance band for high artistic purpose. The instrumentation expanded as time went on. Three saxophones became four, two altos and two tenors, the section's sound vastly deepening when baritone came into widespread use in the 1940s. The brass section too expanded, growing to three trumpets and two trombones, then to four and three, and eventually four and even five trumpets and four trombones, including bass trombone.

This instrumentation may vary, and of late years its range of colors has been extended by the doubling of the saxophone players on flutes and other woodwinds, the occasional addition of French horn (Glenn Miller used a French horn in his Air Force band and Rob McConnell's Boss Brass uses two) and tuba, but structurally the "big band" has remained a superb instrument of expression to the many brilliant writers who have mastered its uses.

The big-band era may be over, but the big-band format is far from moribund. The "ghost" bands go on, though the revel now is ended, and their greatest actors are vanished into thin air: Tommy Dorsey, Woody Herman, Duke Ellington, Count Basie, and more. The Artie Shaw band goes on, though Shaw does not lead it. It is the only ghost band that has a live ghost. (Woody Herman seems to have invented the term "ghost band" and swore his would never become one. It did.)

Curiously, none of the ghost bands has the spirit, the feel, of the original bands. In ways I have never understood, the leaders of these bands somehow infused them with their own anima. Terry Gibbs has attested that, sometimes, when the crowd was thin, Woody Herman would skip the last set and let the band continue on its own; and it never sounded the same as when he was there, Terry said. The current Count Basie band does not have the "feel" of the original. There are of course two things without which a Basie band is not a Basie band: Basie and Freddie Green. But those conspicuous omissions aside, Basie was able to get a groove from that band that eludes his successors.

Far more interesting than the ghost bands are those regional "rehearsal bands" that spring up all over the country, and indeed all over the world, or the recording bands assembled to make albums and, afterwards dissolved – at least until the next project.

As we end the twentieth century, the evolution of jazz *as the art of the soloist* has slowed and, in the example of many young artists imitating past masters, ceased completely. There is an attempt to institutionalize it in concert halls through repertory orchestras such as that at Lincoln Center led by Wynton Marsalis, the Liberace of jazz; and a brisk concomitant interest in finding and performing, when possible, the scores of such "arrangers" as George Handy.

There is an inchoate awareness that it somehow isn't quite kosher to imitate the great soloists of the past, though that hasn't deterred some of the younger crop of players from appropriating a little Bubber Miley here, a little Dizzy Gillespie there; but it is all right to play music by jazz composers of the past, because written music is *meant to be* re-created by groups of musicians. And so the emphasis in the current classicalization of jazz is to a large extent on the writers for past jazz orchestras. Thus jazz is being institutionalized as "classical" music has been, the latter for the good reason that Beethoven couldn't leave us his improvisations; he could leave only *written* music to be *re*-created by subsequent players.

Much of this re-creative work in jazz is rather sterile. It lacks the immediacy, and certainly there is none of the exploratory zeal, that this music had when the "arrangers" first put it on paper. The new stuff being composed and/or arranged is much more interesting. And in any case, all too much of it is focused on Duke Ellington. This incantatory fervor for Ellington has precluded a fitting concert recognition of Fletcher Henderson, Sy Oliver, Eddie Sauter, Ralph Burns, Bill Finegan, Billy May, and so many more who certainly deserve it. Unnoticed even by the public who admired them, these writers ("arrangers" seems a pathetically inadequate term) were building up a body of work that is not receiving the homage that is its due.

Thirty years ago, it seems to me, the writers in the jazz field were not taken seriously at all by some people. All was improvisation, the illusion being that jazz *was* fully improvised, rather than being made up of carefully prepared pieces of vocabulary, what jazz musicians call "licks" – chord voicings, approaches to scale patterns, and the like.

The influence of the big-band arrangers has now spread around the world. The format itself survives, of course, though rarely in full-time bands. It is found in the work of certain bands that come together from time to time, such as in the Clarke-Boland Big Band, now alas gone, based in Germany and led by the late Kenny Clarke and the wonderful Belgian arranger and composer Francy Boland. It is encountered today in the Rob McConnell Boss Brass in Toronto, and in Cologne in the WDR (for Westdeutsche Rundfunk) Big Band. Some years ago, I saw a Russian television variety show that included a big band, playing in the American style – not doing it well, to be sure, but doing it. The format survives in countless bands imitating Glenn Miller.

With the end of the big-band era, various of the arrangers for those bands found work elsewhere. Many of them began writing for singers. Marion

Evans, alumnus of the postwar Tex Beneke–Glenn Miller band, wrote for Steve Lawrence, Tony Bennett, and many others. So did Don Costa, who wrote for, among his clients, Frank Sinatra. Sinatra's primary post-Dorsey arranger was Axel Stordahl and, later, Nelson Riddle, alumnus of the Charlie Spivak band. Peter Matz, alumnus of the Maynard Ferguson band, wrote for just about everybody, as did the German composer Claus Ogerman, particularly noted for his arrangements of Brazilian music. On any given work-day in the 1960s, musicians were rushing around New York City and Los Angeles to play on these vocal sessions, a last hurrah (as we can now see) for the era of great songwriting, a sort of summing-up of that era, the flower reaching its most splendid maturity just before it died.

Some of the arrangers, for a time, got to make records on their own, instrumental albums in which they were allowed to use string sections. Among them were Paul Weston (whose deceptively accessible charts are of a classical purity), Frank de Vol, Frank Comstock, and most conspicuously Robert Farnon.

Many of these arrangers and composers began to influence motion picture music. They turned to film for money, and for a broader orchestral palette. They included Farnon, Benny Carter, Johnny Mandel, Billy Byers, Eddie Sauter, George Duning, Billy May, Patrick Williams, Michel Legrand, Allyn Ferguson, John Dankworth, Dudley Moore (whose gifts as a composer were eclipsed by his success as a comedian and actor), Johnny Keating, Frank Comstock, Pete Rugolo, Oliver Nelson, Roger Kellaway, Lennie Niehaus, Shorty Rogers, Lalo Schifrin, Tom McIntosh, Quincy Jones, J. J. Johnson, Duke Ellington and Billy Strayhorn, Mundell Lowe, and Henry Mancini.

These people introduced into film-scoring elements of non-classical music that had been rigorously excluded. The medium had been dominated by European concert-music influences. Early scores appropriated the styles and techniques of Tchaikovsky, Mendelssohn, Brahms – and sometimes their actual music. Later the twentieth-century Europeans had an influence, up to and including Bartok and Schoenberg, though probably no one was ripped off as much as Stravinsky, whose 1913 *Rite of Spring* is still being quarried by film composers. In his scores for the TV series *Mission: Impossible*, Lalo Schifrin used scale exercises he had written for his teacher Olivier Messaien at the Paris Conservatory.

The appeal of film scoring to "jazz" composers and arrangers is obvious. Most of them had extensive classical training, and strong tastes for twentieth-century European composers, especially Ravel, Debussy, Stravinsky, and Bartok. (William Grant Still, essentially a classical composer but also an arranger who scored "Frenesi" for Artie Shaw, studied with Edgard Varèse as far back as 1927.) This familiarity with the full orchestra inevitably led to a sense of restriction with the brass-and-saxes configuration of dance bands. Despite a general hostility of many jazz fans toward string sections as somehow *effete*, many of the leaders wanted to use them, and some tried to do so, among them Artie Shaw, Tommy Dorsey, Gene Krupa, and Harry James.

These experiments were doomed for two reasons. The first was a matter of orchestral balance. A 100-member symphony orchestra will have a complement of as many as 60 string players. This is due to complex mathematical relationships in acoustics. Putting two instruments on a part does not double the volume of the sound: far from it. To balance the other sections, a symphony orchestra *needs* 60 string players. But the instruments of a standard dance-jazz band can drown even the 60 strings of a symphony orchestra, as appearances of jazz bands with symphony orchestras have relentlessly demonstrated. (In the recording studio, of course, a turn of the knobs will raise the volume of the string section to any level desired.)

As far back as the 1940s, such arrangers as Paul Weston, Axel Stordahl and, in England, Robert Farnon used their work with singers as a means to explore string writing. Indeed, strings had been used in the 1930s and early 1940s by singers such as Bing Crosby. But the uses of strings behind singers became much more subtle and sophisticated in the 1940s, 1950s, and 1960s with the writing of such arrangers as Nelson Riddle, Marion Evans, Don Costa, Marty Manning, and Patrick Williams. Some jazz fans abhorred the string section; musicians know there is no more subtle and transparent texture against which to set a solo, whether vocal or instrumental.

No bandleader could afford the large string section needed to hold its own with dance-band brass-and-saxes. And so those bands who embraced them in the 1940s tried to get by with string sections of twelve players or fewer – and on the Harry James record "The Mole," there are only five. There was something incongruous, even a little pitiful, in seeing these poor souls sawing away at their fiddles on the band platform, completely unheard.

During World War II, with his US Army Air Force band – when money was no object, because all his players were servicemen – Glenn Miller was able to deploy fourteen violins, four violas, and two celli: a total of twenty strings. But this was still hopelessly inadequate against the power of the rest of the band.

It was in film that former band arrangers were able to experiment with the uses of jazz and classical orchestral techniques, for the money they needed was there, along with a pool of spectacularly versatile master musicians who had been drawn to settle in Los Angeles for its movie and other studio work. To this day, some of the most successful fusions of jazz and classical influences have been in the movies, including such scores as Eddie Sauter's "Mickey One" and Johnny Mandel's "The Sandpiper."

That era is gone: gone completely. The singers of quality are of no interest to the record companies; neither are the songs from the great era of songwriting, the songs of Kern, Porter, Warren, Rodgers and Hart, Carmichael, Schwartz. Thus the superb orchestras that used to be assembled in the 1960s to record such songs with such singers are a thing of the past. Even in the movies, the change has been total. There are no longer excellent studio orchestras on staff, and orchestral writing of any kind is comparatively rare in films. The producers long ago discovered that they could use pop records as scoring. Pop records and synthesizers. The long-chord drone of synthesizers, not even skillful but sounding like slightly more developed Hammond organs (which were used for dramatic underscore in the old radio soap operas) are heard in movies today. Only a handful of composers, and "real" musicians, are able to derive their living from movie work, or from recording.

A story circulated rapidly among musicians a few years ago. A musician was called to play on a recording session that utilized a large "acoustic" orchestra. Afterwards he was asked what it was like.

He said, "It was great. We must have put two synthesizer players out of work."

A film composer was asked to submit some themes to the director of a movie. He gave him five. The director waxed enthusiastic. The next day he told the composer he was throwing out three of the themes. Why?

The director said he had played them for his daughter, and she had disliked those three.

"How old is she?" the composer asked.

"Five."

The brilliant comedy writer Larry Gelbart, creator of *M.A.S.H.* has said that in the movie industry today, you're dealing with foetuses in three-piece suits.

The president of the movie branch of Warner Bros has stated publicly that he shows script ideas to his 14-year-old son. If his son doesn't like them, he throws them out.

Yes, the era is over.

Some years ago, I went with Henry Mancini to a Hollywood party at which we encountered Pete Rugolo, his close friend, one of the original architects of the Stan Kenton band and career, and himself an enormous if unsung influence on American music. As unfashionable as it has become to give any credit whatever to Kenton, his band's innovations and style have been cannibalized endlessly by composers who would never admit its effect on them. It isn't politically correct.

I hardly knew Pete Rugolo, but when I found myself in conversation with him at that party I decided to tell him a story.

When I was a young newspaper reporter in Hamilton, Ontario, in which city I was born, I went to hear one of the bands I liked at the Hamilton Armory, a regular station in their tours. I fell into conversation with the band's arranger, whom I recognized from his photo in magazines. He suggested we go upstairs and sit in the balcony that, as I recall, surrounded the big main assembly room: that way we got out of the crowds of listeners who pressed close to the bandstand. I found him a most pleasant man, and I was in awe that he would even talk to me. At that age – I was 19 or, at the most, 20 – one is full of uncertainty and sensitivity; rejection, above all rejection from hero figures, can be devastating. But he was most gracious to me, and I suspect the memory of his kindness, talking to me as if I actually knew something, probably influenced me to go deeper into this music and write about it.

So, after telling him this story, I said to Rugolo, "Do you know who that arranger was, Pete?"

"No," he said, keenly interested.

"You."

Growing up in Canada, I was subject to that peculiar psychological ailment that is the country's curse, its much-chronicled national inferiority complex. It was inevitable, to be sure, because Canada was completely overshadowed by England, the United States, and France. The novels we read were American or British; so were our movie heroes. We saw countless wartime movies about the valiance of British and American fighting men, and never saw a picture about our own tragedy at Dieppe. If occasionally a movie did deal with Canada and the war, the Canadians in it were portrayed by American or British actors, as in the case of *Captains of the Clouds*, with James Cagney, Dennis Morgan, Alan Hale, and Brenda Marshall, not one of whom had a Canadian accent. Indeed, when the Americans wanted to cast an Englishman in some military film, they made him a Canadian; and the British, with comparable tin ear, would sometimes cast Americans as Canadians. Curiously enough, there was a large pool of Canadian actors in Hollywood, but none of us in Canada knew who they were. Thus too our literature. We admired novelists of every nation but our own, and I was a young adult before I learned that the great Morley Callaghan was a Canadian.

The same with music. I grew up on the songs of Kern, Gershwin, Porter, Arlen, Warren, sung by American singers or played by American bands.

In such an atmosphere, it is little wonder that so many of us acquired by osmotic absorption an impression that Canadians were irrelevant in the arts (except painting, at which we demonstrably excelled) and perhaps incapable of them. I had no idea that the most significant city in post-World War II arranging and orchestration was Toronto, a tedious and sanctimonious dullard of a place in those days. For Robert Farnon and Gil Evans were both born there, and they were the pervasive powerful influences in the postwar arranging world. And Percy Faith, who had significance enough of his own, would be important if only because of the influence he had on Farnon, and he too was born in Toronto. And my friend since our high-school days, Kenny Wheeler, would turn out to be a considerable influence on jazz composition at the end of the century, although when we were two kids listening to Miles Davis and Dizzy Gillespie, we assuredly did not foresee that. Kenny too was born in Toronto.

A final point.

This book is by no means an attempt at a survey of composers and arrangers: such a work, if its entries explored the subjects to the same extent these essays undertake, would fill a shelf of books. It is not even a complete collection of my writings thus far on the subject. Essays on Duke Ellington, Benny Golson, Benny Carter, Paul Weston, Dave Brubeck, and Horace Silver are to be found in others of my books.

The book is dedicated to all those musicians who, in solitary and often silent commune with sheets of score paper, have with tiny pencil markings enriched so many of our lives.

2

Come back last summer:
Kenny Wheeler

The lakes and the rivers shaped our lives. We were surrounded by Lake Huron, the Detroit River, Lake Erie, Lake Ontario, and the Niagara River. Insular we surely were, made more so by an invisible line that runs through the lakes and down the rivers from somewhere around Sault St. Marie to a point a little east-northeast of Massena, New York, demarking the border between Canada and the United States.

The Niagara River leaves Lake Erie at Buffalo and flows north 28 miles, descending 326 feet in the journey, 167 feet of it in the plunge over Niagara Falls. It then flows seven miles between the walls of the Niagara Gorge, churning with rapids for much of that distance, and another seven miles across a flat alluvial plain to debouch in Lake Ontario. It drains the upper lakes, Erie, Huron, Michigan, and Superior, whose combined surface is 260,000 square miles.

The strip of land approximately 30 miles wide lying east of the river between Lakes Erie and Ontario is called the Niagara Peninsula. A few miles north of Buffalo is Niagara Falls, New York, a shabby colorless city that gazes across the gorge at Niagara Falls, Ontario, a shabby garish city dedicated to relieving tourists of money. About ten miles east-northeast of Niagara Falls is St. Catharines, Ontario, whose name is mis-spelled in every piece of writing about Kenny Wheeler I have ever seen. Its chief distinction is that the zipper was invented there.

In its expansion, St. Catharines has absorbed Port Dalhousie, a little lakeside town – a village, then, really – that had a small amusement park in which there was a dance pavilion, ten cents a dance, where the kids used to go on summer evenings. The park has long since disappeared. An interurban trolley connected Port Dalhousie, St. Catharines, and other communities. I used to ride it to Niagara Falls to hear bands at the arena there. Like all such trolleys in North America it has been dismantled, and the Niagara Peninsula is criss-crossed with freeways.

The Niagara Peninsula is divided into two distinct regions by the Niagara

Escarpment, a sudden rise in the land that runs far to the west and whose tree-covered precipitate face has been designated a protected area by the Canadian government.

Early in the nineteenth century, to circumvent the obstacle to shipping presented by Niagara Falls, a canal was built to connect Port Dalhousie to Chippewa Creek, which gave access to the Niagara River above the falls. From there on it was smooth sailing upriver to Lake Erie. The early canal soon proved inadequate, and further versions of it were built. The present canal, with lift locks that make it in many ways more impressive than the Panama Canal, was opened in 1932. Remnants of an older canal, locks built of great stone blocks, are scattered about the land, grasses and wildflowers growing on their bottoms. They are like artifacts of another age, a sort of abandoned maritime Stonehenge.

These were the realities that set the flavor and the character of the area, which is peculiarly bland. The people of St. Catharines, a population of about 35,000 when I was a boy and about 125,000 today, were for the most part parochial, shallow, and aloof. If you found anyone who held interests in common with you, such as jazz, you made a friend, perhaps for life.

One afternoon in 1945, as World War II was ending, I was visiting the bedroom of another young jazz fan, a boy named Tommy Fancy. Tommy had spent some time in a tuberculosis hospital, but had at last been discharged. He still was required to get plenty of bed-rest. One day there was another boy there: his name was Kenny Wheeler. His family had just moved to St. Catharines, and I must have been one of the first kids he met.

I was 17, he was 15. He was of slight build and looked younger than his age, as he does to this day. I remember that we listened to Sarah Vaughan and Frankie Laine in that room. "Tommy was a big-band freak," Kenny told me a while ago. "I still get a Christmas card from him every year."

Interviewed for an article about him in the March 1998 issue of *Jazz Educators Journal*, Kenny said, "I have always been attracted to the more 'orchestral' bands, such as Ellington, Kenton, and earlier Gil Evans. As a composer of jazz tunes, I have also been attracted to Wayne Shorter, Horace Silver, Billy Strayhorn, John Taylor, Bill Evans, and quite a few others. I cannot specify individual works; but there was a Gerry Mulligan tentet recording with a ballad that I took to pieces, and I learned a lot about jazz harmony from that experience." I can remember listening to some of that music with Kenny, particularly some of the writing of Gil Evans for Claude Thornhill.

Kenneth Vincent John Wheeler was born on 14 January 1930, in Toronto, which is about 30 miles due north of St. Catharines across Lake Ontario. Toronto seemed like the faraway big city, though it was in fact quite provincial. In those days there was nothing to see from Port Dalhousie (which we pronounced "d'loozy"), but now on clear days the tall buildings of Toronto rise distinctly out of the flat plain of water. I never felt at home in St. Catharines: neither did Kenny.

He was the fourth of eight children in a Catholic family of mixed Irish, Scottish, English and German descent – three girls and five boys, born just over a year apart over a ten-year period. Their father, Wilf, was an accountant and part-time musician, and their mother played piano by ear.

Kenny's sister, Helen Jelley, said: "My father worked for car dealerships – office management and accounting. We lived in Windsor for two years, where he worked in a war plant. When that folded up in 1945, we came to St. Catharines. He worked for Murphy's auto dealership. We lived at 21 Salina."

The house is a two-storey red-brick dwelling with a pillared porch. It is 50 yards from Yates Street, which ran seven blocks or so along the brow of the valley through which flowed Twelve Mile Creek. The swells lived there, the richest people of the town, and although some of their daughters and sons attended our high school, they seldom spoke to us members of the lower orders. "Yates Street was only a few doors away," Kenny said. "But it seemed like a million miles.

"I guess my dad was born in Toronto. Or maybe Belleville. Belleville rings a bell." It is 40 miles or so east of Toronto, on the north shore of Lake Ontario.

"I don't know what my father did before. He tried to become a professional musician. He played around New York a little bit. But I don't think he did what you'd call jazz jobs, although he knew how to play jazz, I think, in those days. But he played like, I suppose, Jewish gigs up in the Catskill Mountains and all that stuff. I'm told he played in one of the Paul Whiteman road bands."

"Whiteman had a number of road bands," I said. "Just as Lester Lanin had a number of bands."

Kenny said, "Lester Lanin came to London once and did a record I was on, just third or fourth trumpet. We were just going to start a tune and the guitar player says to him, 'Mr. Lanin, I think there's a wrong note here.' And Lester Lanin says, 'Wrong notes, I don't care. My first record had a million wrong notes and it sold millions of copies, One two . . . '"

We both laughed. The Lester Lanin stories are endless.

"How'd you get started on trumpet?" I asked.

"My dad just came home with a cornet one day and gave it to me. He didn't say, 'Play it,' or anything. I took two or three weeks looking at it, lying on the bed, and then I picked it up and tried to play it. I thought I'd better get myself a book. So I started playing out of a book. Something kind of simple. My father showed me a couple of things, but it wasn't like he was my teacher on a regular basis. He just left me to do it. I guess I didn't get a teacher until we moved to Windsor.

"In Windsor this guy had a navy band. He was teaching kids from 13 to 18 or something. I remember I had my own actual real uniform. Navy whites and all that stuff. I was, I guess, 14, and I looked about 7. I had one of those little faces, y'know. Marching up the street with my cornet and my uniform on, very proud. He kind of took a shine to me. I played all the wrong notes physically, but I had a good technique. The lip was wrong. I stuck my tongue through my lips, which you're not supposed to do. You're supposed to keep the tongue back behind the teeth. And he used to try to get me to . . . " Kenny made the motion of spitting a bit of tobacco off the end of the tongue. "But I could never get the hang of that."

"Did you eventually?"

Again the laughter. "I'm almost there now! I came to some compromise years ago, where it's not too damaging for me to do whatever I do.

"My father, playing trombone, was interested in the Tommy Dorsey–Glenn Miller type of thing. I was already a great fiddler with the radio. By doing that, you'd hear Glenn Miller, and stumble on something a bit different, and you'd say, 'Wait a minute, what's that?' This was jazz, I guess. So I started to get a liking for that stuff.

"Then we moved to St. Catharines."

Helen said, "My father played trombone and baritone sax. He worked in dance bands, polka bands, marching bands. He encouraged us all to learn music.

"All my brothers, except George, the oldest, play semi-professionally. George became captain of the *Meisner*. It was the biggest ship on the Great Lakes. I think it carried iron ore. George retired and the *Meisner* was sent to India to be scrapped."

Those Great Lakes ships hauled wood to the paper mills near St. Catharines and ore to the great smelters. They were long, rust-colored ships, and their names were romantic to us, because they went to far places.

Kenny said, "My second brother, Wilfred, named after my father, is still a semi-professional musician on trombone and piano. He still lives in St. Catharines. He just retired, too, from accounting. Paul, my other brother, plays clarinet and baritone.

"My father was always a very careful man. He encouraged us in music, but he always said, 'Make sure you have another profession handy, something to fall back on.'

"I tried. I had several office jobs in Toronto, but they all seemed to last about three months, and then I'd come back home again. I went to Detroit and got a job in a supermarket. The manager eventually just had to look at me and he turned blue with anger. I was one of those fumbly type people that keep knocking things over. Eventually he said, 'Why don't you go back to Canada?' So I did."

"I remember you in that high-school orchestra," I said. "I never could understand how you stood it. I think you were the only trumpet in it. It was a weird instrumentation, anything they could find. Lots of fiddles and no cellos. That orchestra was so out of tune all the time. But I guess you were getting some kind of experience."

"Yeah, that was it," Kenny said.

Kenny and I attended the St. Catharines Collegiate Institute and Vocational School, sometimes called St. CCI. I hated that school, and its principal, a man with a ruddy face and pate surrounded by a clamp of white hair. He looked like a beardless Santa Claus, but there the resemblance ended. He was a cruel man who intimidated the school's population of about 1,300.

"Wilson Salter," I said.

"That was his name!" Kenny said.

"He strapped me once," Helen said.

"He strapped me two or three times," I said. "But I'm surprised that he strapped a girl." Salter was a drunk, a man unfit to supervise the education of the young, whom he ruled by intimidation. The school was devoid of morale. Even its football team was listless. The physical plant was a long, yellow-brick structure with heavy stone pillars running in a vaguely Roman style about four stories up a portico that faced west. Across the street was a candy and sundries store that carried a weekly magazine containing the lyrics to the hit songs, which I memorized by the hundreds.

"Wilson Salter was a bad son of a bitch," I said to Helen, and then to Kenny, remembering how we both wanted to get out of that town, "Didn't you used to go over to Buffalo and sit in with groups?"

"I don't know if I actually sat in," Kenny said. "I used to go over to Buffalo regularly for lessons. There was another bandmaster. This guy ran a military band. He was a bit of a con man, in a way. He used to get me to do musical problems, y'know, weird problems to do with theory. And I'd spend a long time doing that, and I enjoyed that, but I used to think, 'Well what's this got to do with a trumpet lesson?' He wasn't really very good, but I liked him a lot, and he said to me one summer, 'Do you want to come to New York with the army band?' I said, 'I can't do that, I'm a Canadian.' He said, 'Don't worry about that.' So I went to the Catskill Mountains with this army band, only because he said we'd get two days off at the weekend, and I knew I could get to 52nd Street, which seemed like a dream to me.

"When the weekend came, Friday night, a bunch of us got the train and I got off at Grand Central Station and practically flew up to 52nd Street. I was 17 and looked about 12, and I had this American army uniform on. People looked at me as much as to say, 'What's this kid doing with the army uniform on?'

"I went straight for, I think it was, the Three Deuces where Charlie Parker was playing with Miles. That would be '47, I guess."

"You were the first one who turned me on to Miles," I said. "I was listening to Dizzy and Bird. Of course I didn't understand that music first time I heard it."

"I didn't either," Kenny said. "It took me three or four listenings. I remember in New York, this is my great claim, I spoke to Charlie Parker. I went up to him at intermission and I said, 'Where's Miles?' And he said, 'He's out back.' And that was the extent of my talk with Charlie Parker. I couldn't find Miles."

"Did you know him eventually?"

"I met him once," Kenny said. "I think he probably knew of me, through Dave Holland." It was a typical Kenny Wheeler remark.

Anyone who has ever known Kenny, in those days or now, in St. Catharines or London or New York or Toronto, will tell you of his lifelong reticence, his almost disabling shyness. I asked Helen once, when Kenny wasn't around, "Was Kenny like other members of the family, or different?"

"Different."

Kenny studied at the Royal Conservatory of Music in Toronto – trumpet with Ross MacLathan and harmony with John Weinzweig, one of the pioneers in Canadian serial composition. "I studied harmony with him," Kenny said. "I used to come over from St. Catharines to Toronto to study with him. Traditional harmony, Paul Hindemith's book. I was probably just one of a hundred students he had. I know I enjoyed it. I thought he was a great teacher."

There was little work for Kenny in those days.

"I suppose you could get a job a week in a dance band, if you were lucky," Kenny said. "Maybe two. It wouldn't be enough to live on."

"When your dad was playing in the 1920s," I said, "there was all that theater work, but with the talkies, it all went, and with the Depression it got worse. Now in St. Catharines, there was that band that played at the little pavilion by the lake in Port Dalhousie . . . "

"Bruce Anthony," Kenny said. "I played in that band. He was the slightly more jazzy of the big bands. It was nothing to do with jazz, really, but it wasn't quite so commercial as the other bands. There was another band, Murray Morton. My dad used to play for him.

"I used to go over to Toronto to play Polish weddings and stuff like that. I don't think I was a good enough jazz player to actually play with the jazz guys in Toronto, and I was much too nervous anyway to even sit in. I would be shaking, if they'd let me sit in. And I don't think I was good enough anyway. Some people like Herbie Spanier were in full flight then. I considered them far above me. But I was good enough to do Polish weddings."

Desperate for work, Kenny played some non-union gig at a club in downtown Toronto. I spoke about it to Helen: "I seem to remember he got hauled up on charges by the union."

"Yes," she said. "It was the Club Norman. I think he lied about his age." At 20, Kenny wouldn't have been allowed to enter any place in Toronto that served liquor, much less permitted to work there. "One of his so-called friends," Helen said, "a part-time musician from St. Catharines, went there to see him and then squealed on him. He's the one who went to the union.

"Kenny was expelled. Dad was very uptight. He worked for the union for years. He was sergeant at arms. He wanted Kenny back in the union. It cost him quite a bit of money to be reinstated in the union here. Kenny still belongs to the union in St. Catharines, still pays his dues every year. He figures it's better that way, because it's the American Federation of Musicians, and it makes it easier if he has to play in the States."

Kenny was deeply humiliated by the incident.

About then I moved to Quebec to become a reporter at the *Montreal Star*. I made the move for several reasons, one of which was simply to escape puritanical Ontario. There was a solid jazz movement in Montreal, with people like pianists Steve Garrick and Paul Bley, the bassist Hal Gaylor, later with Chico Hamilton and Tony Bennett, clarinetist Al Baculis, a jazz accordionist (the best I ever heard) named Gordie Flemming, the French–Canadian vibist Yvon Landry, and more. Part of the reason was that Montreal was an unabashedly corrupt city whose nightlife was wide open and roaring. Prohibition had never been enforced in Quebec. It had superb restaurants and nightclubs, both dark and intimate and loud and colorful. It had a thriving black neighborhood in which there were two famous clubs, Rockhead's Paradise and the Cafe St. Michel, where you could hear lots of jazz, home-grown and imported. Oscar Peterson was an alumnus of those two clubs, but he had already left that level of work, having made his famous breakthrough with Norman Granz's Jazz at the Philharmonic in September, 1949.

Soon after I moved to Montreal in the fall of 1952, Kenny turned up. "I remember we went by the Cafe St. Michel and you wanted to sit in. There was a Japanese trombone player. I remember being astounded at a Japanese trombone player. The rest of the band was black."

That trombone player, I realized years later, was Butch Watanabe, who had attended Montreal High School, the same high school that produced Oscar Peterson, Hal Gaylor, and Maynard Ferguson. Butch and Oscar were lifelong friends. I urged Kenny to ask the musicians to let him sit in, but he was emotionally incapable of it. I remember sitting with him at a small round table near the bandstand.

"Yeah," Kenny mused when I reminded him of that night.

"I'd begun writing songs by then, or trying to," I said. "I had concepts of songs, because I was beginning to be influenced by the French songwriters. I can't remember: what brought you to Montreal?"

Kenny said, "My piano chops at that time were pretty good. I think you were surprised. I'd had to get up to a certain proficiency to get into McGill University.

"McGill was my last hope. I'd gone home with my tail between my legs so many times. And I thought, 'Well, I could go to McGill University and take this course that would enable me to be a high-school teacher.' That's what I was going to do. And I had to get my chops up on piano reasonably well for that. When I walked around there, I realized there was no way I was going to be a high-school teacher. Never could I do that."

My disillusion with journalism had already set in. I was all too aware of the political dishonesty of newspapers. There would be no great Crusade for Truth and Justice, as in the movies; we reporters were there to serve the secret ends of those who owned the press.

Kenny said, "We decided we were going to go to England, and form a trio, and you were going to sing. It was going to be something like bass, piano, guitar, and you."

"Well," I said, "I'd heard the Jack Parnell Trio on records, and I guess we'd all heard the Ted Heath band. I was familiar with what Bob Farnon was doing on records. There was some sort of music scene going on over there, and Canadians didn't need visas to go there, as we did to go to the States."

Kenny said, "I remember you said there seemed to be bands over there, and they must need brass players. I'll never forget that. That's when it clicked. I thought, 'I've gotta go somewhere, man, and that's going to be it.'"

"You shocked me," I said, "because the next day or something, you'd already bought a boat ticket. This was a fairly radical decision, to dump the country and leave!"

"Well it seemed obvious to me," Kenny said, laughing. "It was the only thing to do. I had decided I wasn't going to back to St. Catharines, no matter what. I just couldn't go back any more."

I said, "I have a vague memory that I saw you off on the boat. Down at the Montreal harbor."

"I think you did."

"I was just astounded that you were doing this."

It astounded everybody. Kenny's father learned of it when he tried to reach Kenny at a boarding house in which Kenny was living in Montreal. He got back a telegram saying Mr. Wheeler had gone to London. Helen said, "The whole family was in shock for two weeks. It was unbelievable. Not Kenny! I don't know about the rest of them, but I was glad. Because I knew it was really important for Kenny, and I was glad to see him do something different."

"It was," I told her, "an act of incredible courage for someone so reticent. I couldn't believe it myself."

Trumpeter and critic Ian Carr wrote, "Although naturally reticent and self-effacing, Wheeler has always had the inner necessity and vision of the true artist, and this brought him early in his career to Europe, the perfect environment for him because it does not have the gladiatorial competitiveness of the American jazz scene."

But that's not why Kenny went to England. He went because we had no hope of getting visas to the United States.

Songs had always fascinated me. One reason is that the song lyric is the most exacting of all literary forms. It is far more difficult technically to fit a lyric to an existing melody and then achieve high levels of emotional expression than it is to write poetry. You must put long vowels on long notes so that singers can sustain them, stressed syllables on stressed notes, weak syllables on weak notes; and in an ideal song, the inflections of the words will match the intervals of the melody in an approximation of natural speech. The poet faces no such problems.

But it is only of late that I have begun to understand what song does in fact do to us. Song slows up emotional experience. Like a slow-motion movie of the flight of a hummingbird, it lets you look at emotion and, with music to help the words, experience it.

Soon after Kenny left for England, a friend heard me singing along with some record. She recommended me for a Canadian Broadcasting Corporation network radio show called *Opportunity Knocks*. It was an amateur show, but at a high level. It was indeed the show through which Oscar Peterson a few years before had made the leap to national prominence. Though I'd had no experience singing and hadn't the slightest idea what I was doing, I was, to my amazement, accepted.

Asked what I wanted to sing, I said, almost without thinking, "Our Love Is Here to Stay." The rehearsal pianist set a key, an arrangement was commissioned. When I arrived at the studio, I found that I was to be accompanied by an orchestra of about 35 men. I was terrified. This was live network radio.

My moment in the show began. I got through the first eight bars without problem. As we approached the B section there was a complex swirl of strings, and I got confused. I jumped in probably two beats early. I was suffering terrible humiliation, and couldn't stop. The conductor heard in his headphones what was happening. He held his palm up to me, signalling me to wait. I felt like a pilot being talked down through fog. All I could do was sing slowly, and then gradually, ever so gradually during what seemed an eternity, I came back into synchronicity with the chord changes.

At the end of the show, I probably went off to some bar somewhere. I do know I vowed I would never, ever try to sing again, and never would I try to write a song. I just didn't have the talent.

Years later somebody gave me an acetate of that broadcast. I listened with trepidation, and when I got to my error, I was amazed at the skill of the recovery. But that error, which loomed so massively in my mind at the time, is the reason I didn't go to England to form a group with Kenny and sing. It took me 30 years to tell him that. I never realized that in England, he was waiting for me. I didn't think I mattered that much to anybody. "Even after three or four months," Kenny said, "I still expected you to come. Suffering away I was in England and I kept thinking, 'Gene'll be here any day, and save me.'

"You seemed so much stronger than I. I thought, 'We'll form this nice trio, and Gene will be singing, and it will be all right.' And then after three or four months, it dawned on me: he's not coming."

"Oh boy, if you thought I was stronger! I must have been faking it, because I was scared to death of the world. One of the reasons I didn't become a singer was terror. I was afraid of being on display. I also didn't think I was any good. Performing is an act of courage. And jazz more than any art. Jazz takes tremendous guts. As a writer, if I turn out something I don't like, I get rid of it. You can't do that in performing, and particularly jazz."

"Yes," Kenny said. "Jazz is instantaneous."

I sat there in silence, digesting it all, imagining Kenny's disappointment as he waited for me in England.

"What happened when you got to England?" I asked at last, feeling bleak, that I had failed my friend.

"I met a trio on the boat," Kenny said. "Johnny Bell was one of them. He's changed his name to Thick Wilson. He plays heavies in the movies. He was the bass player. The guys in the trio on the boat showed me how to find a bed-and-breakfast place. I got a place right in the center in London.

"I got the newspapers and looked where the jazz clubs were. I went around to the clubs, one in particular. People like Joe Harriott, Tony Crombie, Dizzy Reece played there. They had late-night sessions. Eventually I asked to sit in. Nobody said a word when I finished. They kind of acted like I wasn't even there. This did set me into a kind of a shell. They didn't even look at me and say, 'What are you doing here?' Nothing.

"Eventually I started to run out of money and started to get a little bit worried, but the guy who was the doorman there, a young guy – I got friendly with him – he said, "You can come and stay at my place." He was supported by a homosexual guy, which I didn't know until I got there.

"The homosexual guy was very pleasant, and he had no designs on me whatsoever. The young guy was a Scotsman. I stayed there two or three weeks, and then I still had to find some way of making my own way.

"By this time it was Christmas, the end of '52," Kenny said. "I left Canada at the end of September or early October.

"I read that they needed helpers in the post office for the Christmas mail. So I got a job doing that. But meanwhile I'd met Doreen on the telephone. The young Scotsman used to go with Doreen's girlfriend, unbeknown to the guy he was living with. Doreen rang up one day to say that her girlfriend couldn't make this date with the Scotsman. So being young and stupid, I suppose, I started to kid around with her on the phone, and eventually I said, 'You send me a picture and I'll send you a picture.' We sent each other pictures and decided to meet for a date. That's how I met her. I didn't say two words on the first date. She must have thought, 'What the hell is this?'

"I wore a zoot suit and all, because it was still my Canadian influence. With big shoulders and draped trousers!" He laughed. "I must have looked weird in London! But for some reason she liked me.

"I remember one night I came in. The homosexual was hugging a young ballet dancer still in his tights. It kind of embarrassed me, and I thought I'd better start thinking about getting out of here.

"So I got myself a flat and started earning a little bit of money at the post office, getting stronger with Doreen all the time. Then I found Archer Street. This was about the end of January. It was like a market, where every Monday afternoon hundreds of musicians went, and you just stood, and you got work from somebody you knew, or whatever. I started to meet a few musicians there, and eventually somebody said, 'Do you want a job, fourth trumpet?' I said, 'Yeah, I'll take it!' So I got a job with Roy Fox. He was quite famous in England as a commercial bandleader. He liked jazz, and you'd get to play jazz solos in his band. Doreen and I got married 28 March of that year. I had only known her about five months."

"I remember I was getting letters from you," I said. "Not only had you precipitately taken off for England, you'd precipitately got married. And I felt responsible! I thought, 'Oh my God, what have I done! It's all my fault!'"

"Well," Kenny said, "I was quite hopeless with ladies in Canada. I had known a couple of girls, but nothing . . . I was completely hopeless."

"I remember the address on your letters. You lived at Bethnal Green."

"Gales Gardens," Kenny said. "Which is no longer there."

"Now how did you go with Carl Barriteau?"

Carl Barriteau, born in Trinidad 7 February 1914, grew up in Maracaibo, Venezuela. He moved to London in the late 1930s and played with Ken (Snake Hips) Johnson's West Indian Swing Band. He formed his own recording group in the middle of World War II and entertained British and American troops after the war, in Europe, North Africa, and Southeast Asia. Extremely well trained, he was widely considered to be one of the finest jazz soloists in England – *Melody Maker* voted him England's best jazz clarinetist seven years in a row – with a style that many compared to Artie Shaw, both in timbre and style. What I remember is the extraordinary power of his playing; the fact that the musicians liked him; and that he seemed to have a higher opinion of Kenny's playing than Kenny did. He lived the last years of his life in quiet retirement in Australia, dying in Sidney on 24 August 1998.

"I'm not sure when I went with that band," Kenny said.

"I can pin it, because it was the year I came over to visit," I said. "You were with that band in 1954."

"Carl was great," Kenny said. "I loved working for him. I really shouldn't have taken the job, because I didn't have the chops for it. It was a really hard book. There was a front line of about five people. I'd met Art Ellefson in the local jazz clubs. He was born in Moose Jaw. He came over from Canada unbeknown to me, about two weeks after I did. We got to like each other right away. He was the best man at my wedding. He was playing tenor with Carl Barriteau. The trumpet player left, and Art recommended me. I was still in a very nervous state in those days. The broadcasts were live: I wouldn't do them. I told Carl, 'I'll be in the band but I just couldn't do the broadcasts.' My nerves were so bad.

"But I enjoyed it very much. It was hard."

During Kenny's early years in England, I continued writing, and even sold a few short stories, still believing in those days, as all young journalists did, that only fiction really mattered. One of my stories sold to an English science fiction magazine called *Nova*, whose editor was E. J. (Ted) Carnell, prominent in science fiction in England at that period. He was a former dance-band guitarist and loved music. We began to exchange letters.

One morning in Montreal I got called over to the city editor's desk. The *Montreal Star* wanted me to fly to Europe with the Royal Canadian Air Force, as it was called in those days, to write a series of stories on the Canadian forces attached to NATO. I was delighted. Why, I might even get to see Paris! And I would certainly get to see Kenny. I asked if I might take my vacation time on arriving, and then go back to work.

Transatlantic flight still was a little exotic in that year, 1954; indeed transatlantic travel by any means was not all that common. I decided not to tell the only two friends I had in England, Ted Carnell and Kenny Wheeler, that I was coming. I would walk in on them casually, as if it were the most natural thing in the world. We flew in a North Star to Goose Bay, Labrador, then to Reykjavik, Iceland, and then onward. The pilot asked if I wanted to take the co-pilot's seat. I sat there peering through the night at the great horizon ahead, which gradually grew pale and on which at last in the early morning a dark streak appeared. "Ireland," the pilot said, and I remember being amazed that man could take off into the air and travel all this distance and find a predetermined destination. Ireland was real, and it was right where the maps said it was! It looked so green below.

I checked into a Canadian Air Force base, drank with some of the pilots – they flew Saberjets then – and next morning went into London. I telephoned Ted Carnell's office. "I'm terribly sorry," a secretary said, "but Mr. Carnell is out of the city for several days." Lovely. I come all this way and the guy isn't in.

Go to Part Two of the plan. Walk in on Kenny. So I asked for directions to Bethnal Green, took the Tube and emerged above ground. I found the address in a little street of brick row houses. I knocked at the door and Kenny's young wife answered. I introduced myself. She said that Kenny was on the road with the Carl Barriteau band; he'd been gone for some time.

I had discovered that Canadian dollars went a long way. When Doreen told me the Barriteau band was playing Manchester, I said, "Well how would you like to go up to Manchester with me to see Kenny?"

"She thought you were mad, you know," Kenny said. "But she liked you." And she agreed to go. Leaving nothing to hazard this time, I had her phone Kenny in advance.

Kenny said, "Just for her to go out of Bethnal Green at that time was an experience. She's traveled a lot since then, but she'd never been anywhere at that time. She enjoyed the whole adventure. It was something completely new for her. She said you were whistling on the train."

"I was probably whistling Charlie Parker licks," I said. "'Salt Peanuts,' no doubt. Or 'Hot House'."

"You can imagine all the side-glances of the people on the train," Kenny said.

Kenny met the train. We went to several hotels in search of a room for me. Manchester was still recovering from the wartime bombing, there were unexpected green spaces where buildings had once been, and hotel rooms were scarce. By the time Kenny had to go to work, I still hadn't found a room. We went to his gig. I remember the musicians laughing during the breaks. They said Carl Barriteau had such powerful chops that he could play clarinet louder than a whole brass section.

At the end of the evening, Kenny suggested that I might find a room at the theatrical boarding house somewhere on the edge of the city where the musicians were staying. I went there in a car with Kenny, Doreen, and some of the musicians. Alas, there was no room. It was growing late. I told Kenny that I would find something, somehow, and left. It had begun to rain, and I felt as if I were catching cold.

I found a telephone booth and tried to call a taxi. I did not know that you did not call a cab in Manchester at three in the morning, at least in those years. I stood, increasingly miserable and exhausted, in that telephone booth by a main road, not knowing what to do. A great bus loomed out of the night, and I ran out to flag it down. Alas, its head sign said Charter. To my surprise, it stopped. It was empty. The driver, who had a Lancashire accent like my grandfather's, said he was returning from a tour to Scotland, where he had left his passengers. He offered me a ride. He drove to various hotels in downtown Manchester, with me the sole passenger in his enormous bus, and at last pulled up in front of a hotel I had tried earlier. He urged me to try again.

It was a small hotel. In the lobby, I approached a short, slight man in a black uniform, and told him of my problem.

He said to me in the accent I'd grown up hearing, because my father's people were from this part of England, "The' wur a chap that wur supposed to cum 'ere last night. 'Appen 'e won't turn up now. I'll let you 'ave 'is room."

I went out and thanked the bus driver, who declined my offer of compensation for his kindness, wished me well, and drove off.

At the small desk in the lobby, I signed the register. My benefactor, who was probably about 50, said, "Y'know, you don't look all that well, young man."

"I think I'm catching a cold," I said.

"Wot you need is a nice cup o' tea," he said, and poured some from a pot. And, he said, this too would probably help: he poured a hooker of Scotch into it. It certainly did help. As it warmed me, I felt a growing sense of safety.

The man sat down near me. "Tell me," he said, "d'ye think they'll ever send a man to the moon?"

"Well, yes," I said. "Within four or five hundred years, I expect they will. But what makes you ask that?"

"Cum 'ere," he said, crossing the lobby to open a set of double doors. "We've got a convention of those chaps that writes that stuff." He threw a wall switch and lighted a ballroom. All around the room were tables on which there were models of rocket ships, and on easels there were cover illustrations for science-fiction magazines. I blanched.

"My God," I said. "Let me look at your register."

Ted Carnell was in the room next to mine.

Ted was startled and delighted when I introduced myself the next morning. I stayed two or three days, hanging out with science-fiction writers.

Intrigued by Arthur Koestler's fascination with coincidence, I have often wondered what the odds were against my being booked by absolute chance, after leaving Kenny that night, in the room next to the only other person I knew in all Britain.

I went on from there to the Canadian air bases at Gros Tonquin and Metz. I got orders from the paper to go to Paris and write stories on the crisis in the government of Pierre Mendes-France. Paris! My God! I checked into the Hotel California, across the street from the *Herald-Tribune*, and went to work, using the *Herald-Tribune*'s office and a typewriter, never foreseeing that in time Paris would become a second home to me.

I worked there for several weeks, then at last went home to Montreal with the air force. In the spring of 1959, by a sequence of coincidences I became managing editor, and later editor, of *Down Beat*.

"What was happening to you during those years?" I asked Kenny.

"I was with Ambrose for a while. After Carl Barriteau, I was with Tommy Whittle, jazz saxophone player." Whittle, a Scot – a notable number of Kenny's musician friends in England were Scots – also went through the Barriteau band. Whittle joined Ted Heath's postwar band. Kenny said, "Tommy had a real jazz band, eight pieces. He appeared at my door one day and said, 'Would you like to play in my band?' I guess that was the first real jazz band I played in. We had people like Keith Christie and Joe Temperley, who is now quite a big name in New York." Temperley, a brilliant baritonist, is also a Scot, born in Fife 20 September 1929. "That was a very enjoyable situation," Kenny said. "It lasted for a couple of years.

"I also did a couple of nightclub jobs in London, from 10 at night till 4 in the morning. I got an all-night bus back to Bethnal Green. That's when they still had the ladies on the street in London." He pitched his voice high: "'Like a good time, Dearie?'

"There was a great atmosphere in London in those days. When they took the ladies off the street, all that sexual thing went underground and inside. It somehow seemed to coincide with, to me, the deterioration of London.

"After Tommy Whittle, I did various nightclub jobs. But they were commercial. Except you could learn a lot of tunes in a job like that, either a quintet or quartet. You had to come up with new standards.

"I went with Johnny Dankworth in '59, and he went to Newport in May or June."

"July," I said. "Fourth of July weekend. I had been editor of *Down Beat* about eight weeks at the time. You came over to the Newport Festival with the Dankworth band, and I saw you there. That was five years after I'd last seen you, and seven years after you moved to England. It was probably the first band to come over on the exchange from England."

"I think it was," Kenny said. Due to a curious squabble between their respective musicians' unions, groups from the United States were not allowed to perform in England, and English groups were not allowed to work here. Eventually some sort of compromise was achieved, and the Dankworth band was one of the first groups to make the trip to America.

"I was playing the fourth trumpet chair," Kenny said. "I had a couple of solos. I think the whole band was frightened to death of Newport. Nothing like that had ever happened before. Seeing all the big names around. The English mentality is not like the American. The Americans, generally, when they see somebody sitting in the audience with a name, they'll say, 'Oh, I'll play my best for him.'"

"Not necessarily," I said. "One night Stan Getz came in to hear the Woody Herman band, and an excellent young saxophone player just fell apart when he had to play a solo. The Americans may conceal it better. But I think at that time, the European jazz players tended to be very intimidated by the Americans. It used to be said that the European rhythm sections were no good, but that's no longer true. There are lots of good rhythm-section players in Europe."

"Well, even in the old days," Kenny said. "I listen to some of the old records, and the people like Phil Seaman, they were good. But there weren't many of them. Kenny Clare was the drummer with the Dankworth band at that time. He just lived for the drums. He was one of the top session drummers. I think he just wanted to be a jazz drummer, but never really got the chance.

"After that Dankworth started to write for films and commercial things. He started to use people from the band on some of those films. Gradually he got more and more into films and television. Cleo was starting to come up." Cleo Laine, Dankworth's wife, started as the band singer but increasingly she was a star in her own right.

"The next time I was in England," I said, "must have been 1964 or '65. I came to England and worked with Dankworth for a bit. He wrote the score for *Darling*, and asked me to put a lyric on the title theme. He and Cleo had an old converted inn out in the country, and I went out there for a few days and wrote the lyric. That film came out in '65."

"I don't think I saw you then," Kenny said. "I started to get into the studios too, through the odd session with Dankworth. At that time, there was a lot of studio work around, so I got into that. I was never one of the top calls. Those guys were working three sessions a day, recording or TV or something. My limit was about six or seven a week, which still gave you a good wage to live on, much better than the average man.

"I studied a bit with Richard Rodney Bennett. He was a great teacher. The first thing he did when I walked in was to say, 'Sit down, I'm going to play a lot of different musics for you. You don't have to tell me what composer it is, just tell me what you like and what you don't like.' I thought that was a great way to start. We got into serial writing. I wrote some pieces for flute, oboe and clarinet on a three-note series, which were accepted by the Promotion of New Music Society and performed, but I never heard them.

"After a while I said, 'Do you think a musician needs counterpoint?' He said, 'Yes, but I would be too bored to teach it to you.' That's when I went to study with Bill Russo, who lived in England and had a regular Saturday morning band.

"He was a very stimulating man. His lessons were great. He got very angry if you didn't come with a lot of work done. You didn't even have to pay in cash. Instead you could do editing. That's when I realized how important it was to be neat. He would give you scores to edit. If the dynamic wasn't just under the note, you put a tick beside it. All the little things like that: if the crescendo didn't go right to where it was supposed to. It spoiled me. Because music after that, I realized, is so messy. Most people didn't take care in sessions that things were right. With him, what was there was perfect.

"I studied baroque counterpoint with him. He was a wonderful teacher. That helped me a lot. But after a couple of years he went back to the States.

"Then I started to get busy. A lump came up in my mouth, and I thought, 'That's it, it's cancer.' But it was an impacted wisdom tooth and it set up a pouch of poison. I was in the hospital two or three days, but they said, 'You won't be able to blow a trumpet for about three months.' There was a big hole, and they put this packing in. Which was okay, except when they had to put a new one in and pulled the old one out. It was like they were pulling out something from the bottom of your toes.

"Mentally, it was a great period. Because Dankworth said, 'While you can't work for three months, would you like to write an album for the band?' That's when I wrote that album called *Windmill Tilter*. It turned out to be one of the most productive three months of my life. For all this music I'd been sort of hearing and wanting to write for a big band did sort of come together for that album. That was made in 1967." The album, based on *Don Quixote*, is now out of print, but at the time it went far to establish Kenny as an arranger and composer.

"By this time," he said, "I was a much better trumpet player and not quite so nervous. But I still couldn't play what I guess you might call be-bop, although it was my roots. I was never a good be-bop player. I was getting very frustrated, because I wanted to play more, and in Dankworth's band you got maybe two 32-bar solos a night.

"It got to the point where I didn't care what kind of music I played as long as it was jazz of some kind. So I went up to the Little Theater Club, and I heard these guys playing what they called free jazz, and I hated it on sight. But I went a few times, and eventually they asked me to sit in. And it was great. I don't know whether I enjoyed it, but it felt therapeutic. When I finished, I felt like I'd got rid of something. I wouldn't say it was good or bad.

"I got more interested in free music. Those guys, people like John Stevens, Evan Parker, Derek Bailey, Barry Guy, who are now kind of the fathers of the free jazz movement in Britain, were in touch with the free jazz players in Europe, and that's how I got my entry into Europe – through free jazz.

"After many years of that, somebody said to me, 'Oh, I didn't know you played changes.'"

He'd been playing be-bop, or a form of it, with Joe Harriott, Ronnie Scott, Tubby Hayes, and others. But by the early 1970s, he was considered one of the most important figures in the free-jazz movement. Yet he retained his links to a more traditional jazz, working in groups led by Ian Carr, Mike Gibbs, and John Taylor. He played in the Clarke-Boland Big Band in Cologne and wrote for Maynard Ferguson's British band. He co-led, with saxophonist and clarinetist Tony Coe, a group called Coe, Wheeler & Co., and with singer Norma Winstone and the Manchester-born pianist John Taylor formed a group called Azimuth. He has worked with the Globe Unity Orchestra, the Anthony Braxton Quartet, the United Jazz and Rock Ensemble, and the Dave Holland Quintet. It seems there is nothing in modern jazz that he hasn't played. One of the best descriptions of his playing and writing comes from Ian Carr. Carr, yet another Scot, has an extra insight into Kenny's work because of his own trumpet and fluegelhorn skills.

"He became a complete brass virtuoso with a technical mastery of trumpet from the lowest to the highest registers, and tremendous stamina. He composes and arranges for very large ensembles and for small groups, and both his playing and his writing have a powerful individual atmosphere which has spawned many disciples – a kind of buoyant, romantic melancholy. Immensely self-critical, he finds it easier to like his writing than his playing, and has said, 'I don't have any solos of my own that I like completely, only those that are not as bad as others . . . perhaps the solos on *Dear Wan* I can live with.'"

Kenny told me, "I'm trying to get simpler. I think having a strong technique helps you to get simpler. I am trying to get clearer and simpler. A lot of people shake their heads and say, 'I haven't a clue what he's trying to do.' But a lot of people do understand it. I couldn't put it into words. It's not strict be-bop, but it's be-bop rooted. Louis is the grandfather and Dizzy's the father of it all."

"You must be aware of your technique."

"Well it's got to do with relaxing," Kenny said. "I'm learning more how to relax when I play, and that's why it's better. You could never be as tense as I was years ago and improve, that's for sure.

"I never got much chance to play conventional jazz. Then somebody played me a record of Booker Little, and that helped me a lot. He sort of opened up for me a new way, his compositions and his playing. They were different, but they were still be-bop. So I thought, 'Oh, you can do things differently and still be in the tradition.' That gave me courage to search out and have faith in my own thing and not feel guilty because I couldn't play strict be-bop. And I found that the one helped the other. If I did get a normal sort of jazz gig, with tunes, I felt the free jazz helped that, and also that helped the free-jazz gigs. Somehow the free jazz helped loosen me up on changes, and those gigs brought my playing in free jazz in a bit, where it was more controlled."

"Well," I said, "you're talking about the artist getting rid of inhibitions, and I know that you and I had plenty of them. How repressed were we all in Canada? I've talked to Christopher Plummer about this. He said, 'It's a wonder any of us got out of there with any of our talent intact.' The one thing you're not supposed to be in Canada is different. God forbid you should want to be visible. Humility is the Canadian ideal.

"Maynard Ferguson lives down the street from me in California. I saw him at his mailbox one day. I slammed on the brakes and leaned out the window and said, 'Hey, Maynard, why did the Canadian cross the road? To get to the middle.'

"He was hanging on the mailbox with laughter. Tell that to an American and all you'll get is a blank stare."

One of the things that amazes everyone about Kenny is the sheer effortless volume of his playing. His long-time associate at the Banff School of Fine Arts, pianist, composer, and bassist Don Thompson, with whom Kenny has recorded, told me that Kenny a few years ago made a guest appearance with a big band in Toronto. Its members were essentially the same people who play with Rob McConnell in the Boss Brass, and that, needless to say, is a powerful brass section. Kenny rehearsed one of his compositions with the band, and then said in his reticent way, "I think I'll play a little on this." He picked up his fluegelhorn and drowned the whole brass section.

"Kenny's an absolute original," Don said. "He can play one note and you know it's him. He's two people. He's that quiet person, and then when he picks up his horn, he just explodes, like a giant. The power of his playing – and his harmony, and his writing, and everything – are so intense that it's scary.

"There's something rhythmically he does that is strange. His phrases don't end or start when you think they're going to. They always go where you don't expect, notes and rhythms and everything. Nothing is ever what you think it's going to be. You can't predict anything."

The late Red Rodney told me, "Kenny Wheeler to me is one of the most magnificent of all the trumpet players we have. He's very lyrical and he's very modern, with a melodic bent in everything he does. He's a cult hero of all the young, up-and-coming players. And I'll tell you, I'm part of that cult. I love him."

Saxophonist Jane Ira Bloom said, "What I hear is sincerity – and a unique voice. Kenny Wheeler could be playing a trumpet, or a saxophone, or a violin, I could tell it's him. It's his voice coming through that instrument. And he has a great deal of harmonic imagination, which I find very refreshing, in his music, in his orchestration, and in his own playing. It's almost completely lyric. And it's effortless. The virtuosity is invisible, and that's the way it should be. The instrument disappears. The fluency of that instrument sounds so easy.

"There's magic in him."

She had been engaged to do a concert tour with Kenny. She said, "I just can't wait to stand beside that horn and listen to him."

Saxophonist and composer Bill Kirchner said, "He's the most in-tune fluegelhorn player I ever heard."

Brazilian trumpeter Claudio Roditi said, "Kenny Wheeler keeps improving. I've been following him for many years. He just keeps getting better and better."

One of the people who has worked with Kenny is John Abercrombie. John told me: "At ECM I recorded with different people. I recorded with Dave Liebman and I did my own record with Jack DeJohnette and Jan Hammer before Jan Hammer went over into rock-and-roll. Then Manfred Eicher, who founded ECM, called me up one day and said he wanted to do this project with Kenny Wheeler, and Kenny wanted to use guitar, either me or Ralph Towner. Ralph Towner plays acoustic, nylon-string classical guitar. I play electric guitar. Then I figured Kenny maybe didn't know what either one of us really sounded like. He didn't seem to care whether it was electric or acoustic. As a result we both wound up on the album.

"It was mostly me, because ultimately I think he wanted somebody to comp and play more like a piano. That's when I first met Kenny. I remember getting together in a little hotel room in Oslo with Kenny and Dave Holland. Kenny played me some tapes of music he'd done, and showed me the music he planned to record. I looked at it and said, 'This looks interesting. This looks hard.' I took it back to my room and worked on the voicings and tried to understand what he wanted. We did the album in a day. It's called *Dear Wan*. It's a neat record. That was with the Norwegian saxophone player Jan Garbarek. Dave, Jack DeJohnette, Jan, Kenny, and myself. Ralph Towner played on one or two pieces.

"Kenny's tunes are hard. But they're so melodic, and they make so much sense, that you can play them. Kenny writes a tune that's got all these odd-ball chords, but it's held together with this gorgeous melody.

"Have you heard *Windmill Tilter*? It's a great record. All English musicians. An amazing record. You can hear where Kenny's going to go. The first time I heard it, I said, 'Kenny, you sound a little like Booker Little on this.' And he said, 'He was one of my big influences.'

"I've done three albums with Kenny now, and we've also done several tours. I'm just amazed at how strong and how consistently he plays. I was saying to Randy Brecker, 'Kenny plays so strong. So loud – so much sheer volume that comes out of the horn is incredible.' I asked Randy as a trumpet player if he had any idea why Kenny plays that way. We thought maybe he just hears that way. We thought he hears the trumpet as vocal. I can't even describe it. Most guys play *in* the time: Kenny just plays *across* the time, almost consistently. It almost reminds me, although it doesn't sound like it, of a rock-and-roll guitar player. When I play the guitar loud, it gets a sustained, singing quality. And I almost think that's what Kenny goes for. He goes for this powerful sound. It's lyrical, but it's powerful. It's not quiet and timid. It's very forceful.

"The leaps he makes! He'll be playing a line and then leap into another register. Kenny told me he felt he'd never really mastered be-bop. And I think he goes beyond be-bop.

"And he's totally self-effacing. According to John Taylor, who's very close to Kenny, when they did the big-band tour of England for his sixtieth birthday, Kenny was amazed at how many people came out."

Kenny remarked to me at one point, "Well to me, if you haven't got sound and time, you might as well forget it. You have to have both of those before anything else."

I said, "There's something about your approach to pitch that I can't figure out."

"I never do have trouble with intonation," Kenny said, "unless somebody in a band starts to say, 'Well we're not really in tune.' Then I'm completely lost. Because once you decide prematurely to do this and say, 'I'm flat,' you have a problem. I never touch my tuning slide from one session to another. Something in the lip must adjust it. Especially when you're playing with a bass player like Dave Holland, who is very strong on pitch, and you've got that underneath you. It makes it a lot easier.

"You're apt to get these people in big bands saying, 'Look, fellows, we're behind.' I can't do those things preconceived. I'm behind, okay, I'll rush everything. I can't do that. You just play, and the intonation is right or the time is right, and that's why I say that sound and time are the main things. When I say sound, I mean not only a good quality sound but the intonation as well. You can't think about time."

In 1990, Kenny sent me a two-CD album he'd made for the ECM label, titled *Music for Large and Small Ensembles*. The musicians on the sessions included John Abercrombie, guitar; John Taylor, piano; Dave Holland, bass; Peter Erskine, drums; Norma Winstone, vocal lead; Derek Watkins, Henry Lowther, Alan Downy, and Ian Hamer, trumpets; Dave Horler, Chris Pyne,

Paul Rutherford, and Hugh Fraser, trombones; Ray Warleigh, Duncan Lamont, Evan Parker, and Julian Arguelles, saxophones; Stan Sulzman, tenor saxophone and flute; and of course Kenny on trumpet and fluegelhorn.

I put it on the stereo system and started across the living room. In the first bars of the opening – in which you can hear the evidence of the baroque counterpoint he studied with Bill Russo – I paused. The first side of the first CD is a seven-part suite for big band. As it unfolded, going into the second and third parts, I became transfixed, standing utterly motionless as I listened.

In Part II of the suite, titled "For H.," Kenny comes in on fluegelhorn. He can do things with the upper register of that instrument that no one else can do. Whereas virtuoso brass players climb to high notes, Kenny seems to start above the register of the instrument, up in the inaudible range, and then come diving down, like an aircraft breaking out of clouds. It's eerie, and he does it all the time. But above all, as the suite unfolded, the writing mesmerized me.

"What about the big-band writing?" I asked.

"About '69 or '70," he said, "I got the feeling I would like to write for a big band that involved the various styles of the people I'd been playing with. I'd always admired Keith Christie, who was known as a traditional player, although I would not have called him that, and Evan Parker and Derek Bailey who were free-form players. And I liked Norma Winstone. But I didn't want to have a band singer. I thought about writing for her like a horn in the band. And that's how I got started with the big band. The BBC give you one half-hour broadcast a year, and they don't pay for rehearsal time. So you've got to ask the guys to do free rehearsal. I guess I must have done that since 1969 probably about fifteen or sixteen times in twenty years."

He used Winstone as a wordless lead on the sections.

"I realized I had to use some studio brass guys. It was three trumpets in the beginning and three or four trombones, and I had a mixed front line of trumpet, voice, and a couple of saxophones. I had to use some studio guys. I wanted some people whose intonation was good. The drummer I had was Tony Oxley, who's been doing a lot of playing with Cecil Taylor, and he'd played with Bill Evans. He's a great drummer, but he doesn't conform at all, he's very loose. For these sessions guys, it was very difficult, playing in a band like this, a combination of inside and a lot of outside playing. The drummer never gave you 'one'. It used to be really funny, to look at all their feet going in different places. 'I've got "one"! I've got "one"!' But I loved the effect of it, I thought it was great, the whole looseness of this big band. I never thought, 'Well, I'm doing something new here.' But I guess it was new, having more like a quartet rhythm feel rather than a tight feel. I couldn't stand that tight big-band feeling. I liked the idea of good quality music played very loosely – I guess getting more towards Ellington, a bit. Since then the big band has probably got less free and more conventional."

I said, "You're aware, surely, of the stature you've acquired."

"Well, amongst musicians," he said. "It's nice to be accepted by a lot of musicians. Maybe in the last two or three years I could feel the media getting a little more interested. But they still find little ways to put me down. As if I don't really know what I'm doing. In Canada and England, particularly."

I said, "But the most vicious criticism in the world is written in England and Canada. I don't think they really know how to praise."

Kenny said, "It's almost like, well, we've said enough good things, we'd better say something put-downish.'"

Kenny's sister Helen is the one who watches most closely over Kenny's history. She has every record he ever made. She told me that Kenny's son and daughter are named Mark and Louanne. "Louanne is named after Doreen's mother, who was named Louise. The 'Anne' comes from my middle name. Mark works for a travel company. Louanne is married to a businessman who owns a restaurant in London. They have a villa in Portugal.

"Doreen is just what Kenny needs, a totally different temperament. She's very outgoing and easygoing. Seldom gets upset. Kenny can get very up-tight. He can get very moody, Ken. She knows how to keep him on an even keel. The thing about Kenny is that he knows when he's been that way, moaning and groaning, and he always apologizes. He knows when he's got down and got everybody else down.

"I think it's because Kenny has such deep feelings about things. The saddest thing was when Dad died. Dad died 12 January 1983. It was just before Kenny's birthday. Kenny flew over from England. We didn't want him to come. It was a long way to come. He wanted to. We kept Dad laid over an extra day, so Kenny could be here. Kenny went to the funeral parlor all on his own. I remember walking in and seeing Kenny sitting all by himself by the coffin, just staring. It was such a sad picture, to see him. Kenny was so upset by Dad's dying."

I told Helen that I have been bothered all my life by Kenny's move to England. Would he eventually have found his way to the United States and found an earlier and greater recognition?

"Maybe if you hadn't suggested it and he hadn't gone to England," Helen said, "he'd have come back to St. Catharines. And that would have been a catastrophe for him."

Perhaps in the end, Ian Carr was half right. It was not in search of a non-competitive world that Kenny went to England: at the time, he and I simply couldn't get visas to the United States. But England is a softer country than the United States. Kenny had no precognitive intuition about the right place for him. He went to England almost by accident because I said something in the Cafe St. Michel.

But what if the musicians had asked him to sit in that night?

"I couldn't have done it anyway," Kenny told me recently. "My hands would have been shaking."

To return to St. Catharines would indeed have been catastrophic for him. Had he done so, he might have ceased playing for ever.

"Doesn't it seem ironic," I said a day after he made an album with Don Thompson, "to be recording jazz in Toronto all these years after being ignored here?"

"Yes, it does, really," Kenny said. "I had a walk around the east end yesterday, and the streets came flooding back from when I was a kid. I still don't feel anything in Toronto, I don't feel I'm any kind of celebrity, although the last time I played, the place was packed. I played with Dave McMurdo's big band. But the times I played before, about three times in ten years, nobody came. I wonder what would happen if I played in Toronto now, whether anybody would come."

"I think the Canadian condescension to Canadian talent is still here," I said.

Kenny said, "One critic in England, speaking about ECM artists, accused them all of being very rich. Which certainly is not true. I've just got a little house, I'm not rich."

"For all the years I've lived in the States," I said, "I still feel the identity with Canada."

"Yeah, I do too."

And so he comes home regularly. Sometime in the early 1970s, when I was living in Toronto and, having overcome at least some of my fear of performing, doing a lot in television, Kenny came home. It was a rainy summer. Kenny lamented that he liked to come home to sit in his mother's back yard in St. Catharines and soak in the sun. This summer it hadn't been possible. I said, "It's a drag. It's been like this all summer, and yet last summer was just beautiful. Endless sunshine."

And with his slightly bizarre sense of humor and slightly English accent, he said, "Well then, I guess I should go back to England and come back last summer."

Kenny and Don Thompson have been among the most important teachers at the Banff School of the Arts. Don tells me that between them, they have produced about 75 per cent of the finest younger jazz players in Canada. Renee Rosnes passed through that school.

I thought this was typical of Kenny, who by then was in his fifties: he told his wife, "I think perhaps by now I may know enough to teach."

When I told him that I was pleased for him, he said in that shy way that hasn't changed since we were in high school, "I just wish it had happened maybe ten years earlier." I couldn't help remembering the two of us in the St. Michel, he with his horn on his lap, yearning to play, and no one asked him.

On 28 May 1999, Kenny began a three-night engagement at Birdland in New York City leading a mixed American–British band of superb players. Composer Bill Kirchner said the next day:

"The band sounded excellent. Kenny's writing and playing, of course, are totally personal. Kenny himself is self-effacing to the point of being comical. He left all the conducting and announcements to one of the tenor players and stood only when playing solos."

But the best Kenny Wheeler story I know came from a friend of ours in St. Catharines, a former drummer named Rod North.

During one of Kenny's periodic returns to St. Catharines, he went with Helen and Bryon Ball, his nephew and son of his sister Mabel, to a jazz club. One of the musicians recognized him and started an effusive introduction from the bandstand. Something to this effect: "Ladies and gentlemen, we have with us tonight a real jazz celebrity! He is a composer, an arranger, a trumpet player . . . "

Kenny sank lower in his chair.

"A man who left St. Catharines to become one of the great jazz musicians of our time!"

And Kenny sank lower still.

"Ladies and gentlemen, may I present . . . Mr. Kenny Wheeler!"

Kenny jabbed Bryon with an elbow and said, "Stand up!"

3

Music by Faith:
Percy Faith

In the mid-1970s, the CBS Records Group negotiated a reciprocal arrangement with the Russian label Melodiya, which gave the company access to that extensive and very important catalogue of Soviet classical recordings. What did the Russians ask for – and get – in return? At the head of their shopping list were the albums of Percy Faith, he of the "mood music" with the pretty strings and woodwinds, of latter years called "elevator music."

Percy has been gone for more than twenty years. He died of cancer at the age of 68 in March, 1976. He was an immensely successful musician, but that he was also an influential one was not widely recognized, and for that matter still isn't. Percy Faith was one of the first arrangers to bring to the orchestration and performance of popular music the skills, scope, and instrumentation of classical music. He did this before even Morton Gould. He was doing it as far back as the early 1930s. Over a period of 30 years, Percy recorded for Columbia a probable 65 albums, not to mention all the charts he wrote for singers, including Tony Bennett and Johnny Mathis.

"None of my albums," he said, "ever went into the red, despite the large orchestras I used." He did know the number of films he had scored: eleven. One of those scores, the one he wrote for a dreadful movie called *The Oscar*, proves beyond question something most of his albums did not: that, given the chance, Percy Faith was an elegant and highly lyrical composer.

The best songs of the late 1930s and 1940s were superior to the orchestrations applied to them. The writing, particularly accompaniment for vocals, was often awkward if not downright primitive, with strange instrumental balances and clumsy voice-leading. The good writing was found in the big bands, jazz and otherwise, but it was limited to trumpets, trombones, saxes and rhythm section. When Artie Shaw, Tommy Dorsey, Harry James, and Gene Krupa added string sections to their bands, the effect was often unsatisfactory. The strings were too few to balance the brass, and the other instrumental colors – those mixed from classical woodwinds and horns – were not even in the palette. The effect was simply that of a dance band with added strings, a format that Paul Weston would develop to glorious effect in a series of albums for Capitol in the 1950s and 1960s.

The influence of Percy Faith comes into American music through another figure, Bob Farnon.

"I learned a lot from Percy," Bob said. "I admired him very much. I admired his taste. He especially taught me what to leave out. I studied his writing. I was playing second trumpet and the jazz solos, and I appreciated his inner lines, which were so nice. These were the things that rubbed off on me."

Percy's later career was enormously successful. He was proud of the fact that every one of his albums for Columbia Records, his arrangements of current pop material, made money. But they are compromised albums, since some of the songs he arranged were trash, and his is a curiously blunted career. He rarely got the chance to show how good a composer he was, and the only instance of it on record that I know of is the album on Columbia (long since out of print) of his score for *The Oscar*. It is a superb score, and, interestingly, shows his skill at counterpoint, with marvelous inner lines. This is something he shares with Bob Farnon and Gil Evans.

Percy had a far more extensive academic background than Bob. Like Glenn Gould and unlike Bob, he was a product of the Toronto Conservatory of Music. But, like Bob, he studied for a time with Louis Waizman. Neither Glenn nor Percy had affection for the Toronto Conservatory. Glenn told me once, "Whatever musician I am, it is in spite of, not because of, the Toronto Conservatory." And Percy said, "I was ready to jump two or three years ahead of what they were doing. But I was told by my harmony teacher, 'You must learn the basics. You must learn Bach, all the preludes and fugues, on the piano, then orchestrate them for string quartet, for brass quartet. Learn Beethoven. Learn that foundation, and then when it's become a part of you, forget it and go on.'" He entered the Toronto Conservatory at the age of 14, and performed the Liszt *Hungarian Rhapsody* at Massey Hall in 1923, when he was 15.

He began conducting for radio in 1931, and when the Canadian Broadcasting Corporation was organized, he went to work for it almost immediately. Wonder of wonders, they let him attach his name to the show. It was called *Music by Faith*. Possibly he got away with it because the title seemed allusive to religion. From the very beginning Percy used not dance-band instrumentation but the "classical" kind of orchestra for which he later became known in the United States, with traditional woodwinds rather than a sax section. Percy hired Bob for the show; Bob was 17.

When I told Percy that Bob had always said that he, Percy, was one of his great influences, he said, "The strings were always quite busy in anything I wrote. But the trumpets had many, many bars' rest, and I gather that Bobby did a lot of listening.

"I had added six girls to the orchestra. I wanted certain sounds. The budget wouldn't allow for extra percussion and woodwinds, and I found I could get girls to sing for five dollars each per show. They did nothing but vocalize at first, in conjunction with three or four flutes plus a vibraphone and celesta. We got a great sound. People thought it was an organ or some kind of electronic instrument."

My memory is that Percy said he hired six singers; Bob says the group was sixteen. Whatever it was, it was apparently effective.

"Once this clicked," Percy said, "the CBC suggested, 'Since you've got them, why don't we hear something with lyrics?' So I turned the girls over to Bobby, and I said, 'Let's do one number a week.' But since we were so avant garde, I said, 'I don't want any ballads. Let's do nothing but out-of-left-field tunes like "Where Oh Where Has My Little Dog Gone?"' So Bobby started writing these vocal arrangements for me, and they were fantastic. With the band and six girls, it really swung."

A legend persisted in Toronto music circles that Bob would set an empty chair beside him in the brass section, and, while the orchestra was rehearsing for a broadcast, use the tacet passages in the trumpet charts to write vocal arrangements on that chair. Both Bob and Percy confirmed the story. Percy said that he and the other musicians found it disconcerting.

"After one of our broadcasts," Bob recalled, "he took me out into the lounge and said, 'Bobby, I wish you wouldn't do that. I find it somewhat soul-destroying to watch.' It was *naïveté* on my part. I didn't realize it was bothering him. But I stopped doing it."

Though Farnon attests to Percy's influence on him, their writing is not especially similar, as you can hear immediately on comparing the charts they wrote on "How Are Things in Glocca Mora," but sometimes there are similarities, as in a trick of using vibes with flutes. Percy wrote a stunning chart on "Younger than Springtime" that particularly reveals their relationship. For an intro, he establishes a melody consisting of (in G) F-sharp, G, E, F-sharp, in eighth notes, which he assigns to the flutes. In the first eight bars of the tune, which is played by solo violin, the motif is used as a counterline. The counterline is developed chromatically, in a way Farnon might do. A variant of it is used even in the release. The connective figures are, again like so many of Farnon's, in half-steps. At the end of the tune, he introduces a glorious variant on his own variant, now played by the piano. Then, reprising the front strain in high strings, Percy assigns his countertheme to the low strings, throwing it for a coda to oboe. It unifies the whole. It is beautifully intelligent writing, logical and consistent throughout.

Percy Faith was born 7 April 1908 in Toronto. He began studying violin at 7, piano at 10, aspiring to a career as a concert pianist. From 1920, when he was 12, he worked as a pianist accompanying silent movies in Toronto theaters, and he played in dance bands until about 1926. Then he burned his hands severely, and that ended his concert ambitions. He could, however, still write, and he began working as an arranger. From 1935 to 1938 he was arranger and conductor on various Canadian Broadcasting Corporation programs.

In 1940, a CBC executive ordered the budget for *Music by Faith* cut, despite its success. It was one of the few Canadian productions to be carried regularly to the larger audience of an American network. Percy, who all his life had a crusty streak, was angered.

And by an accident of timing, the National Broadcasting Company was at that time auditioning conductors to replace Josef Pasternak, conductor of a show called *The Carnation Contented Hour*. (Older Americans and Canadians still remember its theme song: "Won't You Wait Till the Cows Come Home?") Pasternak had died and Percy, now 31, auditioned in Chicago, was hired for the summer, confirmed as permanent music director of the show in September, and gave up his position as, in his own bitter words, "the token Jew of the CBC". He stayed with *The Carnation Contended Hour* through 1947, becoming one of the top arrangers of popular music in the United States. Eventually he became virtually the house arranger for Columbia Records from 1950 to 1959 and in Los Angeles from 1960 to 1976, and he recorded a total of 45 instrumental albums for that company.

But his pioneer work had already been done in Toronto. "As a matter of fact," he said, "as late as 1955 I recorded some arrangements that were, practically note-for-note, arrangements I did in Toronto in the '30s.

"But it's all changing now. Jerry Goldsmith said that the art of film scoring is gone – scoring in the style of Max Steiner, Alfred Newman, or his own. And he's right. It's an electronic world now, and I've been studying the Moog, the Arp, the Fender-Rhodes piano. I use them in my recordings sometimes.

"When you walk into the record studio, the sound stage, you don't see any big string sections, any 90-piece orchestras for the main titles. You'll see three or four keyboard men, the finest in the country, all sitting around with synthesizers and electric pianos and the E-3 Yamaha organ, which can practically simulate any orchestra sound, and that's your score." One can only wonder what Percy would think if he were alive to see the equipment available now; and to note that early in 1985 his brilliant friend Jerry Goldsmith had a score thrown out of a movie, to be replaced by electronics. But Percy certainly saw what was coming.

"With 32-track equipment, one man or a group of four or five men can come up with some fabulous sounds. And so you're into a new study. It is a pity, but that's the way it is today, and you either go along with it or be dropped."

Percy adapted to changing fashions in music with apparently effortless facility. For one thing, he understood rhythm sections. And he had a knack for picking the right musicians to play his music, with a leaning toward jazz players. When he toured Japan, the pianist in the orchestra was Alan Broadbent. The emphasis in his writing was usually on strings and woodwinds, but he wrote extremely well for brass and his brass sections could swing.

"I do three albums a year," he told me in 1974. "There is a rock influence in the things I've done in the last few years. I've just had to. You cannot sell Gershwin, you cannot sell Rodgers – they've had it. The Establishment won't buy it, and the young people aren't interested, so you've got to give it to them their way."

His prognosis for movie music was equally gloomy. During the time of the great movie studios, there was a key figure in the production chain, the music director. Himself a musician, he functioned as intermediary, arbitrator, and translator between the producer and director and the composer. By the mid-1970s, with the gradual breakdown of the studio system, this figure had vanished and the composer was forced to deal directly with producers and directors, who usually have little or no understanding of the dramatic function of music in film.

"That's what's going on now," Percy said. "And so I haven't done a film score in three years. I'd just as soon do my recordings, do a few concerts, play some golf and fish, rather than get involved with directors and producers who really don't know anything about music and will admit it to you but will stand over your shoulder while you're writing. That's a terrible amount of pressure to be under."

Percy's son, Peter Faith, was a widely respected agent for film composers.

"Peter is involved with a film right now where they've done three scores, by three very well-known writers," Percy said. "One of them was Dave Grusin, who is a great, great talent. Dave was brought in after they threw out the first score.

"The producer was practically standing over his shoulder all the time, wanting Dave to play the score on the piano as he was writing it. So at the recording session, on the scoring stage, when they were in rehearsal, Dave called the producer out to stand beside him in front of the orchestra, and said, 'I want you to listen to this, because I don't want to waste any time.'

"Dave played four bars and stopped and turned to the producer and asked, 'What do you think of it so far?' This is in front of the orchestra! So the producer is a little stunned, because he isn't in an office with Dave, where he could clobber him, he's in front of 30 or 40 men. He asked, 'Well, isn't there more?' and Dave said, 'Sure.'

"So Dave said, 'Okay, boys, bar five.' And then he went on and played bars five, six, seven and eight, and stopped again, and said, 'What do you think of it so far?' And the producer turned around and walked out, figuring that he was being had."

I have no idea how many people heard that story from Percy and Peter Faith. Certainly I told it to a few musicians. It took on the proportions of minor legend, until finally, running into Dave Grusin one day, I asked him if this classic tale of a composer's sarcasm were true. Dave confirmed that it was, but said he wasn't really being sarcastic. Sensing the situation, he simply wanted to save time.

Dave's score too was thrown out of the film. "Now they're working on another one," Percy said. "I'd hate to depend on that form of composition for my bread and butter."

But that is precisely the misfortune of Faith's career. He was not adept at the machinations of Hollywood. He was too testy and blunt for the Byzantine politics of the industry. So he was never given the film assignments his talent deserved and thus never received his due as a composer. The films he did get were minor and are by now forgotten, such things as *The Love Goddesses, I'd Rather Be Rich*, and *The Third Day*. As far as I know, none of them was ever recorded, with a single exception: *The Oscar*.

A turgid soap opera of a movie about a ruthless actor who aspires to win the Academy Award, the film is worthwhile only for Percy's music. The album derived from it, issued on Columbia like all Percy's albums, reveals him as a wonderful melodist. Not all arrangers can write melody: but Percy could. There is a great variety of styles in the score, from a Latin piece featuring a solo alto to a jazz waltz that swings nicely. The way Percy uses trombones for rhythmic pops in this tune is particularly deft.

The love theme of the film is one of the most glorious melodies I have ever heard, and I am surprised that jazz musicians have not taken it up. It was given lyrics by Jay Livingston and Ray Evans and called "Maybe September," and its most well-known recording was by Tony Bennett. Tony's version of it was in his *Movie Song* album. Percy didn't write the exquisite chart; Larry Wilcox did, and the conductor was Johnny Mandel. The track was borrowed from Tony's album and included in the Columbia album of the film score. It is one of Tony's finest performances. No doubt the melody inspired him. A rangy tune with big leaps, it isn't easy to sing, which may be why so many singers have ignored it.

It has an unexpected construction. The body of it is in A B A B1 form. As it comes to the resolution, it suddenly takes off into a totally new melody, sixteen bars long. "I just felt the need for it there," Percy said, without any further justification.

The instrumental version of the tune is scored for strings, oboes, and flutes, with vibes adding touches of color. What is most arresting is the linear writing. Although the track is harmonically interesting, it is even more enchanting for the movement of the bass and inner lines, in which Percy's years of immersion in Bach become evident. The attention to detail is part of what makes this track so lovely, right down to articulation markings for the strings.

According to the format of his recordings for Columbia Records, Percy arranged the current hits of the day, and therefore his albums constitute a documentation of the decline of great melodic writing in America, in Tin Pan Alley and in film scoring. Broadway material simply disappears from his repertoire as the theater ceased to produce hits, and then film-writing starts to follow it down the tube.

Percy came about as close as anyone in music ever did to being able to make a silk purse out of a sow's ear. But he was not at his best when he was handed trash. Percy could not, for all his professionalism, get creative juices flowing fully for such material as "Song Sung Blue" or Francis Lai's "Love Story," and in a song such as "Windy" he could descend into the deepest corn. A lot of what Percy did was garbage – high-class garbage, to be sure, but garbage nonetheless. Percy apparently approached a lot of this material cynically, giving it the treatment it deserved, putting his public on and perhaps also the brass of Columbia Records who didn't know the difference. There is no other explaining it. His taste was too unerring for him not to be aware of the worthlessness of the worst material and his own treatment of it. *The Oscar* proves that. You could detect his respect for a tune, or lack of it, in the first two bars. Given superior material such as Jerry Goldsmith's "Love Theme" from *The Sand Pebbles* or Johnny Mandel's "A Time for Love," or Richard Rodgers' "Younger than Springtime," Percy's writing was gorgeous, and very moving. And always there was that lovely linear writing, the heritage of Bach.

There is something sad about the career of Percy Faith, for all the success of it. It was full of frustration. He was frustrated at the CBC because of limitations imposed on him, and then the cutting of his budget. He never ceased to be Canadian, but he never ceased to be annoyed about it either. Like Bob Farnon, he said he couldn't go home again, except for occasional appearances with symphony orchestras. "When you've lived in a mansion," he said, referring to the recording budgets and large orchestras he had in the United States compared with what one could expect in Canada, "you can't go back to living in a two-room flat."

He never got the chance to fulfill his true potential as a composer.

In a way, Percy was lucky to die when he did. Were he alive, he'd be unemployed.

4

À la claire fontaine:
Robert Farnon

As World War II was grinding to its close, a young Canadian army captain named Robert Farnon, a former jazz cornet player, was turning out a series of arrangements and compositions that for the rest of the century would profoundly influence arrangers around the world, and nowhere more than in the United States. He is the most influential Canadian musician ever born. Despite the admiration in which he is held in other countries, despite the fact that in Britain he has received the Ivor Novello award five times, no major Canadian magazine has ever so much as published an article about him and he has never received an important award in his native country.

There were in England at the time three bands of the Allied Expeditionary Force, established on the direct order of General Dwight D. Eisenhower. The British Band of the AEF, as it was called, was led by George Melachrino. The American Band of the AEF – the name it eventually acquired after several previous designations – was led by Captain, later Major, Alton Glenn Miller, as he signed his official military correspondence. The Canadian Band of the AEF was led by Captain Robert Farnon.

All three bands had something in common: they used more or less standard dance-band instrumentation augmented by string sections. It was the kind of orchestra no civilian dance-band leader could afford. But in the military, where money was not an object and the musicians were in uniform anyway, the leaders of these bands, none of them more than Miller, were able to reach out and commandeer all the available talent they wanted.

Miller had the biggest name and the biggest band, peopled by musicians of the stature of Mel Powell on piano, Ray McKinley on drums, Peanuts Hucko on tenor, and Bernie Privin on trumpet. And because of the huge pool of superb American musicians Miller was able to draw on, his was the best of the three bands.

Farnon said, "In our band we had a great number of musicians but not many very good ones. Five trumpets, five trombones, six saxophones, rhythm, and a big string section. But some of the fiddle players held their instruments down on the chest. No kidding. Some of them said, 'I can't read, I'll just listen to you' to the man next to them.

"Our string section wasn't anywhere near up to the standard of the Miller band. He had guys out of the New York Philharmonic."

Miller's wartime band was the best he ever led, and in the opinion of Ray McKinley, with whom I discussed this, it was "the best band ever to play popular music in America, and probably in the world."

But much of the best writing was that being done for the Canadian band. The Miller band had a number of arrangers; the Canadian band had only one, Bob Farnon and, given the heavy schedule of the band – four or five broadcasts a week on the BBC, as well as concerts and dances for the troops – the sheer quantity of his output is amazing.

The reverence in which Farnon is held by arrangers and other musicians, not to mention singers, is unlimited. They have long referred to him as the Governor, or just the Guv, and I heard one arranger say in a radio interview, "He is God."

When someone unfamiliar with Farnon's music asked Rob McConnell who he was, Rob said, "He is the greatest arranger in the world."

André Previn long ago called Bob "the world's greatest string writer." André said that when John (then Johnny) Williams was a young studio pianist in Los Angeles, he asked a question about string writing. André gave him a Farnon album, telling him to take it home and listen to it. Late that night, Johnny called him back to ask what the hell Farnon was doing at such-and-such point in one of the tunes. André said, "I don't know, but if you figure it out, call me back."

Years later, I ran into John Williams and, to be sure my memory was accurate, asked if the story was true. He said, "I don't remember, but say it is anyway. I'd be honored merely to be mentioned in the same breath with Robert Farnon."

When, in January 1995, in Miami, Eileen Farrell was overdubbing her voice on orchestra tracks recorded in London – her fourth CD with Farnon arrangements – I asked her how these albums had come about. She replied: "In interviews, people have always said, 'You've done opera, you've done television, you've done radio, is there anything that you'd like to do next?' And I'd say, 'The one thing I want to do before I die is to make a record with Robert Farnon.'

"Oh God! He just gets right into your soul! What he does with the chords, and his phrasing, is not to be believed. And he has such great musicians in London, and of course they just adore him."

Farnon was born in Toronto on 24 July 1917. His hair has long been white, and he has become quite portly. He continues to work on a schedule of writing and recording and, in Europe, concerts, that would crush far younger men. Comparatively recent albums include one with George Shearing, *How Beautiful Is Night*, named for one of Farnon's pieces, released on Telarc in 1993, as well as Joe Williams' 1994 *Here's to Life* on the same label. Gitanes records has issued a J. J. Johnson album, *Tangence*, recorded with Farnon in London in 1994. In 1992 Reference Records issued a new recording of the suite drawn from Bob's score to the movie *Captain Horatio Hornblower* and other concert music, including the *Rhapsody for Violin and Orchestra* and the exquisite *À la claire fontaine*. And of course older works continue to be reissued. In 1993 Reprise brought out in CD an album with Farnon charts called *Sinatra Sings Great Songs from Great Britain*, recorded in London in 1962. Arranger and film composer Allyn Ferguson said, "That's my favorite vocal album."

Bob said: "Sinatra wasn't in the best of voice. He had just come back from a world tour, and then he'd been doing two concerts a night at the Royal Festival Hall for children's charities. He came down to the studio to record at two o'clock in the morning. There were people everywhere. They were beside me on my podium. I could hardly move for fear of stepping on their hands. They were seated on the floor, crawling in amongst the players. I never saw anything like it. He loved it. But he just wasn't happy with his own voice."

Sinatra never allowed the album to be released west of the Atlantic, and it remained in a limbo of legend until the 1993 CD edition.

The body of Farnon's work in all genres has been enormous. But the actual scores had been treated with criminal negligence by the various publishers through whose hands they have passed. Many of them were available only in incomplete versions or poor photocopies. Some were lost in a fire at Chappell's in London. They have at last found a savior. Jeff Sultanof, an American with a prodigious background as composer, arranger, and music editor – who wasn't even born when some of these charts and compositions were written – has been working as a labor of love, with Bob's involvement and co-operation, to restore them. British conductor John Wilson is working with Jeff.

Meanwhile, a highly active Robert Farnon Society with members all over the world continues to publish its *Journal into Melody*. (The title is a play on that of one of Bob's compositions, "Journey into Melody.") The *Journal* is well past its 120th issue, and one of the society's members has prepared a full Farnon discography, a huge job.

Farnon, of mixed Scottish–Irish background, is the second of three brothers. Brian, the oldest, was long the music director of Harrah's casino in Lake Tahoe. Dennis too is a composer and arranger. For some time he lived in the United States, where he made big-band records. He is chiefly remembered in the US, however, for scores to the Mr. Magoo movies and the Bullwinkle television cartoons, all of which make him a great deal of money. He married a Portuguese girl and lived in Lisbon for some years, but after her death, he met a girl from Holland and moved there with his three children.

Brian is six years older than Bob, Dennis six years younger.

"Both our parents were musical," Bob said. "My mother played very nice piano, and my father played violin. They used to have musical evenings. They'd bring over a cellist and play trios. We'd sit at the top of the stairs, just Brian and myself, and listen to them play. It seeped into our blood."

Brian, who, being the elder brother, remembers some of Bob's childhood better than Bob does, said, "My mother was a really fine classical pianist who couldn't fake her way out of a bag, but she could read anything. My dad played sort of a hoedown Irish fiddle, strictly self-taught. And he sang pretty good, too, in a typical Irish tenor style. There was a friend of his who was a barber in a little town just north of Toronto. Every Sunday he would come down, bring his wife and his cello, and they'd be in the front room. And we would be listening to it, wondering where it came from."

There must be a longevity gene in the Farnon family. Brian, who was born on 27 November 1911, speaks with the voice of a man of perhaps 40. He is witty, laughs exuberantly, and remains fully committed to life, although he retired from his job at Harrah's in 1984 after 25 years there. He lives in Stateline, Nevada.

"My father died when I was 12 and Bob was 6," he said. "He left my mother with five children. Nora was the oldest, at 13. He left my mother an insurance policy that was probably worth 20,000 dollars, which at that time would be a fair amount of money. But she was conned out of it by some guy selling her shares in a chinchilla farm somewhere up in the northern part of Ontario. Naturally, she lost all the money, and she had to go to work.

"We were in such bad shape that we had to move out of the place we were living and go to live with my mother's mother, in the heart of Toronto. Her maiden name was Menzies: Scottish. We moved then to the east part of Toronto, near the Woodbine race track. Do you remember the Laura Secord candy stores?"

"Sure," I said. "There are still a few of them left."

"There *are*?" Brian said in amazement. "Well, my mother worked at one of the Laura Secord stores, behind the counter, selling candies. We needed the money. I got one year of high school and then had to quit. I got a job at Weston's biscuits at, I think it was, nine bucks a week, pushing a cart around.

"One day my mother and I went to a movie, a double feature. Between the pictures, a guy came on-stage playing a banjo. Then he put it down and picked up a saxophone. Then they had the second movie. As we walked home, she said, 'What did you think of the saxophone and that banjo?' I said,

'They sounded all right.' I wasn't the slightest bit interested. She said, 'Well, if you work hard at your job and they promote you, I'll rent either one of those, and you can learn to play it, if you like.' I said, 'Oh that's nice,' and I forgot completely about it.

"But fate's a strange thing. Two months later they did promote me from the factory into the office, into the cost department. I probably got two bucks a week more. I told my mother I was now in the office. She hugged me and said, 'You *are*? Well now, what about those two instruments? Would you like to try one?' I said, 'Well, I don't know.' She said, 'Which one do you want?' I said, 'Well let me try the banjo.'

"Well, when you start to play the banjo, the steel strings almost kill your fingers. I said, 'No, this hurts my fingers. Let me try the saxophone.'

"She rented a saxophone, a King she got somewhere. I started, and I liked it. I practiced on it and practiced on it.

"Now Bob at the time was going to school. He said to our mother, 'If he can have something, why can't I?'

"She said, 'All right, I'll rent something for you. What do you want? He said, 'I'd like to play the drums.' So she rented him a drum set. That's how he got into the music business. At that time there was no such thing as music in schools. Nothing. Bob took a few drum lessons and he got himself a set of vibes, from where I don't know. All of a sudden I'm hearing these good melodies coming out of the vibes, he's playing a bit of jazz on it – all self-taught. Not a lesson."

Brian insists that those few lessons on drums amount to almost all the formal musical education Bob received; everything else was self-taught. In this Bob is like Gil Evans.

"I found the fingering on the saxophone," Brian said. "My mother being a fine piano-player would get a sheet of piano music and play it, and I would try to find the corresponding note on the alto. That was fine as long as I was standing there playing with my mother. But then a friend of mine who played tenor sax said, 'Why don't we play some duets?' He got some alto and tenor duets. But when I tried to play the alto parts, I was in the wrong key. It's a different transposition. He finally got me a saxophone method. I taught myself the fingering and that's how I got in the business. I formed a little band right in that neighborhood, around Woodbine and Balmy Beach Canoe Club.

"The young fellow I played duets with played tenor. We got hold of another guy who played alto. We had three saxes, a trumpet player, trombone, tuba, piano, and Bob played drums. We rehearsed and sounded pretty good and we asked one of the people at the Balmy Beach Canoe Club if they'd listen to us. They did and they said, 'Yeah, you sound okay. We'll give you some work.'

"Some of the people from Malvern Collegiate started coming around." Malvern is a high school with some interesting alumni, the most famous by far being Glenn Gould. "We started getting some dates. We got a job at a Masonic temple. We played there every Saturday night.

"One night a lady said, 'I have a summer place up near Sarnia, named Crinnian's Grove.' She offered us a job. We accepted it and played there for the summer season.

"Then we got a job at the Silver Slipper, near the Humber River. We had a pretty good band. Somebody heard the band and liked it and we got more work."

Bob said: "Brian was the influence on me and Denny. When I was 12, Brian got me into his dance band playing drums. Denny fancied the trumpet." And Bob was laboriously teaching himself how to write.

Then came a significant gig.

When Bob was 15, Brian's band played at the Brant Inn. The Brant Inn, in the tiny town of Burlington, was a nightclub on the shore at the exact western end of Lake Ontario. Its elaborate décor effected the look of the deck of an ocean liner. It was one of the key locales in the circuit through Ontario where name bands played. Burlington is now a large city, and where the Brant Inn once stood there is a neighborhood of red-brick apartment buildings in a style that might be called North American Ubiquitous.

Bob's *modus operandi* was to write out each part separately, the different sheets spread out on a table and even the floor.

"I'd write a note here, a note there. It took ages," Bob said. "I had never heard of a musical score. Don Redman's band came to the Brant Inn. And Don Redman showed me a score. What an eye-opener that was. That simplified everything! And from then on I wrote scores."

Bob's only other formal training, beyond those drum lessons, was a few lessons in counterpoint with Louis Waizman, the librarian of the Toronto Symphony. Bob said, "I don't mean to be immodest, but he was teaching me what I already knew. He was telling me formally what counterpoint was."

Bob played drums with Brian's band for about three years. Then: "I fancied playing a melodic instrument, and Jimmy Reynolds, who was a trumpet player, gave me one of his old cornets and I learned the fingering and I gave up the drums for the rest of my playing days."

While they were playing the Silver Slipper job, Geoffrey Waddington was forming a band to play in the Imperial Room of the Royal York Hotel in downtown Toronto, a grand old palace owned by the Canadian National Railway.

Brian said, "He auditioned me and Bob and we joined his band at the Royal York. Bob was doing some pretty good writing. Bert Pearl was the pianist in the Geoffrey Waddington band."

"That was really the beginning," Bob said. "I never looked back."

Born in England and raised in western Canada, Geoffrey Waddington began studying violin at the age of 7. He won a scholarship to the Toronto Conservatory of Music and toured as a violinist. In 1922, he became a conductor on radio station CKNC, and when the Canadian Broadcasting Corporation took over its facilities in 1933, he became the new network's music director. He formed that band to play at the Royal York in 1933. And that's when Bob joined him.

"About 1937, Bert Pearl did a program for the summer season at the CBC," Bob said.

It was a reflection of a bizarre national characteristic that the CBC would not let the show that Bert Pearl founded be referred to as *The Bert Pearl Show*, although that was the name Farnon thinks it should have had. It was given the faceless name *The Happy Gang*. In the arts in Canada, and particularly at the CBC, one was supposed to be anonymous and grateful that you were even allowed to make a living.

The Happy Gang stayed on the air for 22 years, from 1 p.m. to 1.30 p.m., five days a week, and Bob was with it from the time it started until he joined the army in 1943. I have often said that I never heard Bob Farnon play trumpet – or cornet – but I realize that can't be true, because I occasionally heard the show when I was home sick from school; and furthermore, its personnel played a concert in a lacrosse stadium in St. Catharines, Ontario, where I grew up. I was there. I simply never heard him play jazz.

The show had an improbable instrumentation, including piano, violin, electric organ, and cornet, and a singer named Eddie Allen, and I thought the music was pretty corny. "On one occasion," Bob said, "we advanced the clocks ten minutes in the studio, and when Bert thought we were on the air, we all started swearing. It was a terrible thing to do to him. He had a hangover, and he was a nervous guy anyway." Pearl, like so many Canadians of talent, went to the United States. He worked in TV production in Los Angeles, where he died.

During Bob's period with Geoffrey Waddington and *The Happy Gang*, he started doing studio work as well. And one of the jobs he held was in a CBC orchestra led by Percy Faith.

Brian recalled: "We were playing at a place called Lake Chemong, up near Peterborough, with probably nine guys. This was the first time I really got an inkling of how well Bob wrote. He brought to a rehearsal one time an arrangement of a Duke Ellington tune, something so full of close harmonies, almost everybody in the band playing a different note. At that time I thought, 'How can this guy think of these things and put them down?' He was probably 17. When he was 21 he wrote his first symphony."

This piece, actually titled *Symphonic Suite*, was premiered on 7 January

1941, by the Toronto Symphony Orchestra, and later was performed by the Philadelphia Orchestra. Bob's *Ottawa Symphony* was premiered a year later by the Toronto Symphony.

Percy Faith told me that Bob once played drums on *Music by Faith*. "Our drummer was Harry Nicholson," Bob remembered. "He got sloshed one night and cracked up his car and they put him in the jug for a week. So I played drums for Percy."

"And quite creditably," Percy said.

"Well I knew Percy's book anyway, so it wasn't that difficult," Bob said. "During all the time I was a session musician, working with Percy and Sammy Hershenhorn and other conductors, I was also with *The Happy Gang*," Bob said. "I played vibraphone as well as trumpet with *The Happy Gang*, though I didn't play all the tuned percussion."

In 1939, Dizzy Gillespie came to Toronto in the Cab Calloway trumpet section. Bob Shuttleworth, a pianist and dance-band leader, invited to his home some of the Calloway musicians, including Dizzy and Cozy Cole. "That's where I first met Dizzy," Bob said.

The musicians began jamming.

"I'll tell you something about that night that Bob won't tell you," Brian said. "Even though he's incredible, Bob's kind of shy and doesn't want to push himself forward. He was just sitting there, like I was, enjoying it. Finally, somebody said, 'Bob, why don't you play something?' Bob said, 'No, I just want to listen to Dizzy.' Dizzy said, 'Come on, play.' So Bob played. And after it was over, Dizzy said, 'I don't feel like playing trumpet again for the rest of my life.'"

But he did resume playing, with Bob. "We jammed all night," Bob said. "We became firm friends and always were."

Never having heard Bob play jazz, I once asked Dizzy about that night. He said Bob was a marvelous trumpet – or cornet – player and, chuckling, added, "I'm *glad* he gave up trumpet."

"We met just before the war," Bob said.

The war began for Canada in September of 1939. Geoffrey Waddington went into military service and became the music director of the Canadian Army show, a recruiting show that played across Canada. Bob said, "Geoffrey wanted me as the arranger of all the music. I went in as a captain, and replaced Geoffrey as musical director when he left. That was in 1943.

"The show, after it played Toronto and right across Canada, went overseas. I stayed behind, forming another unit of different small groups which were to go to not exactly the front line but pretty close to it, spread across Europe as the Allies advanced. They were groups of ten or twelve men, to work with dancers or singers. We were months at the Victoria Theater in Toronto, rehearsing.

"When we got to London, we didn't break up into small units at first. We started to do BBC broadcasts, five or six a week, and we became known as the Canadian Band of the Allied Expeditionary Forces. Miller was already there.

"Miller had that big orchestra with strings and broke it up into a swing band as well as smaller units. We did the same sort of thing. We had a choir show and a Dixieland band show and a string show. That's how we were able to do so much entertaining in one week. There was a lot of writing to do as well as a lot of organization."

There was another American band in England at the time, a navy band led by Sam Donahue. It had evolved out of the band Artie Shaw had organized and led in the South Pacific, where it had undergone hardship, sometimes performing in forward areas under Japanese sniper fire and sleeping under ponchos in the rain with the GIs. When Shaw was given a medical discharge – among other problems, a shell explosion had destroyed one of his eardrums – along with Dave Tough and some others, Donahue was assigned to continue the band. Testimony to its excellence under his leadership comes from many sources. Farnon is one of them. "Just between you and me," he said, "it was the best band of the lot. It was a swinging band. It had great players. A lot of the guys in our band who were good jazz players would go over and play with them when they could."

Glenn Miller flew to England on 21 June 1944, and reported to SHAEF (Supreme Headquarters, Allied Expeditionary Force). The band came by troop ship, disembarking on 28 June. Miller at first stayed at the Mount Royal Hotel in London; the band was billeted in a block of requisitioned flats in Chelsea. Miller felt the band to be very vulnerable: one flying bomb hitting the flats could wipe it out entirely. Miller immediately began efforts to move the band out of London to Bedford, a wartime center for BBC broadcasting. It was said by some that Miller was personally afraid of the flying bombs. But in the first place, any rational man would be; and in the second, Ray McKinley told me that if Miller had had his way, the band would have been playing at the front lines at the earliest possible time. And perhaps Miller was prescient. Soon after the band left London, a bomb did land near the flats where they had been living.

When the Canadians under Farnon arrived, they were allowed no such luxury: they stayed in London through all the bombing.

Farnon and Miller could not have been less alike. Miller was a martinet with high connections in the military, took his rank very seriously, and used both. Farnon's style was different. He was unimpressed by the military and identified himself with his men. He had a taste for practical jokes. In the days when men's trousers had buttoned flies, it was a sophomoric joke to walk by someone and flip his fly open with a crooked finger. Bob would do this during inspections and then say to the bandsman with mock severity, "Soldier, you're improperly dressed." The band found it funny.

One of the band's trumpet players was the late Fred Davis, who after the war gave up music for a career in Canadian television. Fred had a small gig on the side, playing with a combo drawn from the larger orchestra at a British officers' dance. For some reason, the band's pianist couldn't make the job. Fred asked Bob if he would fill in on piano. Bob donned his battledress. The British and Canadian battledress – from which the Eisenhower jacket was derived – was identical for officers and enlisted men: only the insignia on the shoulder denoted the difference. Thus Bob in battledress seemed at a casual glance to be an enlisted man. But three crowns, or pips as they are called, said he was a captain.

Hardly anyone had arrived for the dance. A young British lieutenant started to badger Fred Davis to start playing. Fred protested that there wasn't an audience yet. The lieutenant continued his harangue. Bob got slowly up from the piano, walked to the front of the bandstand, and shoved his shoulder under the young man's nose. Fred Davis and the other musicians remembered the incident long afterwards. Even Bob remembers it: "He slunk away with his tail between his legs. We never saw him again that night. It was a great feeling, that." It is the only incident anyone remembers of Bob pulling rank.

Legends about him abounded after the war. One of the musicians told me that Bob would listen to short-wave radio from the United States, take down the new songs in rapid notation, and arrange them for the band's broadcasts.

"You are aware no doubt," I said to him in 1984, "that you are admired by a lot of musicians for a non-musical reason, namely the reputation you had for being adept with the ladies."

"Are you running that tape recorder?" Bob said with mock alarm and a touch of laughter.

"Yes."

"You're quick, aren't you?"

"Yes. Now, there's a story I heard about your powers of musical concentration – compartmentalization of thought. I was told that the wartime band was rehearsing and you were sitting at a table writing something else and somebody came up and said that your wife was arriving from somewhere and your girlfriend from somewhere else, and you said, 'Put my wife in such-and-such a hotel, put the other in such-and-such, and send them both flowers,' and went on writing."

"Oh," Bob said, laughing, "that's not true. At least I don't think it's true. Well, wait a minute. It could have happened. You know, I once had three girls all named Pat. And I didn't have any trouble at all. It was easy to go from one to the other."

"And what is your wife's name?"

"Pat!" Bob said.

"That's what I thought. Is she one of the three Pats?"

"No!"

"Does she know about your colorful past?"

"Oh sure. Of course. And I know about hers too." The laughter lasted what seemed a long time.

One reason for Eisenhower's appointment as Supreme Commander of the Allied Expeditionary Force was his reputation for diplomacy. He had to co-ordinate the work of men of high ego, particularly General Bernard L. Montgomery on the British side and General George C. Patton on the American. This gift of diplomacy extended into questions of morale and entertainment.

The American, British, and Canadian forces were integrated under his command. He told SHAEF Command, well before the D-Day invasion of the continent on 6 June 1944, that he wanted to set up a radio service for these forces, with regular broadcasts on the BBC, mostly of music, variety shows, and news. The contents of these broadcasts would reflect the ratio of these forces that constituted the main armies of the AEF: 50 per cent American, 35 per cent British, and 15 per cent Canadian. These broadcasts were to be beamed only to the troops, and would not even be announced until late on D-Day. They went on the air the next day, 7 June. The technicians were all from the BBC, and a BBC transmitter in Devon was used. The announcers were drawn from the three countries. The program material was provided by the US Armed Forces Network, the BBC, and the CBC. Much of the material was on transcriptions, large discs revolving at 33⅓ rpm.

And when Glenn Miller and what was then called the Army Air Forces Band arrived, arrangements were immediately made for them to broadcast live on this new network. But the brilliance of the Miller band soon brought pressure from the British press, particularly the music press, demanding that its programs be broadcast to the British civilian population as well. This was soon arranged, and all three bands – Miller's, Farnon's, and Melachrino's – were heard throughout England. Miller was already a household name in Britain; the obscure Canadian Robert Farnon soon became one.

In December the Miller band was to move to the Continent. On 4 December, Miller wrote to his brother Herb saying, "By the time you receive this letter, we shall be in Paris, barring of course a nose-dive into the Channel." He really does appear to have been prescient.

Miller planned to go on ahead of the band. On 15 December Miller and Colonel Norman Baessell left for Paris in bad weather in a Norduyn Norseman, a single-engine high-wing monoplane piloted by Flight Officer John Morgan. The band went to Paris three days later. Miller's plane had disappeared but, Ray McKinley told me, the band was not informed of this for more than a week. As far as the musicians knew, Miller simply hadn't arrived. Pre-recorded material with Miller's voice announcing it continued to be heard on the BBC, sustaining an illusion that Miller was alive. Miller and the plane in which he was flying were never found.

Farnon said, "The three bands were to do a Christmas show together. Our band and the Melachrino band were at the Queensbury Club in London. Miller was supposed to do the broadcast from Paris. The audience at the Queensbury Club were getting very restless, so I first played our book through, the whole show that we were supposed to do on the broadcast. Then Melachrino did his. And we still didn't go on the air. And then finally the news came through that Miller was missing and Jerry Gray was going to take over and do the show. About two hours late, that Christmas show was broadcast."

The war ended eight months later, and Bob faced a decision. The men of the Glenn Miller band shipped home: the Canadian band stayed on.

There was little for Bob to go home to. He had a name now as an arranger and composer in Britain, none in Canada. There was no film industry, and no music industry – certainly no recording industry – to speak of in Canada. Nobody was going to offer him the kind of large orchestra he liked to write for.

Bob said, "I saw the opportunities in England for writing for film. And that was my crowning ambition, to write a movie score, even though I knew nothing about it."

But first he had to get over the emotional effects of the war, all that he had seen of London under the flying bombs. He orchestrated the French Canadian folk song "À la claire fontaine." It was one of the most affecting and effective of all his pieces, serene and beautiful and pastoral. "I wanted to forget about all the horror of the war, all the bloodshed," he said. "And that seemed a good way to do it."

And then his dreams began to come true.

"Even when I was still in uniform," he said, "I was asked to do a couple of scores for Crown film units – war epic jobs. One of the film composers, Allan Gray, asked me to write the title music for a film. That helped a bit. And then I met a lady who would be my third wife, Pat.

"She was a casting director for Herbert Wilcox, and I badgered her for ages to get me in there, even just writing one cue. Eventually, in 1947, Wilcox made a musical called *Spring in Park Lane*. And he had to drop his music director, who was a bit of a fuddy duddy. So Pat finally succeeded in getting me in to do that score."

She would be more than a business associate. As Bob put it, "Our romance blossomed in the autumn of 1954."

Released in 1948, *Spring in Park Lane,* starring Anna Neagle and Michael Wilding, is a well-regarded comedy that still turns up on television, and of course makes royalty money for Bob.

"That started my film work," Bob said. "I did three films with Herbert Wilcox, all musicals, as composer, orchestrator, and conductor.

"We were working at Elstree, where Warner Brothers were starting to make films. The Warner Brothers people heard the musicals I did for Herbert Wilcox and asked me to do the score for *Where's Charley?* with Ray Bolger. They were very pleased with that. I asked them could I do a dramatic picture. They said, Yes, and they gave me *Captain Horatio Hornblower.*"

The film, starring Gregory Peck and set during the Napoleonic wars, a sea saga bearing a vague resemblance to the life of Lord Nelson and based on a novel by C. S. Forester, came out in 1951. The score contains one of Bob's loveliest pieces, the "Lady Barbara" theme. It is also one of his most performed.

But film composers, with a few exceptions such as Henry Mancini, remain anonymous figures to the public. Bob now had a name in Britain, thanks to the BBC.

"The big-wig at Chappell Music was named Teddy Holmes," Bob said. "He came down with a movie director friend of his to hear one of the army broadcasts, one of the symphonette things I wrote. They were fairy tales. One of the pieces was "Jumping Bean," although it did not have that title at the time.

"I was demobbed in the spring of 1946 and stayed in England. Even before the war was over, I went up to see Teddy Holmes and went to work.

"Teddy Holmes had the Queen's Hall orchestra doing movie music recordings. He asked me if I would like to write something for the Chappell library. I first wrote a thing called "Willie the Whistler." He liked it, and I went on to do "Portrait of a Flirt" and other things. Eventually I wrote more than 500 compositions for the library.

"It wasn't long after the war that the BBC asked me to do a regular broadcast, an hour every Sunday. I wrote six or seven charts a week. It was a lot of writing. But then, when you're that age, you can do it.

"I continued to do that for the BBC for a long time, with Vera Lynn. And that got me into Decca. Vera Lynn was so big then. She was called the Forces' Sweetheart, because she was the favorite of the troops."

The Decca relationship began with arrangements for various British singers, Gracie Fields as well as Vera Lynn among them. Finally the Decca executives said, "How would you like to do an album of your own?"

"Some of the charts I recorded," Bob said, "I'd written for the BBC. Ones that had turned out well. After that I did no more vocal albums. It was all orchestral from then on."

English Decca was a separate company from American Decca. And when they decided to enter the American market, they could not use that name. They incorporated a new label for North America, London Records, that became known for superiority of sound and quality of pressings, putting out LPs by the Ted Heath band and some small jazz groups, such as the Jack Parnell Trio. I bought quite a number of those records, astonished to find that the British could play jazz at all; and even more so, that they could play it well.

But I did not become aware of the Farnon albums until the early 1950s. I was not the only one discovering them. I have never met an arranger from that time to this who did not have some or all of those albums: *Flirtation Walk, Cocktails for Two, Light 'n' Easy, By a Waterfall, Sunny Side Up, Something to Remember You By, Stardust, From the Emerald Isle, From the Highlands*, and *Porgy and Bess* among them.

The instrumentation on those albums was usually strings, five saxophones doubling woodwinds, harp, percussion, including vibes, and rhythm section. *Porgy and Bess* was for full symphony orchestra.

"The English musicianship was in some respects remarkable," Bob said. "They were the best readers. They still are. Fantastic. It's always been my contention that the American musicians can *interpret* our style of music so much better, but the British read it so much better.

"It's better now. They finally got the message."

And they developed people like the remarkable bassist Chris Laurence, who is on most or all of the Farnon records of recent years, and drummers like Martin Drew and the late Kenny Clare.

I once observed to Bob that the only thing that has dated in those early London albums is the rhythm section sound. The rhythm sections of the old recordings had a plodding quality.

"The only album we had a good drummer on was *Sunny Side Up*," Bob said. "We had Phil Seaman. A serious drunk. Finally killed himself with a needle. Did you know him?"

"No, just of him."

"Pissed all the time. He was the one who was in the pit of *West Side Story* in London, and he fell asleep during a ballad. Someone nudged him for a cue coming up, and he grabbed his stick and accidentally hit the big gong. And he stood up grandly and said, 'Ladies and gentlemen, dinner is served.' He got fired that night."

Excepting *From the Emerald Isle* and *From the Highlands*, most of those albums were made up of standard popular songs. But the elegance of the orchestration was astounding. The tunes were mostly done at dance tempi, with dance-band brass but with flutes and other "classical" woodwinds (with occasional saxophone soli), a string section, and touches of color from vibes. Bob uses vibes for color more than any arranger or composer I've ever heard. All the arrangements were harmonically beautiful and notable for exquisite voice leading, every little line going somewhere intelligent, and very musical. Recently I got these albums out, though they are hissy and worn, and listened to them anew. They remain as fresh as ever, nearly 50 years after they were made. One of their qualities is that even in melancholy or wistful ballads, there is a certain sunniness about them. It perfectly reflects Bob's personality.

I heard various influences in the writing, particularly and obviously Ravel and Debussy. They were affecting arrangers everywhere, to be sure, as was Stravinsky, who had a great influence on Ralph Burns and Neal Hefti. I thought I heard touches of Sibelius, particularly in the way Bob used woodwinds; and later, when I asked him if he were a big Sibelius buff, he said, "Yes indeed."

"And Delius?"

"Oh yes!" Bob said in Miami. "All the French school. Fauré, Satie, Debussy, Ravel, and Delius, as you say. And Tchaikovsky. He was an influence in the early stages of my writing career. He could really write a tune." He sang two or three Tchaikovsky themes in illustration.

"And then I got on to Bartok, although I went through a Stravinsky period too, his ballet music. I didn't like some of his avant-garde music.

"I had the pleasure of meeting Bartok in 1945. It was an evening at the MacDowell Club in New York. MacDowell's wife owned the club: she started it after her husband's death. Bartok was there, and some of them did a Bartok quartet, with Bartok and his wife playing the two-piano part. He was very ill by that time. It was a highlight of my life to meet this man: it was like meeting God.

"I so adored his music. I admire the way he developed the folk song of Hungary – so much better than Kodaly did. His orchestration, of course: and then his gentle use of atonality. He never overdid it, like some. He didn't go wild. He used it for a purpose that was very effective. He didn't write it mechanically, mathematically: he wrote it from the heart, even though some of it's atonal, and that's rare. In a lot of atonal music, the composers are the only ones who enjoy it. The musicians on the whole don't enjoy playing it. I found that out in my travels.

"I was invited to a session, produced by his son, Peter Bartok, a wizard recording engineer. They were recording most of Bartok's major works. It was such a pleasure to get to know him and talk about his father."

Probably no one on earth, at this point, knows the Farnon canon as well as Jeff Sultanof, for no one else has studied the scores as closely as he has in the process of restoring them.

"What I started to do was to get the main pieces that everyone knew, such as 'Jumping Bean' and 'A Star Is Born,'" Jeff said. "And I wanted to get to some of the classic arrangements he did for English Decca. They were recorded *pretty* well, but I would never want to think about transcribing them. A lot of it had been destroyed in a fire at Chappell in 1964. For example, 'Yes We Have No Bananas,' which is a classic arrangement, went up in flames. They had to put that catalogue back together, particularly the symphonic music. It took them years to find out what they'd lost.

"I knew that Bob had a huge library, a lot of it stuff that he was using for concerts. I made up a basic list and told him that I wanted to prepare definitive editions of these things: for instance, 'Jumping Bean.' That had been published with only a piano-conductor part. You could get the parts but you could not get the full scores.

"Having been in publishing, I can tell you that the publisher was at first looking to get some extra mileage out of those pieces. Obviously there was some demand for them. They had been done for the Chappell library. They were recorded with a relatively small orchestra, basically two flutes, one oboe, two clarinets, one bassoon, two horns, two trumpets, three trombones, not even a tuba, maybe two percussion, maybe a tympani, harp, and strings. Except for rare occasions, the instrumentation was pretty consistent. Whoever did them at Chappell made his own piano conductor parts, because Bob said he never saw them.

"I was looking to study these things. I knew they had printed only parts. So I would put scores together, and find errors. The only way you could see there were errors was if you saw them with the other parts. And as happens in publishing, these things never get corrected."

The other problem was that all the Farnon pieces were out of print. Jeff became involved in this restoration project while he was the editorial director of the Warner Brothers print-music division. Warner had long since bought Chappell.

"I took this on on my own," Jeff said. "The people at Warners didn't even know I was doing this. And the reason I was doing it was because I wanted to study the music. And I wanted to conduct it. I have heard performances of these things that were atrocities because the conductors had no scores. They were working from violin parts or piano-conductor scores.

"I got some of the material from the rental library – Schirmer had it at this point. It had gone around to so many rental agents, from pillar to post. A lot of these pieces were unknown in the United States. Whatever little you could find was mostly in bad photocopies. And some titles were completely missing from the library. One that was missing was 'Gateway to the West.'"

"Gateway to the West" is one of Farnon's many Canadian pieces, among them "Canadian Rhapsody," "Prairie Sunset," "Cascades to the Sea," "Alcan

Highway," "Toronto City March," and "North of the French River." "Gateway to the West" was used as the theme for the David Susskind television show.

"First I had to find out what was physically in the United States that I could Xerox," Jeff continued. "Then I went to our British facility and got more from them. And I went to work on these pieces, in consultation with Bob. I've completed 51 of them now."

This labor of love led to a friendship with Marc Fortier, a fellow conductor, composer, and arranger who for several summers had conducted the Montreal Pops Orchestra. Marc too was interested in performing a good deal of the Farnon material but couldn't get his hands on it.

Marc talked to the Chappell office in Toronto, swiftly learning that this branch of the company wasn't interested in Farnon's music – yet another of the slights Farnon has experienced in his native land.

"Even in England," Jeff said, "the attitude was that the music didn't get rented all that much, so why bother? Much of the stuff I did get from them was unplayable because it was unreadable: that is not unusual in rental libraries. A lot of pieces circulate in very poor condition.

"Take, for instance, Bob's piece 'Colditz March.' Bob originally wrote it for a BBC series. It's a terrific march. There was one score that I received that he had written for the television series. In order to expand it for symphony orchestras, he wrote a second score, in which he filled in extra parts. There was no full score that contained all the parts: on top of which there was never a viola part – we had to add one. So I was putting together a master score; between the two of us, we finally got a score."

Whereas Jeff has been working to build the scores back up to their full size, Marc Fortier, interestingly, is involved in an inversion of that process, again with Bob's collaboration: he is scaling down the Farnon scores so that they can be performed by smaller community orchestras.

"I look at Bob as a composer who is an arranger," Jeff said. "His mastery of music is almost total. The lines that he writes! His music is extraordinarily linear. Gil Evans wrote that way. The individual parts are wonderful to play: they make incredible sense.

"What really attracted me initially were the arrangements. All the arrangers love his harmony. But his harmony is derived from linear writing. The way he would realize these things for orchestra was just extraordinary. And of course we all know about the string writing – everybody has commented on it.

"But when I actually got these things on paper and looked at them, I realized there is no way you could transcribe them from the records. They're beautifully written for the players. They're beautiful to play. And they're great to hear. There are a lot of little subtle things going on.

"The market that he was writing for at the time was 'mood music.' One of the albums was *Flirtation Walk*. Most of the pieces in it are mezzo-piano, mezzo-forte maybe, with a couple of little splashes of stuff. Then we get to a little dinky song, 'Flirtation Walk,' a cute jaunty little thing. It goes along like most of the Muzak of that time. Then he does an eight-bar transition to a new section with muted brass. That eight bars is some of the finest music you'll ever hear in an arrangement. It is an atonal modulation. It does it in such a subtle way that if you're not listening, it'll fly by you. But if you're listening, you'll ask yourself, 'Where the hell is he going?' And then he lands in this brass thing. And it's genius."

I pointed out to Jeff that some things of Farnon's I've always liked are actually bi-tonal and even walk on the edge of atonality. But the writing is so beautiful that you don't notice how radical it was for the time in which it was written; you are seduced by it. This doubtless reflects Bob's love of Bartok, and the lyrical and subtle way Bartok would use these techniques. But that he applied these things to popular music, and did so 50 years ago, boggles the mind.

Jeff said, "For the listener who is not paying attention, this stuff will go right by you."

One of Farnon's best-known pieces is "Lake of the Woods." It is inspired by one of the most beautiful lakes in Canada. Listening to it in the *Hornblower* album, I caught something I had never heard. Bob paraphrases "Afternoon of a Fawn." Then against it he quotes Prokofiev's *Peter and the Wolf*: the wolf and the deer, living on the shores of that lake. I asked Jeff if he'd ever noticed this.

"No!" he said.

"When we get off the phone, listen to it."

James Caesar Petrillo, the inflexible and dictatorial president of the American Federation of Musicians who had called two disastrous recording bans, both of which helped end the big-band era, made still another lethal maneuver. In the early days of television, he demanded of the nascent stations and networks a 5 per cent trust fund fee to the American Federation of Musicians off the top from the sale of every TV show that used music. This particularly applied to such dramatic shows as *Playhouse 90*.

By then Bob was well advanced in his writing of "library music" for Chappell in London, music that could be used as underscore in movies and television.

His friend Marion Evans (who used Farnon records as teaching tools with other arrangers) said, "I think most of the music on American television during that period was Farnon's. Those original things of his were fantastic. On *Playhouse 90*, for example, the guy from Chappell would arrive with what looked like about six big telephone books, cross-indexed. And the director or producer would say something like, 'I want 41 seconds of Hawaiian music in a chase scene here.' And the guy from Chappell would thumb open the books and go tracing through, and say, 'Okay. Next.' And he would write all this up, like somebody in a shoe department taking an order, and he would go back and build the tracks from Bob's recorded music.

"After a while, the producers began to say, 'We want another composer instead of Farnon now.' And the guy from Chappell would say, 'Okay, we'll use Joe Green,' or whoever, and send them some more music by Farnon. I think he wrote under half a dozen pseudonyms. The best of the things, later on, were recorded for albums."

Marion long ago told me that there was a march by Farnon that for some years was used as a sign-off theme for seemingly half the television stations in America. And of course that meant that ASCAP was collecting money for all these performances and forwarding it to Farnon through the Canadian society, then CAPAC and now SOCAN. That one march alone made Bob an incredible amount of money. Was it, I asked Marion, the "Colditz March?" "I don't think so," Marion said. "He had all kinds of marches. He even had baseball marches. He wrote so many of them, I think he gave them numbers – you know, Baseball March 23. That stuff is played and played and played. Still."

Marion's evaluation of Farnon: "He just simply is the best," he said. "He's a rare combination. Every once in a while, by some biological meeting, some cross-fertilization, we produce an Albert Einstein. We produce somebody who has the talent, the dedication, the training. Farnon had it all. And it was all in one place.

"Plus, through no fault of his own, he found himself in an incredible position in London, where he was standing in front of a large orchestra every day and writing. You do that for a while and you learn. And that's doing it the hard way.

"He had that rare combination of everything. He is exceptional by every standard.

"I think it's not really kosher to analyze Bob in a highly technical manner: it doesn't begin to touch the depth of his talent. Bob has enormous technique, but his talent far exceeds his technique, and so did Mozart's. And that is precisely what you want. Anyone can learn as much technique as Bob Farnon has by going to music school; but they don't have that extra edge.

"Mozart didn't write masterpieces all the time. He sat down and kept writing and let it flow. Bob has a lot of that in him. He's fast. He is one of the fastest writers I've ever known. He just does it, and that's it. He doesn't labor over it. When it's good, it's fantastic."

Bob had married a Canadian girl, Joanne Dallas, who sang with his wartime band. "In 1953," Bob said, "I went back to Canada with Joanne. I was getting offers to work in the States. We moved to Riverside, New Jersey, early in the spring of 1954. I started to write with a very dear friend of mine, Red Ginzler. He arranged an awful lot of shows, such as *Bye Bye Birdie*, and he offered me a show, *The Girl in Pink Tights*, which starred Zizi Jeanmaire.

"Shortly after I began to get established in New York, I got a telegram from Herbert Wilcox, to go back to England and do another film, *King's Rhapsody*, with Erroll Flynn and Anna Neagle. That took me back to England. And then even bigger jobs came up. Warner Brothers wanted me to do another film."

There are certain events that leave an indelible impression in one's life. I can remember the first time I heard a Farnon record. It was in the record department of a furniture store on St. Catherine Street in Montreal. (There were few separate record stores in those days. Records were sold in adjunct departments of furniture stores, which also sold the phonographs on which they were played.)

There had been a few excursions into the full-orchestra presentation of the kind of high-quality popular music that evolved in the 1920s, 1930s, and 1940s, notably Morton Gould's *After Dark* album on twelve-inch 78-rpm records, probably around 1946, and a ten-inch Capitol album by Frank DeVol of music by Jimmy Van Heusen that probably was issued about the same time as the first Farnon albums on London. By the early 1950s, there was a flood of such albums. They became a fashion: albums by Frank Chacksfield, who had a huge hit with "Ebb Tide," the Melachrino Orchestra, led by Bob's wartime colleague, and the Italian-born Mantovani in England; Franck Pourcel and Michel Legrand (whose *I Love Paris* album became one of the biggest hits in the history of Columbia Records) in France; and Hugo Winterhalter, Percy Faith, and Paul Weston in the United States. The level of taste varied widely, with Mantovani's saccharine strings at the bottom; and Faith, Farnon, and Weston at the top. All of them were far more successful on records in America than Farnon. But he was the arranger whose albums arrangers themselves collected, like squirrels gathering nuts in autumn. Bob once said he thought that *only* arrangers bought those albums.

But I had never heard anything like this. The harmony was exquisite, fresh and adventurous; and if I could not analyse the voice leading I could certainly hear it. It was startling stuff, and I got my hands on as much of it as I could.

Bob said in 1984, "I wanted to enhance the popular song. When I do an arrangement of a song, I like to put some thought into it, not just dish it up in two choruses. Make it into a piece of music, a composition, tell a story."

As the Americans were culturally obeisant to Europe and patronizing toward their own composers, Canadians were obeisant to the United States.

But beyond that, the smaller economy allowed no such proliferation of the arts as one found in the United States, and indeed Canada was soaked in American (and to a lesser extent British) novels, movies, songs, and recordings, and it seemed as if everyone famous and accomplished was of another nationality – mostly American.

The psychological effect of this great overshadowing was compounded by a quirk in the Canadian character, the unarticulated tenet that a seemly modesty is the ultimate and perhaps the only virtue. This does not encourage aspirations toward professions where high visibility is a requisite to getting work. Percy Faith left Canada in a state of irritation. The playwright Bernard Slade, whose first dramas were written for the CBC, left in a huff not unlike that of Percy, and never looked back. Lorne Green told me that frustration with the CBC was the main reason he left Canada. Christopher Plummer, who was born in Toronto, shook his head and said, "Oh Lord, it's a wonder any of us got out of there with any of our talent intact."

And so for me the discovery that the novelist Morley Callaghan and the arranger Robert Farnon (I was not yet aware of his compositions) were Canadians were milestones of my life.

"The effect on me was profound," I told Bob in Miami. "It was the discovery that a Canadian could actually do things – because we had grown up in the shadow of the Americans and didn't feel we could."

"I know what you mean," Bob said. "I used to have that same feeling."

In 1954, the *Montreal Star*, the newspaper where I was a reporter, covering fires and strikes and plane crashes and murders, assigned me to do some stories in England and France, and I used the opportunity when I reached London to seek out and meet Robert Farnon.

Bob said that after his brief residence in New Jersey and his return to England to write the score for *King's Rhapsody*, Warner Brothers asked him to do the score for a satiric western with Jayne Mansfield and Kenneth More. The film was *The Sheriff of Fractured Jaw*.

"And that's when I met you," I said. "Muir Matheson conducted the recording session. I was there with you."

"That's *right*!" Bob said.

"I remember having lunch with you and Muir Matheson." It was at some countrified-looking English inn, probably with the half-timbering that seemed so quaint to me then. "We were talking about Wagner and his almost interminable development of themes. And Muir Matheson said with his lofty and precise English accent, and I've never forgotten it, 'Yes, quite. I always want to take a blue pencil to him.'"

Bob laughed aloud, saying, "I remember that!"

"And Pye was at the same time recording an album of your writing, with a Welsh conductor named Jones."

"You're right," Bob said, "Leslie Jones. What a memory you have!"

"No I don't," I said. "What I have forgotten frightens me. That's why I keep trying to get history on paper."

Bob said. "It was the Kingsway Hall studio."

"Didn't they call it the Kingsway Hall Light Orchestra?"

"That's right!" Bob said.

I interviewed Bob at length about his wartime experiences and the rise of his career in England. I took photos. I returned to Montreal, determined to tell his story to Canada. My newspaper wasn't interested. The Sunday supplements weren't interested. The major national magazine, *Maclean's*, wasn't interested. I abandoned the story.

Bob remained in the London area for five years after that, living in Gerrard's Cross in Buckinghamshire. By 1959, he and wife Pat had one child and another was on the way. "We needed a larger place," Bob said. "A friend suggested we go to the island of Guernsey and look around. And it didn't matter where I was. Being a writer, I work at home anyway. We went over one Easter and just fell in love with the place and that was it. We found a property and were moved in within six weeks. It's quite big. It has 21 rooms. It's got granite walls three feet thick, so that it's warm in the winter and cool in the summer."

Guernsey has another advantage: very low taxes.

The house is rather famous; musicians made pilgrimages to it. In 1983, Dizzy Gillespie arrived for a visit. It was the racing season. "We took him to the track," Bob said. "Just for fun he took out his trumpet and played that race-course bugle call before the start of each race, with his trumpet up in the air and his African hat on. He broke up the island, because it's a very small place, and that Dizzy Gillespie was there was very important news."

Bob's preference, as a composer, is instrumental recording. But singers wanted him and began to travel to England to make albums with him. He wrote several for Tony Bennett, as well as *Sinatra Sings Great Songs from Great Britain*. He wrote an album for Lena Horne and Phil Woods, recorded in London in 1976 and released on the RCA label. It is of course out of print. Bob wrote for Sarah Vaughan and Pia Zadora. George Shearing wanted him, and he wrote an album for the pianist recorded by the MPS label; they have since collaborated on several albums. Polydor recorded his *Prelude and Dance*, written for the classical harmonica virtuoso (and Bob's fellow Torontonian) Tommy Reilly, as well as his *Rhapsody for Violin and Orchestra*, with Steven Staryk as soloist.

There was one album that Bob desperately wanted to do, one that he wrote for Dizzy Gillespie and Oscar Peterson.

"We were going to record it in Berlin," Bob recounted. "A piece I wrote for Oscar, 'The Pleasure of His Company,' and 'Private Suite,' which I wrote for

Dizzy. We were going to take over first-chair men because we weren't sure of the musicians in Berlin. First trumpet, lead alto, baritone, and of course Ed Thigpen and Ray Brown.

"Well the guys got talking in London, saying, 'We're going to Berlin to record with Oscar Peterson and Dizzy Gillespie.' And it got to the union. At that time musicians in Britain were not allowed to record in Europe. Well the British union got in touch with the American union and we got telegrams in Berlin, through Norman Granz, saying that if we made the album, we would all be suspended from the unions.

"And so we all went home with our tails between our legs, and the whole thing was shelved, although later I performed the first movement of the piano piece on television with Oscar in London."

But the two pieces have never been recorded, and now, "Private Suite" never will be. Dizzy is dead, and the score has been lost.

Bob and Pat continue to live in their grand manor in Guernsey. Their five children are all grown. Thus far Bob and Pat have four grandchildren.

David, the oldest of their four sons, has an MA in music from Cambridge University. He is a composer and piano teacher. "He teaches wonderfully," Bob said. "His knowledge of music history puts mine to shame. He wrote a lot of music for *The Muppet Show*. When he was first learning, I used to bring him in when I was doing a film. He did some of my copying and also did some work on the short scores that I did. He learned a lot about film. He's coasting along nicely and making a fortune, writing for the music libraries. He's living in Guernsey too.

"Robert, who's number two son, is a recording engineer in London. He's very musical. He didn't study music when he was younger, and he regrets it now. But he loves his work. He has an amazing ear.

"Number three son, Brian, is in Canada. He lives in Vancouver. He is an executive, with his own company, supplying music for films and television.

"Number four son, Peter, is a police detective, in the fraud squad of the Guernsey police. He used to play trombone, and very well. He's a big guy, about six foot six.

"We had four boys in a row and then a girl. Deborah lives in a cottage across from our house. She is a secretary who does temp work to pay for her horses. She loves horses and built a stable that she rents out."

Bob continues to travel extensively, recording and conducting concerts all over Europe. He has done very few concerts in Canada. Over the years I have tried to remove or at least mitigate the Canadian indifference toward him, to little avail. Some years ago, I wrote and narrated a one-hour program about him for the CBC radio network. Ten minutes into the broadcast the time was usurped for a news report about the American astronauts on the moon. The big news was that they were sleeping. This soporific reportage maundered on for the rest of the hour. The Farnon broadcast was never repeated and is now lost.

"What do you think is the reason for it?" Bob said in Miami. "Is it because I went away?"

"No," I said. "It's because you're Canadian."

Bob's most ardent admirer remains his brother Brian.

Brian said, "You have no idea, and Bob has no idea, how insane I am about my brother's work. Bob would never know. When I have tried to tell him, he just says, 'Ah, you're my brother. You're just saying that.'

"Recently I was driving down to Concord . . ." he was referring to Concord, California ". . . and had a jazz program on the radio. Here comes this piece of music with a trombone player and orchestra, and I kept saying, 'God *damn* it, that's gotta be Bob. It has to be.' There was nobody in the car with me. The background chart was incredibly impeccable. It was wonderful. And at the end of it the announcer said, 'That was J. J. Johnson with Robert Farnon and his orchestra.' And I couldn't contain myself. Out loud I said, 'God *damn* it, Bob, I knew that was you.'"

A few years ago, I was invited to do a week-long series of seminars on lyric-writing at a special summer camp near St. Hilaire, Québec, which is about 30 miles east of Montreal in apple-orchard country on the south shore of the St. Lawrence River. The director of that summer camp was my conductor and composer friend Marc Fortier. Marc was born in Jonquiere, Quebec, on 7 December 1940.

I had been under the impression that only English-speaking Canada practiced a demoralizing indifference toward its own arts and artists. Marc assured me darkly that the attitude in French Canada was much the same. Many of Québec's best artists go to Paris, and the brilliant concert pianist André Laplante lives in New York City. Marc too has tried to generate interest in Bob's work in Canada. He has had as much success as I have.

When I reminded Marc that Ann Murray had been given the order of Canada (as has Wayne Gretzky) but Farnon had not, he commented a little tartly: "We are a nation of folk singers," and pointed out that the Montreal Symphony recently received the French Grand Prix du Disque, possibly for the tenth time.

"That orchestra," he said, "is the best symphony orchestra in the world. It is possibly the best symphony orchestra in history. I'm not the only one to say that: many critics have said it.

"But if you go to Place des Arts in Montreal when it is performing, the place is not full, as it should be. There are almost no French Canadians there."

That week in the summer of 1992 was lovely. There were about 30 adult students, half of them music teachers. The camp was housed in the Gault Estate, a vast old stone mansion with a high-peaked snow-shedding slate roof, a handsome building in the French colonial style typical of Québec. It is managed by McGill University. Three times a day we were served gourmet food by the building's staff at a long table whose large window looked out on a round lake on the slope of a forested mountain. One can scarcely imagine a more Canadian setting.

The London Philharmonic recording of Bob's *Hornblower Suite*, which also contains "À la claire fontaine," had just come out. That song runs deep in the French Canadian soul. Marc said that most French Canadians knew it by the age of 3; or used to, in a time before rap and rock. One theory is that it was composed by a fourteenth- or fifteenth-century French juggler. Whoever composed it, it is said to have been sung in Canada by Champlain's men as far back as 1608. It has been orchestrated many times, but no one has treated it the way Farnon did.

Marc analysed it. The melody is extremely simple. Marc said, "It's a ritournelle of four couplets totaling, in four-four time, only six measures, repeated four times. The traditional metronome marking is 80 to the quarter note, which gives a thematic element of nineteen seconds. Robert Farnon made of this a seven-minute symphonic poem: it's a masterpiece."

One night at dinner, Marc played it for us. When it was over, someone at the table said, "Play it again."

The words are about a young man who has lost his love, through no fault of his own, as he sees it.

> À la claire fontaine
> M'en allant promener
> J'ai trouvé l'eau si belle
> Que je m'y suis baigné.

After this swim in the fountain, he dries himself under an oak. On its highest branch, a nightingale sings happily. Sing, nightingale, he says, sing. You who have a heart so gay, a heart to laugh, and I have one to cry. The lyrics are gentle, poignant, and beautiful.

I added another dimension to the experience of that piece that evening. I told my companions how Bob had come to write his version of it: as a gentle transition to civilian life after the horrors of the war.

Many people who lived along the banks of the St. Lawrence remember the troop ships coming up the river at war's end, soldiers leaning over the rails to catch their first view of home, French- and English-speaking alike. Bob uses flutes and clarinets to suggest the nightingale of the story. The introduction uses vibes for a subtle reinforcement of low strings, in a counterfigure that underlies the song's melody, stated in high strings without vibrato. The piece builds to a great and yet controlled climax, and as it subsides, there is what sounds like a distant and half-forgotten bugle call from the muted brass, a receding memory of war. I have no idea whether Bob did this consciously, and by now neither does he, but it *is* the effect it has.

Marc went back to the CD player and repeated it. And he played it yet again. And again. I said, "That's our *Finlandia*," and Marc said, "Yes. It should be our national anthem."

There were six or eight of us at the table. Listening to the music and looking out at the forest and the evening waters, everyone became very quiet. There was one teacher whose face I will never forget. He was burly, and he looked like a tough guy – which thought had to be tempered by the knowledge that he played just about every instrument known to man and was a graduate of the Sorbonne. I watched him struggling to hold back the tears. He failed, and when he did, we all did.

There wasn't a dry face at the table.

In 1997, Robert Farnon was named Companion of the Order of Canada. It is the lowest rank of the Order.

5

He fell from a star: Gil Evans

He was a mysterious man, as elusive and evanescent as his art. He could be maddeningly absent-minded; yet he could be closely attentive and solicitous, and you never knew quite how much Gil Evans was noticing about you. His childhood is an enigma, and there is even a question about his real name. Tall, lank, professorial of mien, he was kind, self-critical, and self-doubting.

Shortly after the 1960 Miles Davis–Gil Evans album *Sketches of Spain* came out, I was talking to Gil on the telephone. The album was suffused with Spanish musical feeling and one track was an adaptation of a movement of Joaquin Rodrigo's *Concierto de Aranjuez*, a concerto for guitar and orchestra.

Nat Hentoff, in liner notes for the album, wrote:

What is most remarkable is the surprising authenticity of phrasing and timbre with which (Miles) plays. It is as if Miles had been born of Andalusian gypsies but, instead of picking up a guitar, had decided to make a trumpet the expression of his *canto hondo*. And Evans also indicates a thorough absorption of the Spanish musical temper which he has transmuted into his own uncompromisingly personal style.

People, I told Gil that day, were puzzled by the album, not knowing whether to call it classical music or jazz.

Gil said, "That's a merchandiser's problem, not mine. I write popular music."

This reply suggested that Gil refused to be trapped in categories. Many "jazz" musicians, including Duke Ellington and Miles Davis, have expressed discontent with the word "jazz," seeing it as constrictive and limiting. But Gil's comment also indicated the breadth of his musical interests. At one period of his life he wrote a great many arrangements for singers, including Helen Merrill and Lucy Reed, and some for the first Johnny Mathis album. Later in his life, he would record an album of material by Jimi Hendrix. Gil's musical interests were inclusive – hugely inclusive – not exclusive.

"I go along with the rhythm of the time," Gil told the Toronto jazz critic Mark Miller in 1984. "Jazz has always used the rhythm of the time, until it becomes formalized . . . Current jazz, now jazz, uses the rhythm of the time."

But for Gil Evans, a man whose music was never "popular" in the strict sense of the word, the assertion that he wrote popular music borders on the inscrutable. Creed Taylor, who produced a number of Gil's albums, thinks he meant the popular idiom, not the extent of the sale. "And that was his concept," Creed said.

Gil told Nat Hentoff in 1957, "I have a kind of direction of my own . . . my interest in jazz, pop, and sound in various combinations, has dictated what I would do at various times. At different times, one of the three has been stronger."

Citing this, the British critic Max Harrison wrote in his book *A Jazz Retrospect* (New York, Crescendo, 1977),

> Such an attitude would obviously prevent Evans from being a member of any self-conscious and organized movement in music for any length of time, and it may be added that he has never been overly concerned with the 'importance' of his writing . . .
>
> Despite their undoubted – if somewhat overrated – contribution to jazz, the swing bands, once established, stood in the way of further orchestral developments. These could only resume when the bands came off the road and orchestral jazz was created by *ad hoc* groups assembled mainly, if not exclusively, for recording purposes. Such conditions allowed far more varied instrumentation than hitherto, a wider choice of repertoire – which no longer had to be orientated to a dancing public – and the application of more diverse techniques of writing. Missing from much of this later music is that feeling of integration which can only be achieved when a group of men play the same repertoire together over a long period, but in compensation the studio players' superior executive skills allowed more adventurous scores to be attempted.

So did improved recording techniques. If you wanted to put classical guitar in front of a jazz orchestra – and Gil did that in the Kenny Burrell album *Guitar Forms* – you could do it. These improved techniques permitted the use in jazz, even with big bands, of the flute.

Gil abandoned the standard jazz instrumentation of trumpets–trombones–saxes–and–rhythm section, using instead flutes, oboes, English horns, French horns, tuba, and a few of the conventional jazz instruments. He enormously expanded the vocabulary of the jazz orchestra.

Gil's childhood is enigmatic. Little is known about his father, but according to Anita Evans, his widow, the mother's maiden name was Margaret Julia McConnachy. "Gil said they were Scotch–Irish. She was one of something like fourteen or seventeen children. That's why she left home at such an early age. Gil said she got on these boats and visited South Africa and Australia."

According to Anita, Gil's mother told him that he had fallen from a star and she found him on a beach. "She told Gil he was her gift, from a star," Anita said. "Gil said that until he was 11, he didn't know anything else."

He was in fact born in Toronto on 13 May 1912. How a man perceives himself becomes part of his perception by others, and Miles Davis in his autobiography says that he met "a Canadian arranger" named Gil Evans.

There is even a question about Gil's real name. The standard references say it was Ian Ernest Gilmore Green. His friend Jimmy Maxwell says it was Gilmore Ian Rodriguez or Rodrigo Green, which suggests some trace of Hispanic lineage. The reference books say he had Australian parentage, but even that seems questionable.

On the evening of 24 November 1984, Gil, who was in Toronto to play a concert of his music with a Canadian band, had dinner with Mark Miller. He said: "My mother carried a mandolin with her. She played folk music. I think they came from Calcutta. They were married in Australia. They moved to Jersey. Then they moved to Canada."

Gil said his father "was a gambler – a horse gambler. My mother told me he'd rent a car and take everyone to the races, but the next week he'd be pawning her jewelry. She always told me never to be a gambler. Well, I've gambled on life."

Apparently his mother moved back to the United States. Gil told Miller: "I came back here (to Toronto) after my first stepfather was killed. My mother moved back here for a little while when I was about 4." Note the reference to a first stepfather. There must, then, have been at least two of them.

The musician who knew Gil earliest and longest is the great lead trumpet player Jimmy Maxwell. Jimmy was born on 9 January 1917, near Stockton, where Gil grew up, and played not only in the band Gil formed there in their youth but continued to work with Gil over the years, including the period when Gil and Claude Thornhill were writing arrangements for the Skinnay Ennis band. Gil met Thornhill through Ennis, thereby beginning an association that produced music as influential in jazz in the last half of the century as that of Fletcher Henderson, Bill Challis, Duke Ellington, and Don Redman in the first half. Gil told Ben Sidran that Don Redman "was one of my first teachers, you know?"

He said, "I lived in a little town in California where nothing like that ever happened. But a man from San Francisco would come up every week to a little record store there and buy all the latest releases. So I was really raised on Don Redman, Duke Ellington, the Wolverines, and McKinney's Cotton Pickers. The Casa Loma band . . . I heard them all. And the radio was a big thing then, in the early '30s. Every day you'd hear a band from New York . . . Don Redman had a great band, wow! He had a big band, but they were packed together tight. Three trombones, three trumpets, four saxophones, they're all bunched up together.

"Don Redman was the original arranger, big-band arranger, of jazz."

Redman, born in Piedmont, West Virginia, on 29 July 1900, the son of a music educator, was a child prodigy who played all the double-reed instruments by the time he was 12. He graduated with a degree in music from Storer College when he was 20, made a living as a saxophone player, then joined Fletcher Henderson's band, for which he wrote. He then joined, played, sang, and wrote for McKinney's Cotton Pickers; he was largely responsible for transforming the group into a major jazz band. He went on to première his own band in October 1931: it lasted until 1940.

Gil told Nat Hentoff: "It was the sound of Louis' horn, the people in Red Nichols' unit, the McKinney Cotton Pickers, Don Redman. Redman's Brunswick records ought to be reissued. The band swung, but the voicings also gave the band a compact sound. I also was interested in popular bands, like the Casa Loma approach to ballads. Gene Gifford broke up the instrumentation more imaginatively than was usual at the time."

Like many composers and arrangers of the time, Gil would slow up records on a hand-crank Victrola and write down what he heard. Where he learned to read and notate music remains unknown.

Jimmy Maxwell said, "He was very cool, very casual. We had a great opportunity to play at the University of California at Berkeley. We loaded into this big old Cadillac. We got the whole band in it and the instruments were in a trailer. Halfway to Berkeley the trailer broke loose and fell upside down. The instruments were smashed and the music was blowing all over the countryside. Most of us got out and almost cried. Gil was standing beside the road having hysterics laughing. He thought it was the funniest thing he had ever seen. He had strange reactions like that."

"He was very trying to his friends," Gerry Mulligan said when he heard that story.

Maxwell said, "Gil had a room in Stockton. He didn't live with his mother. She was a nursemaid for a family who built combines and all kinds of farm machinery." This was the Deere family.

"She was a very nice lady," Jimmy said. "With all Gil's names, his mother called him Buster." (Hence the name of Gil's 1942 chart for Thornhill, "Buster's Last Stand.")

"I didn't know his stepfather," Jimmy said. "No one knew him. He and the mother had separated long ago. He'd deserted her, I think. Gil was out of high school when I met him, out of junior college, for that matter. He went to Modesto Junior College."

"I wonder what he took there," I said.

"That's a good question," Jimmy said. "He was self-taught. I don't think they even had a music course."

Gil told Mark Miller: "I never heard any music until I came to Berkeley High. A high-school chum of mine had his father fix him a basement play-room with a piano, a record player, and a drum set. This was in 1927. So that's where I first heard Louis Armstrong, Duke Ellington, and Don Redman. I fell in love with the music. I'd never heard that music before: only pop music. No classical music either. Where I came from, they'd never *heard* of classical music." This tells us that Gil was living in Berkeley, California, at the age of 15.

Miller asked him, "Were you set from the beginning on being a musician?"

"Soon's I heard Louis Armstrong and Duke Ellington I was, yeah. From then on."

"To be a writer, an arranger?"

"Well, I didn't know what I was going to do," Gil said. "Finally I ended up copying records. I'd play 'em over and over again. I learned how to write some of those things down . . . the Casa Loma band. I started my own band in high school."

Leonard Feather's 1960 edition of the *Encyclopedia of Jazz* says Gil was "raised in British Columbia, state of Washington, and Stockton, Calif." One newspaper story says his father died when he was six months old, but it tells us nothing about who the father was or what he did.

Gil told me that he started listening to bands on the radio in Saskatchewan. I remember Gil smiling ruefully when he spoke of the bitter prairie winters. His mother supported him by working as a cook. Gil told Miller: "She worked in farms and logging camps and mining camps. My mother was maybe five feet tall. She wore a four-and-a-half shoe. And yet she'd get up at three or four in the morning, in one of those mining towns, and fire up the stoves and feed all those men and get them off to work by six o'clock. Amazing."

Mark Miller thinks Gil was about 10 when his mother took him to the United States. Anita thinks he may have been as young as 7. And Gil's mother moved about California as she had moved about Canada. Anita said:

"He attended Burbank High School in Burbank, California, and left there in 1928. But he also attended Berkeley High School. He was down in Burbank, then went up to Berkeley, then over to Stockton. He graduated from Stockton High School in June of 1930. This was the pattern of his mother's changing jobs. I remember him telling me he even went to Hollywood High."

If one pieces the story together from these references, this itinerary suggests itself: Gil's mother must have moved west from Toronto and stayed through at least one winter in Saskatchewan, on to British Columbia on the Canadian west coast, then south across the American border to the states of Washington and Montana (in whichever order), finally south to California with a possible residence in Burbank and Hollywood, then up to Berkeley and finally to Stockton, which is in ranch country some 40 or so miles east-northeast of San Francisco. These movements obviously made an unstable life for a young boy, with no continuity of education. When Mark Miller asked him about his schooling, Gil said: "It changed every year. I went to local schools, always a little school. I used to ride a horse to school in Montana, and I haven't ridden a horse since." That is the only reference to Montana I have discovered, just as the only reference to Saskatchewan came in Gil's conversation with me.

Gil's mother's statement that he fell from a star suggests that she didn't want him to know much, if anything, about his father. And so the details of Gil's paternity and even his childhood sojourning probably can never be determined now: excepting Jimmy Maxwell, there is no one left to ask, and even Jimmy doesn't know that much.

Whatever the details, Gil was, Anita said, "a California guy with that Canadian ethic."

Noah, one of their two sons, told me, "He always referred to himself as Canadian."

And Anita said: "It's true. Gil told me he always felt like a foreigner in the United States. He didn't even become a citizen voluntarily. When he was drafted during World War II, he was given American citizenship automatically." Anita chuckled: "He didn't even own a passport up till then."

Given that he was apparently resident in the United States from an early age, why did he persist in thinking of himself as Canadian?

"His mother programmed him that way," Anita said. "She'd refer to Americans as 'these people.'"

"His sister lived in Canada," Jimmy Maxwell said. "I remember a big event. He'd finally tracked her down. He was very excited about going up to meet her."

This reunion happened during Gil's first marriage, to Lillian. Anita said, "Gil had come late in his mother's life. She was past 45. And he found a sister who was a good deal older than he. He'd been raised like an only child. So this woman was maybe fifteen or twenty years older than Gil. She had married a salt millionaire. She was living the really good life up in Canada. He and Lillian made one visit to her. But the life was on such a different level that they didn't stay in touch.

"She had apparently not forgiven their mother. She said, 'She was an aimless wanderer.'

"But this little lady managed to get all over the world with her spunk. She was dead by the time I met Gil, but she lived to be 90ish anyway."

She must have had an incredibly independent streak. Certainly the evidence is that she would take no nonsense from the men in her life, and apparently there was a succession of them. Whether she married them all or not, nobody seems to know. But her uncompromising individualism may help explain Gil.

Anita said, "Gil told me the first name he remembers having was Gilmore Gustin. That stepfather was after he was 7 years old and in the United States. Mr. Evans came after Mr. Gustin, and Gil took that name."

There was much about Gil that I found Canadian. His perpetual, sometimes infuriating – it angered Jimmy Maxwell – self-doubt seems to me very Canadian. Compare him to Kenny Wheeler.

In any event, on the basis of the testimony of his wife, his son Noah, and of Miles Davis, and indeed my own experience with him, Gil must be perceived as he perceived himself: as a Canadian composer, for all the strong Spanish and western influences in his work, not to mention jazz itself.

Gil wrote very slowly. Nat Hentoff quoted Gil as saying, "I have more craft and speed than I sometimes want to admit. I want to avoid getting into a rut. I can't keep doing the same thing over and over. I'm not a craftsman in the same sense as a lot of writers I hear who do commercials and jazz work. They have a wonderful ability with the details of their craft. The details are all authentic but, when it's over, you realize that the whole is less than the sum of the parts."

Hentoff also cited a comment by Gerry Mulligan: "Gil is the only arranger I've played who can really notate a thing the way a soloist would blow it . . . For example, the down beats don't always fall on the down beats in a solo, and he makes a note of that. It makes for a more complicated notation but, because what he writes is melodic and makes sense, it's not hard to play. The notation makes the parts look harder than they are, but Gil can work with a band, can sing to them what he wants, he gets it out of them."

When the Miles-and-Gil *Porgy and Bess* album came out, Bill Mathieu, a young Chicago arranger who had been writing for Stan Kenton, wrote a review for *Down Beat* in which he said, "The mind reels at the intricacy of his orchestral and developmental techniques. His scores are so careful, so formally well-constructed, so mindful of tradition, that you feel the originals should be preserved under glass in a Florentine museum."

That thoroughness, that surpassing technical command, was in all of Gil's earlier writing; his late work requires further discussion. But he fiddled and fooled with scores, altering a note here, another there, right to the last desperate minute.

Gil's music reflects his affinity for things Hispanic. The Mexican influence is everywhere in California, in the tile roofs and yellow stucco walls, in the very air, in the cuisine, in the love of bright colors, and certainly in the music. Consider his writing in *Sketches of Spain*. Canadian in his own mind though he might be, there was never a more Californian composer than Gil Evans, and to get the real feel of what he was all about, it is helpful to know not just America but California. If the north is in Sibelius, the west is in Gil.

The terrain around Stockton in summer is a dry beige color, a baked land scattered with dark California oaks. It is lonely and vastly spacious country. And Gil spent his latter adolescence a scant 35 miles from Dave Brubeck, a native of that area.

This combination of characteristics – the Canadian and the Californian – prompted me to write that Gil's *Sketches of Spain* made me think of *A View of Toledo* as perceived not by El Greco but by Lawren Harris, a major Canadian painter.

"I'm from Tracy, California," Jimmy Maxwell said. "That's a town about twenty miles away from Stockton. I worked with Gil from 1932 to '36, when I left to go with Jimmy Dorsey.

"Gil copied Casa Loma almost exclusively, either off their records or their radio broadcasts. That whole band was based on Casa Loma: we even had uniforms like theirs. The guys had to double, and we played cornets instead of trumpets. We used to take off from rehearsing to listen to the broadcasts. And we would each be assigned sixteen bars to copy off as quick as we could, if it was a tune that wasn't recorded. And so his arranging at that time was entirely a copy of Casa Loma.

"We kept trying to get ahead. In 1934, we went to Lake Tahoe and played there for the summer. Then we went back to playing casual dates in Stockton. We got a job in the local ballroom, playing five nights a week. And when summer came, we went to Capitola Beach. We were financed pretty much by a friend of Gil's who took us down there. We all worked renovating the ballroom, scraping the wax off the floor and all that stuff, getting it ready. That was kind of a fiasco. The guy lost money. Eventually Gil paid it back to him out of our salaries.

"Then we had a chance to audition down at Balboa Beach. We all drove down to Balboa Beach in this one car with a trailer, everybody sitting on each other's laps for 450 miles. We auditioned that afternoon, and the guy said, 'Okay, you can finish out the last two weeks of the season.' Then he said, 'You can stay through the winter, but it only pays twelve dollars a week.'

"The band just hung on at Balboa Beach, or maybe they made more in the winter, after I left.

"All the bands used to come down to see us. Benny Goodman came down, and all the guys from his band. The Casa Loma band came down to hear us. By that time, we were copying Benny Goodman. As soon as Benny made 'Sometimes I'm Happy' and 'King Porter Stomp,' Gil copied them off. Some of the other guys copied some arrangements. I copied some Ellington and Lunceford arrangements. 'Dream of You' was one I copied; and 'Solitude.' Gil copied one of Ellington's, 'Sweet Dreams of Love.'

"I was zipping around the country. I got a wire from Gil to come back with the band. I went back to Balboa Beach for a while.

"Benny had fixed us up with Music Corporation of America. We used to go in every week and talk to Norman Doyle, who was our representative. We'd say, 'When are you going to get us a really good hotel spot?' And Norman Doyle would say, 'Are you guys really ready?' And Gil would say, 'I don't know, we could be a little more polished.' We could have killed him. Norman didn't know anything. If we had told him, 'Yes,' he'd have put us in.

"I used to get into some pretty bad arguments with Gil because I didn't think he was pushing enough. But Gil was like that. He was terrible about finishing arrangements. When he first came to New York, I was doing pretty well, and I got him several assignments, people who were thrilled at the idea of him writing for them. Patti Page. I was on the staff orchestra at Columbia Broadcasting Company. He'd take a job to write an arrangement and he'd never show up. They'd have a specific date to broadcast that tune, and they'd say, 'Where's your friend Gil?' I'd call him up, and he'd say, 'Oh Jesus, you know, I forgot all about that.' He screwed himself like that.

"Getting back to the thing with Norman Doyle: it kept going on. Finally, Skinnay Ennis left Hal Kemp's orchestra and he was out in Hollywood, going to start a band." Skinnay Ennis was a drummer and an odd, kind of corny, singer with Kemp.

Jimmy continued, "Music Corporation told Skinnay, 'Listen, we've got a band ready-made for you, if they're interested in doing it. We've got this band down at Balboa Beach.' I wasn't in the band then. Skinnay liked the band and he said he'd take it over.

"As far as I know, Gil gave him the entire book and didn't charge him anything. He just wanted to see the guys work. That's how Skinnay got hold of the band. Gil gave it to him."

Gil's band had lasted from 1933 until 1938, when he was 26.

"When Skinnay took the band over," Maxwell continued, "he brought Claude Thornhill to write the vocal arrangements for him. The band went to the Bob Hope radio show. Mannie Klein played in it the first year, but then the next year he wasn't there and I played first on it. We went on tour during the summer of '39. Benny Goodman was in the Victor Hugo, where we'd been playing with Skinnay – a very fancy restaurant in Beverly Hills. It was a place all the movie stars came to. It had very good food and dancing till one o'clock. That's where we played the whole winter and did the Bob Hope show. I did that for two years.

"I wanted John Hammond to bring me to New York. I heard Mezz Mezzrow was going to start a mixed band. I didn't have the nerve to go on my own. John said to come around to the studio and audition – not just sit in – with Benny Goodman, so he could hear me. I went with Benny.

"Gil stayed writing for Skinnay. Skitch Henderson came in as the piano player. Gil wasn't that much of a commercial piano player. When Skinnay brought in Claude Thornhill, he and Gil hit it off right away. They had great admiration for each other. According to Gil, he learned a lot from Thornhill. I don't think Gil had any formal or classical training on writing, though he certainly knew more about writing than anybody who went to college. He would copy things off Debussy records. Casa Loma did that; they had something from César Franck as an introduction to something. Duke Ellington had a lot of that French influence, which he got through Willie the Lion Smith, whom he said he owed so much to. Willie knew all that stuff.

"Gil learned a lot from Claude in the sense of 'Do a little of this, do a little of that. Don't overdo this or that.' Not actual writing, because by that time, harmonically and structurally, Gil knew what he was doing. He wouldn't write difficult fingerings for saxophones, for trumpets. That's why it took him so long. He labored over every inch of it. He wasn't one of those guys who would just sit down and say, 'Well this is a C seventh chord, I'll write such and such.'"

As well as writing for the Skinnay Ennis band on the Bob Hope show, Gil wrote for the Chesterfield Supper Club and the orchestra conducted by Paul Weston. Paul remembered: "We did five shows a week with Johnny Mercer and Jo (Stafford, later Paul's wife) and the Pied Pipers, it involved a hell of a lot of arrangements – five, fifteen-minute shows a week. Gil did some work for me then.

"We lived in the same apartment, Casa Argyle, on Argyle Street north of Hollywood Boulevard, two blocks west of Vine Street. Skitch Henderson, Axel Stordahl, Sammy Cahn, and a bunch of guys lived there."

"How was he about delivering charts on time?"

"He was all right," Paul said. "He knew when we went on the air. Every arranger does everything he can think of, go to the bathroom, sharpen pencils, walk around the room, go out in the yard, anything but start the head-hurting creative process. And Gil just waited longer than some others. But Gil always got it done.

"Gil was very quiet with a sly, cute sense of humor. We would get laughs out of the same kind of jokes and musicians' talk.

"Even then, when he was writing for me and Skinnay Ennis, I think he wanted to go beyond the five saxophones, six or seven brass custom of the way everybody wrote in those days, and get into different kinds of unisons and combinations of instruments that were easier to work with in the context of jazz orchestration than in commercial orchestration. I don't think he was ever terribly comfortable with commercial orchestration such as we had to do for records and radio at that time. He was looking further than that. And I don't think at that time he had much sense of his own worth.

"Then he got the call to go to New York with Thornhill."

I said, "I was told that you had to lend him the money to get there."

"Ah," said Paul, who was the kindest of men, "don't put that in there."

"Why not?" I said. "Gil was notorious for being casual with money, including the money he lent people and forgot. Maybe that's why he was so often broke."

"Well, okay," Paul said. "You know, I never saw him again after he left California."

Thornhill formed his band in 1939. Gil, who knew the owner of the ballroom at Balboa, recommended the Thornhill band to play there. He told Nat Hentoff in 1957, "Claude had a unique way with a dance band. He'd use the trombones, for example, with the woodwinds in a way that gave them a horn sound." Pointing out that Thornhill had the band play without vibrato, except for expressive purposes, Gil said: "I think he was the first among the pop or jazz bands to evolve that sound. Claude's band was always very popular with players. The Benny Goodman band style was beginning to pall and had gotten to be commercial. I haunted Claude until he hired me as an arranger in 1941. I enjoyed it all, as did the men.

"The sound of the band didn't necessarily restrict the soloists. Most of his soloists had an individual style. The sound of the band may have calmed down the overall mood, but that made everything feel very relaxed.

"Even before Claude added the French horns, the band began to sound like a French-horn band. The trombones and trumpets began to take on that character, began to play in derby hats without a vibrato.

"Claude added the French horns in 1941. He had written an obbligato for them to (an Irving) Fazola solo to surprise (him). Fazola got up to play; Claude signaled the French horns at the other end of the room to come up to the bandstand; and that was the first time Fazola knew they were to be added to the band.

"Claude was the first leader to use French horns as a functioning part of a dance band: that distant, haunting, no-vibrato sound with the reed and brass sections in various combinations. Claude deserves credit for the sound. My influence, such as it has been, was really through him. His orchestra served as my instrument to work with. That's where my influence and his join, so to speak.

"In essence, at first, the sound of the band was almost a reduction to an inactivity of music, to a stillness. Everything – melody, harmony, rhythm – was moving at minimum speed. The melody was very slow, static; the rhythm was nothing much faster than quarter notes and a minimum of syncopation. Everything was lowered to create a sound, and nothing was to be used to distract from that sound. The sound hung like a cloud."

"This kind of sound," I asked Jimmy Maxwell, "that floating Thornhill sound," I said. "Do you have any thought on who originated that? Was it Gil or was it . . . ?"

"Gil! One hundred percent."

"He originated that sound?"

"Absolutely!" Jimmy said. "No question of it. It was Gil. He wrote some beautiful things. 'Blues for Texas' or 'Texas Blues.' It was a record Jack Teagarden had made with the Charleston Chasers, Benny Goodman and Teagarden. Gil did an arrangement on it. He had the sound of coyotes on the French horns."

Duke Ellington said of Thornhill, "I wonder if the world will ever know how much it had in this beautiful man."

Thornhill was born in Terre Haute, Indiana, on 10 August 1909, and thus was five years Gil's senior. He claimed to have studied piano at the Cincinatti Conservatory and the Curtis Institute, but there is evidence that he invented this background. Certainly he recorded with Bud Freeman and Billie Holiday and played with Benny Goodman, and he wrote arrangements for various bands, including that of Benny Goodman. He first recorded as a leader in 1937, and in 1940 formed a band that lasted until 1942. Gil wrote for that band.

The war interrupted both careers. Gil spent three years in the army and Thornhill played piano in the Artie Shaw navy band that performed in the South Pacific and evolved into the Sam Donahue band that Robert Farnon heard in England. Thornhill re-formed his own band in 1946 and immediately hired Gil to write for it.

"I always considered Gil my best friend," Jimmy Maxwell said. "I even gave my son his middle name after Gil. When my son was born, Gil had just got out of the Army. He came and lived with us three or four months. We had an apartment on London Terrace in New York. Unfortunately it was a two-room apartment. My wife and I slept in the living room and Gil stayed in the room with the baby. He played piano all night, and sometimes I stayed up all night and played records with him. My wife was at the limit of her endurance. After three months, I had to ask him to get his own place.

"Gil was very charming and very sophisticated-seeming. Compared to the rest of us, you'd say he was an intellectual. He read. He had two or three favorite books. He had a book called *Genius*, and he was a great admirer of *The Seven Pillars of Wisdom* by T. E. Lawrence. Another favorite was a mystery story called *The Cadaver of Gideon Wick*. Another was *A Generation of Vipers*, which had just come out, the first put-down book."

Gerry Mulligan said, "Claude wrote 'Snowfall,' 'Adios,' 'Portrait of a Guinea Farm.' Claude had great humor in his writing. He was very funny, for being such a shy man. The bulk of the book that is known and identified as being by Claude Thornhill was by Bill Borden. Those arrangements were deceptively simple. They just sounded so logical and so simple, but they were very, very tastefully done, and perfect for the band.

"Gil wrote 'Anthropology,' 'Donna Lee,' and 'Yardbird Suite' for Thornhill. My favorite was 'Lover Man.' Another ballad he did – and he did another version for the nonet – was 'Moondreams.' But my favorite was 'Lover Man.' It included about ten sharps, I think! But it was so beautiful."

Mulligan said, "There was always at least one clarinet going, and in some things they used two clarinets. You know, in the original band, Claude had four saxes and two clarinets: Danny Polo and Irving Fazola. You can't beat that for sound. Fazola had the most beautiful sound in the world and Danny was right next to him. Early on it was three trumpets, two 'bones, and either one or two horns. Two, I think. Even in the early band it was two horns and two clarinets. It changed."

Ira Gitler, in his 1985 book *Swing to Bop* (Oxford University Press), quotes Lee Konitz:

> The thing about that band that is most important, I suppose, in this whole transitional period, is that Gil was, in fact, teaching the men how to play be-bop . . . Although I thought of Claude's band as basically a ballad band. That was its forte . . .

Thornhill was an enigmatic man with a quirky sense of humor and a drinking habit. Konitz said: "He was a shy guy. His wife traveled with him quite a bit of the time. So they were off by themselves. Gil conducted the rehearsals."

Gil said of Thornhill, "He could play the piano with no vibrato, and that's what the band did. He could make the piano tone fit into the arrangement."

The piano, of course, *has* no vibrato. And yet anyone who ever heard Thornhill's cool, detached, quite lovely piano sound knows what Gil meant. And Brew Moore said, "Claude was some kind of freak genius. He could take the worst out-of-tune piano and make it sound in tune."

Gitler quotes Thornhill:

> Perfect intonation in the sections and balance of the overall sound of the orchestra were emphasized. With the exception of certain pieces in our arrangements, the

orchestra played almost without vibrato. Vibrato was used to heighten expressiveness. Even before we added French horns to the band, the feeling and sound were there; the trumpets and trombones, often in hats, imitated the sound, and did it quite well.

Thornhill added tuba to the band around the end of 1947. He hired Bill Barber; that sound, with a tuba bottom, would be in almost everything Gil wrote for rest of his career, and the tuba player he used was often Barber.

Gerry Mulligan said, "I didn't play with the band that much. I was arranging for Claude. And then at one point I went on the road with him for a few months. I think that was 1947."

"And I'm pretty sure you were in it when I saw the band," I said. "And that was '47. I'm sure Lee Konitz was in the band and I guess the drummer was Billy Exiner. I was in absolute awe of the sound that band was putting out."

"Yeah," Gerry said. "People don't know what we're talking about when we say that. They say, 'Yeah, well, mm-hmm.' But the band was orchestral. It wasn't a band."

Gil said: "Claude was a complex arranger. After the war he never really got writing again. He leaned on me, and he didn't want to. I let him because I wanted the experience. He liked the modern jazz, but it wasn't what he wanted to play. He wanted the old 'Where or When,' 'Snowfall,' style. He liked things to float and hang – clarinets moving very quickly over a sustained background."

Gil said the instrumentation after the war was three trumpets, two trombones, two French horns, a tuba, two alto saxophones, two tenors, baritone, and a separate flute section. The French horns had been Thornhill's idea, but Gil added the tuba and flutes. Its vibratoless sound, Gil said, made the band compatible with be-bop, and in turn made it attractive to the boppers, who were also interested in Gil's harmonic practices, including the use of minor ninths.

Gil told Ben Sidran: "Up until that time, with the swing bands, mostly the harmony had been from Fletcher Henderson, really. Where you harmonize everything with the major sixth chords and passing tones with a diminished chord, you know. So that was how things changed with be-bop."

Gil often recommended his friends to Thornhill as arrangers, among them Gerry Mulligan, Johnny Carisi, and Gene Roland. Sidemen in that band included Roland, Lee Konitz, Red Rodney, Lou Mucci (who would be on many of Gil's later dates), and Rusty Dedrick. Gil told Nat Hentoff: "My final leaving was friendly. The sound had become too somber for my taste, generally speaking, a little too bleak in character. It began to have a hypnotic effect at times. The band could put you to sleep."

In 1959, when Miles Davis and Gil were planning *Sketches of Spain*, I commissioned journalist Marc Crawford to write an article for me at *Down Beat* on the relationship between Gil and Miles. We called the piece *Portrait of a Friendship*. Miles was in Chicago, visiting his then in-laws. He told Crawford on the telephone, "I don't like discussing Gil. I got too much respect for him to do that. It's almost like asking a man to discuss his wife." But then he relented, and when he and Crawford sat down to talk, Miles said: "I first met Gil when I was with Bird, and he was asking for a release on my tune 'Donna Lee.' He wanted to make an arrangement (of it). I told him he could have it and asked him to teach me some chords and let me study some of the scores he was doing for Claude Thornhill.

"He really flipped me on the arrangement for 'Robbins' Nest' he did for Claude. Gil had this cluster of chords and superimposed another cluster over it. Now the chord ends, and now these three notes of the remaining cluster are gone. The overtone of the remaining two produced a note way up here. I was puzzled. I had studied the score for days trying to find the note he heard. But it didn't even exist – at least, on paper it didn't.

"We've been friends since that first meeting. He's my favorite arranger, yet he's never really made money out of the business."

Crawford wrote that Gil's "income seems to wind up some $500 a year under what his needs require."

In a 1979 interview, Gil said, "I got here (to New York) in Christmas of '46, intending to stay a couple of years, and stayed over thirty."

Gil remembered that he got off the train, left his bags in a check room, and went, as so many others did, directly to 52nd Street where, with its line-up of jazz clubs, on the first night he met such of his heroes as Ben Webster, Erroll Garner, and Bud Powell. Of that time in his life, he said, "People pour into New York City – right? – for their careers, to seek their fortune. Everybody comes here and you put yourself in an area where you figure you're gonna meet some other people that do the same thing. I came here from California, which had been my home for a long time, after I got out of the army, because I wanted to pick up on my trade, what I did and what I like, to get into jazz more. I wanted to make all kind of connections.

"It's like the butterfly. The butterflies all meet out in the redwoods in Big Sur in October. They come flying in from everywhere. I just happened to be there one time, and I never did see anything in my life like it. They must have been in the billions. Some of them meet and some of them don't, right? That's the way it happened here. (Miles and I) happened to have the same kind of an ear for sound, a certain sound. I could appreciate his sound, and he could appreciate my sound in the orchestra. There was a certain emotional connection.

"The thing about him is that he can play from the lowest note on the trumpet to the highest and it all has the same sound. It all belongs to him, even though you go up through different registers. Naturally you sound different below middle C than you do above on account of the intensity. But it's all in the same family, so that you never get a break. You especially notice it when he's playing a solo and he's 'way up high and he decides to come down. He never falls down. Some people can be 'way up there and they can't get back down again – gracefully, I mean. But he has a way of just stepping, tripping, all the way back down again.

"When he first started out he didn't have the sound he had eventually. You fill it in. You breathe harder into it. You fill the horn up, soon as you know how you want it to sound. But that thing has to come along. You can't just wake up one day and say, I've been struck by a new sound, and you do it. He had to gradually get that thing. It was like it needed to have more flesh and blood to it. It was very stark at the beginning. It's a developmental thing. You watch it as an interested bystander. Later he had more of the melancholy cry that he wanted to get."

And he said, "I feel very tight, very close with Miles. I'm very happy that we met. It was a great thing. A big thing in my life. I mean, the *biggest* thing in my musical life and my career. The biggest thing that ever happened to me."

Gerry Mulligan was 20 when he wrote for the Claude Thornhill band and first came under Gil's influence. Gerry was living in Philadelphia when Gil suggested that he move to New York, and, until he made other arrangements, live with him.

Gerry said: "I wound up sharing the room with him. We took turns using the piano, we took turns using the bed, and there was always a succession of guys in and out. We'd be working on charts, and there were conversations going on. Davie Lambert was a regular. He was scuffling around, doing odd jobs. He always had his little daughter in tow. John Benson Brooks was a regular. John Lewis used to come by, when he was in town. Then the guys from Claude's band when they were in town, Danny Polo and Billy Exiner."

Mulligan, Johnny Carisi – who also had been writing for the Thornhill band – John Lewis, Lee Konitz, Max Roach, and Miles Davis were part of the ongoing seminar, if that's the word, conducted by Gil in that apartment on 55th Street in New York. One of the regulars was Johnny Mandel.

"It wasn't really an apartment," Mulligan said. "It was a big basement room. To get into it, you go down five steps of an entry-way. To the left is a Chinese laundry. You go behind the laundry and make a dog-leg turn and go into the giant room with pipes running through the ceiling. There were a few steps up to a little back courtyard, which was an air space more than anything, and a fence. It looked like it was out of *My Sister Eileen*, only no curtains on the window. There was a sink on the right and a little compartment where the toilet was. As you went in the door, the bed was in front of you, the piano was to the right."

Gil, in an interview with Ben Sidran, said, "I left the door open for two years. Just left it open . . . I never locked it. So sometimes I'd come home and I'd meet strangers. And most of the time I met people like Miles and John Lewis. George Russell.

"We talked a lot about harmony. How to get a 'sound' out of harmony. Because the harmony has a lot to do with what the music is going to 'sound' like. The instruments have their wave form and all that, but the harmony means that you're putting together a group of instruments, and they're going to get their own independent wave form, right? You can't get it any other way except as an ensemble playing together.

"So Miles and I talked about that lots of times. And played chords on the piano."

Mulligan said, "It was a special time, to be part of a scene like that where a whole bunch of young people gravitate together by some kind of mutual interests. Even as diverse as our individual approaches were to it, our main interest was focused around music and ways to improve it and improve ourselves.

"Johnny Carisi and I were always at each other's throats. It was very intense."

Carisi said, "We used to fall by. And between Gil and Mulligan, I think they conceived that (nonet) instrumentation, which is kind of logical from a very practical instrumental viewpoint. It's six horns which are more or less octave arrangements of each other. Certainly the trumpet and trombone, it's the same pitch an octave apart. The alto and baritone, the same thing. The French horn and tuba, because the tuba is, in a sense, although not exactly, if you want to really go deep into it, a big French horn . . .

"Gerry wrote more than anybody. Gil wrote a couple of tunes, either his own or he mostly did arrangements of other people's things. John Lewis did a couple. Gerry did some of his own and (George Wallington's) 'Godchild.' And I wrote about three things, two of which never got on because . . . they never had enough rehearsal time to ever actually work them out, but 'Israel' was the one that really got a good shot at it."

The instrumentation of that nonet, six horns in three groupings in the same families, is parallel to that of Stravinsky's *L'Histoire du Soldat*, which also is built around six instruments in three groupings, in that case clarinet and bassoon, cornet and trombone, and violin and bass.

Pianist and arranger Gene DiNovi was a regular at Gil's pad. Gene recalled: "I used to hang around in front of Nola's Studios on Broadway, to see if enough guys could be assembled to hire some space and blow. On a good night guys like Tiny Kahn, Red Mitchell, and Al Cohn would show.

"One summer evening I stood there for a long time, but no one showed up. So I went to the second floor of Nola's and opened the door of one of the long studios. And there I found a rhythm section, doing nothing but playing time. The players were Barry Galbraith on guitar, Joe Shulman on bass, Gil Evans on piano, and Billy Exiner on drums. It was the Claude Thornhill rhythm section plus Gil. There were no horns. Just those four people playing time, perfecting that rhythm section. And they were playing so closely that you got the feeling that if one of them died, the rest would commit suicide. Gil graciously asked me to play. Being your basic nervy kid from Brooklyn, I said, 'Sure. What do you want to play?' As I recall, somebody said, '"All the Things You Are."' We started. Not until long afterward did it occur to me that that was the first time I was truly *accompanied*. They were listening to me and expected me to listen to them – what Gil called interrelated playing . . . But my most vivid memory of the incident is seeing Gil with his ear *in the piano*. A lesson in listening.

"On other nights Miles Davis, Stan Getz, Brew Moore, Tony Fruscella, John Carisi, and other young Turks would show up. If the Thornhill band was in town, that rhythm section would be at Nola's in the evening. Afterwards we'd go back to Gil's apartment and listen to more music. The conversations – particularly the exchanges between Gil and Billy Exiner – expanded a lot of minds. And it was in that apartment, of course, that what became known as 'the cool' was born. We never used the term, indeed never even heard it.

"You might see Bud Powell at the piano, playing a Bach invention in his own way. One night Charlie Parker came to the door and asked for five dollars for his cab fare. He listened to Prokofiev's *Scythian Suite* on the phonograph and said, 'I don't even scratch the surface.'

"Or Dave Lambert would be there, writing an arrangement. Gerry Mulligan and I would go out for something to eat, continuing the conversation begun in the apartment. Wonderful tenacious Johnny Carisi would keep everybody's minds alert.

"And Billy Exiner, somehow, was the father of all of us, though Gil's was the mind we minded. It was a beautiful time."

Gerry said, "Gil was a man with a vision. He was a gentle person. And we all looked up to him as a source of strength and insight. And he was that, to all of us."

"It was collective," John Lewis said. "Me and a lot of others, we used to go to Gil's place between sets. A lot of the people, Gerry Mulligan and Lee Konitz, had already been friends and worked together in Claude Thornhill's band. It was through them I met Gil and became friends with Joe Shulman and Billy Exiner and Barry Galbraith. Gil was the inspiring influence. He was doing things we had heard with Claude Thornhill. And it seemed to be possible to translate them to a smaller group too, taking just the essentials. And we were young, things were much different then economically. It was cheap to rent studios. And we all just wrote music, 'cause we just enjoyed doing it. It had nothing to do with any commercial business. Whoever had some money paid for the rehearsal or whatever. It was a co-operative.

"Gil was a catalyst. He was a wonderful, wonderful human being."

"Perfect," Gerry Mulligan said. "And he *was* a catalyst. We had a relationship to each other, insights into each other, and we learned from each other in ways that we wouldn't have done if we hadn't had Gil as a catalyst and a focal point. Young guys today have no place to turn for direction. The only place they've got to turn is to the business itself. And that's a great place to turn for some kind of philosophical and idealistic direction in your music – to the record companies! It's good luck Charlie! That's what it's devolved into. There's no Jim and Andy's, there's no Charlie's Tavern. The only place they come across it is in schools, which of course today there are lots of. That is subtracted from the reality of having to get out in the workplace.

"What you learn as an arranger writing for a band is quite different from what you learn writing in school. Writing as a professional for a leader, you've got to please that leader. And you've got to please that audience that the band is going to play for. And you've got to be able to do things that allow the guys in the band to channel what they can do through this form that you lay out. One of the things I always tried to do was, in the midst of these requirements, to please myself. It's a hell of a challenge.

"John Lewis is absolutely right. Gil was our catalyst."

Jimmy Maxwell too remembered fondly those Bohemian days in Gil's pad: "Charlie Parker hung out there all the time. I'd come over there some mornings to see Gil and Charlie would be sleeping, maybe on the bed, maybe on the floor. Sometimes there'd be a couple of guys sleeping on the bed."

Of Gil's unceasing self-doubt, Jimmy said, "He couldn't finish his arrangements because he thought they just weren't good enough."

I asked Gerry, "How did Miles get to be the leader on those recordings?"

"He made the phone calls," Gerry said. "He made the phone calls for the rehearsals. He made everybody get in and play.

"Some of the tensions that would build in the group! You had a bunch of strong guys, each with his own ideas. So as leader, Miles should have turned around to the band, and said, 'Do it this way.' But he didn't do that. John Lewis would keep trying to tell him, 'Miles, you went out and got the gig for this. This is not a rehearsal band any more. If you want to be the leader, then you've got to be the leader.' Miles would say, 'Bullshit, man. Problems have got to take care of themselves.'

"John said, 'But it doesn't happen like that.' John also used to give him hell because we never got paid for any of those charts. None of them. John said, 'We wrote the stuff for ourselves, this was a rehearsal band, and that was great. Now you've recorded this stuff and we're supposed to get paid.' We never did. I never got a penny."

In his autobiography, Miles said, "Monte Kay – " the late Monte Kay would later manage the Modern Jazz Quartet " – booked us into the Royal Roost for two weeks. When we opened up at the Roost, I had the club put up a sign outside that said, 'Miles Davis's Nonet; Arrangements by Gerry Mulligan, Gil Evans, and John Lewis.' I had to fight like hell with Ralph Watkins, the owner of the Roost, to get him to do this . . . We played the Royal Roost for two weeks in late August and September of 1948, taking second billing to Count Basie's orchestra.

"A lot of people thought the shit we were playing was strange. I remember Barry Ulanov of *Metronome* magazine being a little confused about the music we played. Count Basie used to listen every night that we were there opposite him, and he liked it. He told me that it was 'slow and strange, but good, real good.' A lot of the other musicians who used to come to hear the band liked it also, including Bird. But Pete Rugolo of Capitol Records really liked what he heard and he asked me if he could record us for Capitol after the recording ban was over."

The reference was to the second recording ban called by James Caesar Petrillo, president of the American Federation of Musicians. Both bans are now seen to have caused tremendous damage to music, particularly jazz. Most of Gerry Mulligan's writing for Thornhill, for example, went unrecorded and is lost.

Saxophonist / composer / arranger / author Bill Kirchner, who teaches jazz composition at the New School, wrote in a paper delivered at a conference on Miles Davis held on 8 April 1995, at Washington University in St. Louis, Missouri, that the group that grew out of those sessions in Gil's pad was an anomaly: "It recorded only a dozen pieces for Capitol and played in public for a total of two weeks in a nightclub, but its recordings and their influence have been compared to the Louis Armstrong Hot Fives and Sevens, and to other classics by Duke Ellington, Count Basie, and Charlie Parker. Though its personnel changed frequently, many of the nonet's members and composer-arrangers became jazz musicians of major stature. Most notable were Davis, trombonists J. J. Johnson and Kai Winding, alto saxophonist Lee Konitz, baritone saxophonist and arranger Gerry Mulligan, pianist and arranger John Lewis, pianist Al Haig, drummers Max Roach, Kenny Clarke, and Art Blakey, and arrangers Gil Evans and John Carisi . . .

"The *Birth of the Cool* sides were recorded in three sessions on 21 January and 22 April 1949, and on 9 March 1950. Issued initially as single 78s and eventually in various LP collections, these recordings had an enormous impact on musicians and the jazz public. Principally, they have been credited – or blamed, depending on one's point of view – for the subsequent popularity of "cool" or "west coast" jazz. Indeed, composer-arrangers such as Mulligan, Shorty Rogers, Marty Paich, and Duane Tatro *were* inspired by the *Birth of the Cool* instrumentation and approach.

"A good deal of their music, though, was more aggressive and rhythmic than some critics would lead us to believe – the frequent presence of such impeccably swinging drummers as Shelly Manne and Mel Lewis alone insured that.

"But the *Birth of the Cool* influence extended far beyond west coast jazz, and frequently appeared in all sorts of unexpected places. In the '50s, east coast composer-arrangers such as Gigi Gryce, Quincy Jones, and Benny Golson produced recordings using this approach, as did traditionalist Dick Cary, who used the style in orchestrating a set of Dixieland warhorses. Thelonious Monk, with arranger Hall Overton, used an almost identical *Birth of the Cool* instrumentation for his famed 1959 Town Hall concert. The format was proving to have all sorts of possibilities for creative jazz writing.

"Gil Evans spent much of the rest of his career expanding on the innovations of his Thornhill and *Birth of the Cool* scores."

What is generally overlooked is a point made by Max Harrison: that the "cool" did not begin with those nonet sessions. "There has always been cool jazz," Harrison wrote in his essay on Evans. "Far from being a new development of the 1950s, this vein of expression, wherein the improviser 'distances' himself from the musical material, goes back almost to the beginning. The clarinetists Leon Roppolo of the New Orleans Rhythm Kings and Johnny O'Donnell of the Georgians, two bands that recorded in 1922, both avoided the conventions of 'hot' playing, as did other prominent jazzmen of that decade like Bix Beiderbecke and his associate Frank Trumbauer, and this is true of several prominent figures of the 1930s such as Benny Carter, Teddy Wilson, and particularly Lester Young."

Lester Young himself attested to the influence of Beiderbecke and Trumbauer on his work, and Miles acknowledged that of Bix, not directly on him but indirectly through Bobby Hackett, one of two white trumpeters who helped shape him. The other was one of the hottest of the players to come out of Louis Armstrong, Harry James, a striking jazz soloist when he was not playing the lugubrious ballads on which his later fame rested.

It is also well to remember that Miles much admired Benny Carter, and had played with Carter's big band and small group in the mid-1940s.

Miles was not doing well in the early 1950s. He had a heroin habit by now. He recorded with Charlie Parker, Sonny Rollins, J. J. Johnson, and others, and played in clubs, but his career seemed to be going nowhere.

For a while Gil did club dates and wrote arrangements for singers' nightclub work. He told Ben Sidran, "There was a vocal coach named Sid Shaw, and he had me and a piano player named Jimmy Lyons, and we would go around to these different people's houses, and Sid would pick out the songs that he felt they should sing in their act, and we would write the music for them. So I did quite a bit of that."

And, although he had never been trained as a pianist, he did a lot of piano jobs. "I went out and played weddings and beer parties, and I played downtown at a place called the Nut Club ... One Sheridan Square ... So I worked there for a year, just to get the practice of playing. And we had drums and tenor, so I would play the bass part. It was good experience for me. Seventy-six dollars a week. Incredible."

Gil remained unmarried, and it was probably a good thing. It would be hard to imagine any woman living in a one-room dump with musicians wandering in and out at all hours, lying around in groups sleeping, endlessly talking and listening to records and plunking on the piano in the process of writing charts.

He finally married at the age of 38. The year of that marriage, then, was 1950, a year after the "cool" had been born.

One of the habitués of Nola's studio was singer Helen Merrill. Given a chance to record an album for the Emarcy label, she asked for Gil Evans as her arranger. Producer Bobby Shad said "No!" He told Merrill that Gil had no sense of time in the studio and always ran over budget. How this reputation had come to be is unknown: Gil hadn't recorded much and Miles, not he, had been in charge of the nonet sessions.

Merrill says, in her liner notes for the 1992 CD reissue of the material, recorded in three sessions toward the end of June, 1956, "Bob was right ... the album took a long time in the studio and there was no way of rushing it." What, three sessions for twelve tracks? That's not a long time, and certainly not in comparison with rock-and-roll practices. "In those days," she continued, we recorded live (as I still do) and getting a balance of the orchestra took a long time ... and then Gil would do his rehearsals on studio time ... "

But that's standard practice. The American Federation of Musicians allows no rehearsal scale. Music is rehearsed in the studio with the clock running at full recording scale.

"Gil was a self-taught musician," Merrill says. So is Robert Farnon; so is Gene Puerling, and many more. There is something about that term that suggests inferiority or ignorance or wrong practice; but some people are so brilliant they don't even need teaching. Gil was one of these prodigies. Merrill continued: "And giving direction to the band members often consisted of using poetic phrases that had to be communally deciphered. It was beautiful to behold the adoring faces of his loyal musicians and the love their guru had for them."

The album consists mostly of ballads, particularly the slightly arty songs beloved of girl singers at that period, such as "He Was Too Good To Me," which is *not* one of Larry Hart's best lyrics. One point of curiosity: this is one of the few examples on record of Gil's string writing. He uses strings at one point as if they were a sax section.

The one other example of his using strings that I know of is found on two tracks of a single by Al Martino, recorded around 1952. The tunes are "Wae Paesano" and "Melancholy Serenade." This is not, you may be assured, a record you would want in your collection. The former tune, with some unidentifiably Latin beat and a vocal group – probably the Dave Lambert singers – is horrible to the point of the laughable, and how Gil managed to write the chart with, as it were, a straight face is testimony to his fortitude and his understanding of how bad work had to be to make it in the commercial marketplace. "Melancholy Serenade" is not really a bad tune, though not a particularly good one either. Jackie Gleason wrote it; it was the theme of his television show. But it's interesting in that it shows that Gil had a grasp of conventional string writing, if he chose to exercise it. Above all, these two sides prove that Gil could have become a rich man writing trash had he chosen to do so. But he didn't: he went down a much lonelier road. That took courage, or perhaps a simple unconsidered independence – like his mother's.

Another point of curiosity: Helen Merrill sings "Where Flamingos Fly," a composition by John Benson Brooks, who had been a member of the group that hung around Gil's pad in the late 1940s. The introduction is interesting – Gil would use it again – for it is a direct quotation of the opening figure of the first movement (and in the same key, E minor) of Prokofiev's *Sinfonia Concertante for Cello and Orchestra*, Opus 125. Referring to those times in Gil's pad in the late 1940s, Gerry Mulligan said: "We were all crazy about Prokofiev."

Of the early 1950s, Gil said, "I was really waiting around for Miles, to tell you the truth." He said, "We didn't see each other in any regular way until about 1956. That's when we got together and decided to do an album. We made it in 1957." The album would be *Miles Ahead*. "I never thought of it in terms of history," Gil told Mark Miller. Others did, including André Hodeir, who wrote its liner notes, and George Avakian, who produced the album for Columbia Records.

Helen Merrill says in her liner notes to the album she did with Gil:

I also played a part in the resumption of the Miles Davis–Gil Evans albums that followed. Miles and I were on tour together, and I suggested that he think about recording with Gil again. He was very intrigued by the idea and those beautiful albums followed . . . Miles loved Gil and adopted him as a kind of surrogate father after the death of his dad, whom he adored.

George Avakian told me: "I signed Miles to Columbia sixteen months before I could release anything by him. He was with Prestige. I worked out a deal with Bob Weinstock, who owned Prestige, whereby we could record him, then hold the masters back until the Prestige contract expired. Which was fine with Bob, because he knew he would ride on all the publicity Columbia would give Miles.

"I told Miles that we were going to call the first album, which would be with the new quintet, *'Round Midnight*, because that was the tune that knocked everybody out at Newport when Miles played it as a walk-on at the 1955 festival. The second one, I told him, we'll call *Miles Ahead* because of the publicity campaign that you're miles ahead of everyone else and you're moving ahead and all that sort of thing. But it has to be very different from the quintet because Bob Weinstock will be recording the quintet like crazy to finish up the contract.

"About three or four months after I signed Miles, he did a guest spot with Gunther Schuller in an album called *Music for Brass*. Miles plays solos on two compositions, by J. J. Johnson and John Lewis. I said, 'Let's do something similar.' I asked him if he wanted to revive the nine-piece band. And he wasn't too keen about that, and I said, 'You're right, that would just be going back to something you've done. Let's go beyond.' And so I steered the conversation to the size of orchestra Gunther had used. And I suggested there were two arrangers who could handle it. One would be Gil, and the other would be Gunther. Miles said, 'I'll do it with Gil.' I said, 'That's perfect.' And that's just what we did.

"I asked him to save one composition without a title so we could call it 'Miles Ahead.'

"The recording went quite slowly because, as you know, Gil was a very slow worker. But it turned out to be quite fabulous.

"The first day of the first session, I saw a new machine in the control room. It was a two-track machine, which in those days was called binaural. The word 'stereo' wasn't used yet. We were told that the engineers were given the machine by Ampex to try out, and they were to report back how they liked it.

"Well we made a balance at the beginning of the first session and just held that all the way through and recorded in two-track as well, with no intention of ever using it. As it turned out, everything couldn't be used in stereo anyway, because Miles wasn't able to execute all the solos live. He overdubbed some of them. Since we had only one two-track, we couldn't make a two-track master. That's why the first edition on CD has a lot of different solos. All the editing notes were gone, the original scores were gone."

That is why there are two versions of the album on CD. Connoisseurs have complained that the solos on the first CD edition were not those of the original album; they were alternate takes and the solos weren't the best Miles played on those sessions. The second CD conforms to the original LP. The boxed set Sony released in 1996 of all the Gil Evans / Miles Davis recordings finally presented the original album in stereo.

Its ten tracks were edited into a seamless whole, one tune flowing into the next, a technique that Columbia had used in Michel Legrand's *I Love Paris* album, but much more significantly in this case, since it is used to unite the pieces in a kind of long two-movement suite. The orchestra was large: five trumpets, three tenor trombones, one bass trombone, two French horns, tuba, alto saxophone, bass clarinet, and two clarinets doubling flutes. The bassist was Paul Chambers. Lee Konitz, who had been in the nonet, was the alto player, and Johnny Carisi was in the auspicious trumpet section, which also included Taft Jordan, Ernie Royal, Bernie Glow, and Lou Mucci.

Despite its size, however, the band was essentially an expansion of the nonet, and its two French horns and tuba revealed its historic roots in the Claude Thornhill band.

One of the pieces in the suite – André Hodeir called them mini-concertos – was Dave Brubeck's tribute to Ellington, "The Duke." Dave attended the session. He and Gil had never met. They chatted about California, about growing up not far apart. Then Gil said, "Brubeck. Do you have a brother?"

"Yes," Dave said. "Howard." Howard became a music educator, head of music in the Santa Barbara, California, school system.

"Yes!" Gil said. "He played drums in my band in Stockton."

By now Miles had fully developed the tone that would make him instantly recognizable – and often imitated – for the rest of his life. At one point, when Miles was playing the Village Vanguard in New York, Gil said to him during an intermission, "Miles, it just occurred to me. I don't know if you ever thought about it or not, but you're the first person to change the tone of the trumpet since Louis Armstrong."

By the time of *Miles Ahead*, the tone was distant, melancholy, and almost devoid of vibrato. What vibrato there was usually came at the end of notes, and it was narrow, rather slow, and very controlled. On *Miles Ahead* he played fluegelhorn, which fattened his sound. Yet the album got some bad reviews. But, again, Max Harrison, in his essay on Gil, took the album's true measure. He wrote:

(The musicians) are treated largely as a body of individual players, and the chords are composed of the most varied tone-colors, which are dealt with according to their natural intensity, some being allowed greater prominence than others. In this respect one is reminded of Schoenberg's *Orchesterstucke* Op. 16 . . . and it indicates the development of Evans's musical language that whereas *Moondreams* is reminiscent of aspects of Richard Strauss, here one thinks of Schoenberg.

"Moondreams" and "Boplicity" were Gil's only charts in the *Birth of the Cool* sessions.

Harrison describes the effect of Gil's scoring as

that of light imprisoned in a bright mineral cave, its refinement such that at times the music flickers deliciously between existence and non-existence. No matter how involved the textures, though, it always is possible to discover unifying factors as an altogether remarkable ear is in control, ruthlessly – and almost completely – eliminating clichés. Complaints that these Davis–Evans collaborations produced unrhythmic music were due to faulty hearing, and the widely quoted metaphorical description of the textures as "port and velvet" is inept. Despite its richness, the orchestral fabric is constantly on the move, horizontally and vertically; it is unfortunate that some listeners cannot hear music's pulse unless it is stated as a series of loud bangs.

Two untrue things were commonly said of Gil. The first was that he was not a composer, he was "only" an arranger. The second was that he could function only at a high level as an accompanist to a soloist, above all Miles Davis, but also Cannonball Adderley and Kenny Burrell, around both of whom he built albums.

Three albums in the next two years offer persuasive disproof of both theses. The first of these, *Gil Evans & Ten*, was recorded for Bob Weinstock's Prestige label. Since the first of its two sessions, held on 6 September, followed by a little over three months the last of the *Miles Ahead* dates, this album tends to disprove yet another of the myths about Gil Evans, that he was a dilatory writer. To be sure, he was no prodigy of speed, but the album verifies what Gil said, that he had more craft and speed than he liked to admit. He could indeed work very slowly, when he chose to. But as his work as far back as the Chesterfield Supper Club show with Paul Weston indicates, he could also turn it in on time when he had to.

Technique is a two-edged sword. It can lead an artist into the trap of casual superficiality. But in the more thoughtful and conscientious practitioner, it is a tool of deep exploration. It was commonly said that Miles was a great artist but not a great trumpet player. He was a great trumpet player *for what he wanted and intended to do*. I would quote something Charles Aznavour taught me when I was writing with him a lot. Charles said, "We build our styles not out of our abilities but out of our limitations." Miles did that. Gil used his considerable orchestral chops to explore, not to hurry. The album was done in three sessions in the fall of 1957.

The band, as the title indicates, is much smaller on the Prestige sessions than the band on *Miles Ahead*, but Gil is still feeling his way deeper into his own musical realities. There are some seemingly unlikely tunes involved, Irving Berlin's "Remember," the Rodgers and Hart song "Nobody's Heart," and Cole Porter's "Just One of Those Things." But these very tunes, familiar as they are, only help to make clear that Gil was a true composer. His arrangements amount to recomposition. "Nobody's Heart" is completely transformed.

The problem is that the term "composer" has been so misused in the last few decades, as has the word "concert" – solo stand-up comics give "concerts" – that it has lost its original significance. In my youth, it meant somebody who did composition, full-scale and finished works for individual instruments or chamber groups or orchestras; and it applied almost exclusively to classical music. One of the men in jazz whom the term fitted accurately was Duke Ellington. But in the aspiration to status that transmogrified janitors into custodians, hairdressers into stylists, and used cars into pre-owned vehicles, even rock-and-rollers began to refer to themselves as "composers". What Gil was not was a songwriter: he wasn't a writer of full-scale melodies. But like Beethoven building a massive piece out of a four-note theme of only two tones in the Fifth Symphony, Gil was able to build big structures on simple thematic fragments, as in his "La Nevada" and "Las Vegas Tango," integrating the improvisations of soloists into these pieces so perfectly that they sound written.

"I left Columbia in early 1958," George Avakian said. "One of the first things I wanted to do was record with Gil again."

Avakian produced one Gil Evans album for Pacific Jazz: *New Bottle Old Wine*, for which Gil wrote charts on jazz standards ranging from W. C. Handy's "St. Louis Blues" to Dizzy Gillespie's "Manteca." The orchestra consisted of three trumpets, three trombones, French horn, tuba, and one reed instrument. The drummer on one session was Philly Joe Jones; on all others it was Art Blakey. And nothing reveals how far Gil had progressed from standard big-band arranging than his chart on "King Porter Stomp," utterly unlike the famous Fletcher Henderson arrangement of it.

"They went more easily than the sessions with Miles," Avakian said. "For one thing, it had been done once already. There were no jazz recordings of that scale before the *Music for Brass* album. So it was a strange thing for everybody. Gil was much more at ease, having done one album with a large orchestra already. And I think the same thing for Cannonball. He was more relaxed than Miles. Miles was kind of nervous about the whole thing. I don't know whether it was because Cannon was a more relaxed person generally. But those sessions went much more easily." The album was completed on 26 May 1958.

Gil said in a 1979 radio interview, "It's succession rather than growth. I don't feel any taller than I was when I did the arrangements for Cannonball. And yet I'm different now. It's a succession of phases you go through, but they don't necessarily add up to progress or maturity. I don't feel bad when I hear that album that I made with Cannonball. I liked those arrangements and the way he played and everything and the fact that we did the whole album in nine hours with no rehearsal. It came off in a dumb-assed studio that you could hardly hear the bass or anything, it was outrageous. But when I hear it now, I like to hear it, it sounds good to me. It's a good thing, it's *done*, and you go on to the next thing. A masterpiece is just a successful experiment. You never hear of the unsuccessful ones."

Gil did a second album for Pacific Jazz, again of older jazz tunes, this one titled *Great Jazz Standards*. The instrumentation was essentially the same as that of the previous album. Again, Gil wrote charts on standards, but these of more recent vintage, such as Monk's "Straight No Chaser" and "Django" by his old friend from the nonet days, John Lewis. This album also contains the first recorded performance I know of Gil's "La Nevada," a classic example of the way he could build something big on a small fragment, and in this case only one chord, G minor thirteenth.

By now, Gil Evans albums – coming at a rate of approximately one a year – were anticipated events in the jazz community. He was becoming legend, this tall, gangly, soft-spoken, gentle and self-effacing man who didn't take his own music that seriously, for all the meticulous care with which he made it. It was evident to everyone with ears that he was unique.

And then came his next great collaboration with Miles Davis.

Well before the release in 1959 of Otto Preminger's movie version of *Porgy and Bess*, the studio began a publicity campaign as inflated as the picture itself. All sorts of recordings of the opera's music came onto the market; but the best remembered is the album that Gil and Miles made for Columbia. That album is one of the highest mountains in jazz. Every bit as good as musicians thought it was when it came out, it has not dated. Roger Kellaway said, "Gil was one of the great masters of the twentieth century. And I am *not* limiting that to jazz."

On *Porgy and Bess*, Gil used four trumpets and four trombones, Cannonball Adderley on alto and Danny Bank doubling bass clarinet and alto flute. Phil Bodner and Romeo Penque doubled flute, alto flute, and clarinet. The rest of the band comprised three French horns, tuba, bass, and drums: no piano. And by now one thing is obvious: Gil used slightly different instrumentations on each album. The saxophone section, *per se*, no longer existed for him. Charles Edward Smith, in his notes for the album, observed that

Gil thinks of the music in its entirety, as a painter thinks of a canvas. Indeed, when he speaks of depth or density of sound, impingement of instrumental tone, the dynamics of structure and the particular requirements of each theme, the resemblance to descriptions of pictorial art is striking. And when one recalls Picasso's dictum that a painting is alive, the parallel is completed.

The final session of *Porgy and Bess* took place on 18 August 1958. Given the weight of *Miles Ahead* and *Porgy*, these collaborations with Miles were now seen as Events, and arrangers (among others) were waiting to see what they would do next. The first of the sessions for *Sketches of Spain* was held fifteen months later, on 20 November 1959. The album was completed in March 1960.

The planning of that album must have begun not long after the release in 1959 of *Porgy and Bess*. Miles described the genesis of the album in his autobiography:

In 1959 I was in Los Angeles and went to see a friend of mine named Joe Mondragon, a great studio bass player, who lived in the San Fernando Valley. When I got to his house, he played this recording of *Concierto de Aranjuez* by this Spanish composer, Joaquin Rodrigo, and said, "Miles, listen to this; you can do this." So I'm sitting there listening and looking at Joe and I'm saying to myself, Goddamn, these melody lines are strong. I knew right there that I had to record it, because they just stayed in my head. When I got back to New York, I called up Gil and discussed it with him and gave him a copy of the record to see what he thought could be done with it. He liked it, too, but said we had to get some more pieces to fill out an album. We got a folklore record of Peruvian Indian music, and took a vamp from that. This was *The Pan Piper*. Then we took the Spanish march "Saeta," which they do in Spain on Fridays when they march and testify by singing. The trumpet players played the march like it was done in Spain.

According to Nat Hentoff, Miles and Gil listened extensively to Manuel de Falla's 1915 ballet music *El Amor Brujo*, from which Gil adapted "Will o' the Wisp" for the album. Gil read several volumes of books on Spanish music, particularly flamenco, and on the life of Spanish gypsies, and listened intensely to various ethnic recordings. Miles said later, "He made that orchestra sound like one big guitar."

It was about this time that Miles played a gig at the Cloister, a club in the Rush Street area of Chicago. He stayed with the family of his then wife, and it was there that Marc Crawford, who had been a foreign correspondent, a staff writer for *Ebony*, and entertainment editor of *Jet*, interviewed Miles for *Down Beat*. Miles was listening with bursting enthusiasm to Arturo

Benedetti Michelangeli's recording of the Ravel G Major Piano Concerto. He'd called Gil in New York and asked him to fly out to Chicago to spend time with him.

He told Marc, "You know, my ambition has always been to write like Gil. I'd give my right arm to do it – no, my left one, because I'd have to write the notes down."

He continued: "Gil is my idea of a man. Say you had a friend who was half man and half donkey, and suppose he even wore a straw hat and you said, 'Gil, meet George.' Gil would get up and shake his hand and never care what George looked like."

His meaning was clear. Gil was devoid of racism of any nuance. It simply didn't exist in him. His second wife, Anita, said that for this reason he hated to be in Los Angeles. She said that almost invariably when she and Gil would be riding in a car, they would be stopped by that city's notoriously racist police: a white man and a black woman. "It infuriated him," she said.

"We were in California in 1963 when Miles and Gil wrote music for the play *The Time of the Barracudas*. Then we were in California in 1964. We came to Los Angeles from the Monterey Jazz Festival. We stayed in a place either on Sunset Boulevard or Hollywood. It happened mostly on Sunset Boulevard. I wouldn't mention it if it happened only once or twice. But it was an inevitable thing to be followed by a police car. We were stopped even with the children in the car."

Miles told Marc Crawford, "You know, in New York we go over to each other's house, but we don't drop our problems on each other. When Gil is writing, he might spend three days on ten bars of music. He'll lock himself up in a room of his house, put a 'Do not disturb' sign on the door, and not even his wife Lillian – " the interview was done at the time of Gil's first marriage " – can come in. It's torture for her when he's writing. It's like he's out to lunch. Sometimes he'll get in there and play the piano for twelve hours. He's not only a composer and a hell of an orchestrator, he just knows instruments and what you can get out of them. He can use four instruments when others need eight ...

"People always want to categorize music – jazz, classical. Put labels on it. But Gil says all music comes from the people, and the people are folk. Therefore all music is folk."

Gil arrived. He was already white-haired and, Marc wrote, his six foot-plus frame filled the doorway. He told Marc, in a moment alone with him, that he considered Miles a true artist, adding, "and there are very few of them in the world today. I also think he's a pretty fine specimen of the human animal in most things he does."

He again defined himself as "a commercial arranger" and said that "what I write is popular," surely one of the oddest claims any artist ever made for himself. And he told Marc: "I only work for Miles and myself."

Nat Hentoff, who attended the sessions that winter, described Gil as resembling "a gently aging diplomat who collects rare species of ferns on weekends."

He wrote: "Though always polite, he is in firm control of his record dates and insists on hearing exactly what he has written."

One of Gil's staunchest admirers was a young and boyish-faced ex-trumpet player and former Marine Corps officer with a degree in psychology from Duke University. Creed Taylor was proving to be one of the most astute record producers in the business, with a knack for getting from musicians performances that were simultaneously of the highest artistic merit and yet had considerable commercial appeal. His "product" usually sold well. And Creed had been following the work of Gil Evans since the Thornhill days. Indeed, Creed saw that band when it played Duke. "I remember standing there with goosebumps," Creed said. "That was the '49 band."

Creed had founded the Impulse label and established the pattern for his career. He was not "an" a&r man for a label. He would always be the sole a&r man, running the label completely, not answering to a front office somewhere. And one of the artists he now wanted to record was Gil.

The first album that came of this was *Out of the Cool*. Gil turned to old associates for two of the pieces. He did a new version of "Where Flamingos Fly" by John Benson Brooks and "Stratusphunk" by George Russell, who had shared arranger credits with Gil on a Lucy Reed album for Fantasy. Gil orchestrated Kurt Weill's "Bilbao Song" for a third track, and used two of his own pieces, one called "Sunken Treasure" and a new version of "La Nevada." It is interesting to see how the orchestral colors in "La Nevada" differ from those in the same tune in the *Great Jazz Standards* two years earlier for Pacific Jazz. The same figure from Prokofiev that Gil used in the Helen Merrill album opens *Where Flamingos Fly*.

Creed Taylor left Impulse to run the Verve label, which had been purchased from Norman Granz by MGM records. Creed was the sole a&r director of Verve. One of the albums he made there was *The Individualism of Gil Evans*. The original LP contained five tunes. Gil turned again to Kurt Weill for "The Barbara Song," which has a strange and haunting reflective quiescence about it. Gil had an eerie ability to write the sound of quiet. The other tunes included his own "Las Vegas Tango," "Flute Song," and "El Toreador;" and "Hotel Me," a co-composition with Miles Davis. The total running time of that album is 32 minutes and 29 seconds. But for the CD edition, the vaults were searched and a great deal of material that Creed and Gil had abandoned was included, those "special bonus" tracks that flesh out CD reissues. At first I thought Gil and Creed were right about the rejected material, but the more I hear it the more I value it, particularly "Time of the Barracudas," interesting for, among other things, the excellent Wayne Shorter tenor solo. And "Spoonful" has some predictably fiery playing by Phil Woods.

I no longer remember whether it was Creed or Gil who asked me to write the liner notes of that album, but I do remember that Creed set aside an audition room for us, and Gil and I listened to the tape together. I wrote at the time:

> Without doubt the most individualistic and personal jazz composer since Duke Ellington, Evans is held in near-reverence by a wide range of composers, arrangers, instrumentalists, and critics. This feeling is only intensified by the fact that he is a rather inaccessible man – not unfriendly, or anti-social; just politely, quietly inaccessible – whose output has been small, and all of it remarkable.

As we listened to "Las Vegas Tango," Gil said, "It's a plain traditional minor blues." There was nothing plain about it. Gil said, "I used this title because it had a kind of open sound like the plains, to me. I grew up in the west." A gorgeous, big-toned, melancholy trombone solo by Jimmy Cleveland emerges from the orchestration. The melody, in its opening phrase, is so perfectly suited to the composition that I asked Gil if it was written. "No," Gil said. "That's his." One of the most striking things about the track is the way Elvin Jones dances across the cymbals, drawing from them all the varied sounds of which they are capable.

I asked Gil why he so often used Spanish titles for his tunes. He answered: "I don't know. Perhaps because I can't find English titles for them. I've always inclined to Spanish music, but I didn't really absorb it from the Spanish. I got it from the French impressionists – and, of course, the Spanish impressionists, like de Falla."

Creed Taylor told me at the time that he'd had trouble getting that album done. Gil did not have the public name that Miles Davis did and limited sales could be expected. MGM allowed Creed a budget of only $10,000. These were, to be sure, early 1960s dollars. Gil would have to bring the album in at whatever cost he could and keep the remainder for himself. Gil fiddled with the scores on the dates to the point that he ran it over budget and ultimately lost money on the album.

"That sounds right," Jimmy Maxwell said when I told him that story, and he too commented on Gil's endless fiddling with charts on the dates.

"That's what happened with the Patti Page album and all the others. Gil never had a lead sheet even. He wrote everything on two lines, one line for the brass and one line for the reeds, and then the copyist had to separate them."

The *Individualism* album was released in 1964.

George Wein recounted an incident that gives an insight into Gil's character.

"I'd known Gil for years, but we were never that close. We weren't buddies. I got a serious attack of gout. And I was in pain. It was in my knee. And one night at my apartment, 9.30, there was a knock on my door. Not even a ring from down below. I opened the door and it was Gil.

"I said, 'Gil! What are you doing here?'

"He said, 'I heard you've got the gout. Cherries are very good for the gout. I brought you this bottle of cherries. Maybe they might help you.'

"Isn't that a beautiful little story? I never forgot."

This sweetness of Gil's nature, this affection for others, apparently didn't mean much to his first wife, Lillian. According to Jimmy Maxwell, she could not abide Gil's close friendships with other musicians, and she brought about a temporary estrangement between the two of them. Jimmy said: "Gil's wife and our side had a falling out. She accused us of being faggots. She was an awful drunk. After they separated she'd call me up and cry. Couldn't I get her back with Gil?"

Finally, Gil and Lillian were divorced. And Gil met Anita Cooper, a native of Staten Island. "My family have been in New York for generations," she said.

Anita was working on her doctorate in psychotherapy. "But I was getting my degrees just to please the family," she said. "My true love was always music." She has been a singer, songwriter, and producer. "I met Gil at Birdland the night before George Washington's birthday when John Coltrane was playing there. It was the very night Coltrane met Alice. She was playing with Terry Gibbs. She was then Alice McLeod.

"We got married in 1963. We went out to Fire Island. So it was over the Memorial Day weekend. Noah was born on 21 March 1964. Miles was born on 5 July 1965.

"The *Individualism* album came in '64, a little before Noah came. And '65, the year Miles was born, was the *Look to the Rainbow* album with Astrud Gilberto."

The quantity of Gil's output thinned after *Individualism*. He organized a band that played Monday nights in New York. He listened to the current pop music and, along with music of Charlie Parker and Charles Mingus, played some of it. A lot of people were puzzled by what he was doing. In 1969, he recorded the album *Gil Evans* (later called *Blues in Orbit*) and in 1977 *Priestess*.

In time Gil incorporated electronic instruments into the group. Examples from this phase of his work are to be found in Evidence albums titled *Gil Evans Live at the Public Theater*, Volumes 1 and 2. It contains a lot of long and self-indulgent solos by band members.

At one point Gil performed in concert with Miles Davis, including an evening at the Hollywood Bowl. Gil phoned me and invited me to the concert; I attended it with Roger Kellaway. We thought we were going to hear the classic charts from their great albums, but they did not even appear together. Their two groups played separately. My son, who was then playing keyboards in a rock group, attended the concert, along with some of his young friends. They were seated around Roger and me, along with some younger jazz players whom Roger knew. I didn't know what to make of the music; I certainly didn't like it. And then one of the young musicians said, "This isn't very good jazz." And one of the rock musicians said, "It isn't very good rock, either." All I can remember of the concert is that there was a good deal of synthesizer sound.

Roger and I went backstage afterwards to pay our respects to Miles and Gil. I was uncomfortable because I couldn't say that I had loved the music. Gil probably sensed it. In any event, he hugged me, and I remember feeling how thin he was in my arms. I believe that it was the last time I ever saw him.

In 1984, when Mark Miller asked how many scores he had for his New York band and the concert he was doing in Toronto, Gil said there were about twenty. If it were not for the take-downs by other arrangers, we would have much less of Gil's music than we do. The amount of it that exists in his own handwriting is not great, although more of it is turning up.

When the Kool Jazz Festival wanted to present an evening of tribute to Gil, the scores for his earlier work had to be reconstructed by John Oddo, Manny Mendelson, and Mike Patterson from recordings, hardly an easy task with music of such textural density and subtlety. The concert was presented as a Gil Evans Retrospective on 3 July 1983, at Avery Fisher Hall in Lincoln Center.

During the last three years of his life, Gil worked with an amanuensis and orchestrator. Maria Schneider had been one of the students in composition and orchestration of the late Rayburn Wright at the Eastman School of Music, along with John Oddo, Manny Mendelson, and Mike Patterson. Gil was looking for an assistant. In 1985, she telephoned him. She started working for him as his copyist, and then she began reorchestrating some of his pieces for standard instrumentation. As he became more familiar with her music, he gave her greater responsibility.

"I tended to get nervous about getting everything done," Maria said. "Gil tended to be very relaxed. I think we were good for each other. He was always telling me to loosen up, but if I'd been as loose as he was, I think I'd have been the last person he wanted working for him."

Maria was his assistant on assembling the music for the Paul Newman film *The Color of Money*. It seems as if Gil was always concerned about the health of his acquaintances and friends. "We had a recording session," Maria said. "In the morning I came over to his place in the West 70s between Central Park West and Columbus. I was supposed to finish up some stuff. I had a back problem. We were trying to get out the door. He was finishing up some bit of writing. We were late. The limo was there waiting, and his son Miles was there.

"Gil was in his underwear. Miles said, 'We've got to get going.' Gil said, 'No, wait, Maria's back hurts.' He said, 'I've got the perfect book.' He pulled out this yoga book and started showing me the proper way to sleep. He spent a lot of time reading to me and showing me the proper position to sleep . . .

"Finally we got to the Nola studio on 57th Street. The guys were just kind of walking around. It was Gil's band, thirteen or something. Gil started reprimanding them for not working on the music and practicing. He said, 'You know, we got detained. We've been busy writing this music. I'm so disappointed in you.' They were all upset, because they loved and respected Gil. They looked like beaten puppies. But they loved him so much . . .

"Gil was so interested in all cultures and all sorts of music. He took in so much stuff: he was a synthesis of that. All these unique things came together. Gil listened to so many different things, he was interested in many things. He had a book on African face painting. He had a mind that soaked up everything: an interested man.

"Before he died he wasn't really talking that much to his friends. Sometimes when we worked together, I didn't get a real chatty thing going. There were nights when we'd sit and listen to music, but in general I felt that if we weren't doing work, I didn't want to bug him. In a way that was maybe a mistake. Sometimes I think Gil wanted me to relax and spend time with him, but I had this way I looked up to Gil, I didn't want to be in the way, I just wanted to help him.

"One day he called me up. I said, 'How're you doing, Gil?' He was telling me how he wasn't feeling well and was worried that something was really wrong, and he'd been to a doctor. I kept thinking he was going to say we were doing a project and could I come over. But it wasn't that. He just wanted to talk. That was the last time I ever talked to him. After that he got really sick. Gil was very fragile at the end. He became very thin . . . "

Maria was one of the arrangers who reconstructed Gil's scores for performance at the Montreux Jazz Festival in 1991. Gil Goldstein did a great deal of this writing, working from sketches that Gil's sons dug up, material that hadn't been seen in 30 years. One score that Maria did was "Miles Ahead."

"Just in putting that together," she said, "each individual line is so beautiful. Sometimes the vertical chords that result from the horizontal lines on their own are so strange, but everything has such gravitational pull. Everything is moving ahead. Something feels tense, but it's going some place. It's a real feeling of forward motion. In Gil's writing, every line makes such beautiful musical sense.

"Another thing is the surprise element. There was one thing I orchestrated for him, it went from one note in anticipated eighth notes that got real fat. He wanted the instruments with low tessitura to go into their highest range and the instruments with high tessitura to go into their lowest range. He pushes instruments out of their normal tessitura, and you get a real character. You get something in the tone besides the obvious.

"Gil used to say that the marvelous thing about Miles' tone is that it was Miles' tone in every register, from bottom to top. There wasn't that division of sound. And Gil was so sensitive to tone. That's what he liked in Miles. He said over and over again that it was the tone."

The Montreux concert was held in 1991, with Quincy Jones conducting the music and Miles Davis as the soloist. Gil was dead by then. There are two views of what happened there. According to some of the people who attended that concert, it went extraordinarily well. Anita Evans said, "It was as close to levitating a room as I have ever experienced. There were more than a thousand people, French, Swiss, Italians, some Americans. In the room, it was awesome. Because the musicians were so sensitive. Many of them European. They were floating. Everyone was almost in tears of happiness, shimmering with joy. As Miles said, there was no reason for him to go back and play what had already been played. Gil would have been so happy. It went off the way Gil would have liked it. It wasn't a carbon copy of what had happened 30 years before."

The television show derived from it was a different matter. It was shot in a gloomy sort of fashion. The balances on the band were flat and dull, even allowing for the limitations of television speakers. Miles sat in a chair and played the passages he still could execute: he was sick by then. Wallace Roney, beside him, played the passages he could no longer manage.

Fortunately, the old records have been reissued by Sony in a five-CD package of all the collaborations of Miles Davis and Gil Evans. Also included are some tracks that were never issued, including music they wrote together for *The Time of the Barracudas*.

Most of the important scores have now been reconstructed and the music continues to be performed. In 1993, Maria Schneider conducted the Gil Evans Orchestra, augmented for the event, at the Spoleto festival, playing the *Porgy and Bess* music, among other things.

Maria's admiration for Gil's work is almost universally shared by composers, and most critics. An exception is Stanley Crouch, and since Crouch is "artistic adviser" to the Jazz at Lincoln Center program and controls Wynton Marsalis, who runs it, this extraordinary body of jazz composition will never be performed there.

Crouch expressed his contempt for Gil Evans in an article titled "Sketches of Pain," and subtitled "The rise and fall of Miles Davis," published in *The New Republic* on 12 February 1990.

Of the *Birth of the Cool* album, which Crouch calls "the highly celebrated but essentially lightweight nonet sessions," he says,

Heard now, the nonet recordings seem little more than primers for television writing. What the recordings show us, though, is that Davis, like many other jazzmen, was not above the academic temptations of Western music. Davis turns out to have been overly impressed by the lessons he received at Juilliard when he arrived in New York in 1944. The pursuit of a soft sound, the uses of polyphony that were far from idiomatic, the nearly coy understatement, the lines that had little internal propulsion all amounted to another failed attempt to marry jazz to European devices. The overstated attribution of value to these recordings led the critical establishment to miss Ellington's "The Tattooed Bride," which was the high point of jazz composition of the 1940s.

(Gil, surprisingly, never met Ellington. But one day he received a call from Ellington. Ellington said that Gil was his favorite jazz writer. Gil was thrilled.)

Crouch says:

It is true that those albums with Evans also reveal that Davis could be taken in by pastel versions of European colors (they are given what value they have by the Afro-American dimensions that were never far from Davis's embouchure, breath, fingering); if Davis's trumpet voice is removed, in fact, a good number of Evans's arrangements sound like high-level television music.

What is Afro-American about Miles' trumpet fingering, or anyone's for that matter, is a mystery; the one trumpet, or rather cornet, player who used an unorthodox fingering of his own invention was Bix Beiderbecke. As for embouchure, you put your lips together and buzz into the mouthpiece. And it is totally new to me that African Americans breathe differently from anyone else. I thought we all did it with our lungs.

Miles, by the way, studied trumpet with William Vacchiano, for 40 years the principal trumpeter with the New York Philharmonic.

No work of art is diminished by its imitations. Much to the contrary.

Despite his admiration for Gil's work, Max Harrison had reservations about "Sketches of Spain," saying

Evans' boring rewrite of the first movement of Rodrigo's *Concierto de Aranjuez* was a strange miscalculation. So, too, was the bogus flamenco of *Saeta* and *Solea*, although these were solo vehicles for Davis in which Evans had little part . . . (An) altogether finer expression of Evans's taste for Iberian music is "Lotus Land," a track on the *Guitar Forms* album that he made with Kenny Burrell.

But all criticism, excepting technical analysis, is subjective, a sort of Rorschach test of the critic. "Boring" is a subjective word, the response of the writer, not a fact about the music. Bill Kirchner, a composer and teacher of jazz composition, thinks Gil actually improved that movement of the Rodrigo concerto. "It's more interesting," Bill said.

Though Harrison's essay on Gil was written 30 years before the Crouch piece on Miles, it might have been in response to it. "In fact," Harrison wrote,

> this music increasingly happens on several levels at once, recalling the multiplicity of events in Charles Ives's work. For instance on "Las Vegas Tango," a gravely serene piece from the *Individualism* set, things happen close up, in sharp focus, others take place in the middle distance, some murmur far away on the horizon, and the exactness of Evans's aural imagination is such that we can hear it all, every note, every vibration, carrying significance. Yet one gains the impression that he feels music, like other forms of truth, should never be understood, that there should always remain some further element to be revealed. Note the gradual, almost reluctant, disclosure of the melodies of "La Nevada" and "Bilbao Song", or the way the theme of "Joy Spring" is not heard until right at the end.
>
> These endings, many of which fade, like beautiful sunsets, as we look at them, in turn suggest by their very inconclusiveness that Evans, again like Ives, has an Emersonian dislike of the spiritual inactivity which comes from the belief that one possesses a truth in its final form. It is tempting to think that in achieving the lyrical resignation of "Flute Song" or the alert tranquillity of "The Barbara Song" Evans uses sounds rather as Mallarmé uses words – as mirrors that focus light from a hundred different angles to his precise meaning. But they remain symbols of meaning rather than the meaning itself, and much is left to the imagination. If the listener is unwilling, or, worse still, unable, to exercise this faculty then he will soon be left behind.

Robert Farnon is intimately familiar with Gil's writing. Gil was equally familiar with Bob's. Each was well aware that the other was born in Toronto. I don't think either ever had enough ego to contemplate the effect they jointly had on arranging and orchestration in the latter half of the twentieth century. But Gil wanted to meet Bob, and Bob wanted to meet Gil, and each of them knew that I knew the other. I wanted to arrange their meeting. I thought it would be of some historical import. It was not to be: when I saw Bob in Toronto in 1984, Gil had been there and gone only a few weeks before.

Gil's gradually fading health caused him to undergo surgery in early 1988. Afterwards he left New York's winter to recover in Cuernavaca, Mexico. Instead of recovering, he contracted peritonitis, and he died there on 20 March: he was not quite 76.

"Gil was my best friend," Jimmy Maxwell said. "I don't think a day goes by that I don't think of him. When I'm practicing or something I'll think, 'Gee, I wish he could have heard me do that.'

"He did a lot of nice things. Somebody told me a story. When he went to England for a presentation, he said, 'Louis Armstrong was the greatest trumpet player that ever lived, and Jimmy Maxwell swung that Goodman band single-handed. He's a blowin' ass.'

"When I was with the Gerry Mulligan concert band, Gil'd come in, and say, 'God *damn*, Fen – ' he called me Fenimore ' – you finally made it, you're really doing it. Beautiful.'"

"Gil loved him like a brother," Anita said. "He was family to him in his heart and his head and it never changed. I've never known whether Jimmy Maxwell knows how much Gil cared for him."

Gil touched lives in ways that even he didn't know. For example: at one point I got a note from him, mailed from Norway, where he was doing a series of concerts. It was written on a small sheet of ocher-colored music paper, taken from one of the sketch pads composers commonly carry in case they want to jot down ideas. The note said simply: "Keep on doing what you're doing. And don't smoke so many cigarettes. Love, Gil."

I had been trying to quit smoking for years. That laconic note, so typical of Gil in its understatement, was like a benediction. I held it in my hands, read it several times, and never touched another cigarette.

"If it were not for music," Anita Evans said, "I think it would all be over by now. Music is the magical medicine for all our souls and spirits.

"Gil's still here, really. I still think he's up in his studio."

In 1996, the contents of three cartons that Miles Davis had left in a storage facility in Philadelphia were cataloged and appraised. They contained the scores and parts to all the music Gil wrote for Miles. New editions, derived from this cornucopia, have since been played all over the world. That same year, the Hal Leonard Corporation published a folio of Gil's music derived from his manuscripts.

6

I hear the shadows dancing:
Gerry Mulligan

When I became editor of *Down Beat* in May 1959, I telephoned one of my predecessors, Jack Tracy, by then a producer for Mercury Records. I asked him who, of the various musicians I would soon have to deal with, might give me a problem.

"Three guys," Jack said. "Buddy Rich, Miles Davis, and Gerry Mulligan." He added that, personally, he liked all three, but all three had prickly temperaments, and you had to accept them as they were; none of them more so than Buddy Rich. Perhaps because Jack had forewarned me, I had trouble with none of them, and indeed became very fond of all three.

Two of them – Miles Dewey Davis and Gerry Mulligan – were alumni of the Gil Evans "seminars" on West 55th Street, and of the *Birth of the Cool* records.

Among the bands I particularly liked in my late adolescence were those of Claude Thornhill, Elliot Lawrence, and Gene Krupa. Mulligan wrote for all three.

Gerry said, "I met Gil probably when I was arranging for the Krupa band. I knew about his writing before that. I used to visit Gil with Claude's band when I was working for other bands. One time I came back to New York after leaving one of the bands; it might have been when I left Tommy Tucker. And I stayed at the Edison Hotel. My room was on an air shaft on the west side of the building. And every morning about 10 o'clock, the band started to rehearse, because Claude was just back from the service and they were reorganizing. I would sit hanging out the window, listening to the rehearsals. A friend of mine, a guitar player from Texas, would come by, and we'd listen to the rehearsals.

"I went back to Philadelphia, to write for Elliot Lawrence's band. And I lived there for a while. I got a postcard from Gil saying, 'What are you doing living in Philadelphia? Everything's happening in New York. Come back.' So I did. I stayed in a succession of rooms. Finally Gil said, 'Stay here.'"

One of the records by the Krupa band that I liked was "Disc Jockey Jump," and I had bothered to note who wrote it: Gerry Mulligan. That was probably the first time I heard his name. I would soon hear it again: in the writing and playing credits on the so-called *Birth of the Cool* album.

Thirty-three years later, in early 1992, Mulligan would re-create that album for the GRP label, with John Lewis again on piano but Wallace Roney replacing Miles Davis, and Phil Woods replacing Lee Konitz.

Mulligan's interest in the format of those sessions continued beyond the *Birth of the Cool* sessions, and in January 1953, in Los Angeles, he recorded an LP made up almost entirely of his own compositions, including "Westwood Walk," "Simbah," "Walking Shoes," "Rocker," "A Ballad," "Flash," and "Ontet." I was becoming very, very conscious of this Gerry Mulligan, thinking he was one of the most important composers in jazz – though who was I to judge? I not only loved Mulligan's writing – I soon knew all those charts by memory, and still do – I loved his work as a soloist. He played a sort of rollicking, charming, unpretentious kind of piano, and he produced lovely solos on an instrument usually considered unsuitable for solos: the baritone saxophone, which he played with a light and highly individual tone that is now imitated all over the world.

That ten-inch Mulligan LP was part of the sound-track of my life at that time. By then I knew from pictures what Mulligan looked like: a tall young man with a brush-cut and a body almost cadaverously thin.

By then Mulligan had a quartet featuring Chet Baker on trumpet, which played Monday nights at a club called the Haig. The group had made its first recording for Dick Bock's Pacific Jazz label in August of 1952, a little over four months before the tentet record. The group startled critics because it used trumpet, baritone, bass, and drums, but no piano, always considered essential to communicating the harmony of a tune. Much was made of this "odd" instrumentation. It lay not in arcane musical philosophy, however: the Haig's owner could not afford more than four men. Red Norvo had played there with only vibes, guitar, and bass. Mulligan also got along without piano.

The rapport between Baker and Mulligan was remarkable. The emphasis was on counterline, and it seemed to free both horn players for ever more imaginative flights. Michael Cuscuna wrote in the notes for a CD reissue called *The Best of Gerry Mulligan with Chet Baker*,

The limitation of two voices (and sometimes a third with the bass) seemed to ignite Mulligan's already fertile mind.

Whether remodeling a standard or introducing an original, Mulligan stretched his limits and came upon a sound that was not only new and stimulating, but also incredibly fascinating and accessible to the general public. Four months after their first recordings for a then eight-week-old label, they were stars beyond the jazz world with full-page features in magazines like *Time* and choice engagements around the country.

Mulligan was then 25.

So much legend has grown up around Chet Baker that his musical brilliance is often overlooked. Baker was a heroin addict: so was Mulligan. Mulligan would eventually break free of it, but Baker would not, leading a strange, bohemian, itinerant existence, hocking his horn from time to time, sometimes without clothes, sometimes even without shoes, surrounded by people who seemed fascinated by the morbidity of his existence. He got his teeth knocked out by dope-pushers for failing to pay what he owed them. He spent time in a jail in Italy. A story went around that when he met pianist Romano Mussolini, son of the murdered dictator, he said, "Hey, man, sorry to hear about your old man." I thought the story surely was apocryphal, but I asked Caterina Valente about it, and she said, "It's not only true, I was *there*. It was at the start of a tour."

Time ravaged Chet Baker. I encountered him only once, when he came into Jim and Andy's bar in New York to beg money, which the musicians willingly gave him. He looked bad. By the end, that clean-cut all-American-boy face was a barren desert landscape of deep lines and gullies. He died from a fall from a hotel in Holland. It is widely believed that he was thrown from the roof by elements of the Dutch underworld, among the roughest in the world, for not paying a dope bill.

Whatever the cause of the death, the legend obscures the talent, and part of that legend is that he was just a natural who couldn't even read music. Mulligan was adamant in rejecting this.

Much of the music that quartet played was Mulligan's own. Only a few leaders, among them Dave Brubeck, Horace Silver, John Lewis, and Duke Ellington, have devoted their recording careers so extensively to their own compositions. What Baker was called on to do was very complex.

Mulligan told me: "People love to say Chet couldn't read: he could read. It's not a question of whether he couldn't read chords or anything like that. It's that he didn't care. He had one of the quickest connections between mind, hand, and chops that I have ever encountered. He really played by ear, and he could play intricate progressions."

"I presume that in blowing, you're playing by ear too," I said.

"Well at my best I'm playing by ear! But I often am saddled with thinking chords, until I learn a tune. And I have to learn a tune some kind of way. And, really, my connection between my ears and my hands is not that quick. Sure, when I've got a tune firmly under hand – which is different from having it firmly in mind – I'm playing by ear. It's taken me a long time to connect up."

"You said he could do that fast?"

"Yeah. Yes. Oh yeah."

"You'd run a tune by him and he'd get it?"

"Oh yeah. And in any key. He had incredible facility. Remarkable. So it's obvious that at some point in his life, Chet Baker practiced a lot. It's all well and good to be able to do that. You're not born able to do that. You're maybe born with a facility to learn quickly. It's like Charlie Parker. Everybody thinks Charlie came along full-blown, there he was. But as a kid, he was a heavy practicer. And Chet must have been too."

In view of its importance in jazz history, it is surprising to realize that the quartet with Chet Baker lasted only a year. Mulligan was arrested on a narcotics charge and sent to a California honor farm for three months, after which he returned to New York, where he established a new quartet with trombonist Bob Brookmeyer instead of Baker. With Jon Eardley on trumpet and Zoot Sims on tenor, the group recorded for Mercury as the Gerry Mulligan Sextet. But the quartet continued, growing constantly better, and it lost none of its momentum when Art Farmer succeeded Brookmeyer. The group (with Bill Crow on bass and Dave Bailey on drums) can be seen at Newport in the pioneering film *Jazz on a Summer's Day*.

And meanwhile, Mulligan made a series of albums for Norman Granz according to a formula Granz found appealing: mixing and matching various pairs of musicians. Mulligan recorded with Thelonious Monk, Stan Getz, Ben Webster (one of his early heroes), Johnny Hodges, and Paul Desmond, a particularly close friend.

When I joined *Down Beat*, I was well aware of the extent of the heroin epidemic in jazz: yet the subject was kept hushed. I did a good deal of research on the problem, asking many of the former addicts I was coming to know how and why they had quit. Al Cohn told me that an infection from a dirty needle settled into his eye, resulting finally in its surgical incision. "Losing your eye will make you quit," Al said in his sardonic fashion. Zoot Sims told me that he got into a car with a girl he was going with, left New York, and went through withdrawal in motel rooms as he made his way home to California.

And, later, when I knew Mulligan well enough, I asked him too how he quit. Gerry, not entirely surprisingly, took an intellectual approach to the problem. He met a New York psychiatrist who was interested in the problem of addiction. The psychiatrist said he could lose his license for what he was about to do. He said that he was going to supply Gerry with good syringes and medical morphine to replace the dirty heroin of the street. At minimum it would remove the danger and dark glamour from the practice. Morphine isn't as strong as heroin, but it's pretty good, as you know if you've ever had it in a hospital.

Gerry was playing a gig in Detroit. At intermission he went into the men's room, and he was inserting his nice clean medical syringe into his nice clean bottle of morphine when he stopped, thinking, "What am I doing to myself?"

He telephoned Joe Glaser, his booking agent, in New York, and told him to get him out of the job on grounds that he was sick. "And I'm going to be," he said. And he simply quit, going through the sweats and shudders and nausea of withdrawal. I always thought this was a remarkable act of courage. But Gerry said, "What else could I do? It was destroying the thing that means the most in the world to me, my music. I had a reason to quit. Had I been some poor kid in a Harlem doorway with nothing to look forward to even if he does quit, I don't think I could have done it."

I saw Gerry in person for the first time at the Newport Jazz Festival on the Fourth of July weekend of 1960. He had just organized what he called the Concert Jazz Band. In a flurry of publicity, it was to make its début at Newport. The big-band era was ended. Nobody – well, almost nobody – tried to launch big bands any more. The ballrooms and dance pavilions were gone, or no longer booked bands. *There's a dance pavilion in the rain, all shuttered down*, Johnny Mercer wrote in the lyric he set to Ralph Burns' "Early Autumn." A new big band?

But I wanted to hear it: anything Mulligan did seemed likely to be innovative, as indeed that band was. I was backstage in a tent, talking with Dizzy Gillespie, when the first sounds of the band came to us. It was raining torrents. At stage left, the United States Information Agency had set up a shelter, a sloping canvas roof, to protect their television and recording equipment. They were recording the whole festival. The stage was chin high.

The band began to perform Bob Brookmeyer's lyrical arrangement of Django Reinhardt's ballad "Manoir de mes rêves." In front of the stage, rain danced on a garden of black umbrellas. An imaginative cameraman panned across this audience in the rain, then across the stage, coming to rest on a great puddle, in which an upside-down Mulligan was playing an exquisite obbligato to the chart, leading into his solo. I was watching both the image and the reality. It was one of the unforgettable musical moments of my life.

I returned to Chicago, where *Down Beat* was headquartered. The Mulligan band was booked into the lounge in the Sutherland Hotel on the South Side. It had a largely black audience and booked the finest performers in jazz, black and white alike. Its disadvantage to performers was that they had to play on a high stage in the middle of the racetrack-shaped bar, and a band of thirteen had little room to move.

The group was startlingly fresh. Later Gerry told me he didn't think it was really a concert jazz band; it was a first-rate dance band. But he underestimated it. It was a gorgeous small orchestra, with a sound unlike any other. Gerry told me that he had previously tried to make small groups, such as the sextet, sound like big bands; now he wanted a big band to play with the fleet levity and light textures of a small group. Unfortunately, its book contained little of Mulligan's own writing. He found himself so busy running and booking the band that he didn't have time to write. Much of the burden of the composition and arranging fell on Brookmeyer, himself one of the most brilliant writers in jazz.

Something was going on during that Sutherland gig that none of us knew about, except, I think, Brookmeyer.

Gerry was going with and for some time had been in love with actress Judy Holliday, a gentle woman and one of the most gifted comediennes in American theater. She had just undergone a mastectomy. Gerry was playing the Sutherland in the evenings, then catching a red-eye flight to New York, sitting at her bedside as much of the day as he could, then getting an afternoon flight back to Chicago to work. He must have done all of his sleeping on the plane, and if he was drained and short-tempered at the time, it is hardly a wonder.

Some time during that week, I went upstairs with Bob Brookmeyer for a drink in the "band room," a suite of two or three rooms assigned by the hotel. Mulligan was in a bedroom with bassist Buddy Clark, whom I also knew by then, and they were in the midst of a heated exchange. Buddy shouted, "I'm getting sick of it! I'm tired of pulling this whole goddamn band by myself!" And Mulligan told him he wasn't pulling it by himself; he was getting plenty of help, and who the hell did he think he was? "I felt badly about that," Gerry told me some time later. "I didn't know Buddy was sick." Neither did anyone else, including Buddy. He had a rectal problem for which he later underwent surgery, and, he told me, his discomfort had made him short-tempered. He regretted the incident as much as Gerry did.

Mulligan, whose hair in those days was reddish-blond, came out of the bedroom and stopped in his tracks seeing me, a stranger, in the band's midst.

"Who are you?" he said harshly.

I told him.

"Oh God," he said, "that's all I need: press."

"You don't think I'd write anything about this, do you?" I said. And I never did, until now.

Mulligan stormed out, and the band played its next set.

I do not recall where next I encountered him, but by then everyone in the profession was crossing my path. By the time I moved to New York in July 1962, I knew him fairly well.

His influence, and through him that of Claude Thornhill and Gil Evans, had spread around the world. He had been a considerable influence on the development of the bossa nova movement in Brazil, for example, and that is aside from all the baritone players on the planet whose sound resembled his.

There is no questioning this influence of Mulligan on Brazilian music. I had just returned from a tour of South America, and in Rio de Janeiro had met João Gilberto and Antonio Carlos Jobim, both virtually unknown in North America, except to a few musicians such as Bob Brookmeyer, Zoot Sims, and particularly Dizzy Gillespie, always aware of developments in Latin American music. It was said that the album made by Bud Shank and Laurindo Almeida called *Brazilliance* had also exerted an influence, but American critics tended to deny this, probably on the politically correct grounds that West Coast jazz was unimportant, and even Bud Shank said to me once, "The Brazilians didn't need me." But Bud (who incidentally played alto on the Mulligan tentet album) was wrong. Claudio Roditi, the superb Brazilian trumpeter, told me that in the period of bossa nova's gestation, almost the only jazz records available in Brazil were those on Dick Bock's Pacific Jazz label. The Shank–Almeida album, he said, was indeed an influence. But the major influence, according to Gilberto and Jobim, was Mulligan, and the influence on Gilberto's singing was that of a French Caribbean singer – from Martinique – named Henri Salvador, whose work I knew and loved.

Jobim told me that part of the ideal of the bossa nova movement was to achieve acoustical rather than electronic balances in the music, one of the keys to Mulligan's thinking. Jobim told me at the time, "The authentic Negro samba is very primitive. They use maybe ten percussion instruments and the music is very hot and wonderful. But bossa nova is cool and contained. It tells the story, trying to be simple and serious and lyrical. João and I felt that Brazilian music until now had been too much a storm on the sea, and we wanted to calm it down for the recording studio. You could call bossa nova a clean, washed samba, without loss of the momentum. We don't want to lose important things. We have the problem of how to write and not lose the swing."

Jobim came to New York that autumn for a Carnegie Hall concert of Brazilian musicians and, backstage, Gerry became one of the first American musicians I introduced him to. We were often together after that. Jobim's song "O Insensatez" begins with the chord changes of the Chopin E-minor Prelude and, as a send-up of Jobim, Mulligan recorded the prelude as a samba. Jobim and Mulligan remained friends to the end of their days, and Gerry would see him whenever he went to Rio de Janeiro.

Gerry was not, as everyone seemed to think, living with Judy Holliday. She lived in the Dakota, on West 72nd Street at Central Park West, and he lived a block away.

I saw more of Gerry after Judy's death of cancer, which devastated him.

We both lived on the West Side, and, aside from Jim and Andy's downtown, we had two or three favorite restaurants in the area of Broadway and the West 70s and 80s, halfway between his apartment and mine, which was on West 86th. A lot of my lyrics, including those written for Jobim tunes, had been recorded by then.

Gerry loved theater, and we thought we should try to write a show together. We looked for an appropriate subject, and one of us came up with the idea of the relationship between Diamond Jim Brady and Lillian Russell. I learned that Brady's house had stood approximately across the street from my apartment on West 86th a few doors in from Central Park. It had long since been replaced by an apartment building.

One of my happier memories is of that period when Gerry and I ran around to libraries and pored over books, absorbing the life of Diamond Jim, getting inside his mind, acquiring a feel for the New York of his time. We sketched out a script, and I think it was a good one. We wrote some songs. Gerry arranged a meeting with Hal Prince. The receptionist said, "Are you *the* Gerry Mulligan?"

And Gerry said, "I'm the only one I know."

She showed us in to see Hal Prince. And Hal Prince told us that a Diamond Jim Brady project was already under way, with Jackie Gleason set to play Brady and Lucille Ball as Lillian Russell.

We left Hal Prince's office feeling crushed, and no doubt stopped somewhere for a drink. Gleason and Ball would be perfect casting. All our excitement had been killed in an instant, and I suppose Gerry thought, as I did, of all our work being left to molder in a drawer. This would be the second disappointment of that kind for him. He and Judy Holliday, who was a gifted lyricist, had written a musical based on the Anita Loos play *Happy Birthday*. And although the songs were superb, Gerry had never been able to get anyone interested. One producer told him it could not succeed because the setting was an Irish bar. And, he said, "The Irish go to bars. Jews go to theater."

Gerry and I abandoned our Diamond Jim project. The show with Gleason and Ball was never made; it vanished into that limbo of unfulfilled Broadway projects.

One night Gerry and I went to see Stephen Sondheim's *Company*. Later we went to the Ginger Man for drinks and a late dinner. "I hate him," Gerry said. I said, "Me too." For Sondheim had done both music and lyrics, and both were brilliant. Long after, Gerry laughed when I recalled that night and said, "I've been trying to hate him for years and can't. He's too good."

One night in Jim and Andy's bar, Gerry said he had tickets for a new play and asked if I wanted to go with him. We ran down 48th Street to get to the theater by curtain time. We saw Jason Robards in *A Thousand Clowns*. The co-star was a young actress named Sandy Dennis. She and Gerry would be together for years, and then separate. Sandy is now dead, like Judy, of cancer. And like Gerry.

Being of English origin, I had for some time been noticing the scarcity of WASP English influence or even presence in American music, particularly jazz. Once, over dinner, I said, "Mulligan, you and I must be the only WASPs in the music business."

And, laughing, he said, "Speak for yourself, I'm an Irish Catholic."

Because he was not actively so, I asked him if he felt himself to be Catholic. He thought for a minute and said, "No. But I do feel Irish."

All this led to a series of observations on the ethnic origins of the Europeans in American jazz and popular music. Irish, Scottish, Welsh, yes; Polish, German, Jewish, Russian, just about any nationality you could mention. But very few English. Even those who bore "English" names, such as Joe Farrell, Louis Bellson, Eddie Lang, Will Bradley, and Glen Gray, had changed them to escape the prejudices of America.

It was during one such discussion that Gerry and I discovered we had arrived independently at the same conclusion: white American jazz musicians tend to reflect their ethnic origins in the style of their playing. And although this is not a universal verity, it often will be found to be true. Gerry told me that once, when he and Judy were listening to Zoot Sims, who was Irish, she said, "There he goes again – playing that Barry Fitzgerald tenor." And she imitated Fitzgerald's laughter, Ah-ha-ha-ha-ha, on a falling melodic line. It is a remarkably perceptive insight. But, even more to the point, listening to Gerry on a taped interview, I once heard him say something with the exact, momentarily falsetto, inflection of Barry Fitzgerald. And one part of Gerry's family came to America nearly a 150 years ago.

But speech patterns persist for long, long periods, and the accent of Normandy still echoes the speech of the Viking conquerors who settled there 1,000 years ago, and is in turn the source of the French Canadian accent. Perhaps the speech of Marseille descends from the Phoenicians. You will hear subtly Swedish inflections in Minnesota, even in those whose people have been there a long time.

I hear, I am certain, an Irish quality in Mulligan's playing and writing. It couples whimsy with melancholy, sadness with exuberance, it is at once lyrical and witty, and it is above all eloquent. I find that all very Irish.

In his last years Gerry led a quartet *with* piano. He continued to write for all manner of formations, including full symphony orchestra. An album on the Par label called *Symphonic Dreams* was recorded in 1987 by the Houston Symphony under Erich Kunzel. One of my favorite of Gerry's albums is *The Age of Steam* on the A&M label. Like the late Glenn Gould, Gerry had a fascination with trains. His Christmas cards usually showed one of the big old steam trains, often in a winter setting.

Proust points out somewhere in *Swann's Way* that fictional characters are transparent while the persons we know in life are opaque. Even those we know well are mysteries. We are mysteries even to ourselves.

So who was Gerry Mulligan? Where did he come from? Why did he love the old trains?

After 1969, Gerry and I never lived in the same city. I moved to Toronto for a few years, then to California. Once he came up to Toronto for a few days, and we did a television show together. We always stayed in touch. On my way to Paris, with a stopover at Kennedy airport, I called him from a phone booth. The conversation lasted an hour; it was mostly about Irish history.

An aristocratic Italian photojournalist named Franca Rota was assigned to cover him on a 1972 recording date in Milan: that's where they met. After their marriage, they lived in a house in Connecticut and an apartment in Milan, not far from the great cathedral and from the castle of the Sforzas, now a museum. I had lunch with them in Milan in 1984. By now Gerry did not smoke or drink. He never was a heavy eater, but his diet had become disciplined to the point of the Spartan. He told me I shouldn't use salt.

In the spring of 1994, we found ourselves on a jazz cruise of the Caribbean, with time for conversation, a little as in the Jim and Andy's days of memory. I asked him about things we had never discussed, in particular his family. I was aware that his relations with his father had been somewhat uncomfortable. It will usually be found that a gifted musician was encouraged by a parent or both parents, but not Gerry.

He was the youngest of four boys, in order: George, Phil, Ron, Gerry. All three of his brothers became, like their father, engineers, and Gerry's father wanted him to be one.

"Don't you think that's affected your work?" I said, thinking of the sense of design in all Gerry's writing and playing.

"Some of the attitude of the builder, the constructor, I suppose," he said.

"What did he do exactly? I asked.

Gerry said, "By the time my father was mature, they had started to use engineering to improve efficiency and practices in factories. It was the beginning of the time-study period. The pejorative term for what my father did was 'efficiency expert'. Of course, the companies hated to see people like that coming because they knew they were going to have to work hard. And it meant that a lot of people were going to lose their jobs because they streamlined the procedures. So he was schooled in all sorts of engineering.

"I remember when I was in high school in Detroit, he put himself through night school in aeronautical engineering, just to increase his own abilities. But he had his peculiarities. He had this image of having an engineering business with his sons. Dynasty time. My brothers fought that battle pretty well. My oldest brother didn't want to go to engineering school, and my father was only going to send him to school if he studied engineering. And I think he finally knuckled under and went and was very unhappy in engineering. The brother after him liked it, so it was all right.

"My father had a kind of strange attitude. I have realized in recent years, he was kind of anti-education and anti-intellectual. It was too bad, because he missed a lot of things. At the point where I started to be in contact with other musicians, especially the people with education, which I didn't have – have never had – I heard Ravel's *Daphnis and Chloé*. My father's response was, 'Ravel only ever wrote one piece, and that was the *Bolero*.' Well you realize you can't have much conversation with people who think like that."

"There's a similarity here," I said. "My father had the same anti-intellectual attitude. He once said, 'An intellectual is like a man in a white suit who can't change a tire.'"

Gerry mused on that for a moment, then laughed – he liked to laugh, often a short sardonic chuckle, and there was a kind of effervescence in his voice – and said, "If I'd been smarter when I was young, and my father had come right out and said that to me, I'd have said, 'Yeah, well I want to be the man in the white suit. Let somebody else change the tire!'" And he laughed again.

I remembered the Gerry Mulligan wind-up doll Bob Brookmeyer invented. You wind it up, put it on the table, and it sends for room service. Gerry later amended that, satirizing himself: "Hello, room service? Send up the concert."

"What was your father's name?" I asked. "And where did the family come from?"

"His name was George. His family was from Wilmington, Delaware. His family must have come over here from Ireland in, probably, the 1850s or thereabouts. My mother was half Irish. Her mother was born in Germany, and her father's family was Protestant Irish. So I came along with a built-in dichotomy.

"I was born in New York, but before I was 1, my father picked up the family and moved to Marion, Ohio, where he became an executive with a company called the Marion Steam Shovel Company: the biggest business in town, a big, big, big factory. To this day, you'll see older equipment with that name on it. And then he was with another company that made Hercules road rollers and stuff like that. So we were out there until I was 10 years old and in about fourth grade." Laughing, he added: "So I always say I did 1 to 10 in Ohio.

"After that he went with a big company, May Consulting Engineers, still one of the biggest, based in Chicago. He did a lot of jobs for them. And because all these jobs would take a year or two, we wound up going with him. From Ohio he went to a job in Puerto Rico for a winter.

"Meanwhile, my grandfather, who was a retired locomotive engineer from the Pennsylvania Railroad, had died. He and my grandmother lived in South Jersey. So we went there for a while.

"My father then went to Chicago. We were there for one school year. I started to go down the garden path, because what was available there was four theaters that had big bands playing. I was old enough to get on the El and go downtown. We lived at 4200 North, near Sheridan Road. Not far from the lake. I went to the grade school whose claim to fame is that Joyce Kilmer and Janet Gaynor went there. I spent my time learning how to run fast. I was the country bumpkin. I guess it was the beginning of various kinds of ethnic warfare. The kids were ganging up on other kids, and I guess I looked like a likely subject, because they'd chase me and beat the hell out of me if they could.

"Then my father went to a job in Kalamazoo, Michigan: we were there for about three years. That's where I first got some training on an instrument, barring the one semester in second grade in grade school that had piano lessons. At the recital, I would get halfway through a piece and forget it. About the second time I started over they came and took me offstage, like amateur night at the Apollo. And the nun told my mother, 'Just save your money. He will never play these things the way they were written.' A nun had said it to my mother, therefore it must be the truth.

"In Kalamazoo, I wanted to take trumpet but I got side-tracked onto clarinet. I liked clarinet, because I liked Artie Shaw a lot, and I liked the Thornhill band, with Irving Fazola. I loved the sound of Irving Fazola, and one thing led to another. I wrote my first arrangement in Kalamazoo.

"I went to a public school the first year in Kalamazoo. There was a kid who lived across the street who could play trumpet. He could play things like "Carnival of Venice" and "Flight of the Bumble Bee." I was the most envious kid you ever saw. I admired him and we were best friends.

"The next year they sent me downtown to the Catholic school. The school was right next to the Michigan Central tracks. Every day I'd go out for the recess just as the Wolverine was going by. I used to see the people sitting in the dining car, with the white tablecloths and the silverware. The Wolverine was a very classy train on the New York Central. For a long time the Wolverine had the fastest schedule of any train in the country. Those were the Michigan Central tracks, but the Michigan Central was part of the New York Central. A great train, going by. And here I am in this filthy play-yard in the freezing cold. I was envious then, too."

"Does that explain your fascination with trains?" I asked.

"Well it runs in the family. My father's family had been with the B&O and the C&O, and on my mother's side, her father was a locomotive engineer with the Pennsylvania Railroad. The Irish built a lot of the railroads in this country. So I came by it naturally.

"The next year, they put up a new building and the school moved over there. They decided they were going to have their first school orchestra. They got a teacher and everything, and I learned the basics of the clarinet, and now we had an instrumentation not to be believed: probably a trumpet, a clarinet, two violins, and God knows what. An ungodly conglomeration. So I sat down and wrote an arrangement of "Lover," because I was fascinated by the chromatic progressions. I brought it in to play, and like a damn fool I put the title "Lover" on the top of it. The nun took one look at it and said, 'We can't play that.' So I never heard my first chart.

"But what's more interesting is what prompted me to write an arrange-ment in the first place. I don't know the answer: I just wanted to do it. I figured I could do it. I'd figured out how to make a transposition chart. I had one of those charts that you put behind the piano keys when you're a kid starting out. I guess I was in about the seventh grade at the time. A lot of us who were arrangers, there was always a kind of fraternity among arrangers, because of the recognition of the similarities. There are things that you know how to do and don't know how you know. I knew the basics of orchestration without having to be told."

"Could you, in grade seven, actually listen to a record and hear the chord content?"

"A lot of it, sure. The thing that I liked about the bands was the textures. I always was hooked on that. What you do with a single instrument is nice. What you do with a whole bunch of instruments becomes an interesting challenge to make it all add up to something cohesive. And to turn this thing that deals with a lot of mechanics into music is a miracle.

"If somebody had said, 'You can't do it,' it might have stopped me. But nobody did."

"Let me get this straight," I said. "As a kid in grade seven, you could simply hear the contents of arrangements on records, hear the voices, without lessons?"

"Yeah."

"To me, that's weird. Henry Mancini was the same. He could just hear it. He told me, and Horace Silver did the same thing, that he'd play records at slow speeds until he could figure out what was in the chords."

"I wasn't that smart," Gerry said. "I did it the hard way."

"Your parents were not musical?"

"My mother and father were both born in the '90s. So they were in their twenties and thirties in the '20s and '30s of this century. And they both learned enough piano to be able to play.

"My father could read, but he read like an engineer. He could sit down and play a piece of music, but he'd miss all the accidentals, play lots of wrong notes, and just go happily along. But my mother played very nicely. She liked pretty music."

"Obviously you left Kalamazoo eventually," I said.

"We went from Kalamazoo to Detroit. There wasn't music proliferating in the schools. There was no such thing as jazz courses. And no such thing, really, as available lessons on an instrument. Music was a very separate and separated thing.

"But there was music around. Detroit is where I got totally hooked on boogie-woogie piano players. I loved Meade Lux Lewis and Pete Johnson and Pinetop, that whole era. It was such a joyful, funny, dynamic music. In Detroit we had at least one thing: the Michigan Theater played bands. That's one of the days I can pinpoint accurately: I know where I was on the seventh December, 1941. It was Sunday and I was at the Michigan Theater to hear Erskine Hawkins. I loved that band.

"I didn't realize it then, but Erskine liked a very thin sound. And apparently he liked guys in the section to have that sound. As a consequence, when they played even reasonably high, it sounded exciting: it sounded piercing. A high C with a thin sound really sounds high. Then later on, I wrote things for bands with guys with incredible chops; they could play a high C that was so fat that it didn't sound high. They had to go up to an altissimo G or something before it really started to sound piercing. It finally dawned on me that a fat sound on trumpet somehow diminished the impact of the highness of the note. Took all the excitement away. Erskine's band had a crackling excitement, and mainly because the trumpet players had a thin sound: it was great.

"From Detroit we went to Reading, Pennsylvania. My father was working for a company that made an alloy of beryllium and copper. It was valuable because it's non-sparking and they can make tools for working around refineries or any place where sparks are dangerous. It's also unaffected by altitude or temperature. When I finally got a saxophone and clarinet, I wanted him to make me a set of springs, because that alloy never wears out, but he never did.

"I worked at that plant one summer as the mailboy. I saved my money and bought my first clarinet. I went to a teacher at the music store where I bought it and went through the exercises with the books. Sammy Correnti: a wonderful man. Sammy also transcribed a lot of the players he had known in the '20s and '30s.

"One day after I'd been taking lessons with Sammy for a while, he brought in an arrangement he had written in the early '30s on a piece called "Dark Eyes," written for three brass, three saxes, and three rhythm – two altos and a tenor, two trumpets and a bone. He said, 'Here, take this and revoice it for four brass and four saxes.' I did. His attitude was, 'You can do this, so do it.' It wasn't 'You can't do it.'

"We had these things to learn, jazz choruses. I learned Artie Shaw's 'Concerto for Clarinet' solo and his solo on 'Stardust.'"

"Just about every reed player I ever met learned that 'Stardust' solo," I said. "Billy Mitchell told me he could still play it. Did you start working while you were in Reading?"

"Yeah. I started working professionally in Reading. I put together a quartet in high school. My brothers had a good time driving us around to our gigs, because all of us in my group were too young to drive. I was back there a few years ago. I went out to the church where we used to play for dances.

"But I wanted to have a big band. So I started collecting stock arrangements. Then they used to do manuscript charts of various bands. I had things from Les Brown's band, from this band and that band. We used to get gigs. I'd get these guys together and rehearse. Then it would be a mad thing. The band would be playing from 8 p.m. to 11 p.m. in a gymnasium some place, and my brothers would be racing back and forth. This guy could make it from 8 p.m. to 9 p.m., then they'd have to pick up his replacement.

"In Reading there was a piano player named Dave Stevens, who played with one of the studio bands in Philadelphia. I was a sophomore in high school, but I was playing with the professionals in town.

"Pennsylvania was a blue-law state, which meant that no entertainment was allowed on Sundays: no movies, no stage shows, no nothing. But it was all legal in private clubs, so private clubs proliferated all over Pennsylvania, which meant that there was work for musicians in Pennsylvania when work was dying out everywhere. I remember we played the Fifth Ward Democratic, the Third Ward Republican, the Polish American, the Irish American. Name it, all the ethnic groups in town, the labor unions, and they all had their own clubs and each one of them would hire a band, and a couple of them even had big bands. The Eagles had a thirteen- or fourteen-piece band. That was the most desirable one in town. I used to play in the band at the Orioles. These were good musicians I played with: I was very lucky."

I said, "Well this bears on what Bill Challis told me. He said that in the '20s, around Wilkes Barre, the musicians played dances in clubs. The coal barons had their clubs, the miners had their clubs, and the miners loved to dance. And when you think of all the musicians who came out of Pennsylvania, all the guys who came out of Pittsburgh and Philadelphia, the Dorsey brothers, Benny Golson, Henry Mancini, Billy Strayhorn, Red Rodney, it's a remarkable list."

"That may well have been a factor," Gerry said. "The blue laws and the clubs. Not only that, after the war, when work started to fall off for musicians, there still was that outlet in Pennsylvania for professional musicians."

I said, "Artie Shaw told me that in the heyday of the bands, you could play a solid month of one-nighters in Pennsylvania."

"Hmm. Well, those are all things that are impossible for people nowadays to understand. How many bands there were. There really was a lot of music available."

"What came after Reading?"

"From Reading, we moved to Philadelphia, and I found myself in West Philadelphia Catholic High School for Boys. About 2,000 boys, and no girls. That was the first time I had encountered that, and I hated it. Especially because down the street two blocks was the girls' school, and they started rehearsing their symphony orchestra in October for a concert in April. Envy again. There was no music in the school I was in.

"Dave Stevens of Reading had told me to go down to see Johnny Warrington, who had the house band at radio station WCAU. I took myself down to WCAU and saw Johnny. Now I think what kind of bemusement it must have fostered in him, to have this junior high-school kid come in and say, 'I want to write for your band.'

"And sure enough, he assigned a piece to me and said, 'Make me an arrangement of this. It will be for our Saturday night show.' I took the piece and spent a couple of weeks writing the arrangement. I brought it back. He went over it with me and he said, 'Well, let's see, you could have done this, you could have done that. Why didn't you do that here? Take it back and rewrite it and bring it back.' So I'd lucked into a teacher, somebody who helped. And he bought it and played it and assigned me something else.

"But the way that I got it written was even wilder. I really hated the school. There were a couple of teachers I liked and a couple of subjects that were fascinating. I had looked forward to chemistry as being probably an interesting subject, because you had laboratory work and it would be fun doing experiments. I had a teacher who ruined it for me. He spoke in a monotone, and he was a very dull man, and I remembered nothing.

"The school was taught by Christian brothers. Brother Martin was in charge of the band. When I transferred into this school and talked to Brother Martin, he never even asked me or even suggested that I play with the marching band. He explained that the marching band was not very good. The guys only went out for the band to get a letter and go to the ball games free. He said, 'The facilities are here. Any time you want to use the band room, it's yours.'

"Because it was such a big school, we had staggered lunch breaks. There were four lunch breaks. I had one of my own and three others. I started a band out of what I could get out of this marching band. I would have one of them come to my class and say, 'Brother Martin wants Gerry Mulligan in the band room.' So I would spend three out of the four lunch breaks in the band room, writing my chart for WCAU."

I said, "People forget that aside from the radio networks, which not only used to broadcast the big bands but had symphony orchestras on staff, even local radio stations employed bands, and pianists, and small groups. They generated their own music. They didn't just play records, as they do now. Radio was a tremendous generative force for music."

"Oh yeah. And given the opportunity, bands in all kinds of work tried to do their best. That's not to say all bands were good. There were a lot of sloppy bands around. But the best of them, which was a lot of them, were always trying to make music better. We always felt we could learn something, try something. So it was a good time for bands, all through the '30s and '40s.

"This brings up one of the areas where musicians got into a wrongful kind of relationship to the rest of the society, because of the attitude of the musicians' union. The union started in Chicago, and it was very much like a gangster organization, the way it went about doing things. For instance, their attitude in a town like Philadelphia. They would go into a radio station like WCAU and say, 'How many musicians do you employ?' The station might say something like, 'We employ ten.' And the union would say, 'All right, from now on you employ thirteen. How much are you paying them?' And the station might say, 'We're paying 75 dollars a week.' And the union might say, 'From now on you're paying 100.' It was done without discussion, it was: This is the way it's going to be or we'll pull the music out altogether.

"You'd be surprised how many radio stations said, 'Well, screw it.' And they got rid of the musicians. Those kinds of practices, I think, did musicians a great disservice. It made an antagonistic relationship that was harmful and wrong. And of course Petrillo, who was very much a dictatorial type, arbitrarily, against the advice of many people in the union, including the bandleaders, pulled the recording ban. That was the *coup de grace* for the big bands. Of all the times when he pulled it, when the guys were coming back from the service and needed all the help they could get!"

"But you still had WCAU and Johnny Warrington," I said. "Were you still in high school?"

"Yeah. In fact, at the school, I decided to put a band together. There were a lot of clarinet players in the marching band. There was only one kid who had a saxophone. I went and bought an alto so I would have at least two saxophones. We had a bunch of trumpets and we had one kid who played decent trombone. I wrote arrangements for the band, using this instrumentation. It came out sounding like Glenn Miller, because it was heavy on the clarinets. But because of that, I made something happen in the school, and we became the heroes that year, playing at various schools, playing at their assemblies. We even went down and played at the girls' school. So I suppose the girls' school was envious that we had a dance band and they only had a symphony orchestra.

"I went into the senior year. Chemistry had been destroyed for me, and I was bored to tears by the rest of the school. In senior year they had physics. They had lecture classes: it was like college – you're a big kid now. I go into the lecture room for the first thing on physics, and who have I got? The same guy who ruined chemistry for me. My mind did a trick on me that day, and I realized it started this at other times and it frightened me. Have you ever forgotten how to do something automatic, like tying your shoes or tying your tie? I watched this man. His lips were moving but I forgot what words meant. I totally lost the connection with language. I got up at the end of the class and went down to the office of the school and said, 'I'm leaving school. I have my father's permission. I'm going on the road with a band.'

"I didn't have a job and I didn't have my father's permission. I went to see Brother Martin, who didn't try to talk me into staying. He's one of the people I wish I'd had sense enough to keep contact with. He must have been a remarkable man. He didn't do any of the judgemental things that all the other grown-ups I remember from childhood did. He really treated me like a human being with the intelligence to try find my own way and as someone determined to find my own way.

"I went home and told my family what I was doing. My father didn't put up a big argument because, I think, he had lost his taste for trying to direct us. And obviously I was so far removed from his ideal of engineer that I didn't even warrant consideration.

"I thought unkindly in later years that he was probably relieved: he wouldn't have to think about paying to send me to college of any kind.

"I really would have liked to go to music school, but I never even broached the subject with him. I knew it was out of the question. That's what I mean by anti-intellectualism. I don't understand having that kind of an attitude toward your own kid. I never was that way with my own son, and can't be that way with young people."

(Gerry had one child, Reed, a son by his first and brief marriage to Arlene Brown, daughter of Lew Brown, of the Henderson–Brown–DeSylva songwriting team.)

He said, "I like to help young people have whatever opportunities there are, in whatever ways I can, without pushing them, without telling them – the way Sammy Correnti did with me.

"I was now out of school, with no job to go to. I had to get a job in a hurry so I didn't have to go back to school ignominiously.

"I had met an agent named Jimmy Tyson. He was the agent for Alex Bartha, who had been the bandleader on the Steel Pier in Atlantic City for maybe fifteen years. What I didn't know was that every year he had this desire to take the band on the road and be a name band. I was infected with that! He promised he was going to take me on the road with him. Great! This was the job I thought I had. So I went down to see the agent. Jimmy said, 'Alex has been saying that for years. He's not going to take a band on the road.'

"And I thought, Oh God. I parked myself in the office of Jimmy Tyson's agency and waited for somebody to call up. Every band that came through to play at the Earle Theater, somebody would call up and say, 'I need a trombone player,' or something. And I would hear Jimmy say, 'Do you need a tenor or alto player?' I was playing tenor and alto then. And nobody ever did.

"Then Tommy Tucker came to the Earle. Same thing. He didn't need a saxophone player. So Jimmy said, 'Well do you need an arranger?' And Tommy Tucker said, 'Send him around, let me talk to him.' So I met Tommy Tucker backstage at the theater. He gave me a try. He signed me to a contract, 100 dollars a week for two jump or three ballad arrangements. Ballads being fewer pages than the jump tunes. Copied: I had to do all the copying."

Mulligan's career detour through the Tommy Tucker band has occasionally raised eyebrows: it seems somewhat incongruous.

The band, whose radio broadcasts began with the signature announcement, "It's Tommy Tucker Time!", was in that group that drew votes in the *Down Beat* poll's King of Corn category, usually won by Guy Lombardo. To the hip fans of the bands, that is to say those who thought they were hip (or, in those days, hep) there was a sharp division between the "jazz" and "mickey" bands, the latter including such as Blue Barron, Freddy Martin, Sammy Kaye, Russ Morgan, Kay Kyser, Shep Fields and his Rippling Rhythm, Lawrence Welk, and Wayne King. But to the professionals, the demarkation was not that sharp. I know saxophone players who thought Freddy Martin was a fine tenor player, and Benny Carter told me that one of his favorite saxophone players was Wayne King, not because what King did was jazz but because it was excellent saxophone playing.

Mulligan too has this breadth of view, and I was always baffled by his stated admiration for the Guy Lombardo band, which he shared with Louis Armstrong. I was baffled, that is, until I actually saw the band in the 1970s and got to know Guy late in his life. I realized with a start, after only a tune or two from the band in person, that what I was hearing was a museum piece: an authentic, unchanged, perfectly preserved 1920s tuba-bass dance band. And it did what it did extremely well. It was, as Gerry had always insisted, a damned good band.

Many of the "mickey" – meaning Mickey Mouse – bands contained excellent musicians, and some of them, including the bands of Kay Kyser and Sammy Kaye, could play creditable swing on occasion. Some excellent arrangers cut their professional teeth in those bands. George Duning, for example, wrote for Kay Kyser. And for a short time, Gerry Mulligan wrote for Tommy Tucker.

Gerry said, "That was my first experience on the road with a name band as an arranger. That was 1945, I guess, and that would make me 17 going on 18. It was the last year of the war. We traveled by cars. When we hit a town, I would be out of the car like a shot and into the hotel. Is there a room with a piano? It was always a search for a piano. And I never managed to make the three ballads or two jumps a week. But I got pretty close, wrote a lot of music for Tommy. It was a three-month contract.

"We did a lot of one-nighters. We did a month or six weeks or something at a big hotel in Chicago. I was a pig in mud. All the bands were coming through. Billy Eckstine's band came to a downtown theater, with Dizzy playing trumpet with him. Earl Hines had a great band. Artie came through and Lena Horne was singing with him.

"My arrangements for Tommy started to get more and more wild, although I think Tommy liked what I did. There's one thing of mine on a Hindsight record, taken from an aircheck. It's called 'Brass Hats.' I used plungers and hats. Years later, when I heard this thing, I fell off my chair, because I had copied Erskine Hawkins' 'After Hours.' I didn't mean to copy it, but it was very close.

"After the three months, Tommy said, 'It's been very nice, and you've done a lot of good things for the band, but I think you're ready to move on to another band because I think my band is a little too tame for you. I want you to know, Gerry, that if you ever want to go into business or anything like that, I really would be glad to help you – in anything except a band.'

"I never got to see Tommy after he retired, and then I found out a few years ago where he was, because a lot of friends went to Sarasota and saw him. I no sooner found out where he was than I read that he had died. I did call up his widow, a lovely woman. They were great people, and he was good to me.

"That's one thing I was lucky about. The men that I worked for were such *nice* people: Tommy Tucker, Gene Krupa, Claude Thornhill, Elliot Lawrence.

"After I left Tommy, I went back to Philadelphia. Johnny Warrington was no longer at WCAU. Elliot Lawrence had taken over. Elliot had been kind of a child star in Philadelphia. He had been the bandleader on the Horn and Hardart kiddies' hour. He kind of grew into the bandleader job."

And Mulligan began to write for Elliot Lawrence. In the 1950s, some of the writing he did for Lawrence was re-recorded in an album for Fantasy.

"It was all right," Gerry said of that album. "But it wasn't as good as some of the performances the band did at the time. Once, at a rehearsal, they played some of my music so perfectly that it made my hair stand on end. There was a unison trombone passage. The Swope brothers were in the trombone section. The section sounded like one trombone, the unison was so perfect."

Gerry was born on 6 April 1927. Earl Hines and Louis Armstrong had not yet made their pioneering records. The Duke Ellington band would not open at the Cotton Club for another eight months. Though the Paul Whiteman band was immensely popular, the so-called big-band era had not dawned. Benny Goodman was still with Ben Pollack. The Casa Loma Orchestra would not make its first recording for another two years. And network radio had just come into being. Some people still owned crystal radios.

Like Gerry, I grew up, ear to the radio, on the sounds of the big bands in the 1930s. Network radio was an incredible cultural force, presenting – live, not on records – music of immense cultural diversity, almost every kind of music that America produced, and making it popular. Network radio made Duke Ellington and Benny Goodman famous and, a little later, Glenn Miller. It made Arturo Toscanini and James Melton household names. On Saturday afternoons, the broadcasts from the Metropolitan Opera could be heard everywhere from the Mexican border to the northern reaches of Canada.

How long jazz has been with us depends on how you define jazz. If you refer to Buddy Bolden's music, which you have never heard (nor has anyone else) or Scott Joplin's rags, as jazz, then it begins early in the century. Others would call this earlier music proto-jazz. But jazz begins at least by the late teen years of the twentieth century. If you define it even more strictly as the art of the great, improvising soloist, then it begins in the 1920s, and its principal founding figure is Louis Armstrong. As Dizzy Gillespie said of Armstrong, "No him, no me."

So if you accept Armstrong as the defining figure, then jazz was, as Bud Freeman used to argue, born in Chicago in the 1920s. Gerry Mulligan was born with jazz, just before the big-band era.

The big-band era lasted roughly ten years, from 1936 to 1946, when the major orchestras began to disband. If you want to push it back to the 1920s, with Whiteman, Goldkette, and early Ellington, then it is longer. And its influence persists, with the fundamental format of trumpets, trombones, saxophones, and rhythm section still in use. The evolution of that instrumentation is like that of the string quartet or the symphony orchestra: it works, and will live on. But as a vital part of America's commercial entertainment, the era has long since ended.

It was an era, as Woody Herman used to say, when "jazz was the popular music of the land."

Many years ago, Gerry said to me that the wartime gasoline tax had helped kill the big bands. And a thought occurred to me: I said, "Wait a minute, Gerry, the kids who supported the bands didn't have cars, and since they weren't making them during the war, our fathers certainly were not inclined to lend theirs." And it was precisely during the war years that the bands were most successful, even though many of the best musicians were in the armed forces. The dance pavilions and ballrooms were packed during those years with teenagers and uniformed servicemen and their girlfriends.

How did we get to the ballrooms and dance pavilions? On street railways and the inter-urban trolleys. And the street railways and trolley lines were bought up and dismantled by business elements whose purpose was to drive the public into automobiles and buses: this helped kill the ballrooms.

And network radio was dying as the broadcasting industry discovered how awesomely lucrative television advertising could be, and to the purpose of attracting ever larger audiences began seeking the lowest common denominator of public taste.

When the big-band era ended and the musicians went into nightclubs to play in small groups, their admirers followed them, for they were now over 21 and could go to places where liquor was served. But a younger audience could not follow them. A few nightclubs tried to solve the problem. Birdland had a bleachers section where young people could sit without drinking liquor. But this was at best a Band-aid, if you'll pardon the pun, and knowing the names of the musicians was no longer an "in" thing for young people. They were turning at first to "How Much Is That Doggie in the Window" and "Tennessee Waltz," then to "Blue Suede Shoes" and "Hound Dog." The Beatles were coming.

The exposure of jazz to a new, young audience was restricted. Thus you will find that by far the largest part of its audience today comprises older people. There are some young admirers, to be sure, and they always give one hope. But the music is hard to find; they must seek it out. It is no longer common in the culture. It is not on the radio in most areas. And fewer and fewer radio stations are presenting jazz. When I met Gerry Mulligan in 1960, he was only 33 years old. I know lists are boring, but I would ask you to read this one: Pepper Adams, Nat and Cannonball Adderley, Gene Ammons, Benny Bailey, Dave Bailey, Chet Baker, Kenny Barron, Keter Betts, Ruby Braff, Bob Brookmeyer, Ray Brown, Ray Bryant, Monty Budwig, Larry Bunker, Kenny Burrell, Frank Butler, Donald Byrd, Conte Candoli, Frank Capp, Ron Carter, Paul Chambers, Sonny Clark, Jimmy Cleveland, Jimmy Cobb, Al Cohn, John Coltrane, Junior Cook, Bob Cranshaw, Bill Crow, Kenny Davern, Arthur Davis, Miles Davis, Richard Davis, Alan Dawson, Willie Dennis, Gene DiNovi, Eric Dolphy, Lou Donaldson, Kenny Drew, Allen Eager, Jon Eardley, Don Ellis, Booker Ervin, Bill Evans, Art and Addison Farmer, Joe Farrell, Victor Feldman, Maynard Ferguson, Clare Fischer, Tommy Flanagan, Bob Florence, Chuck Flores, Med Flory, Carl Fontana, Vernel Fournier, Russ Freeman, Dave Frishberg, Curtis Fuller, Stan Getz,

Benny Golson, Urbie Green, Gigi Gryce, Jim Hall, Slide Hampton, Herbie Hancock, Jake Hanna, Roland Hanna, Barry Harris, Hampton Hawes, Louis Hayes, Jimmy and Tootie Heath, Billy Higgins, Bill Holman, Paul Horn, Freddie Hubbard, Dick Hyman, Frank Isola, Chuck Israels, Ahmad Jamal, Clifford Jordan, Richie Kamuca, Connie Kay, Wynton Kelly, Charlie Kennedy, Jimmy Knepper, Lee Konitz, Teddy Kotick, Steve Kuhn, Steve Lacy, Scott LaFaro, Pete La Roca, Lou Levy, Mel Lewis, Melba Liston, Booker Little, Dave McKenna, Jackie McLean, Mike Mainieri, Junior Mance, Johnny Mandel, Herbie Mann, Warne Marsh, Don Menza, Jymie Merritt, Billy Mitchell, Blue Mitchell, Dwike Mitchell, Grover Mitchell, Red Mitchell, Hank Mobley, Grachan Moncour, J. R. Monterose, Buddy Montgomery, Jack Montrose, Joe Morello, Lee Morgan, Sam Most, Paul Motian, Dick Nash, Oliver Nelson, Jack Nimitz, Sal Nistico, Marty Paich, Horace Parlan, Sonny Payne, Gary Peacock, Duke Pearson, Ralpha Peña, Art Pepper, Walter Perkins, Charlie Persip, Oscar Peterson, Nat Pierce, Al Porcino, Bill Potts, Benny Powell, Seldon Powell, André Previn, Joe Puma, Gene Quill, Jimmy Raney, Frank Rehak, Dannie Richmond, Larry Ridley, Ben Riley, Red Rodney, Mickey Roker, Sonny Rollins, Frank Rosolino, Roswell Rudd, Willie Ruff, Bill Russo, Don Sebesky, Bud Shank, Jack Sheldon, Sahib Shihab, Wayne Shorter, Horace Silver, Andy Simpkins, Zoot Sims, Jack Six, Jimmy Smith, Victor Sproles, Alvin Stoller, Frank Strazzeri, Ira Sullivan, Grady Tate, Arthur Taylor, Toots Thielemans, Edmund Thigpen, Bobby Timmons, Cal Tjader, Ross Tompkins, Cy Touff, Nick Travis, Stanley Turrentine, McCoy Tyner, Leroy Vinnegar, Cedar Walton, Wilbur Ware, Randy Weston, Bob Wilber, Phil Wilson, Jimmy Woode, Phil Woods, Reggie Workman, Eugene Wright, and Leo Wright. What do they have in common? They were all actively performing in the United States in 1960, the year I met Gerry. And they were *all* under the age of 35. And that is by no means a complete list.

Max Roach, Sonny Stitt, Terry Gibbs, Sarah Vaughan, Paul Desmond, and Shorty Rogers were 36, and other major figures, such as Dave Brubeck, Milt Jackson, and John Lewis were under 40. Indeed, if you add to the list all those under 40 who were at the peak of their powers, factor in all those who were not well known to a national public, such as Gene Allen, Wayne Andre, and Phil Bodner, all the excellent jazz players of Chicago, such as Jodie Christian, Eddie Higgins, and Larry Novak, whose names have never made it into the encyclopedias, and then remember that almost all the pioneering and founding figures, including Duke Ellington, Count Basie, Don Redman, Benny Carter, and Earl Hines, as well as such lesser figures as Frank Signorelli, were alive, you see that the depth of jazz in the United States in that year was astounding. The problem is that we took it for granted, and looked on genius as a commonplace.

By comparison, the current jazz revival is very shallow indeed and merely imitative. This is not to say that there are no excellent young players. But none of these figures is original, and whereas the Ellington music was a constant adventure in innovation and the bands of the 1940s were ceaselessly pushing into the future, all that is now embalmed in jazz repertory programs that concentrate on the music and styles of the past. The jazz of the past has become, truly, a classical music, disinterred from its original context.

You start to wonder if jazz has at last run its creative course, as Oscar Peterson a few years ago predicted it soon would. Not that the new reconstituted food doesn't contain nourishment for a younger audience that is just now discovering jazz. But it hasn't much savor to those who grew up in its great age of innovation and remember its unmistakable individualists. And Gerry Mulligan lived through almost the entire history of jazz. It is against that background that he should be understood.

To jazz musicians, of course, the question "Where is jazz going?" has always been anathema. But a new question arises: "Where has jazz gone?" I put it to Gerry. He replied: "Where jazz has gone relates to where the country has gone. It's pretty hard to separate the progress of one without taking the other into consideration.

"There are a number of things going on in our society that we wonder how they're going to turn out. We have no way of knowing what the effects are because we've become a society of guinea-pigs, trying out new technologies. We've had a whole century of it, and God knows where we are. A rather precarious psychic state. By that I mean the numbers of things that have changed, not just in the ways people live but in the ways their minds work.

"I've been conscious of it lately because, doing university level courses of jazz history, I've found it's very hard to get people to imagine the world that musicians inhabited in 1910 as compared to now. It's hard for people to imagine how different everyone's life was, how life must have been before there was artificial music being thrown at them from every side. All along the way, there were the good and bad accumulations of the various technologies and the industries that grew out of them and the effects that they've had. Many of the effects of the phonograph record and radio were the very elements that made jazz develop the way it did; they probably were responsible for making it into an art form and not just being forgotten as an offshoot of popular music, something of a passing character.

"There were, even early in the century, statements that jazz was immoral and would lead to the breakdown of society as we know it." He laughed. "Listen, with the outcome we see, the state of our popular music, they may well have been right.

"However, I make a big distinction between what jazz was and is and what's going on in popular music.

"At this end of the game, where big business is involved with exploiting whatever available audiences there are – and you usually start with the kids now – they've affected people's thinking about what music is, what music should do, how music should be used, and what music sounds like. So, unless you take the one into consideration, you can't figure out the other.

"Sometimes, of course, I wonder if it's just the usual generational sour grapes. A young generation comes along and they tend to put down what you're doing. You look at 'em with a kind of jaundiced eye and say, 'Well, young whipper-snappers, in my day they said jazz was an immoral music and now they're saying it about rock.' After you examine that, one has to carry through to what has happened to the content and the intent of popular music. Two elements come to mind. One is the music itself, which, a great deal of the time, as you know if you ever see MTV, is calculated as a destructive force, breaking down the good old enemies, the middle class, the bourgeoisie, and all of those causes of all our troubles. It's a music that's based on raw emotion, or at least the illusion of raw emotion. This is very prevalent in that music, easy ecstasy. There's the matter of volume: if you do it loud enough it sounds like you're having fun. And distortion. The day that somebody discovered the intensity that happens to the sound of a guitar when you overamplify it, they created a new world of easy access to excitement. You don't have to work for it, you don't have to think about it, you don't have to develop a craft, man. It's there, it's built into the vacuum tubes and the transistors. The equipment.

"Then there is the actual content of the words. We see a couple of generations that have grown up on a dissatisfaction, a disaffection, with the society that produced them. You only have to watch sitcoms to realize that the parents are always bumbling idiots and the children are all smart-talking, wise-cracking little bastards. So we've got an odd view of what our culture is and should be. These forces don't give a damn. The people who are exploiting our kids don't care about the effect. In fact they'll fight to the death to prove to you that violence on television doesn't have anything to do with violence in the streets.

"If people are so busy convincing themselves of nonsense like that, how can you persuade them to assume responsibility for anything? This has become the key to our time. It's always: 'It's not my fault.' We have become a nation of victims. It's always somebody else's damn fault. This is what has led to all this political correctness crap. You mustn't hurt anybody's feelings! Bullshit, man. What has that got to do with the real world?"

"The television people," I said, "try to convince you that their commercials can alter public behavior by selling products, but the entertainment part of their programming can't. It's a contradiction in their position. It's nonsense."

"Well," Gerry said, "there's a lot of the texture of our social structure that is just as contradictory. This is why you can't say what is going to happen to jazz without observing the society that produces it.

"There are a couple of things that have come out of the educational things I have done. I've been very interested to learn how it appears to other people, usually younger than I am. People come to some of these college classes because they want to go to school or they're interested in the subject. But a lot of it has to do with students who are looking for an easy credit." He laughed.

"It's fascinating to see how people react to their own time, to see how aware they are that they're being ripped off, to see whether anything can be done about it, or to contemplate the future. There is a lot of questioning about where we're going. We see immense changes going on in the United States and don't know what to make of it all.

"One thing I do know: in the States, people are terribly insular. Jazz musicians, a lot of us, travel around the world a lot, so we see a great deal more of the world than the average Statesider. We come home and realize that people have a very, very unrealistic view of the world. We're politically awfully naïve, and we are being manipulated at all points by the press and various other special-interest groups. It's an oddity. I don't know whether to worry about the suppression and repression from the right or the left or whether just to accept them both as the enemy equally and try to protect my niche in the middle. Because I know that I am the enemy. Anyone who walks the middle ground is gonna have very strong enmity from both sides."

I mentioned that Nat Hentoff had written a new book whose subtitle is: "How the left and the right relentlessly censor each other."

Gerry said, "That's interesting that a writer like Nat should arrive at that, because when he was first writing, he was very much a writer of the left. My feeling was always: I don't care what color the uniform is and I don't care whether your ideology is leftist or rightist, man, when you come around and tell me what I can and can't do, it amounts to the same thing. I don't care if you're beating me up in the name of Lenin or Hitler, it hurts with the same kind of bruise."

I said, "I met someone to whom that actually happened, a Hungarian symphony conductor, I can't think of his name. He told me, 'I've had my nose broken twice, once by the Nazis and once by the Communists, and it felt exactly the same both times.'"

"Perfect. I sometimes wonder if this is why Americans have dedicated themselves to such sloppy dress. Dress styles today have gotten to the point of grotesque. A lot of these things, it's very hard for me to get a grasp on. You read the expensive magazines and you see the advertisements of the expensive companies. Giorgio Armani, he's got these beautiful young men lying out on the beach – with torn jeans! Wait a minute, man? What are you trying to sell here?"

"Torn jeans," I said.

"Anything to be *in!*" Gerry said. "It's a peculiar time. But then I wonder what it must have been like to live through some of the strange transition periods of cities or countries. Germany in the '20s must have been an insane place to be. And then in the '30s, the insanity came out of the closet. There have been a lot of times like that, the idiocies. Look at Bosnia. What must it be like for intelligent people to live through this? Or Argentina under the colonels? We've had such insane things happen in the world. And I wonder why. Why? Why do people want to do that to each other?

"The Puritans of New England would meet strangers at the city limits, and if they were Quakers or Catholics, they'd grab them and put them to the stake, because they were heretics. And always with the admonition, 'I'm going to burn you at the stake, but understand, this is for your own good.'"

I said, "You've got the same thing with the anti-abortion people on an overpopulated planet, what I call the kill-for-life crowd."

"Absolutely!" Gerry said. "It's taking on the kind of ridiculous stature that one would expect. This is why the whole movement for political correctness is a dangerous thing.

"It is the justification of the suppression of other people's rights and opinions in what appears to them to be a good cause. And I say, 'Whatever reason you burn me at the stake, I'm sorry, the cause is not good enough.'"

I said, "We can't talk about jazz alone, I agree. We have to talk about the evolution of the big bands, the movie industry, network radio, which were all interlinked. Bands on radio, bands in the movies, playing songs from Broadway shows. Network radio, which young people today cannot grasp, was a major linking force in the American culture . . . "

"Absolutely," Gerry said.

" . . . whereas later, disc jockey radio became a force of destruction."

"Absolutely. That's exactly what I'm talking about. The effect of radio in the early days, when it was still struggling to find its audience and find itself, was good. But the man who invented Top Forty radio . . . "

"Todd Storz of New Orleans," I said.

"I'd rather not know his name," Gerry said. "I'd rather think of him as someone anonymous hanging by this thumbs somewhere."

"No, he's probably swinging in a penthouse. Or a mansion."

"It's rather remarkable," Gerry said. "He succeeded in destroying radio and music with one idea."

When I was at *Down Beat*, I met all the founding figures of jazz, most of whom were still alive. I had conversations with Duke Ellington, Coleman Hawkins, Don Redman, Ben Webster, Benny Carter, and many more. But Gerry not only knew them all, he recorded with a great many of them. What

Gerry and I know of early jazz history comes largely from the people who made it.

I said, "When our generation is gone, there will be no more direct oral links. Future writers will be getting it all from secondary sources, such as newspaper and magazine clippings and previous books, some of the material very unreliable and sometimes downright wrong."

Gerry said: "I remember John Lewis and I walking down 55th Street one day. We'd just left Gil Evans' place. John said, 'Gerry, there's one thing you've got to understand. Jazz as you and I know it and love it will die with our generation.' And I of course reacted with indignation, saying, 'How can you say that, John?' He just smiled like the sphinx and said, 'Remember this. We grew up playing with these men. We've had the chance to sit and play with them as professionals, we traveled with them, we know them, and knew how they thought and arrived at it. After we're gone, it will all be hearsay and records.'"

I said, "Bill Crow told me once that the older musicians told him that on record sessions in the 1920s, drummers had to back off, because if they played hard, it would jump the cutting needle. So we can't really know how those rhythm sections sounded live."

"Sure," Gerry said. "Because of these lectures I've been giving, I've been doing a lot of listening to old things, in some cases to records I'd never heard before. I've become very conscious of what those drummers were doing. A lot of those dates through the '20s were done with brushes, brushes on a telephone book, anything to make an illusion of propulsion without knocking the needle off track. You seldom could hear the bass, which is mostly, I think, why the guys used tuba or bass saxophone, 'cause they had to be heard."

"Rollini, for one."

"Rollini was already into something else. He was a line player. I didn't remember hearing him. I probably did when I was a kid, because I listened to all those bands on the radio every night, and Rollini played with a couple of bands I remember hearing. But later on I had a record of Red Nichols' band, with Jimmy Dorsey on clarinet, Miff Mole on trombone, Adrian Rollini on bass sax, Joe Sullivan on piano, and I think it was Davey Tough on drums. There were two sides of an old ten-inch that Jon Eardley gave me. He said his father had made a copy for me. And it was 'The Battle Hymn of the Republic.' The first side starts out as a slow thing, with Joe Sullivan playing it as a kind of a blues piece. And you turn it over and they take it up and make it into a swing piece. And Adrian Rollini plays an entrance to his chorus on it, which knocked me over, because it sounds so much like an entrance of Charlie Parker's on 'Blues for Norman,' recorded on one of the Granz tours." Gerry sang the Parker passage. "It was almost the same phrase that Adrian had played on that record."

"Do you think he might have heard it?"

"That could be, because Bird was all ears when he was a kid."

"He said he hired Chet Baker because his playing reminded him of Bix."

"I loved Louis's comment when he heard Bix. I have to paraphrase. He said they were aiming for the same thing. Which seemed very odd to people, because their styles were so totally different."

I said, "Everybody talks about how pretty Bix played. But he had a real sting on the edge of his tone."

"Oh yeah. But we can only have the impression we get from the records. This is something I was very conscious of, listening to the records he made with Frankie Trumbauer. Those were intricate arrangements. And they were intended to be – highly sophisticated music. And again, they suffered because they had to hold the rhythm section back. So it's likely that those things neither sounded nor felt quite the way they do on the records. Bix's sense of style and form alone were obviously unique. I would love to have heard his sound.

"You know, Bird had an incredible ability to sail through pretty complicated progressions, especially if the progressions were going somewhere – not just a sequence of chords, but a true progression. I was listening to some Tatum records the other day and it suddenly dawned on me: I wonder how much time Bird spent listening to Tatum? Because Tatum could do that. He could do the *damnedest* transitions, and the damnedest alterations. It will make your hair stand on end! And even when he was doing it fast, it was such a remarkable sounding thing.

"Bird had a tremendous amount of facility in a lot of directions. He had so much facility, I've always thought he really didn't know what to do to survive. He didn't know how to be a beginner again. He needed to move on from where he was. It wasn't satisfying enough. And he became more and more frustrated. He loved a lot of different kinds of music. He loved things like Debussy's *Children's Corner*. Whenever he would come by Gil's place, he would want to listen to some parts of the *Children's Corner*."

"I was told he loved Prokofiev's *Scythian Suite*."

"Oh God yes! We were *all* hooked on the *Scythian Suite*. It was the Chicago Symphony, and it was a dynamite recording of it. It's a wonderful, dynamic piece. It was a youthful piece of Prokofiev's. There are a few pieces that different composers wrote around the time *The Rite of Spring* was written, but so much has been said about the outrage caused by *The Rite of Spring*, this supposedly chaotic music, that people didn't pay much attention to other pieces. And I think the *Scythian Suite* is one of those. But it's a piece that just swings relentlessly from beginning to end. It has a momentum, a forward propulsion to it, through all the movements, through tempo changes and everything. And that particular recording was very good. I've heard a lot of recordings of it since then, but it's impossible to get that one any more. Every time I see a recording of it, I buy it. But I'm always disappointed. I say, 'That's the wrong tempo!' One man's opinion."

And he laughed at himself, as he was wont to do.

If some of those in the audience now in its forties, growing jaded with a rock-and-roll that has now survived for 40 years – four times as long as the big-band era – are discovering jazz and saying "Oh wow!" to young players whose every influence Mulligan and other older jazz musicians can instantly detect, that's all right. Imitative jazz will doubtless continue for some time.

But Gerry's generation lived through an era of innovators, Hines and Tatum and Wilson and Cole and Powell and Evans, Hawkins and Webster and Young, Armstrong and Berigan and James and Dizzy and Miles, Redman and Carter and Sauter and Evans, each with a thumbprint you could not miss. The experienced ear can detect Benny Carter in two bars; no one of the new generation has that kind of individuality.

I try to resist thinking about the 1960s, but sometimes I can't help it, and I remember all the friends Gerry and I have lost, including Zoot and Mel Lewis and Nick Travis and Willie Dennis, all of whom were in Gerry's Concert Jazz Band.

When I wrote a piece about the end of the big-band era, which is in my book *Singers and the Song*, I used a phrase of Johnny Mercer's "Early Autumn" lyric. I called it "Pavilion in the Rain."

This essay, Gerry told me later, caused him to write a tune he called "I Heard the Shadows Dancing." Then Nancy Marano told Gerry she wanted to record the tune. Gerry called and asked me to put a lyric on it. And so I did. I remembered seeing abandoned pavilions on beaches and in parks, where the ferris wheels no longer turned. I used those images in it.

Gerry was even slimmer than in his youth, but he wore a beard, and the strawberry blond hair had gone as white as paper. Did he have regrets? Who doesn't? I daresay he regretted that he and Miles Davis never got to do the tour they had planned to perform the *Birth of the Cool* music. Miles got sick, precluding it, and Gerry toured without him.

Another regret, apparently, was our abandoned Diamond Jim Brady project. A few years ago I asked if he still had the music. He had lost it. The lyrics? I lost them. The script? Gone.

"We should have finished it," he said on the phone one day.

Other regrets?

"I wish I'd gone to music school."

Then, in early November 1995, Gerry's current quartet went on a jazz cruise of the Carribean on the SS *Norway*. For months rumors had been circulating that his health was failing rapidly. I heard he was undergoing chemotherapy in Boston. Gerry would tell me it was for treatment of a liver condition consequent of a case of hepatitis years ago.

Phil Woods was on the cruise, performing in the same week as Gerry's group. Phil and Gerry had had their collisions, both of them being very crusty Irishmen. Gerry once hired and fired Phil on the same evening, and at one point he called Phil an Irish drunk, which infuriated Phil at the time. As Phil said to me on the ship, "Talk about the pot calling the kettle green!" (In recent years, neither of them drank anything at all.) They reconciled, of course, and Phil is on the 1992 *Re-birth of the Cool* album Gerry did. Phil also said on the ship: "I love Gerry."

Johnny Mandel came along as a passenger, just to hang with his friends, and the week developed into that, a hangout of Mandel, Phil, Gerry, and me. But Gerry was very weak. His skin now had a transparent look: the veins in his hands stood out quite blue. And he was in a wheelchair much of the time, using a cane the rest of it.

There is a theater on that ship that I don't particularly like. It gives me what Woody Herman used to call the clausters. But I could not miss Gerry's performance there. He hobbled on-stage and sat on a stool. And the quartet began to play. It was one of the finest groups Gerry ever led. And it was some of the finest and most inventive playing I ever heard from Gerry in the 36 years of our friendship, not to mention the years long before we met, when his LPs were high on the list of my favorite records.

The rapport of the group was amazing, particularly Gerry's telepathic communication with the outstanding pianist Ted Rosenthal. I was in awe of what I heard. It had a compositional integrity beyond anything I have ever heard in jazz. From anyone. I do not know what was going on in Gerry's mind, perhaps the atmospheric awareness of his mortality. It is not that his playing was abandoned, although it certainly was free: it was as if he had a total control of it that he had been seeking all his life. There was one piece that he played in which the byplay with Rosenthal left me with my jaw hanging down. I don't even know its name; one of Gerry's pieces. For certainly he was one of the greatest composers in the history of jazz, as well as its primary baritone soloist. Yes, I have known other baritone players who soloed well; but none of them had Gerry's immense compositional knowledge and instinct. So exquisite was the structure of what he, and bassist Dean Johnson and drummer Ron Vincent did, that, afterwards, I told him, "Gerry, I am not sure that this should any longer be called jazz. It seems to be some kind of new end-of-the-century improvised classical music." Franca told me later that he quoted that with pleasure several times.

There were to be two performances by the group that evening. Leaving the theater, I ran into Phil Woods and Johnny Mandel. Both of them felt as I did: they couldn't endure a second performance. Such was the tearing of emotions in two directions: ecstasy at the level of Gerry's music and agony at the frailty of his health. Next day he asked us all to come by his room. And we went up to the top deck. Gerry was never enamored of the sun: with his blond, now white, eyelashes, its glare bothered him. But we went up, and I took a camera. Franca photographed the four of us. There were days in the 1960s when you could have found the four of us together in Jim and Andy's bar in New York, one of the favorite hangouts of jazz musicians in the 1960s. Mandel and Gerry had been friends since they were habitués of that Gil Evans pad on West 55th Street. As Franca took the pictures, I think we were thinking the same thing, that the four of us would never be together again.

On New Year's Eve, the last evening of 1995, he was cheerful and said he was feeling well and lectured me a little about taking care of my own health. Had I been fully alert, I would have realized that that call – warm and affectionate, more overtly so than was typical of Gerry – was a farewell. I later learned he had called Bill Holman, Johnny Mandel, and other friends about the same time.

On the morning of 20 January 1996, I received a telephone call from Franca. When I heard her voice, with its slight Italian accent, I asked, "How's Gerry?"

And Franca said quite softly, "Gerry's dead." She paused for a breath, then said, "He died a few hours ago." As she told me later, he slipped away between 10.45 p.m. and 11 p.m. on the night of 19 January.

I burst into tears at her words. Yes, yes, I should have known. He had been lying to all of us. Why didn't Gerry admit to his friends us that he had liver cancer? Perhaps he wanted no sympathy. When our close friend Paul Desmond was terminally ill with cancer, Gerry had kept me posted on his condition. It seems that all the highways to New York City's main airports run past cemeteries, and Paul left orders that he be cremated, saying with that sardonic wit of his that he didn't want to be a monument on the way to the airport. Perhaps Gerry didn't want to hear the hushed voice of solicitous inhibition in conversations with his friends. Whatever his reasons, he didn't reveal his true condition, and so I was at the same moment quite unsurprised and totally surprised by her news. Certainly I was shattered, and it was for more reasons than the loss of a friend. As you grow older, you get, if not inured, at least accustomed to such tidings.

But she had lost her husband, and I tried to control my feelings out of concern for her. Then she said, "Gerry always thought of you as his brother. He would say, 'I have to talk to Gene about this. He'll know what I mean.'" And that only made matters worse; I cried quite helplessly after that. I wanted to get off the phone, but Franca wanted to talk, and the least I could do was listen.

She told me something Gerry had said to her that will remain with me as long as I live. He said, "A life without ethics is meaningless."

Gerry could be feisty; and he did not suffer fools gladly. But he was at heart a kind, warm man.

The best evaluation of Gerry that I saw in print after he died was a column by Robert Fulford in the *Globe and Mail*. He noted that Gerry's "boyish eagerness" made him always eager to participate in whatever kind of jazz was being played, and quoted Whitney Balliett's wonderful remark that Gerry would "sit in with a treeful of cicadas."

Fulford wrote of the first Mulligan quartet's "inventive charm and rueful humor." He said:

Over about seven years, the Mulligan quartets demonstrated that there were more possibilities in jazz than anyone had imagined, not all of them necessarily momentous. His own tunes were amiably sophisticated essays, musical equivalents of James Thurber's stories or Ogden Nash's poems. The sounds Mulligan made colored their era. And when I heard the original records . . . four days ago, they sounded as fresh as they did more than four decades ago.

Gerry Mulligan . . . was a catalyst, a splendid performer who was also the cause of splendid performances by others. John Lewis . . . once remarked that Mulligan's influence was so vast and general that it became hard to spot. It melted into the music of the time, became part of the climate.

Yes. What began with Gil went out to the whole world. Including Brazil.

On that New Year's Eve 1995, Gerry told me how much he loved my lyric to "I Hear the Shadows Dancing." "It makes me cry," he said. The lyric is about the vanished big-band era that nurtured and shaped him.

On 12 February 1996, a memorial service was held in New York at Saint Peter's Church. It was titled *A Celebration of the Life of Gerry Mulligan*. Many of his old friends and musical associates, including Clark Terry, John Lewis, Chico Hamilton, Dave Grusin, Jackie and Roy Kral, Art Farmer, Bill Crow, Dave Bailey, Lee Konitz, and more, performed. George Shearing and Dave Brubeck, with whom Gerry had often toured, played piano solos. The speakers included George Wien, Herb Gardner, Elliot Lawrence, and Alan and Marilyn Bergman.

I couldn't be there. Franca arranged that the last song Gerry and I wrote be performed, the lyric he told me on New Year's Eve made him cry. It was sung by Annette Saunders, accompanied by Ted Rosenthal on piano. I realized later that I had written it on 13 February 1991, five years and one day earlier. The lyric goes:

A ferris wheel abandoned,
a silent roller coaster,
a peeling carousel
whose painted horses revolve no more.

Within a grove of willows,
in shadows made by moonlight,
a dance pavilion dreams,
its shutters fastened, the music gone.

It dreams of bygone dancers
who filled the floor with motion
and fell in love to songs
that almost no one remembers now.

The ferris wheel reverses,
the carousel runs backwards.
The horses start to prance,
the roller coaster begins to roar.

Then softly from a distance
the blended sound of trumpets,
and saxophones and drums.
A wondrous music returns and then
I hear the shadows dancing once again.

7

The pioneer:
Bill Challis

The roads of eastern Pennsylvania tend to run west-southwest, in conformity to the contours of the land. They slip down the valleys between the long ridges of the Appalachians, the Blue Mountains, and the Tuscaroras. The Susquehanna River, in the upper part of the state, wiggles a path to the southeast for a while, but then it gives up about halfway between Scranton and Wilkes-Barre and follows the imperative of the mountains and, finally, having picked up some strength from the added waters of the Juniata, reasserts its will and swings back on a southeast course near Harrisburg and empties into Chesapeake Bay in Maryland.

Even the little roads, and indeed particularly the little roads, follow these contours of the land. The modern freeways, of course, reflect man's passion for imposing straight lines on the planet, but the characteristic back roads of eastern Pennsylvania run as they do because of the mountains.

It is only at first discovery that one is surprised at the number of musicians who came from this part of the country; on examination, one discovers a reason for it. But produce them it did: Fuzzy Farrar, Russ Morgan, the Dorsey brothers, Les Brown and his brothers, and somewhat to the north, in New York State, the trombonist Spiegle Willcox.

Bill Challis is from this part of the country, both in Wilkes-Barre on 8 July 1904. *The New Grove Dictionary of Jazz* devotes a short biographical entry to him. John Chilton, in his *Who's Who in Jazz*, allots him only nine lines compared with 31 for Doc Cheatham farther down the same page. Leonard Feather's *Encyclopedia of Jazz* fails completely to mention Challis.

Only Digby Fairweather, in *Jazz: The Essential Companion*, takes something close to the measure of the man. "(He) played a central role in creating a style for Paul Whiteman's great orchestra of 1927–1930," Fairweather says, being one of the few writers to give that band its fair due.

Challis's highly (if occasionally determinedly) modernistic arrangements were always charming at least, as well as ingenious, and often much more . . . (It) could be argued that most of Challis's work is much more complex and daring than the contemporary output of (Don) Redman or even Duke Ellington, neither of whom was faced with writing for orchestras as huge as Whiteman's. Even the more contrived moments in Challis's 1920s work are hard to dislike, and his settings for (Bix) Beiderbecke, (Frank) Trumbauer and their brilliant contemporaries are often ravishing.

Bill Challis was not only a major architect of the Whiteman band, he performed the same service for Jean Goldkette and even helped shape the band of Fletcher Henderson. He was one of the pioneers of the saxes-and-brass orchestra out of which the big-band era grew. He is one of the most overlooked and underestimated men in jazz history.

Challis and Russ Morgan were alumni – along with Tommy and Jimmy Dorsey, pianist Itzy Riskin, and lead trumpeter Fuzzy Farrar – of a Pennsylvania dance orchestra called the Scranton Sirens. They knew each other early.

Dance bands were burgeoning all over America to supply the music required by the dance craze catalyzed by Vernon and Irene Castle and their famous black music director, James Reese Europe, after World War I. Given the quality of the musicians who came out of it, the Scranton Sirens must have been a very good band. Not very far to the north, Spiegle Willcox was playing in local bands in pavilions and dance halls.

Challis began writing for the Jean Goldkette band in 1926. His arrangements were far ahead of their time, harmonically and rhythmically, and highly admired by musicians. A strange thing happened to those Challis charts for Goldkette.

The Goldkette arranging staff included Russ Morgan and a violinist named Eddy Sheasby. Sheasby, who at one point shared conducting duties with Frank Trumbauer, was a volatile, temperamental drunk, and even the musicians, tolerant though they often are of human vagary, didn't like him. Something set him off. Nobody seems to know what. In a fit of rage he disappeared just before an important engagement in St. Louis. The band's library, including the Challis arrangements, went with him. Goldkette saw him several years later, but the band's book was never recovered. Its loss contributed to the orchestra's eventual collapse.

When Paul Whiteman hired Challis, he asked the arranger to reconstruct his Goldkette pieces. Challis adapted the charts to Whiteman's larger instrumentation. All the Challis charts for Whiteman are in the Williams College library. In 1975, a Carnegie Hall concert resurrected some of the Goldkette music. Then a young New York bassist named Vince Giordano, who had studied arranging with Challis, urged his mentor to re-create some of his Goldkette charts with their original instrumentation. Withdrawing some of the Whiteman versions of the charts from Williams College, Challis went to work to scale them back down to the size of the Goldkette band, thirteen men. Giordano put together a band to record the material, made up of musicians sympathetic to the music of that earlier era, including Bob Wilber and the late Dick Wellstood. One of the trombonists had a special affinity for the music: Spiegle Willcox had first played it with Goldkette 60 years before.

The resultant album is called *Bill Challis' The Goldkette Project*. It deserves the attention of students of arranging and researchers in the history of jazz.

A reassessment seems inevitable because of the reissue on CDs of all sorts of significant material that has been hidden away for decades. The new technology of sound processing is making it possible to hear details of writing that were previously all but inaudible. In the case of Robert Parker of Australia and latterly of England, he has been able to turn the sound into quite creditable stereo.

One of the discs in the Columbia Records release list is devoted to Bix Beiderbecke, with emphasis on the band called Frankie Trumbauer and His Orchestra, which recorded for OKeh in 1927. Several charts are by Challis, including "Ostrich Walk," from the repertoire of the Original Dixieland Jazz Band, Hoagy Carmichael's "Riverboat Shuffle," "Three Blind Mice (Rhythmic Theme in Advanced Harmony)," and two with the eerily awful vocals of Seger Ellis, "Blue River" and "There's a Cradle in Caroline." The album also contains the famous "Singin' the Blues," whose impact on musicians was comparable to that of Armstrong's "West End Blues." The Columbia annotation attributes this chart to Fud Livingston, but it is the work of Challis. Dan Morgenstern, in his annotation of a Fletcher Henderson reissue on the Bluebird label, attributes the chart to Challis. Furthermore, yet another reconstruction of the chart is heard in *The Goldkette Project*.

One might suggest that Challis, for some obscure reason, lied in claiming the chart was his. But, as we shall see, Challis from his earliest days was a man in whom modest self-effacement amounted almost to a serious defect of character. Challis wouldn't lay claim to what he did do, much less take credit for what he didn't. He says he wrote that chart. It is interesting to compare the original Trumbauer–Beiderbecke 1927 version of the tune on Columbia, a previously unissued take of a 1931 Fletcher Henderson recording of the Challis arrangement (with Rex Stewart reproducing the Bix solo) now out on Bluebird, and the version in *The Goldkette Project*.

The Robert Parker albums include a compilation of New York recordings from the 1920s, one of which is Paul Whiteman's "San," another Challis chart, recorded on 12 January 1928. The CD reissues should also cause a reevaluation of Whiteman, a dartboard for jazz buffs for these many decades. That Paul Whiteman could not play jazz and merely stood there and waved a stick is not necessarily relevant. Dizzy Gillespie has repeatedly attested that Lucky Millinder, who was not a musician, was a first-rate bandleader.

Cab Calloway, a singer, not an instrumentalist, had a crackling great band.

To be sure, Whiteman's band could be ponderous, but not always and cer-
tainly not in all its recordings. The personnel on "San" is only ten men:
Charlie Margulis on trumpet, Beiderbecke on cornet, Bill Rank on trombone,
Jimmy Dorsey on cornet and clarinet, Trumbauer on C-melody saxophone,
Min Leibrook on bass sax, Matty Malneck on violin, Carl Kress on guitar, and
Harold McDonald, drums. The pianist is Challis, who didn't consider piano
his instrument. "San" is a delight to this day, and one of the reasons is the
quality of the writing. And it swings.

There is something else we should note at once about Challis. He was the
man who transcribed the five Bix Beiderbecke piano pieces, "In a Mist,"
"Candlelights," "Flashes," "In the Dark," and "Davenport Blues." Without
him, we would not have those pieces, and perhaps not even Beiderbecke's
piano recording of "In a Mist."

We wouldn't have them without Whiteman, either: Whiteman made the
deal with publisher Jack Robbins to put these pieces out, whereupon Bix and
Challis went to work to get them on paper. Nor would we have the Challis
charts for Goldkette without Whiteman. He was a natural target, with that
rotund face with its pencil mustache, so easily caricatured, and he was later
mocked by the jazz writers for that press agent's title King of Jazz. He was
privately modest on the subject of jazz, but he was a perceptive appreciator
of the music, hired some of its best white players, and made the public pay
some attention to it. I have never met a musician who worked for him, or
even knew him reasonably well, who didn't like and admire him. That
includes Bill Challis, who lives in quiet retirement in the little community of
Harvey's Lake, Pennsylvania.

I passed Scranton on Interstate 81, heading southwest toward Wilkes-Barre,
which is nineteen miles further down the Susquehanna River. My father
worked briefly in one of the coal mines in this area just about the time Challis
left it to write for Goldkette. That was before I was born. He quit – he said the
Pennsylvania mines were terribly unsafe, far below the standards of those in
England – and went back to playing music for a living until the Depression
and the arrival of the talkies dried up the work. My dad said that in those
days, you'd see miners resting on their haunches along the roadside, waiting
for their buses to work in the mornings, the same posture you saw in the
mining country of England and Wales. It's the only way to rest in a narrow
coal seam. It occurred to me on that freeway that my dad may well have
heard the Scranton Sirens.

You don't see miners resting easy on their haunches in Pennsylvania any
more. The pit mines are gone; the coal is extracted by the ruthlessly efficient
process of strip mining.

It wasn't just the reissue of so many records with Challis charts that had set me on this quest into coal country. His name had been coming up more and more. Then Hank Jones expressed the view that Bix had exerted an influence on arrangers through Challis. And Benny Carter, who first wrote for Fletcher Henderson probably in 1926, when Challis was with Goldkette, had said to me in New York, "Bill Challis and Frank Trumbauer were my idols."

That alone gave him significance.

I pulled off at Wilkes-Barre, passed through the city, and headed out into the country, following directions from Evan Challis, Bill's younger brother, keeper of the flame and family historian. Evan pronounces his name "Even." He says there are two pronunciations of the name in Wales. The family is Welsh on the mother's side, Huguenot on the father's. Thus the name Challis is French.

I arrived at Harvey's Lake. It is a little lake, ringed by a road and rows of summer houses and boat docks. It was deserted on this April afternoon, not a boat in sight. I could not find the house. Bill Challis lived with Evan and Evan's wife Elizabeth. I telephoned and at last found the address.

In a camel-hair topcoat, almost shyly holding up his hand to tell me I had come to the right place, he stood on the front porch, overlooking the road perhaps 30 feet below the house, and the lake that shone beyond it. As I climbed the steps and looked back, I saw, beyond the lake, among the houses that rim it, the skeletal form of a roller-coaster, from which no happy screams have emanated in years; it is abandoned. To anyone who grew up along the Great Lakes, as I did, a lake is a body of water you can't see across, and this one, Harvey's Lake, is a mere puddle, a postage stamp of water, narrow and a couple of miles or so long. Still, a sign by the highway as you approach it proclaims it the largest natural lake in Pennsylvania. It is not the largest in area but in terms of content of water: it is very deep.

Once upon a time, when you could get here on the inter-urban electric trolley from Wilkes-Barre, there were three dance pavilions around its rim, and two more between the two communities, five in all. But the trolley was long ago dismantled, the pavilions died, and the sounds of bands no longer drift across this water in the evenings. Bill Challis played C-melody saxophone in bands that worked these pavilions. He was in high school then.

At the top of the stairs, I shook hands with him, having the curious sense – this happened when I met Rudolph Friml, too – that I was touching history. In Friml's case, the thought occurred to me that his hand had shaken that of Dvorak, which had shaken that of Liszt, which had shaken that of Beethoven, which had shaken that of Mozart. I was five handshakes from Mozart. In the case of Challis, I have no idea how many he shook hands with. Certainly with Fletcher Henderson and Bix. And no doubt Rex Stewart and Coleman Hawkins on the night of the legendary confrontation of the

Goldkette and Henderson bands at Roseland. I looked into a face with clear skin, thinning white hair and, inside the one lens of his bifocal glasses, a dark eye-patch. As I learned, the sight in the right eye was going.

The four issues from April to July 1929, of the British journal *Melody Maker* presented an extended analysis by Al Davison of Paul Whiteman's recording of "Sweet Sue," a Challis arrangement. Davison, whose prose was tortuous, wrote that

> modern rhythmic music has arrived at a stage where at its best it is worthy of being considered as a form of music which is by no means valueless even when adjudged with the highest of artistic standards in mind. In fact, at such a stage has it arrived that it is plain to see that it is more than likely that shortly the influence of the general atmosphere of modern dance music, and more particularly perhaps the subtleties of interpretation which produce what we broadly term dance rhythm, will have a strong effect on the work of the great master composers of tomorrow.

With notated examples, Davison analysed the orchestrator's harmony, including minor ninth and thirteenth chords, intimations of the whole-tone scale, and his voice-leadings, going through the chart almost bar by bar. The tone of the article, which in total covered eleven pages of the publication, is ecstatic. Bix got a copy of the article. He brought it to Challis and said, "Hey Bill, read this." What Bix had noticed was that Challis' name was never once mentioned: the arrangement was attributed to Ferdé Grofe.

Another man came out of the house to join us. This was Evan Challis, whom I had talked to these several times on the phone. I apologized for the intrusion, but they dismissed this and said, "We want to take you to lunch." And so we left immediately for a little family restaurant part-way back to Wilkes-Barre and sat down amid a clink of dishes and soft string music from the Muzak. A Jobim tune.

Bill was born in Wilkes-Barre on 8 July 1904, Evan on 29 August 1916, the sons of a barber. There were two more boys and a girl in the family, but only Evan and Bill survive. You could sense immediately the friendship between these two brothers.

How did Bill get started writing?

"We had a band here called Guy Hall's Orchestra," Bill said. He spoke softly and slowly. "He wrote 'Johnson Rag.' He wrote a couple of other things too. I was just a kid, in my junior year in high school. He had a guy who played tenor sax in the band. The saxophones were just new. I got a hold of a C-melody sax. I was a good saxophone player. Russ Morgan was around then, nine miles down the road from Wilkes-Barre. He played trombone. Jimmy Dorsey and Tommy too, their father was a teacher."

"They were from the lower coal fields," Evan said. "Shenandoah." Jimmy in fact was born the same year as Bill Challis. Evan said there had always been a strong brass-band tradition in this area.

"I think the miners and their gals used to like to dance," Evan said. "They'd dance at the drop of a hat. Every night, there was a dance with somebody's band playing. In all these towns, Plymouth and Nanticoke and Wilkes-Barre and Scranton. The outside dance pavilions and then, in the winter time the halls, there was dancing going on all the time."

"Where did you study arranging, Bill?" I asked.

"I didn't study. I more or less just picked it up. I was a faker, a real faker. I studied with a fellow here named Fritz Anstette. Czechoslovakian. He taught clarinet. Most of the guys around here that were talking saxophone at the time said, 'Go down to Old Man Anstette.' I went down to him. It was a buck a week or something like that. He had a son who was an oboe player, another son who was a trumpet player, and I think some of the girls played piano.

"He started on me, showed me all about the saxophone. I had a very good tone. I figure he was the one who taught me to develop a tone. Long whole notes and low tones. Sooner or later I came up with a pretty good tone. That's what got me my job with the Scranton Sirens. Russ Morgan was in the band, playing trombone.

"I went with Guy Hall's band. He had five guys. Sometimes he expanded to three trumpets, two trombones, three saxes, and the rhythm section, with string bass, piano, and banjo. Guy was the drummer."

Evan said, "Bill wrote an arrangement of 'Blue Room.' That arrangement had a history. Guy Hall had all those men for an occasion. They'd play the top club in town, the Westmoreland Club, where all the coal barons were members. They'd have a ball there. Playing gigs around town, it was five pieces, but they augmented it for big occasions. Bill wrote the 'Blue Room' arrangement for that larger band. Bill was still going to high school. He'd play summers with Guy Hall."

"We'd play the pavilions around here," Bill said.

"After high school I went to Bucknell, about 65 miles down the river at Lewisburg. I took pre-law. I was going to go to law school at the University of Pennsylvania in Philadelphia.

"At Bucknell I wound up with my own band in my second, third, and fourth years. As the band augmented – and I did my best to augment it – I had to write for the extra instruments.

"The guy who had the band before me had five pieces. In my first year I was the second saxophone. The guy who played trombone doubled on saxophone. When I got the band in my second year, it got to be six guys. Then I got another saxophone player and a trumpet when they came to school. The band began to build up. It got to be three saxophones and trumpet and trombone and piano. We had no bass. Then a guitar player came to school. We did a little rehearsing, putting some tunes together. I had to write out the extra parts for the three saxophones. I wrote for the C-melody, the alto, and the tenor. Then I got another trumpet player and a bass player. So I had a rhythm section, three saxophones and three brass. We wound up with eleven or twelve pieces. It was practically a complete band.

"By my senior year, we had some harmony in the band. It sounded like a bigger band. If necessary, I would write the trombone, which was closest in the register, so that the guy had to play the melody. If we wanted four parts, the saxophones would play the other three. We always had a band that sounded like it had a lot of guys. Itzy Riskin wrote that I was the one who brought that around.

"We played mostly for the girls in the sororities. They squawked a little about raising the price on them, but they paid it, and we had no problem. Each time we got another guy in the band, I had to write the part."

Challis graduated from Bucknell, his mind on going to law school. "I sent in my tuition money," he said. He returned home for the summer and played for Guy Hall, then joined a band led by Dave Harmon out of Williamsport, Pennsylvania. "Dave Harmon's band played battles of music with the Wolverines," Evan said.

"I heard Bix then," Bill said. "I liked him. I didn't know him."

"Jean Goldkette had a lot of bands out in Detroit, including the band at the Book-Cadillac. When I was with the Dave Harmon band, I visited Detroit. I had a brother there, Lew.

"While I was there, these guys I'd played with in the Scranton Sirens, Fuzzy Farrar, Itzy Riskin, and Russ Morgan, were with Goldkette. I talked to Russ. Russ took me over to Charlie Horvath, who was the manager of the band. Russ said to Charlie, 'Why don't you have this guy make a couple of arrangements? He arranges, too.'"

The Goldkette band comprised three trumpets, two trombones, three saxophones, and four rhythm, including banjo. For recordings it used a violin–guitar duo. Goldkette did not lead the band and only occasionally appeared with it. He was a concert pianist by training who organized bands as a business. Whiteman too had several units. There was another band in the Goldkette stable: the stunningly excellent McKinney's Cotton Pickers, whose music director was Don Redman, one of the major architects of big-band jazz arranging.

Bill returned home to Wilkes-Barre, still intent on law school, but he turned in a couple of charts to the Goldkette band. "I made an arrangement of 'Baby Face.' They sorta liked it. They asked me to make another one, so I gave them 'Blue Room.' It was pretty much the one I'd written, updated. The Goldkette band came through Wilkes-Barre. A friend of mine and I went down to the Cinderella Ballroom to hear the arrangements. Bix and Frank Trumbauer had joined the band. The band sounded great. They'd leave open a space for the cornet and saxophone and Bix and Trumbauer would fill it in like you wouldn't believe."

That "Blue Room" chart is in *The Goldkette Project* album. Let's note that Bill said he'd updated it for Goldkette. But in its essential outlines, it was written when Bill was in high school. He graduated from high school in 1921.

"About a week or two later," Bill continued, "I was going to go down to the University of Pennsylvania." He had spent four years at Bucknell, and this was September 1926, the opening of the school year. Bill was 23. "I got a call from Ray Lodwig. He wanted to know if I wanted to join the band. I said, 'I'm going to go to school.' He said, 'Well, we'd like you to join the band.' They wanted me to be the fourth saxophone. They told me to come up to a place in Hillsborough, Massachusetts. The band was staying there. I went up there. I knew a few of the other guys besides Bix and Trumbauer. Spiegle Willcox had joined the band."

In fact, the Goldkette personnel was now remarkable: Fuzzy Farrar, Ray Lodwig, trumpets; Bix Beiderbecke, cornet; Bill Rank and Spiegle Willcox, trombones; Doc Ryker, Don Murray, and Frank Trumbauer, reeds; Itzy Riskin, piano; Howdy Quicksell, banjo; Steve Brown, string bass; Chauncey Morehouse, drums; Joe Venuti, violin; Eddie Lang, guitar; and Paul Mertz, arranger and at times pianist.

Bill continued, "Charlie Horvath told me, 'I can get a million saxophone players. They're a dime a dozen. I only have seven arrangements.' One of the things wrong with the Goldkette band while I was with it, they never had anyone to say, 'I want you to make an arrangement of this or that.' Horvath didn't do it, Goldkette didn't do it. Goldkette didn't even conduct. Ray Lodwig handled the band on the road. We didn't have a systematic way of building up any arrangements."

The 1926 New England sojourn of the Goldkette band has been well documented by Richard Sudhalter and Phillip R. Evans in their biography of Biederbecke, as well as in other books. The promoter, a man named J. A. Lyons, had lodged the band at a place called the Hillcrest Inn, a country house – perhaps what would today be called a bed-and-breakfast establishment – at Hillsborough. The band arrived there on 21 September. It was to play gigs around New England and get ready for an opening on 6 October at the Roseland Ballroom in New York, opposite Fletcher Henderson. Spiegle Willcox has a photo of the band on a wall in his home. The men are seated on the roof of a minibus on the side of which a banner proclaims: "Jean Goldkette Orchestra New England Tour J. A. Lyons Mgr." Wherever the band played during that New England tour, the place was packed with musicians. Such was the band's reputation – and Beiderbecke's.

"Up at Hillcrest, Bix and Trumbauer and I used to take some walks together. I went out on one or two dates to hear the band." No more. That's how little Challis claims for himself. But Richard Sudhalter, whose father, also a musician, several times heard the band during the New England stay, said that the arrangements "that really knocked us out were 'Baby Face' and 'Blue Room,' both of them advanced, beautifully written, and played with enormous spirit." Chip Deffaa, in his book *Voices of the Jazz Age*, wrote,

> Virtually no one had heard this new Goldkette orchestra; it had not yet cut any records; but on (the) New England tour, the band dazzled listeners night after night. And with the hiring of Bill Challis as a full-time arranger, all the pieces came together. Challis's work was downright inspired. His music was graceful, ahead of its time, and he knew how to showcase Beiderbecke and Trumbauer. They played Challis's charts with panache.

Bill said, "We gradually worked our way down into New York and the Roseland Ballroom.

"They said, 'You'll have plenty to do when you get down to New York.' Jesus. It was all, 'Have this out by 8 o'clock.' Most of the tunes I got to do were lousy. Then we'd go down and record: things like 'Hushabye.' It was quite a while before we got a lot of arrangements together."

Lunch ended. Evan and Bill and I left the restaurant to drive back to Harvey's Lake. Bill continued talking in the car.

"When we came to the Roseland, I had made a few arrangements for Goldkette. Fletcher Henderson was opposite us. The story about what kind of trumpet player Bix was was put out by the trumpet players in Fletcher's band. They were sitting in Fletcher's band, Bix was sitting in the Goldkette band. They would have their time up on the stand, and then the Goldkette band would have its set.

"I was there the night it happened. Fletcher had a hell of a band. Don Redman was the arranger and first alto. Rex Stewart was in the Henderson band. Fletcher wanted to exchange arrangements. Ray Lodwig exchanged a few. They listened plenty to Bix. Matter of fact, they tried to get some of our players. They copied a lot from Goldkette."

There was more to it than that. At first the Goldkette band played its commercial material, eliciting titters. Trumbauer, according to Sudhalter, cupped his hands around his mouth, and called to the band, "Okay, boys, let's give 'em the business." They went into "Tiger Rag," then the Challis charts, one after another.

Rex Stewart wrote in his *Jazz Masters of the Thirties*,

> We were supposed to be the world's greatest dance orchestra. And up pops this Johnny-come-lately white band from out in the sticks, cutting us . . . We simply could not compete . . . Their arrangements were too imaginative and their rhythm too strong . . . We learned that Jean Goldkette's orchestra was, without any question, the greatest in the world . . .
>
> You can believe me that the Goldkette band was the original predecessor to any large white dance orchestra that followed, up to Benny Goodman. Even Goodman, swinger that he was, did not come close to the tremendous sound of the Goldkette repertoire, not in quality and certainly not in quantity . . .

And in an interview, Stewart said, "It was pretty humiliating for us, and when the time came for us to go back on, we didn't really know what we should play. They'd covered it all, and they were swingin' like mad. Everything. Bix, for Pete's sake. You know, I worshipped Louis at that time, tried to walk like him, talk like him, even dress like him. He was God to me, and to all the other cats too. Then, all of a sudden, comes this white boy from out west, playin' stuff all his own. Didn't sound like Louis or anybody else. But just so pretty. All that *tone* he got. Knocked us all out."

Fats Waller sat in with Henderson's band that night; Miff Mole sat in with Goldkette. *Orchestra World* wrote, "Most everyone who is anything at all in the music business was present . . . Whoever is responsible for the Goldkette arrangements should be elected to the hall of fame. They are nothing short of marvelous."

The Goldkette boys were anxious to record the Challis charts. It wasn't to be. If we owe it to Whiteman that those arrangements still exist, we owe it to a man named Eddie King – the archetype of the tin-eared record producer – that we do not have the Goldkette performances of them. King didn't like jazz, and he specifically disliked Bix, objecting to his harmonic innovations, his "wrong note" playing. His attitude foreshadowed one that Dizzy Gillespie and Charlie Parker would encounter.

Challis was working hard, turning out charts on tunes King thought would sell, material Bill referred to as "crap."

"Fletcher began to play at Connie's Inn up in Harlem," Bill said. "I was living in Greenwich, Connecticut, then. When I'd go back home to Greenwich, I'd stop in at Connie's Inn. Fletcher and I became good friends. He began to commission some arrangements from me. I wrote a lot for that band. They paid me well. Buster Bailey and Coleman Hawkins and Don Redman and Jimmy Harrison were in the band: it was a great band.

"Don Redman had been the music director of McKinney's Cotton Pickers.

He'd been writing for that band and for Fletcher. He also wrote for the Gold-kette band, and also the Whiteman band.

"Fletcher said, 'I want you to hear this piano player sing.' After the band played a set, they would have this guy play organ or piano and sing. It was Fats Waller.

"After I had been with Goldkette about a year, the word got out that it was going to break up. Whiteman came down to Atlantic City with Bing Crosby. Bix and I were in the band room. Bix asked Whiteman to conduct the band. Whiteman said, 'I don't know any of the arrangements.' I said, 'You don't have to know the arrangements. Just give a down beat.' Bix went up there, and said, 'What do you want to hear?' Whiteman said, '"Tiger Rag."' He turned around to the band, and said, 'One, two . . . ' And Bix started it off. He played the lead. And while he was doing that, who was down at the door? Goldkette. He never stood in front of the band. Very very seldom. I didn't see him, but I was told he was down there watching the whole thing.

"That was our first introduction to Whiteman. He said, 'You can join the band now, if you want. Or you can wait and see how it goes.' Whiteman asked me if I wanted to come directly to the band, or if I wanted to wait around New York. Fuzzy Farrar and some of the guys wanted to wait around New York, do records, and make money. Farrar was a great trumpet player. He could read anything, play anything. He had no trouble finding work. He worked with several bands. But other guys, guys like Ray Lodwig, didn't work much at all.

"Trumbauer and Bix got into a band called the New Yorkers, which was run by Adrian Rollini. That band played at a place called the Whiteman Club, but they were together only about ten days. I went to see Trumbauer and Bix. They were going to join Whiteman when the band got to Indianapolis. They were in the band within a couple of weeks – a very short time. As far as I was concerned, I wasn't in the band yet, but I was traveling around with them. They were playing theaters. While we were in Indianapolis, I think, Jimmy Dorsey took Paul out to wherever Hoagy Carmichael was. They brought Hoagy up to my room. I had a little organ. It belonged to the Whiteman orchestra. They always dumped it in my room, in case I got any ideas. They said, 'I want you to hear this.' Hoagy sits down and plays 'Washboard Blues.'

"Whiteman was taken by it right off. Hoagy sang it and played it on the organ. Hoagy traveled around with us. We got together fairly often, talked. I got to know the tune. Two weeks later, we were in Chicago, and we recorded it. That was my first arrangement for Whiteman. That was the number, and 'Changes,' both my arrangements, that we recorded that day."

We arrived back at the house on Harvey's Lake and settled in a sun porch that overlooks the water. I asked Bill about the Whiteman instrumentation.

As he recalled, there were seven brass – four trumpets and three trombones – and six saxes.

Bill continued, "After that Ferdé [Grofe, Whiteman's chief arranger] gave me a couple of arrangements to do. He gave me 'Old Man River.' I began to get good tunes, nice tunes. And they began to get some nice results. With Goldkette, we weren't an important enough band, it seemed, that we'd get nice tunes to do.

"Bix and I were good friends, but he was a drinker. And I didn't drink." Bix began playing his little piano fantasias for Challis, who was impressed by them.

"He had a very creative mind," Bill said, "and when he played his own music, the second time he played it, he played it differently.

"Paul went to Jack Robbins, the music publisher, about publishing Bix's pieces. Robbins told Bix, 'You have to have this written down, so you have to play it the same way.' Even 'In a Mist,' he played a little differently on the record. I had to insist, when we went over anything, that he play it again, play it again, the same way. We went through all the things that he did, and I'd say, 'Play it the same way again.' We got the things out."

Challis transcribed "In a Mist," "Flashes," "In the Dark," "Candlelights," and one he took off a record, "Davenport Blues." They are all that remain of Bix Beiderbecke's piano inventions.

"The harmonic thinking was radical," Bill said. "It fitted in with what I expected from him. Our thinking was very much alike, harmonically.

"Ferdé was a very good friend of Eastwood Lane's. Bix used to play parts of some of that music over."

I asked, "Is it true that Bix couldn't read? Or that he just read very badly?"

"I think he read badly. I don't say he couldn't read. He'd just sit down and he had to work it out. I would write a chorus for him, or a half chorus. I'd write the harmony. Harmony didn't bother him at all. He could certainly hear it. He knew everything. What the next chord was. And I supplied it to him. The same way with Trumbauer. He could read really, I would say, a little better than Bix. But Bix could read. When he sat down alongside of Fuzzy Farrar and Ray Lodwig, he had no problem following those guys.

"He'd come to a rehearsal. He'd go over the thing. Ferdé would be there. If another trumpet player was there, they'd go over it together. He could read that. No problem reading that. Especially if he was doing it with another guy who could read. He could read some. Some."

Bill made an interesting observation. He said that he had never been too swift a reader, either, adding, "I can't read too well *now*." I have known several composers who wrote with facility but could not read well; Gary McFarland was one of them. Resuming on Bix: "There was always a gin bottle alongside the chair. On the bandstand. Usually a bottle. He didn't get loaded or anything like that. He'd have a nip. Like Harry Barris. He'd take the cork off, put it back down. He'd do that how many times, Jesus.

"He liked guys he could drink with. Frank Trumbauer didn't drink much. Trumbauer was quiet. Bix was a quiet guy too. He certainly was not a talker." (Trumbauer's widow, Mitzi, once amplified on this point. She said, "Frank was an Indian and would never use one word where none would do.")

Bix was listening to Debussy, Stravinsky, Delius, Macdowell, and Eastwood Lane, among others. "He could play most of them by ear," Bill said. "He just did it.

"I'd listen to a couple of things of Bix's and put them in an arrangement."

I remembered what Hank Jones had said about the influence of Beiderbecke on arrangers through his influence on Challis. I wanted to verify the point. "He influenced your arranging?"

"Oh yeah!" Bill said. And you can certainly hear it in the chart on "San." Even in the ensemble passages, he has the band phrasing and thinking like Bix. It is an early and classic example of an arrangement shaped to the abilities of the musicians who are going to play it, rather than generalized ideas of the character of instruments derived from European orchestration treatises. There was no precedent for what Challis, Ellington, Carter, and Redman were doing. They had to explore this form of orchestra, saxes, brass, and rhythm. In "San," we hear true jazz writing, shaped to the idiosyncrasies of the players, and it's brilliant. And it swings.

Bill said, "In those days we did an awful lot with interludes, modulations, and Bix had the whole book, it seemed to me. I don't know where he got that stuff. He knew 'Afternoon of a Faun' backwards."

"What do you think would have become of him if he hadn't died?" I asked. It is a question that has tantalized everyone who has ever given consideration to the short meteoric life of Bix Beiderbecke.

"We talked a lot about writing piano numbers," Bill said. "He wanted to put it down on paper. He wanted to do a lot more than the five numbers."

The days of Bix, Trumbauer, Bill Rank, Venuti and Lang in the lush and largely happy traveling circus that was the Whiteman band, were coming to an end. Whiteman did all that he could for Bix, keeping him on the payroll for many months when Beiderbecke couldn't even play. Whiteman was no puritan about booze, being a toper of proportions himself. But Bix was steadily destroying himself, abetted by hale fellows whose assistance was bitterly resented by Louis Armstrong, among other friends of Bix. "Ain't nobody played like him yet," Armstrong said when Bix was dead. Long afterwards, musicians who knew and admired Bix were protective of him when they were asked about his alcoholism.

"Whiteman started to play a different kind of music," Bill said. "When we went in the band, we made a lot of records. As much as the band played theaters, whenever we'd get the chance, we made records. When we were doing so much recording, Bix and Trumbauer and a lot of the guys were in the band. But when the band started to play concerts and things like that, Bix's spot wasn't so important. It was a lot of written music. And Bix was a great faker. You'd write the background for him, and all he had to do was hear the harmony and know the tune.

"Oh. He was the greatest. All the way around."

"The band broke up in 1930, wasn't it?" I said. "The Depression was on, and Whiteman was having financial problems, and fired a whole bunch of guys."

"I was one of them. That was while we were in the Roxy. The band appeared there with George Gershwin. Eight of us got let out. There was Lennie Hayton, Joe Venuti, Bill Rank, me, a lot more.

"Then Bix died. When Bix died it was . . . too bad. We were in New York, the guys who got let out. I was freelancing. I was working a lot with Nat Shilkret, Willard Robison, Don Voorhees, different guys like that. They'd call me. And I always had the Casa Loma I could write for.

"The Casa Loma was a band that came out of Detroit, patterned after the Goldkette band. But they picked up a few things of their own. Gene Gifford was their chief arranger. They were well managed. Cork O'Keefe was their manager. He and Spike. Spike Knoblaugh. That was Glen Gray's real name, Glen Gray Knoblaugh. We used to call him Spike when he played with the Orange Blossoms in Detroit. They were on the stand opposite the Goldkette band. They were the relief band. Most of their guys were from around Detroit."

In 1927, Goldkette had formed the Orange Blossoms, which soon became the Casa Loma Orchestra. Given the collective influence of the Goldkette band, McKinney's Cotton Pickers, and the Casa Loma Orchestra, a case could be made that the swing era began in Detroit.

Bill said, "I remember I was on the street when I heard Bix was dead. I heard it from the trombone player Boyce Cullen, one of the guys in the Whiteman band. I was up around 72nd Street on the west side. I ran into Boyce. He said, 'Did you hear that Bix died?'

"It shocked me."

Bill stayed on in New York, writing for studio orchestras and the Casa Loma.

As an arranger, Bill was largely self-taught, although this term is dubious: formal teaching to a large extent involves guiding a student to the right books, and some of them find their way without that advice. He said, "I was looking at the orchestration books, particularly Forsythe. I could find a lot of material there. If I wanted to find out how to divide fiddles, of what the fiddles consisted, I found it out of the Forsythe book. Later on I went to Schillinger. Over at Columbia they had practically a Schillinger group. Several of the guys, Glenn Miller, Lyn Murray, Gus Levine, studied with Schillinger.

"Schillinger changed everything around. He was very arithmetical, and I could understand that. Most of the other guys could too."

A lot of musicians were making transcriptions for distribution under pseudonyms to 400 or so radio stations, Benny Goodman and the Dorseys among them. Bill recorded as Bob Conley and His Orchestra. In 1983, the Circle label issued two albums of this transcription material by Challis. The string section comprised ten violins, three violas, and a cello. The sax section (which included Artie Shaw and Larry Binyon), interestingly, was five men, including a baritone. Charlie Margulis and Mannie Klein were in the trumpets, and Jack Jenney and Will Bradley among the trombone players, with Frank Signorelli on piano, Dick McDonough on guitar, Artie Bernstein on bass, and Chauncey Morehouse on drums. Not even that illustrious group could make the Challis chart on "Clarinet Marmalade" swing: the orchestra was too big. The music might be described as pre-Muzak, thick and sweet.

Bill freelanced through the rest of the decade and into the 1940s, writing for Charlie Barnet (for whom he arranged, improbably enough, "Ave Maria"), Mark Warnow, Nat Shilkret, Willard Robison, Lennie Hayton, Raymond Paige, and Glenn Miller. The chart on Miller's "Guess I'll Go Back Home This Summer" is Bill's. He went on staff with Artie Shaw, for whom he arranged "Blues in the Night," "This Time the Dream's on Me," and "Make Love to Me."

"With Artie, you seldom made an arrangement by yourself," he said. "He usually worked on the tune with you. He was right there."

The cordial and even casual mixing of black and white musicians that went on in private and in the recording studio and certainly for arrangers – with Don Redman writing for Whiteman and Bill writing for Fletcher Henderson – still was unacceptable in public performance. Bill said, "The trumpet player we had – Hot Lips Page – Artie cancelled a whole trip through the south because they didn't want to have Page. Guys in the band told me that Page once walked around all night because he couldn't find a place to stay." Shaw too told of the hardships endured; traveling with a white band was hard on Roy Eldridge, too, and particularly Billie Holiday. The segregation of bands came not from the musicians but from the public and, more to the point, the people who booked the bands. The bigots of the Bible Belt would ultimately get Nat Cole's TV show knocked off the air.

In 1936, Bill returned for a time to the Whiteman band, but there was really no place for Whiteman in the Swing Era, when the public expected each bandleader to be an instrumentalist, ideally a hot jazz player. The last of the 185 arrangements Bill wrote for Whiteman was "Sitting on a Rainbow."

He continued with the Casa Loma, by now billed as Glen Gray and His Casa Loma Orchestra. He said, "We got Bobby Hackett in the band for a while, and Red Nichols. Red was a great studio man. If he had a chorus to do, he'd even write the notes out and play them exactly. He was meticulous about what he put down for records. I liked Red: he was a great guy to work with, a great studio man. He wasn't a Beiderbecke, by any means."

The war years came. Bix had been dead ten years. Trumbauer, who had been in the navy in World War I, was now a test pilot. He went back to music briefly after the war, then gave it up and returned to aeronautics. He died in 1957.

Something sad happened to Bill Challis along the way. He was married for a time. How and when his marriage ended I do not know. And I sensed, in my conversation with Evan Challis, that the subject was a sensitive one. I pressed no questions about it.

I stayed overnight in Harvey's Lake, then had lunch again with Evan and Bill. We drove into Wilkes-Barre. Evan and Bill still owned the building on a street corner in which their father had his barber shop. Where the barber chairs and mirrors once were are filing cabinets and shelves holding the memorabilia and some of the music of the life of Bill Challis that Evan collected. I felt strangely moved as I examined charts written in Bill's young neat hand in the early 1920s on printed score paper laid out for three trumpets, two trombones, three saxes, and rhythm section. Bill seems almost indifferent to his place in history. Evan, a salesman by profession and archivist by default, is not.

We shook hands and parted on that street corner in a modest neighborhood where these two soft, gentle men had grown up.

Not long after I got back to California, I received an envelope from Evan and Bill. It contained the transcriptions of "In a Mist" and the other piano pieces that Bill had made for Bix so long ago. I copied them and sent them to Hank Jones.

Once more I was talking to Benny Carter about Bill. I asked him again about Bill's influence. He repeated what he said in New York, his voice inflecting italics, "Bill Challis was my *idol*." And he added, "Will you be talking to him?"

"Yes."

"Please give him my love."

I did.

Bill Challis died on 4 October 1994, in Wilkes-Barre, Pennsylvania, where he was born.

8

A band of arrangers:
Les Brown

Of all the leaders of the "swing era", the one who has kept a big band going longer than any other is Les Brown. Les formed his band, at first with twelve pieces, in October 1938, and four years before that, in 1934, had become leader of the Duke Blue Devils, a college band that recorded for Decca.

Longevity of course is hardly Les Brown's main claim to notice. He led one of the truly great bands of that era, and occasisonal performances even in recent years have demonstrated how alive and well he and the Band of Renown actually are. He has been a bandleader for more than 60 years.

If his band did not produce as many major jazz soloists as other bands did, this is due partly to the stability of its personnel. Musicians stayed with Les year after year after year. Then too, it was chiefly notable for its ensemble work. It was always an arrangers' band, led by an arranger. Frank Comstock, its principal arranger over the years, said, "I'll look in books and see almost no mention of Les. I don't think it's fair. Or right."

Part of the reason that Les Brown is semi-overlooked surely is that he is such a self-effacing man. He claims nothing for himself and nothing for his band, although it has been, year in and year out right into the present, an outstanding group. He once told George Simon that it was a "malted milk band", a perhaps unfortunate characterization that has tended to stick. Doris Day said it was "a milk-shake band," although she may have meant something slightly different by that. She said, "I don't think anybody in the band even drank."

All you'll get from Les is his admiration for others. "What a band!" he said of that led by his late friend Woody Herman. Unlike Woody, Les had only two bands, the one he led in university and the one that, with changes of personnel, continued from 1938 into the late 1990s. Nonetheless, some fine players passed through it, including Don Fagerquist, Abe Most, Geoff Clarkson, Billy Butterfield, Ray Sims (Zoot's trombone-playing brother), Dave Pell, and Ted Nash.

Despite the presence of such soloists, what the Les Brown band was most noted for was consistently excellent playing of consistently excellent arrangements. Jazz fans divided the orchestras into "swing" and "sweet" categories, unsatisfactory designations in that the demarkation was not clear: "sweet" (meaning corny) bands such as those of Kay Kyser (one of whose arrangers was George Duning) and Sammy Kaye employed good musicians and could on occasion turn in creditable performances of the few "jazz" charts in their books. And the "jazz" bands played "sweet" ballads. Furthermore, all of the bands played for dancers. Indeed, a Jimmie Lunceford tune was named "For Dancers Only," and Benny Goodman's theme was "Let's Dance."

Les asserted nothing. He never said his was a jazz band. However, if it was "only" a dance band, it demonstrated just how good "popular" music could be, what levels of excellence and high taste it could achieve. As Terry Gibbs put it, "You never heard Les Brown with a bad band."

Gunther Schuller, in his book *The Swing Era* (Oxford University Press, 1989), wrote that the early Les Brown band

> was decidedly inferior, and thus represents one of the most startling artistic-stylistic transformations in jazz history – an ungainly cocoon into a quite beautiful butterfly.
>
> Brown's earliest recordings from 1936, and even those of his second band formed in 1938 . . . do not suggest in the slightest the level of fine musicianship, technical polish, and healthy swing energy the band could muster ten years later. And . . . the difference was made by the arranger. In Brown's case there were several excellent arrangers involved in the band's transformation, but it was Frank Comstock in particular who, beginning in 1943, turned the Brown band into a crack modern-styled ensemble.

Superior writing came too from Skip Martin, Bob Higgins, who played trumpet in the band and wrote "High on a Windy Trumpet" and "Lover's Leap," and Wes Hensel, a Cleveland native who had come to the band after working with Charlie Barnet and Boyd Raeburn. During more than ten years with the band he wrote, among other charts, "Montoona Clipper," "Flying Home," and "Ebony Rhapsody."

Schuller continued:

> The first intimations of better things to come occur by 1939–40. One hears a considerable improvement over the earlier thumpy rhythmed, thin-toned, and often out of tune performances, in Mary Lou Williams' arrangement of her "Walkin' and Swingin'" and such pieces as "Perisphere Shuffle" and "Trylon Stomp," both written and arranged by Brown for the 1939–40 New York World's Fair (where Brown's band had one of its earliest long-term engagements). But a real

break-through came in Ben Homer's clean, incisive "Joltin' Joe DiMaggio" of 1941, superbly played by the band with a fine two-beat Lunceford swing. There followed such fine scores as "Bizet Has His Day" (one of the few interesting, in this case even witty, transformations of classical material from that era); "Nothin'" from Ellington's *Jump for Joy*, in a clean, lean, swinging arrangement that anticipates the latter's "I'm Beginning to See the Light" of three years later; "Sunday" and "Out of Nowhere" in beautifully crafted arrangements featuring Billy Butterfield in excellent extended solos.

The reason the first Les Brown band to be heard on records is not as good as the one that succeeded it is that it was, like the first Woody Herman band, a co-operative. Woody said that no decision could be made without a meeting of some sort, as often as not in the men's room at some gig.

Les said: "Co-operative bands do not work. Ask Casa Loma. Ask Woody. Ask Johnny Long. I finally got rid of it. I was so happy to make the change."

I put the question directly to Les: "Your bands were always in such exquisite taste," I said. "One of the keys was the writing. Was that because you're an arranger?"

"I think that had *something* to do with it," Les said. "I always made sure that I hired arrangers who were a hell of a lot better than I am! And I sort of confine my arranging to vocal backgrounds. I did a lot when Doris Day was in the band. I know my limitations. I write a jazz chart every now and then. Sometimes it comes off. If it doesn't, it comes out of the repertoire the same night we play it the first time. If I don't like it, I say, 'Hand it in!' But sometimes I'd keep 'em and still play 'em."

Frank Comstock said, "Les has always said that. He always said he was smart enough to hire arrangers who were better than he was and Abe Most because he was a better clarinetist and Ronny Lang because he was a better alto player. That's the way Les is."

Les is a native of the beautiful hilly Appalachian coal region of upper eastern Pennsylvania, in common with trumpeter Fuzzy Farrar, a key figure in the Jean Goldkette band, and Spiegle Willcox, who played trombone with Goldkette when Bix Beiderbecke and Frank Trumbauer were in the band.

He was born Lester Raymond Brown in Reinerton, on 14 March 1912. "My dad was a baker by trade," he said. "But music was what he lived for. It was pretty hard to make a living from music in those towns in those days. And he had four kids. He got married in 1911, and I was born the next year. He was also the town bandleader. Self-taught."

The family background was Pennsylvania Dutch. Les was the oldest of the four Brown children, including their sister Sylvia and Warren Brown, who would one day play trombone in his brother's band and then become prominent in music publishing in New York. The youngest was Clyde Lamar Brown, who acquired the nickname "Stump" when he was in grade six or seven. This evolved into Stumpy when he became a professional musician. He was born on 1 September 1925, in Tower City, Pennsylvania. His father taught him trumpet, baritone horn, then trombone, saying, "Baritone horns can't make a living. There are only two in every concert band." This little remark tells us that their father *wanted* his sons to be professional musicians.

Stumpy said of his parents: "They were beautiful people. My dad taught himself to play all the musical instruments. Trombone was his main instrument. When I was a young boy, he said, 'Y'know, one time I played first trombone over Tommy Dorsey. Of course, I was 21 and Tommy was 12.'"

The Dorsey Brothers too were from that part of the country, and their father, like Les and Stumpy's, was a part-time musician who taught music. Jimmy and Tommy were born in 1904 and 1905 respectively in Shenandoah, Pennsylvania; they were eight and seven years older than Les. These towns are at most 20 or 30 miles from each other, lying in the area's southwest-slanting valleys close to the Blue Mountains spur of the Appalachians. "My dad," Les said, "played trombone with Tommy and Jimmy and their father in Pottsville in the Third Brigade Band." Pottsville is about twenty miles south of Shenandoah. "It was a concert and parade band. Those bands were very popular in the '20s."

Stumpy said, "I'm thirteen-and-a-half years younger than Les. I played in my dad's high school band. In the summertime, in a little town called Lykens, Pennsylvania, the teachers all worked nine months and then had their three months off. Dad would teach the band during the summer. Every fall, the band was always better than it had been at the start of the summer.

"I think my mother was 16 or 17 when they got married. She was not a musician, but she could play the piano by ear. And she could sing. She sang in the church choir."

Les said: "There was a series of towns, between Pottsville and Harrisburg. Tower City, Orwin, which was close to Tower City, Reinerton, where I was born. Most of them had one main street, or at the most three streets. Three thousand people, things like that. Now down to two." He was referring to the depopulation of the area with the decline of the coal industry. "And then Williamstown and Lykens. All the towns put together wouldn't be more than 12,000 population.

"It was sulphur coal mining, done mostly by Czechoslovakian and Polish people. One of my girlfriends at Duke University was from Aliquippa, Pennsylvania, where Henry Mancini was from. I told Hank about that once."

Bill Challis came from that vicinity. "Bill was born in Wilkes-Barre," I reminded Les.

"Paul Specht was also from that area," Les said. "Fred Waring too. I go back to the days of McKinney's Cotton Pickers, Paul Whiteman, and then the Casa Loma. They were my gods for a while, until Benny Goodman came along. I loved the Casa Loma band – and I loved the arrangements of Gene Gifford. And I loved Benny Carter. There's an unusual man. God, I love him! What a talent! I remember when I was in college, listening to his records on trumpet and saxophone. Then I found out he was an arranger and composer. What a musician."

"Did you ever hear the Goldkette band live?" I asked.

"Not live, but I had all their records," Les said. "Glenn Miller played with that band, and the Dorseys. Another band that made some good records was Ted Weems. They were more commercial. But every Friday they'd have the new releases on Brunswick and Victor. The store was right across from my dad's bakery and I'd go by and listen. I couldn't afford to buy 'em, but I heard 'em. Every now and then I'd beg my dad to buy one I really had to have. Fred Waring. McKinney's Cotton Pickers. Bix. When I first heard Bix's chorus on "Sweet Sue," my God!" And he sang a couple of bars of that solo.

"Do you know Spiegle Willcox?" I asked. "He's from just north of there in New York State. He's from Cortland."

"When I was at Ithaca," Les said, "my friend Greg McHenry, a fraternity brother who became the head of the music school, played in the same band with Spiegle. Wes Thomas and his Cornell Collegians, which I played in – tenor sax – after Spiegle had gone out into the so-called entertainment world. He's still living."

I said, "He's still *playing*. All over the world. I've been up to his house near Cincinnatus. Near Cortland."

"When I went back to Ithaca, guest conducting the symphony, not too long ago, Greg called Spiegle to see if he could come down. I did the Prelude to the Third Act of *Lohengrin* at the commencement exercises. They gave me an honorary doctorate and all that. I'd been back to conduct before. And Spiegle came!"

"Most of the guys who became bandleaders," I said, "began as side men with other bands. You didn't."

"Well I did," Les said, "but never with a name band. I went to school from 1926 to 1936, the first three years at Ithaca Conservatory, now Ithaca College." The city of Ithaca, New York, on the shore of Cayuga Lake, is also the home of Cornell University. It is only a few miles north of the region where Les and his siblings grew up.

"That was '26 to '29," Les continued. "Then I had to go back when I was 17 and get my high-school education. I'd left high school to go to Ithaca Conservatory, from the time I was 14 until I was 17, to study nothing but music – composition, theory, orchestration, whatever. And I was saxophone soloist with Conway's Band. Patrick Conway was second to Sousa. I played one summer with him at Wildwood. I was 16 at the time. I had a hell of a lot of technique, I really did.

"During the summer of '29, I met a guy who had been on full scholarship at New York Military Academy for two years, Bob Alexy, who later played with Jimmy Dorsey and Mal Hallett. His recommendation got me a scholarship, and I went there, as my brothers Warren and Stumpy did later on. Johnny Mandel went there with Stumpy. I was class of '32. Warren was class of '34. Stumpy was class of '43. We all finished high school there, on full scholarships."

"Johnny said he knew your mother and father."

"Sure," Les said, "he used to come to visit with Stumpy." (Johnny remembers that a sickly smell of chocolate hung over Hershey, Pennsylvania, home of the Hershey bar.)

I asked Stumpy about the academy. He said, "It's in Cornwall-on-Hudson, seven miles from West Point." Like West Point, the academy is on the west bank of the Hudson River, at that point flowing between great forested bluffs past Storm King Mountain, land that is rich in Dutch history, names, and legend.

"That's beautiful country," I said.

"Especially in the winter, when you froze to death," Stumpy said with more or less mirthless laughter. "I was the leader of the academy dance band. Johnny Mandel wrote arrangements for us and played trumpet in the band. We'd hear a record and want to play it, but there was no stock on it. Johnny would sit down and take it off the record. He was 16."

"Was it a strict military academy?" I asked Les.

"*Very* strict," Les said, laughing. "I ended up being what they called head boy. That was like valedictorian. And that gave me automatic appointment to West Point. I said, 'No thanks! Three years of military is three years too much.' But it was a free education.

"We used to sneak over to the fraternity house at night, when we were supposed to be in bed. We'd find out from the *New York Times* when Paul Whiteman was going to be on the radio, or even Mickey Mouse bands. Whatever bands. Especially Whiteman and McKinney's Cotton Pickers. Or the band coming in from Chicago, Isham Jones. In those days, stations had a hundred thousand watts. I *loved* that Isham Jones band! Golly. Later on, I made some arrangements for him."

I mentioned that Will Hudson wrote "Jazznocracy" for Jimmie Lunceford based on the style of the Casa Loma. "I think that band was more influential than is generally recognized," I said.

"I know it was with me," Les said. "I'd go down to Hershey Park during the summer, and just stand in front of the bandstand all night with my mouth open, listening to them.

"I was supposed to go to the University of Pennsylvania. In those days, during the Depression, they were begging for students. I was playing tenor in a band up in Boston, a week at some park. The Duke Blue Devils was the logo for all the university's athletics, including its football team – and the band was under the direction of a football player called Nick Laney, a very good halfback. In those days Duke had a great football team, with Ace Parker and Freddie Crawford. All-Americans. So the band too was called the Blue Devils. They came out one night to hear our band, and found out that I was getting ready to go to college, and they talked me into going to Duke.

"The reason I went there was that the Blue Devils played for an hour every night between six and seven, and for that you got free room and board. Again, it was 1932, the Depression; I was 20. So my dad didn't have to put up room and board. We used to play enough gigs to make ten, fifteen dollars a week. That would buy as much as 150 does today.

"So I went to Duke. There was no music school. Of course I had finished music school. So I majored in French and minored in history. I liked history and I loved languages. I studied Greek and German. I'd had Latin in military school. And French. I took four more years of French. I can still read it, but I can't speak it now. I wish I'd done more of it. Or taken business administration. Although to this day, business bores me.

"Remember Johnny Long? His was the other band there. He was at Duke at the same time I was, a year ahead of me. He was class of '35, I was class of '36.

"Now Nick Laney didn't know a note of music. He was a nice guy. Good football player. Had a pretty good voice and he sang through a megaphone. And we'd play for fraternity dances, or for concerts. We had four brass, three trumpets and a trombone, and four saxes. Three rhythm, sometimes four with guitar. The instrument you could never hear, because there was no amplification. But you could feel it.

"I played in that band at Duke for two years. Nick Laney finally had his four years of football, and I inherited the band: in September 1934.

"I wrote a lot for that band. All the popular tunes of the day, I arranged. *And* copied. I still do it the way I did in college. Now and then I'll write out a full score. Otherwise, I just do a sketch and copy out the parts myself, because nobody can read my writing. My handwriting is bad enough, let alone my notes. And sometimes I'll change my mind while I'm doing the copying. The guys have gotten used to it.

"I graduated on 10 June 1936."

The prominent record producer Creed Taylor went to Duke because of Les Brown. Creed said, "I was buying his records when I was in high school, including 'Sentimental Journey.' I thought, 'This guy has a band like this and a singer like this and he went to Duke? This has to be the college for me.'

"I played trumpet in that band, although by then it was called the Ambassadors. I had a quintet called, would you believe it, the Five Dukes. Patrick Williams and Sonny Burke both went to Duke."

After graduation, Les said,"We did some one-nighters. We got a job in Budd Lake, New Jersey. It's about 40 miles inland from New York City, toward Delaware Water Gap. We played there from 4 July till Labor Day. I met my wife there.

"On Saturday night, after we finished playing, some of us would head for New York and 52nd Street, just young kids right out of college. We'd make a weekend out of it, because we didn't have to be back until the gig Monday night at 8 o'clock.

"One Saturday night, I told Claire, 'Three of us are going in to New York to hear Basie. We have room in the car, do you want to come?' She said, 'Well, my parents aren't here.' I said, 'Don't worry.' I was very friendly with her parents, who were quite young, in their 30s. I called her home and spoke to her grandmother. I said, 'Tell Ed and Bess that I'm taking Claire in to New York and she's going to be staying with so-and-so. We're going in to hear Count Basie.' I was 27, she was 20.

"That was our first date, although I'd known her for a while. A month later we got married at Lake Mohawk, New Jersey.

"By a lucky coincidence, a guy named Bob Stevens from Decca Records saw a bunch of cars, heard some music, came in, listened to us, and we had a record contract: the first college band that ever recorded for a major label. I had graduated.

"We played Ohio and Pennsylvania," Les said. "We'd stay two or three weeks at a time. The guys were making 60 dollars a week: not bad in those days. They thought it was great, and they were having fun. We ended up at Playland in Rye, New York, in the summer of 1937.

"And then the parents got after them. 'Hey. Get back into school.' And rightfully so. And as I said, it was a co-operative band, and co-operatives don't work. That was the end of it.

"I went into New York, freelance arranged for a few months. I had a four-arrangements-a-week gig with Rube Newman, who was playing the Rainbow Room. Four for 75 bucks. I was pretty fast too. They had a Tuesday rehearsal. I wouldn't start till, say, midnight of Sunday, and keep arranging until I fell asleep around eight in the morning. I'd write on Monday, and I had a copyist right next to me, and we'd just make the rehearsal on Tuesday. The rest of the week, I'd go to the movies, or write a stock.

"There was about eight months, between September and July, when I didn't have a band, the only time I haven't since I took over the Blue Devils. I even inherited the Ford the band had, because nobody else wanted it.

"Then, after that eight months, I went back to Budd Lake with a band, then into the Hotel Edison."

"Had you made up your mind you were going to have a career in music?"

"I think what made up my mind," Les said, "was the Decca contract. And even though we didn't sell many records, we got good write-ups, and it was a pretty good band. And one thing led to another. At the Edison, we were on NBC six nights a week, Monday off.

"I got married a week before we opened at the Edison. The first gig out of the Edison – here I am with a twelve-piece band – and inasmuch as I had gone to school in Ithaca, I knew the guy who booked the bands at Cornell for the junior prom. That was the big social event of the year in that town of 25,000. Everybody in the school went to it.

"This was 1938. Here we are. They had three bands that night. Me and my twelve pieces here. Jimmie Lunceford over here, and Duke Ellington over here. On three different bandstands at Drill Hall.

"I tell you! Was I chagrined! It was awful. They were playing things like 'Jazznocracy.'" Les sang some licks at fast tempo. "They were trying to outdo each other, and here we were, playing our little dance music. I felt caught in the middle between those two great bands.

"But we went on after that. We struggled and struggled. We did a lot of records for Victor, for their Bluebird label. Thank God they haven't re-released them. They weren't up to what they should have been in '38, when you had great bands like Shaw and Goodman. Or the Dorsey Brothers. Our records weren't that good.

"We still had three trumpets and one trombone. Gradually I added more trombones, I added another trumpet. When we were up at Armonk, New York, the whole summer, we were on the air seven times a week: six at night and Saturday at noon.

"Glenn Osser and I lived together that eight months I was freelance arranging in New York. I learned so much about modern arranging looking over his shoulder, more than I did at music school, which taught classical orchestration.

"That Saturday broadcast was big. I'd tell the band to be there at 11 to warm up. We'd go on the air from 12 to 12.30. It was our best shot. One time, I wondered where the engineer was. We had a booth there, because we were on every night. At ten minutes to the hour, I called the station. I said, 'Hey. No announcer and no engineer? We're all here ready to go. Are we off the air?' And the guy said, 'No! You're on!' I said, 'What do we do?' He said, 'Break the lock on the booth, go in and set the dials at 50.' They ran from 1 to 100. He said, 'You do the announcing.' So I did it.

"That afternoon, I got a call from Glenn Osser. He said, 'Les, who the hell was that engineer?' I told him. He said, 'The engineers can ruin you! That was the best balance I ever heard on the radio. I didn't think much of your announcing, but the balance was great!'

"We played the World's Fair in '39 for Mike Todd. And we went into the Blackhawk. We were hired for a month, stayed four months. But it wasn't till 1942 that I made any money.

"I had Si Zentner on trombone, Abe Most on clarinet, Don Jacoby on trumpet, Wolfe Tannenbaum (who changed it to Tayne) on tenor. It was a good little band. Then I started losing guys to the army.

"Eli Oberstein at Victor gave up on us, and rightfully so. Four months after the Blackhawk, our records started to sell, and we had a hit on 'Joltin' Joe DiMaggio.' Vocal by Betty Bonny."

"And when did Butch Stone join you?"

"Butch had been with Van Alexander's band, but Van disbanded and went into freelance arranging," Les said. "Then Butch went with Jack Teagarden. Teagarden gave up his big band too. So Butch went with Larry Clinton. Somebody said to me, 'You ought to go see this guy Butch Stone. He's a great performer.' They were playing Loew's State theater in New York.' I went backstage. Butch said, 'Larry's going into the service as a teacher, a flight instructor. I need a job.'

"I said, 'We're going into the Blackhawk in Chicago in September. Would you like to come?' And I said, 'I also need a drummer. I'd like to have Irv Cottler too.'"

Henry (Butch) Stone was born in Trenton, New Jersey on 27 August 1912; thus he is a few months younger than Les. His parents moved to New York City when he was an infant, and his speech (as well as all the vocal records he made with Les) reflects that cultural conditioning. One of his first jobs was delivering film for one of the studios in the early 1930s. He played saxophone part-time in a band with other semi-pros, one that copied Jimmie Lunceford records. Butch did the numbers that Trummy Young sang with the Lunceford band, and gradually he gained acceptance as a comic singer, occasionally being referred to as the white Louis Jordan.

"A lot of the bands had guys who could step out of the ranks and do a song, usually a comic song, like Louis Prima with Tony Pastor and Tex Beneke with Glenn Miller," Butch said.

I'd never thought about this before, but now that Butch mentioned it, I saw the pattern. Ray Nance with Duke Ellington, Hot Lips Page and Tony Pastor with Artie Shaw, Nappy Lamarr with Bob Crosby, Sy Oliver with Tommy Dorsey and Roy Eldridge with Gene Krupa all filled the same role. Even the "sweet" commercial bands had people to provide this comic relief, filling that dramatic function of breaking the mood as a preparation for serious material to follow. "The bandleaders loved guys like Butch Stone,"

Johnny Mandel said. "They could distract an audience, and the bands were expected to put on a show."

Les was going to add a baritone to the saxophone section anyway, and if he could find somebody who could also do novelty songs, so much the better. Butch perfectly filled the job description, as they would say in a later time.

Butch recalled: "Les told us to go up and see Joe Glaser, who was booking the band. He was a big man in the business. He had a lot of acts that played the Apollo, including Lionel Hampton, and he handled Louis Armstrong. He had an office around 57th and Broadway. On the way over, Irv Cottler and I said we wouldn't take a penny less than a 125 a week. When we got there, Joe Glaser said, 'This band is going places. It's not a band of stars. Everybody gets the same money – 75 a week.'" Butch laughed, remembering. "I said, 'I'll take it.' Irv Cottler said, 'I won't,' and left. He went with Claude Thornhill."

Les said, "I got him later, after the band made a little more money and we were playing the Meadowbrook and Glen Island Casino and the Cafe Rouge." (Irv Cottler is the drummer on many of the great Sinatra records.)

"Adding baritone saxophone, how much did you rewrite?" I asked.

"At that time, the baritone usually just doubled the first, although we don't do that so much in the newer arrangements. Up till then, he just doubled the first sax."

Butch Stone became a mainstay of the band, the dependable underpinning of the sax section and the resident jester, with a flair for singing comic songs, more or less on one note, including "Robin Hood," "Time Will Take Care of You," and a parody on etiquette lessons in which all the wrong things are advocated, "Thank You for Your Very Kind Attention." Another song asserted: "Jack, I'm comin' back in my convertible Cadillac." In 1942 Butch and the band recorded "A Good Man Is Hard to Find," a 1918 song associated with Bessie Smith. It became a hit.

"Butch was the road manager," Stumpy said. "He was always mother hen to the guys, trying to get them good seats on the plane and that kind of thing. He'd go to the ticket agent and say, 'Look, the band has all these instruments and carry-on luggage. Why don't you let us board first and get settled?' And they'd agree."

To which Butch said: "If the musicians are happy, it will be reflected in the music. So when we'd be going through some little town and stop to get something at a diner at three in the morning, and there'd only be a cook and one waiter, I'd go behind the counter and wait on the band. It was just fun. Later, when we started flying, I'd try to see that they got good seats on the aisle or at the window."

One of the band's hits was "Bizet Has His Day." "This was during the fight between BMI and ASCAP," Les said. "And we had to go to PDs." He meant songs in the public domain.

This is a little-understood factor in evaluating the repertoire of those days. ASCAP – the American Society of Composers, Authors, and Publishers – which licenced all the major modern songwriters, demanded more money from the radio stations for the performance of its members' songs.

But the radio industry had prepared an ambush for ASCAP, setting up a company called Broadcast Music Incorporated and signing up songwriters from country-and-western and other fields previously disdained by ASCAP, in preparation for trouble with ASCAP. ASCAP pulled all its music off the air.

BMI immediately became functional, and some observers have seen this as preparing the decline of American popular music to its present nadir. It may have been a factor, but it was one of many. Also significant was the abandonment by the major broadcasting companies of network radio in favor of the rising medium of television. Ironically, this would work to Les Brown's advantage.

During the ASCAP ban, radio stations could play only music licenced by BMI or material that was in the public domain, that is to say music old enough that its copyright had expired, which included folk and much classical music.

"That's why we did 'Bizet Has His Day,'" Les said. (The piece is based on Bizet's *L'Arlesienne Suite.*) "And 'Mexican Hat Dance.' That's why we did Marche Slav by Tchaikovsky. If you didn't record things that were in the public domain, the disc jockeys couldn't play them on the air. We even did 'Old Dog Tray!' 'Bizet' was during that time, 1941."

"'Bizet' was Ben Homer's chart, wasn't it?"

"Yes."

"And where did you find him?"

"He was just out of the Boston Conservatory and he came to me looking for a job.

"Homer was very strange to work with. You'd get a chart about every six weeks. But when you got it, it was a gem. Frank Comstock could do six in a week, if you wanted him to. Glenn Osser could make an arrangement in two hours. And a great one, every time. He had perfect pitch. He didn't have to go to the piano. But I'd say Ben Homer gave us the style."

However, Frank Comstock, born in San Diego, California, on 20 September 1922, became the most important writer for the band. One of Comstock's charts, a reorchestration of "Leap Frog" made when Les expanded the band – this riff tune, based on an octave leap, was written by Joe Garland, who also wrote "In the Mood" – became a hit and the Les Brown band's theme. Later Comstock arranged, orchestrated (for Dmitri Tiomkin, among others), or scored music for films and television shows, though always retaining his association with Les.

"Frank is still writing for us," Les said. "He wrote most of our last album."

Prior to joining Les, Comstock had written three pieces for Stan Kenton. But a more sustained association was with Benny Carter. Comstock wrote for him for eight months until Carter dismantled his band in 1942 and turned his attention increasingly to composition and studio work in Los Angeles.

In 1939, Les encountered a young singer whose work he liked. This meeting would profoundly affect both their lives, its long effect making her a major movie star.

She was born Doris Kappelhoff on 3 April 1922, in Cincinnati, Ohio, and grew up there. Like Ella Fitzgerald, she aspired to be a dancer.

"I loved the movies when I was very young," she remembered. "But dancing was my favorite thing. I started when I was about 4, and I went to dance class four times a week. I sang in personality class at the dancing school. I adored dancing.

"I don't know if I thought about acting. But I thought a lot about movie stars because all kids do, and we played movie stars. And I thought about California, how great it must be. We would see the magazines. It was always sun shining. And I loved the way the movie stars dressed. It was all *exciting*.

"But I don't know if I really thought that I was ever going to do it. I wasn't the kind of person who was a go-getter about being successful and being a star and all of that stuff. I think it's tragic if it becomes the all-important thing in life. It must be tragic for those who don't have a career in that field.

"I was a real mid-western person who thought about home, and getting married, and having a nice family and taking care of my house. I always loved taking care of my room when I was a little girl, and helping my mother to clean. I learned to iron when I was 10 years old. I just thought I was going to be a home-maker. It didn't work out that way. Everything went in a different direction.

"When I was about 12 or 13 we were getting ready to move to California. My dancing partner and his mother and my mother and I had been there to get some new dance routines. We spent about a month in Los Angeles. Oh God, that was the biggest thing in the whole world. We loved it so much that when we came back to Cincinnati, my partner and his mother wanted to move out to LA. The following year we decided that my partner and our mothers would go, and we would see what could happen, and what was in store. Then maybe her husband would come out. My father was not living with us at the time. But my brother wanted to go.

"We were going at the end of October. I was in Hamilton, Ohio, visiting relatives to say good-bye. Four of us young people went out, and the car was hit by a train. It was October the 13th, and it was a Friday.

"I haven't really talked about this very much. I had terrible fractures in my leg. I was laid up about three years. The bones were not knitting, and it was becoming a terrible thing. I couldn't stand on crutches, I couldn't bear the pain. Finally, they started to knit."

Her aspirations to dance were finished. But she could sing, and she began doing so on radio station WLW in her home town. It was there that Barney Rapp, leader of a successful local band with whom she worked at the station, changed her name to Doris Day. Then she joined the Bob Crosby band.

"I was with Bob Crosby a very short time," she said. "They were going out on the road. Bob had a half-hour radio program. There was a gal who was going to be on that show. She was a friend of somebody important. And so they decided that it would be a good idea if she sang with the band."

It's an old show business story. Girl balls Powerful Person, gets the gig. Ironically, the girl who snagged her job did Doris a major favor.

Doris said, "The manager of the Crosby band, Gil Rodin, who was a wonderful person, said that Les Brown had been to the Strand theater in New York and had seen me and would like me to join the band. I said, 'I don't know much about Les Brown.' Gil said, 'He has a terrific band, and he's a terrific person.' So I said, 'Well I'd like to meet him.' I wasn't sure what I was going to do.

"I didn't know the fellows in the Bob Crosby band too well, but they were very nice. I really was looked after. The guys were like brothers to me. They were older. They were all married. And then I found I was going with a very young band, and I was concerned that I would be lonely."

She was 17.

"But then," she said, "Les was always so concerned, and so careful about everything, and he was so dear with my Mom. It was a family scene. From then till now, Les has always been a wonderful friend. We all lived at the Whitby apartments in New York at the time. Claire was there with the babies. We were all so close: we still are.

"It was a good band, and I loved it. We always talk about the laughs we had. When you have 30 or more one-nighters in a row, that's hard. But we still just laughed."

If the band was good for her, she was good for the band. With her vocal, Les recorded "My Dreams Are Getting Better All the Time." He wrote the arrangement. Though the song was not one of the immortal ballads, it was nonetheless a substantial hit.

I said to Les, "I think she is underrated, for all her success. I catch her in an old movie, and I am amazed at how well she sang. When I was in high school, I saw the band in Niagara Falls, Ontario, at an arena. She was gorgeous, and she had wonderful posture. I suppose that was from the dancing. And, I have to tell you, Les, I still remember it: she had the most beautiful derrière."

"Oh sure," Les said, laughing. "We used to call her Jut Butt. She was a good egg to be around. On the one-nighters and things.

"She married a trombone player from the Jimmy Dorsey band, Al Jordan. When he left the Crosby band, he told her, 'All right, get home here.' He was jealous! One time there was a picture of her with the band. She had legs crossed and you could see her knees. He wrote her a letter! She was crying. She showed it to me. I had to write him a note and saying, 'Hey, it's all right, we need publicity, and this isn't bad.'"

It was a period when *Down Beat* heavily emphasized cheesecake photos of the "canaries" or "chirps," as it was prone to call them, who sang with the bands.

Doris left the band, had a baby, then was divorced and returned. "I had to wait until the baby was old enough to take on the road," Les said. "I took her mother with us."

And then came the alchemical combination: Les, Doris Day, and "Sentimental Journey."

"Ben Homer and I wrote 'Sentimental Journey' together," Les said. "It's hard to make guys believe that, because in those days bandleaders were putting their names on material they didn't write – I was offered so many songs. I never would do it. Unless I actually had something to do with the song. In this case, Ben called me and said, 'I'm up at Buddy Morris's office.'"

(The Morris office was in the Brill Building. The building is still there, on Broadway in mid-town Manhattan. Many music publishers had offices there, and it has always had – to me, anyway – a faint aroma of rancid thoughts. In tribute to the savage insensitivity of its typical inhabitants, the author James T. Maher called it "Attila's last outpost.")

"I was living at the Whitby when Ben called. He said, 'I've got a pretty good idea for a tune. Why don't you come on up and we'll write it together? I've got the front part but I can't think of a release.'

"I had nothing to do so I went to the Brill Building. Homer had . . . " Les went to the piano and played a variant on the front strain. In this version, the cell of the tune, the first two notes, drops a sixth. This would increase the range, limiting the number of singers who would be able to handle it. Les pulled this fragment down to a major third, and that repeating pattern is the material of the front strain as the tune finally was published.

Les continued: "Homer said, 'What'll we do about the release?' I said, 'We'll do the Sears and Roebuck change,' which is a four chord to a one chord to a two chord to a five chord." Les played it. "We wrote it in a few minutes. I think I had as much to do with the song as he did.

"Two or three guys wrote lyrics on the tune, but Buddy Morris didn't like them. Then I got a call from Buddy, who said, 'I finally got a good lyric. It's called "Sentimental Journey."' I said, 'That's good. Where did you get that?' He said, 'I'm reading a book. It's a Baedeker of the eighteenth century called *Sentimental Journey*, a guide to the great inns of Europe. I got Bud Green to write a lyric.' Bud Green wrote the lyrics to 'I'll Get By' and 'Once in a While.' And also 'Flat Foot Floogie.' I went up and heard the lyric and I said, 'Great.'

"I had Homer make an arrangement. I said, 'Ben, I want this in thirds, clarinet above the subtone tenor lead, clarinets below.' I'd used that combination in a lot of my own arrangements, and I liked the sound. He came in and it was . . . " Les sang a blatant, loud figure. "I said, 'Stop the band! I told you what I want. Change the first sixteen bars or we don't record the thing.'"

Doris remembered: "We were at the Pennsylvania Hotel in New York. We would rehearse after work, when all the people were out of the dining room. That song suddenly appeared. Les handed me the lead sheet. I thought, 'This is really good.'

"The very next night we had a remote out of New York, about 11.30. And we put that on and, Bang! Right off the bat, I started getting mail about it."

Les said, "People would come up and ask about it. It's a simple song, simple as hell. So we stopped playing it for a while, because we were afraid somebody would steal it before we could record it.

"In November, 1944, we recorded it. Columbia put it out in January 1945. It was just after the Battle of the Bulge. When that was won, we knew the war was over. It was perfect timing. If we'd brought it out earlier, I don't know whether it would have been a hit. I've had so many GIs come up and say something like, 'Hey, I was on a boat docking in New York and it was our favorite song, because we were going home.'"

It reached the top of the popularity charts, a hit so big for Doris as well as the band that it became almost a theme song for her. "Sentimental Journey" made her a star. And so striking were her looks that the movie industry was beckoning. But that was not the immediate reason she left the band. Les said: "She was getting 500 a week, through '44, '45, and part of '46. That's equivalent to 5,000 or 10,000 now. She got so far ahead – she wasn't spending the money – she married one of my saxophone players, George Weidler, and they decided they didn't want to go on the road any more. I understood that, because I didn't want to go either, but I had to."

"Sentimental Journey" came when the bands were already encountering trouble. Costs of travel were rising, and television held a particular appeal to the returned GIs who were marrying and settling down to raise families and thus were less inclined to go out for amusement. Both baseball and movie attendance declined. But network radio, in the last days of its vigor, and soon television, actually rescued the Les Brown band.

"Skinnay Ennis had the Bob Hope radio show until he went into the service," Les said. "Then Stan Kenton had the show. He went into the studio and blew out the walls. Hope said, 'Stan, I love your band, but it's not for us.' Then he had Desi Arnaz, who didn't know a thing about music, but Hope didn't know a thing about music either, didn't know that Desi didn't know.

Desi had a Latin band around town. And so Hope's radio agent, Jimmy Saphier – Hope had the biggest radio show at that time – came in to hear our band and sent a note, asking me to have a drink. I went over to his table, and we got talking about the Hope show. He said, 'Desi Arnaz doesn't know anything about music.' And Jimmy did; he was an ex-trumpet player.

"I said, 'I'd be interested.'

"He said, 'You can make far more money on the road.'

"I said, 'I don't *care*. I want to get *off* the road.'

"I didn't even know Hope. I made the arrangements with Jimmy Saphier. I met Hope in the studio at NBC.

"Doris had left the band in '46. This was spring of '47. Jimmy tried to sell Hope on Doris and the band. Hope said, 'Yeah, she sings well, but how about that band?' I got the job, and Doris didn't. Two years later, she had two hit movies and Hope had to pay through the nose to get her."

She made a series of musicals for Warner Bros, co-starred with Kirk Douglas in *Young Man with a Horn* (the worst movie about jazz ever made except for all the others), played Calamity Jane in the film of the same name. She became increasingly known as an excellent light comedienne and a solid dramatic actress. A drama coach once told me: "It's easier to teach singers to act than actors to sing."

But just as Nat Cole's singing success overshadowed his pre-eminence as a pianist, her movie stardom obscured her excellence as a singer. She not only sang with keen intonation and good time, she always had a sense of the dramatic meaning of a lyric.

"We started on the Hope show in September of '47," Les said. "Come '48, and Bing Crosby was a guest on the show. When Bing and Bob were on NBC together, the rating went sky high.

"We'd do Hope's theme 'Thanks for the Memory,' a monologue, a band number, a skit, a commercial, a song from Bing, another short skit, a five- or six-minute sketch, theme song and out. For our band number one night, we played 'I've Got My Love to Keep Me Warm,' truncated because they only allowed us two minutes. The chart was by Skip Martin. The first chorus was in and so was the piano solo and the last chorus.

"I got a telegram. 'Heard "I've Got My Love to Keep Me Warm" on the Hope show. Go in and record it tomorrow, even if you only do one tune. I want to put it out right away.' It was from the sales manager of Columbia Records. I called him on the phone and said, 'Hey, schmuck, we recorded that two years ago, 1946, while we were at the Palladium. Now look for it.'

"He called back about four hours later. He said, 'We found it, it's great! We're gonna put it out.' About a month later I got a call from the distributor here saying, 'Hey, you've got a hit on your hands.' I said, 'Horseshit.' He said, 'You've got a hit.'

"Most of the bands were folding at the time. We were lucky: we had Hope to keep us warm. You have to be lucky in this business. If Bob Stevens from Decca hadn't come in to hear us, I might not have gone on in the music business. If that guy hadn't been listening to the Hope show that evening, that record would still be at the bottom of the barrel."

As the big-band era came to an end, Les and his band were in an unusual and advantageous position. They had a steady network radio (and later, television) show to provide financial sustenance and at the same time continuous public exposure.

"I went on doing the Hope show for years," Les said, "including the overseas tours. We did eighteen of those tours. Hope would be on radio or television or, early, both, from 1947 until the middle of the '50s. We'd book the summers. Until about 1957, we'd go out each summer for a twelve-week tour, capitalizing on the radio and television shows. We did very well.

"We had Buddy Rich in the band one summer. We got along fine. I even roomed with him at one point. When he had his own band, he introduced me once, saying, 'This is the only leader I never fought with.'

"In 1950, we island-hopped with Hope for 32 days across the Pacific. We traveled in two DC-4s. We did Hawaii for four days, Pearl Harbor, one for each service, on to Johnson Island and Kwajalein and Guam and Okinawa, then Japan, then we went to Korea for two weeks. We were there right after MacArthur invaded at Inchon. They'd pushed the North Koreans up to the Yalu, and we even played in North Korea. We had lunch with General MacArthur in Japan, just before we went over to Korea. He said, 'Don't worry, you'll be safe in Korea. It'll be cold, but you don't have to worry about getting shot at.' I said, 'How about the Chinese Reds?'

"He said, 'Oh, they wouldn't dare.' They dared. But we were on our way home."

The Hope show was not the only TV series on which Les and the band appeared. For some time his was the house band on the Steve Allen show, briefly in 1964 played on *The Hollywood Palace*, and was the house band for the complete run of *The Dean Martin Show*, 1965 to 1974.

"I'm a half-assed arranger," Les said. "But as a conductor, I'm good. That's one thing I'll say for myself. Ask anybody who's worked for me. I have done guest appearances with symphony orchestras, but I'm not really good enough for that. I can do it, but that's just an ego trip." He chuckled. "And my name got me by. But a real symphony conductor? It's one of the toughest jobs in the world. You have to know that repertoire the way we know 'Stardust.'

"But I could follow singers, follow a trapeze act, an elephant act – which I did on *The Hollywood Palace*. I got that experience at the Capitol Theater and Palace Theater in New York, the Strand, other places. We always had to have acts with us. So I got vaudeville experience. Even when

I was in music school, I played saxophone in the pit of a vaudeville house.
    "I think all that paid off. I could conduct, and that kept the band together."

Les has one son and one daughter, and four grandchildren. Les Jr. is much
involved in Les's business enterprises, and he and Les have a warm relationship. Les Jr. runs much of his father's business. At times he sings with the band,
taking it on the road, particularly when Les Sr. doesn't want to go out with it.
    Death becomes part of the late years of anyone's life. One day Les told me
on the telephone that his beloved wife Claire had terminal cancer. He saw
her through the ordeal, and then in June 1996, she was gone. They had been
married 60 years. I ran into him somewhere not long after she had died, and
he seemed to have aged decades.
    A few months before this writing, I had occasion to drop by his home in
Pacific Palisades, California. Les seemed ten or twenty years younger. He was
in the highest spirits. He explained. He and Claire had often played golf with
another couple. The woman, Evelyn Partridge, lost her husband. She and Les
grew closer in their shared loss, and in February 1998, they married. Les was off
to Europe to visit art galleries and music festivals, including that at Salzburg.
    Doris Day, of course, had a phenomenal screen and recording career: she
made 39 films in 20 years. Many of them, such as *Young at Heart*, in which she
starred opposite Frank Sinatra, were box-office hits. Most of her LPs were hits
as well. She formed the Pet Foundation in Los Angeles and remains active in
the animal-rights movement. She did TV shows in 1985. She lives in the
Carmel Valley, near Monterey, California, on an eleven-acre ranch overlooking a golf course near Monterey, and still loves to sing. Her voice remains
youthful and strong and she gives occasional thought to recording again.
    Doris said, "Frank Comstock and I talk on the phone all the time. We
always remember the laughter."
    Frank lives at Huntington Beach, which is down the coast from Los
Angeles and not far up the coast from his native San Diego. Frank, who
wrote a good deal for Doris Day when she became established as a recording
star on her own, said, "Doris is my best friend. When my wife was dying,
hardly a day went by that Doris didn't call.
    "I was talking to Doris just the other day. She said, 'Oh Frank, I wish we
were back on the road again. I never had so much fun in my life.'"
    Why have the three of them, Les, Frank, and Doris, retained a cordial rela-
tionship through all these years? "I don't know," Frank said, with a chuckle.
"Les is not a malicious guy, and neither am I."
    And Doris Day is everything she seemed in the movies and on the records.
You would be hard pressed to find three more decent people.
    "Les is a great guy," Doris said, "and I love him very much."

9

Mandelsongs:
Johnny Mandel

Of all the big-band arrangers who developed into film composers, one of the most successful and, among musicians, admired, is Johnny Mandel. And working through the medium of film, Mandel discovered, somewhat to his own surprise, that he is also a phenomenal melodist.

There are untrained musicians who have this talent, such as Irving Berlin and Harry Warren, and trained musicians who don't. Henry Mancini was a trained musician who had it. By contrast, Nelson Riddle, also well trained, didn't.

Johnny has it all, enormous orchestrational technique and a flair for melody that has produced a considerable body of songs.

"For many years I didn't think I could write songs," he told me once. What has kept some of his songs from becoming the classics they deserve to be is that they are burdened by bad lyrics. One of the weakest is that written by Paul Francis Webster and attached to one of Johnny's finest melodies, "The Shadow of Your Smile." That melody should have had words by Johnny Mercer.

Mercer had written the lyric for Mandel's "Emily." Cleverly, since there is no useful rhyme for the name, Johnny used an unfolding pattern of sound at the end: "As my eyes visualize a family, they see dreamily Emily too." Someone in the publishing division of Warner Bros didn't get it and changed it, and the sheet music went out with "they see Emily, Emily too." A lot of singers have recorded it that way. Johnny was everlastingly annoyed about it.

"Emily" was written in 1964. "It was the first actual pop song I ever tried to write," Mandel said. "It started life as the main theme of *The Americanization of Emily*, a movie with Julie Andrews. The melody sketched her character. Warner Bros wanted a lyric. They said, 'Who do you want for a lyricist?' I said, 'Can I have anyone I want?' 'Yeah.' I said, 'We might as well start at the top. That's Johnny Mercer.' Johnny came in and put a wonderful lyric to it.

"It was an effortless type of collaboration. The song became a hit, with a lot of records, and I said, 'This is fun.' I've never looked back since. That's when I became a songwriter."

Then why didn't Mercer write the lyric for the theme from *The Sandpiper?* "Well, you know," Johnny told me once, "the first six notes are the same as the opening of Hoagy Carmichael's 'New Orleans.' And I'd written with Hoagy and we were friends, and I couldn't do it. Funny part is, Hoagy asked me why I didn't write that lyric. I told him that the two songs had the same opening. Hoagy said, 'They do? I never noticed.'"

And so the main theme of Johnny's score for *The Sandpiper* – a sort of remake of *Rain* (Les McCann dubbed it *The Sandpaper*) in which the seductress is a hippy painter unconvincingly played by Elizabeth Taylor, the schoolmaster she seduces is unconvincingly played by Richard Burton, and the schoolmaster's wife is unconvincingly played by Eva Marie Saint – doesn't have a Mercer lyric. But it has great scenery and a score to go with it.

In 1964, just before it came out, I got a call from Mandel. He was in New York, to sequence the soundtrack album. He asked me to keep him company in the studio, which I gladly did. He told me the picture wasn't too good.

A story circulated that Hugo Friedhofer, when working on *The Best Years of Our Lives*, couldn't think of a thing and so scored a painting in a museum. Hugo denied that: he said that he got the *idea* while looking at a picture.

Rumor had it that Johnny had scored the scenery, not the story, in *The Sandpiper* – glorious vistas of sequestered beaches and water hissing as it slides back down the sand and seabirds crying and great towering conifers and cliffs and spindrift. The scenery, Johnny said, was his problem in that film: "You could shoot *Birth of a Nation* against that scenery and it would get lost.

"I had seen a print of the movie. Big Sur is a stretch of glorious mountainous coast just south of Monterey that I'd loved for a long time. I wrote this and that and tore up everything for I don't know how long. I finally got desperate and said, 'The hell with it,' and went off and saw some other movie. I have no idea what it was, except that it was unrelated to the story and it let me forget about writing. I went to an all-night coffee shop and the melody came out boom! in one piece. This was in the days when they didn't play music in restaurants all the time."

And that tune made me realize that Johnny Mandel was not only a great arranger but a great and distinctive melody-writer.

Tony Bennett fell in love with "The Shadow of Your Smile" and sang it for the executives at Columbia Records. They said it would never go anywhere; the age of rock was here. Tony persisted and recorded it. It became a big song for Tony, and one of the most recorded songs in American history, rivalling "Stardust" – some say exceeding it.

One of Johnny's favorites among his own melodies is "A Time for Love." "Because it just happened. It was written for a movie called *An American*

Dream, totally unrelated to the song, which was heard in a nightclub. It's the only song I know with an AABA form where each A phrase has a different chord structure. And they're not interchangeable. You can't switch them around, they don't sound right, even though the melody is the same except at the end. It returns to major going into the last part, but you couldn't use the chords from the first A section. It has to have more of a feeling of finality."

This song too is marred by a Paul Francis Webster lyric. Webster wrote some good lyrics, including "The Lamplighter's Serenade" (music by Hoagy Carmichael), the brilliant "Black Coffee," and "I Got It Bad and that Ain't Good" (music by Duke Ellington). But he contributed two turkeys to Mandel's catalogue.

Two or three singers have told me they won't do "A Time for Love," as much as they love the melody. It contains such lines as "leaning out of windowsills." You don't lean out of windowsills, unless you're a stone gargoyle; you lean out of windows. And then there's that bizarre phrase "admiring the daffodils above." Are the daffodils in the sky? Or is the windowsill that of a lower Manhattan basement flat and the song's character, face to the bars, is looking up at a flowerpot across the street on a higher windowsill? But the oddest line is: "A time for holding hands together." That's as opposed to holding hands separately? That's a paraphrase of Ring Lardner's observation on "Softly, as in a Morning Sunrise." Is that as opposed to an evening sunrise?

By contrast, Dave Frishberg's lyric for "You Are There" is gorgeous. Johnny said, "The title happened 'way after the melody was written. One morning the song came out in one piece, totally intact, and I didn't have to change a thing. I said, 'What is it? It sounds like something out of a show.' Except that it was never in a show.

"The next step was to get a lyric. Four different writers tried and didn't even come close. Then Dave Frishberg tried and nailed it and it became 'You Are There.' When it comes to problem-solving, I don't think there's a better writer than Dave: he can write anything. Most people familiar with his lyrics have no idea that this side of him exists. He's capable of infinite compassion, tenderness, and sensitivity. Most of his work that people hear is so funny and satiric that they don't realize this side of him is there."

One of Johnny's songs, "Where Do You Start?," was not written for a film. "It was not written for any particular purpose," Johnny said. "I came across a poem, contained within a novel. I can't remember the poem any more. Metrically it set off something that made me want to write a melody to it. The poem itself wasn't a very good lyric, but I set it to music. So I gave the melody, without the poem, to Alan and Marilyn Bergman. And they came up with a lyric, 'Where Do You Start?' What they did might be the best lyric about two people breaking up I've ever heard."

The combined effect of music and an achingly beautiful lyric makes it one of the greatest songs of the past 50 years.

"One of the nicest parts of songwriting," Johnny said, "is that you get to collaborate with so many talented people. The Bergmans and I have enjoyed a relationship that's lasted over 30 years and is still going strong. Our first song was 'Sure As You're Born' in 1966. I had no idea that it would result in this kind of collaboration because it started out as a shotgun wedding." The melody was written for a detective thriller with Paul Newman called *Harper*. This was the main theme, a long melodic line with a lot of harmonic and rhythmic action underneath it, to give a feeling of tension, agitation, and motion.

"During the 1950s and '60s there was a period known as the title-song era. It began with *High Noon*, which was tremendously successful. The geniuses who run the studios figured out that a song would increase the box-office revenues, so the rule of the day was that every movie had to have a song. That period produced gems like 'The Hanging Tree' and 'A Town Without Pity.'

"When I'd completed the score for *Harper*, Sonny Burke, who was head of the music department at Warner Bros, said he thought the theme had to become a song. He got in touch with Alan and Marilyn Bergman. Sonny said, 'Come to the office Monday morning. We'll have it.' I did, they were there, and they said, 'Here is the lyric.' Marilyn sang it. And much to my amazement, it fitted: I didn't believe you could write to that melody."

"The Shining Sea" also dates from 1966. "That one has a bizarre story attached to it," Johnny said. "It began as a love theme for *The Russians Are Coming, the Russians Are Coming*. It was written to describe a love scene during a glorious sunset on a beach. When I took the theme to Peggy Lee, who is not only the incredible singer everybody knows but an extremely gifted lyricist, she hadn't seen the movie; she didn't even know it was from a movie. She heard the music and a day later called me back with the lyric. It described exactly what was happening on the screen. I said, 'You won't believe what you did.'

"Being intuitive is probably one of the keys to the greatness of Peggy Lee, and it shows up in her lyrics. She must have sensed something, because when I took her to see a preview of the picture, she couldn't believe it. It was exactly the way she had pictured it."

Another of Mandel's collaborators is Paul Williams. They wrote "Close Enough for Love" in 1978. Johnny said, "It's from *Agatha*, a movie about Agatha Christie, whose life was as labyrinthine as the stories she wrote. The song had to characterize her, and so it takes many turns. It runs from minor into major, it works its way up and winds its way down on each phrase. This first phrase is twelve bars, although it is not a blues by any means. When it's repeated, it's only eleven bars, because I shortened the ending. It seemed like a stage wait: it didn't seem necessary. Then the bridge goes on its own trip. It goes into major, then resolves. When we needed a lyric, Paul immediately came to mind. Most people don't realize what a lyricist he is. When he got hold of it, he did a marvelous job and it became 'Close Enough for Love,' a play on the old expression 'close enough for jazz.'"

It is widely assumed that Johnny's most successful song is "The Shadow of Your Smile." It isn't. "Suicide Is Painless," written for the movie *M.A.S.H.*, has that distinction. It dates from 1970.

"When I started writing," Johnny said, "one of the first things I heard from other writers was: you can never tell what's going to happen to a song. You never know where it's going to end up. And this is a perfect case in point.

"The song from *M.A.S.H.* started life as a joke. It was written to be sung during the funny last-supper scene in the original movie *M.A.S.H.*, when the Painless Pole, the dentist, has decided that life is over because he can't perform with women any more and he's going to cash it in. Trapper and Hawkeye give him a knockout pill and he's laid out in a coffin. All his friends are walking around the casket to say good-bye. The song was supposed to be played by one of the GIs on guitar and sung by another. So it had to be simple, kind of dumb, with no more than two or three chords. Robert Altman, who directed the film, and I were sitting around talking about it.

"Altman said it should be called 'Suicide Is Painless.' He said he'd like to have a try at a lyric, then came back and said he couldn't do it. He said, 'But I've got an idea. I've got a 14-year-old kid who plays guitar and is an idiot.'

"So Bob's son Michael wrote a lyric, using a Leonard Cohen song with about two chords called 'The Gambler,' as the dummy. The day before we had to pre-record, I didn't have a melody dumb enough. I got desperate and wrote that melody. They made it the theme of the picture, and it became the theme of the television show, and a very important song for me, bigger than 'The Shadow of Your Smile.'"

But of course. The long television series based on the movie still runs on TV around the world, and the airplay money from ASCAP is still coming. Movies are for ever, Hank Mancini used to say, referring to royalties. So is a lot of television.

John Alfred Mandel was born in New York City on 24 November 1925, one of two children. A sister, Audrey, died some years ago.

"My mother was a frustrated opera singer," Johnny said. "My grandparents, who were very Victorian, disapproved: nice girls didn't go on the stage. My mother was very musical, and she was tremendously supportive. My father was a clothing manufacturer, ladies' coats and dresses. He was a gentle soul who loved music, loved jazz. He died of a coronary when I was 11."

Johnny started studying music at the age of 12. "I started trumpet and writing simultaneously," he said. The evidence is that he was precocious at both. When he was 14 he went to bandleader and arranger Van Alexander and asked for lessons.

Alexander, whose mother was a concert pianist, was born in New York City in 1915. Thus he was only ten years older than Johnny, but at those ages, 14 and 24, the gap is enormous. Alexander, educated at Columbia University, arranged for Les Brown, Paul Whiteman, and Benny Goodman. He was 21 when he began writing for Chick Webb in 1936, an arrangement of Fats Waller's "Keeping Out of Mischief Now." In 1938 he wrote the musical adaptation and arrangement for "A-Tisket A-Tasket" that was such a huge hit for Ella Fitzgerald.

"At the time I met Johnny I was arranging for Chick Webb," Alexander said. "I had just started my own band. I was recording for Bluebird." (That band lasted from 1938 until 1943, playing New York theaters such as the Paramount and Capitol. Alexander wrote a number of songs, the best known of which, at one time a particular favorite of jazz singers, was "I'll Close My Eyes." After folding his band in 1943, he moved to California to write for films and television.)

"Johnny contacted me somehow," he said. "He took quite a few lessons with me. There was a lot of talent. I showed him scores, which he didn't know anything about. He took it from there, and look what he's done. And he always gives me credit!"

"I'll tell you what he did for me," Johnny said. "He started me with charts. Van threw me in the water and let me swim. He told me the most valuable thing you can ever tell anyone in this field. He went over to a closet in his apartment on Upper Broadway and pulled out a record he had arranged, and then got a copy of the score from a pile of papers. It was an old Bluebird record, big stuff to me in those days. It was something called 'Hooray for Spinach.' He said, 'This is a score. You can see everything that everybody's playing. Here's what it looks like and here's what it sounds like,' and he played the record. And my eyes bugged out. He said, 'If you can set up an association between what it looks like and what it sounds like, that's the whole trick.'

"After that I went to New York Military Academy." One of his friends at the Academy, which is up the Hudson River from New York City, was Stumpy Brown, Les Brown's kid brother. Les had gone there twelve years earlier, and the other brother, Warren Brown, had also attended the school, all of them on scholarship.

"I went on scholarship too," Johnny said. "The school was very big on band in those days. It was a marching band, and the director was a martinet. But he was a good martinet, and I learned a lot."

There was also on campus an active dance-cum-jazz band, led by Stumpy Brown. When Stumpy graduated, he turned the band over to Johnny, who led it until he graduated.

"During the summers between my junior and senior years, I went with Joe Venuti's band. Then when I graduated in 1944, I played trumpet in the band of Billie Rogers, the girl trumpet player who had been with Woody Herman: a very good musician. Then I went into the band Henry Jerome had during World War II, which was full of young guys.

"Somehow I discovered I was a pretty bad trumpet player. I suppose that happened when I started working with professionals, who played in tune. And I realized I wanted to play trombone. So I played trombone with Henry Jerome, and I never played trumpet again.

"While I was in that band, Leonard Garment and Alan Greenspan were in the sax section. Lenny Garment was studying law and Alan Greenspan was taking economics. When Alan Greenspan left to become an economist, Al Cohn took his place."

Both had notedly successful careers. Greenspan is chairman of the Federal Reserve and Garment eventually became counsel to President Richard Nixon. It is a clue to Johnny's character that he has remained friends with all of these early associates, including the Brown family, Len Garment, and Van Alexander.

"Then I went into the great Boyd Raeburn band," Johnny continued.

"Then came the Jimmy Dorsey band. I played first trombone in that band, and first in the Buddy Rich band, because I could play high and I could play jazz.

"Then I went into the Alvino Rey band when it had twelve brass: that was an experience. It was like playing inside a cement mixer. Alvino was a wonderful guy to work for, and great fun.

"I took a year off and applied to the Manhattan School of Music. They had never had a jazz musician go there. I filled in a lot of gaps in my knowledge of classical music, fugues, canons, and symphonic analysis. I had always listened to this music, but now it made sense to me and I saw there was more to it than a lot of scales. After Manhattan, I went to Juilliard for a semester."

He also studied with Stefan Wolpe, as did Johnny Carisi, and he was one of that group of gifted young musicians who hung around Gil Evans' bohemian pad behind a Chinese laundry, listening to music and talking, dreaming, planning – John Lewis, Charlie Parker, Lee Konitz, Barry Galbraith, Johnny Carisi, Gerry Mulligan – that led to what is now called the *Birth of the Cool* recordings on Capitol. Mandel, however, was not one of the writers for those recordings (possibly because he was in Los Angeles, waiting out his union card). And again, he remained friends with all these early associates.

"I went back to Buddy Rich," he said. "I was in three of Buddy's bands. I started out hating him and ended up loving him.

"I wrote for Buddy and I wrote for Artie Shaw's 1949 band, which had Zoot Sims and Al Cohn and Jimmy Raney in it." That band is remembered by those who heard it as one of Shaw's best.

"In 1948," Johnny said, "I moved to Los Angeles, where I'd always wanted to be. The union was very exclusionist, because of all the movie studio work, and it took you six months to get your card. You couldn't work at music at all for the first three months. I worked as a shipping clerk and wrote at night. I wrote a lot for Latin bands, and there were a lot of good ones around. That's how I got so far into Latin music. I've always had a love of Latin music, which is why I got into the bossa nova movement so early.

"I was working as a soda jerk in a drugstore at Hollywood and Vine when Woody Herman's great Four Brothers band came in to play at the Empire Room around the corner. The guys would come around to where I was working to eat – I don't know why, because the food was lousy.

"Poor Serge Chaloff got so embarrassed seeing me as a soda jerk that once he ordered a dollar-ninety-eight dinner and left me a five-dollar tip. But the guys kept coming in to hang out with me, and when I wasn't slinging food, I started to write for Woody. I never wrote as much for that band as I would have liked to."

But a Mandel composition for Woody, "Not Really the Blues," is one that the Herman bandsmen always loved to play, according to Lou Levy and other of its veterans.

"No sooner did I have my union card than I went right back to New York to work in Chubby Jackson's band, playing not trombone but bass trumpet. After that I went into the studios. I was a staff arranger at WMGM, one of the last, and then I wrote for Sid Caesar's *Your Show of Shows* in the early days of television. After that I went with the Elliott Lawrence band."

He worked with two other arrangers on *Your Show of Shows*. One of them was Irwin Kostal. "Did we ever learn from him," Johnny said. The other half of the "we" was the third arranger: Billy Byers. "Billy was one of the most fantastic musicians I have known," Johnny said. Billy Byers, trombonist and arranger, is almost unknown to the jazz public, in part because he was content to expend much of his brilliant, indeed legendary, talent writing anonymously for, among others, Quincy Jones. Once, in Jim and Andy's, I asked him why he was content to go nameless, as he did, when musicians universally recognized the scope of his abilities. "Quincy's good at the politics and business part of it," he said. "I just want to do my writing."

"Billy used to write on deshon with ink," Johnny said. Deshon is a smooth-surfaced score paper, sometimes called onion skin. It is possible to scrape away a false note with a razor blade. Billy had a briefcase containing his tools. It was notorious that, under time pressure, he could sit down any-where, open his briefcase, set up his two little lights, and start writing. "He didn't use a piano," Johnny said. It was also noted that Billy would, on occasion, write a first trumpet part, then a second, and so forth through the whole orchestra, handing them out as he finished them, remembering what he'd done and never assembling a full score. To be sure, he was not the only one who could do that, but it's a pretty nifty trick.

Johnny said, "There was another way you could erase on deshon, besides the razor blade. You could use a Q-tip and Clorox. I was working on something for *Your Show of Shows* in my apartment in New York. I had a page that was just black with notes. I left the room for a minute or two. When I came back, my cat had knocked over the Clorox, and the page was blank. I went back to writing with pencil, and I've never looked back."

We reminisced some more about the musicianship of Billy Byers, especially his incredible ears.

"I'm not sure he had absolute pitch," Johnny said.

"Yes, he did. He told me about it. He said he could turn it off. If he was playing trombone in a section, he could turn it on or off, adjusting to the intonation of the band."

"I can do that too," Johnny said. "And I have absolute pitch." He said he has a solid memory for keys in major, but it becomes less certain in minor.

"One of the most interesting things about Billy," Johnny said, "was his incredible power of concentration. There could be chaos around him, noise, shouting, music, and he could just sit there and concentrate and write. We worked on a lot of things together."

"How did you happen to go with Count Basie?" I asked.

"In June, I think it was, 1953, I got a call from Basie to join the band on trombone. I joined the band immediately in St. Louis." He was with the band until November, playing and writing. "The experience was so wonderful that it seemed that nothing could ever come close to it. So after I left the band, I quit playing. I came out to California."

His writing was immediately in demand, and his reputation grew. He wrote an album for Frank Sinatra called *Ring-a-Ding-Ding*, another for Peggy Lee of Leiber and Stoller songs, called *Mirrors*. An album of Jerome Kern songs he arranged for singer David Allen (whom he had known since their days with Boyd Raeburn) remains an exquisite rarity in the collections of connoisseurs.

And he began to get into motion-picture composition, including a particular landmark score. Leonard Feather wrote of him: "Mandel's reputation as one of the most brilliant young arrangers was enhanced in '58 by his underscoring for *I Want to Live*, considered to be the first successful integration of jazz into a movie score."

Hollywood, of course, has always typecast its talent. And Johnny became known for his ability to create suspense in scores, and for a long time he got assignments of that kind. At one point I asked him what he really wanted to do. He said: "Write some great ballads. The very first thing I discovered when I began to write songs was that for me they break down into two definite categories: the ones that just come naturally and the ones that I have to manufacture and work at and use craftsmanship to complete. Almost invariably, when I look back, the second kind didn't turn out to be good. It was the first kind, mainly, that did.

"I don't know why a song happens, when it happens. If I start to hear it, I've learned enough to let it come out, let it go wherever it goes, and I assume the role of a caretaker in that I want to make sure I've got it down on paper. In essence what you've got to do is stay out of your own way and let it go. Because for some reason it wants to go there. While it's happening, my main thought is, please let the thing finish itself. Don't let it stop midway and become a fragment. I've got hundreds of great fragments that I can't figure out where to take. The first thing I want it to do is come to a conclusion, or at least come to a place where I can take it and work with it.

"Most of the songs that I've ended up feeling good about have been like that. They happen, and I've learned to let them happen.

"You know, I like writing to lyrics because it pushes me into directions that I might not go otherwise. It's a different way of writing, and it's nice."

This surprised me. I have always believed, and so did Johnny Mercer, that the most lyrical songs are written music first. Few composers can set words to music; Richard Rodgers was one of the spectacular exceptions, and did so when he wrote with Oscar Hammerstein. But I think he wrote his best songs when he worked with Lorenz Hart, at which time the melody came first. For the most part composers, when you hand them a lyric, will give you back a drab recitative melody. "I've lost some good lyrics that way," Johnny Mercer once told me.

Mandel said, "I've learned to listen to that thing that happens, whatever it is. And I don't care what it is. I'm afraid if I knew, it would go away.

"I wouldn't want to give anyone the impression that you just wait for the muse and it just comes out effortlessly: this doesn't happen that often. There are many songs that I have had to manufacturer, hack away at, and yet try to make them sound. I can make a song that sounds pretty good, but at bottom I feel that it's a manufactured item. It isn't all gravy.

"For a good part of my professional life, a lot of what I've done is translating colors and emotions that I see on the screen into sound, and I really don't know how I do it. It seems like something that came naturally to me, probably because I used to feel sensations when I heard other people's music. I don't know what the process is and I really don't want to know.

Again, the superstition takes over. If I know too much about it I have that fear underneath that it will disappear, although I know that isn't the case. You do best if it's instinctive and you have the chops to do it in the first place. I guess I've always been sort of primitive when it comes to dealing with experiences, and I like doing it by the seat of my pants, like the old pilots – rather than looking at the instruments to find out what I should do. All I know is that I really don't know how to put this in a logical, rational, methodical context at all."

Mandel hasn't written a film score in well over a decade. "I don't do it any more," he said. "It just stopped being fun." He'd rather write an album, like the one he did for Shirley Horn, *Here's to Life,* in 1991.

Also in 1991, he did much of the arranging for Natalie Cole's album of songs associated with her late father, Nat Cole. The album, *Unforgettable,* went almost instantly to the top of the *Billboard* chart. It stayed for a long time, like an unscheduled full moon moving only slowly across the sky. In the title song, "Unforgettable," she sang a chillingly beautiful duet with her father. Mandel supervised the complex technical process by which this was achieved. Both albums proved that such music, when the industry allows it to, can succeed in the marketplace.

More recently, Johnny wrote an album for Diana Krall titled *When I Look In Your Eyes.*

Billy Byers and Johnny remained close, in both senses of the word: they were neighbors in Malibu. Sometimes, when pressed for time, Johnny would orchestrate for Billy and at others Billy would orchestrate for Johnny. It reached the point where neither could remember who did what. I mentioned to Johnny that Billy had orchestrated his *Sandpiper* score. He said, "No, I did that one myself."

A day or two later, he telephoned me. He said, "I pulled out the *Sandpiper* score. You were right. It's in Billy's handwriting."

Billy died on May Day, 1996. It was his birthday: he was 69.

The American Society of Musical Arrangers and Composers, ASMAC, is almost unknown to the public. It gives its awards to its own. It is a hidden affair, as it were, not the circus the Academy Awards are. At its dinner on 27 August 1996, ASMAC presented its Golden Scroll Award to Johnny Mandel. In the same ceremony, the society gave the Irwin Kostal Award post-humously to Billy Byers. It is named of course for the arranger with whom Johnny and Billy worked on *Your Show of Shows*. Billy's wife, Yuriko, accepted it. The previous year it went to Van Alexander, its first recipient.

In his impromptu acceptance speech, Johnny, his voice choked, said of Billy Byers: "I think Billy was the best of all of us."

Mandel and I live about 50 miles apart in California. We talk on the phone a lot, it seems. We always did, even when I lived in New York and he in California. Gerry Mulligan's death shook us both badly. I have a photo, taken on the cruise of the *Norway*, of Gerry, Phil Woods, Johnny, and me. Johnny and Gerry had been friends since even before the days in Gil's pad. "Gerry and I started hanging out together around 1946," Johnny said.

When Robert Farnon's name came up in a conversation, Johnny Mandel, one of the most brilliant composers and arrangers jazz has produced, said: "Most of what I know is based on having stolen everything I could from Farnon. I've listened to him and tried to approximate what I thought he was doing. He made strings sound like they always should have and never did. Everybody wrote them skinny. He knew how to write them so that it could wrench at you. I'd never heard anybody like him before and I've never heard anybody like him since. We're all pale imitations of him, those of us who are influenced by him."

Johnny and his wife Martha have lived in a house in Malibu since 1971. Their daughter Marissa is grown-up. The area was not heavily populated when they moved there, but it has grown enormously since then. Their house is sequestered behind a wall and a high wooden gate. Its garden ends at the top of a cliff that plunges down to the beach below.

One day years ago, I was visiting. Johnny and I stood at the end of the garden at the top of the cliff, listening to the flopping of the surf and the keening of terns and gulls. I thought of *The Sandpiper* and the sights of Big Sur and said, "Do you ever get the feeling here that you're walking around inside one of your own scores?"

Johnny said, "Yeah, I do."

More recently I was visiting again. I said, "What do you want to do next?"

"Well," he said, "now I've got this reputation for writing ballad albums for singers, I'd like to get back to writing something that swings."

10

Going home: Henry Mancini

The great scar of the Grand Canyon passed slowly under its wings as the jet coursed eastward at 35,000 feet. It was 12 November 1987. Henry Mancini didn't look out of the window: flying was a part of his life. He had been doing it for years, to record his movie scores or conduct symphony orchestras, to perform in big cities and small, or at the White House for three different presidents, or in London for members of the British Royal Family. Now he was going home – to his original home, not the big house in Holmby Hills or the other one he owned in Malibu or the third in Vail, Colorado, which he visited mostly in the winter, to ski.

"How tall are you, Hank?" I once asked Mancini as we were on our way to lunch. We were in the elevator of the building at Hollywood and Vine in Hollywood, in which at that time he maintained an office. He used to let me use it as a base of operations whenever I came out from New York.

"Six-one," he said, and with an impish grin, added, "Six two when I've got a hit."

It was so like him: quick, witty, sardonic, self-mocking.

Hank was the most successful and certainly the most visible composer in movie history. Most film composers do their work in comparative obscurity. Only the scholars of good movie music even know their names. But Mancini's was a household word.

Some people handle fame well and some don't. Hank handled it superbly: he ignored it. He considered himself supremely lucky. For example: "I've often wondered what would have happened to me if I hadn't needed a haircut that day," he said on another occasion. He had just stepped out of the barbershop at the Universal Pictures lot, when he ran into an acquaintance, Blake Edwards.

They were about the same age, Mancini then 36, Edwards 38. The studio system was coming to an end, and Hank had just lost his job as a staff composer, and he had a wife and three children. He still had a pass to the Universal lot, however, and with nothing better to do with his time, he decided to get a haircut. Edwards asked him about Ginny, Hank's wife, and after a few more minutes of chat, Blake asked, "Hey, would you be interested in doing a TV show for me?"

As Hank told me much later, he wasn't exactly being overwhelmed with offers at the time, and he said, "Yes. What's the name of it?"

Edwards said, "It's called *Peter Gunn*," and Hank said, "What is it, a western?" and Edwards said, "You'll see," and made an appointment with Hank.

It wasn't a western, of course. It was a private-eye story starring Craig Stevens, and it would be one of the most successful series in that genre: certainly it was the most stylish. And it would lead to a profound change in the nature of television and movie music. For it had a jazz score, the first in television history.

I first met Henry Mancini in Chicago in 1959, when he was on a promotion tour for the *Peter Gunn* album and I was the editor of *Down Beat*. This was shortly before the success of *Breakfast at Tiffany's*, and of the song that has ever since been identified with it, "Moon River." It was possible still for songs with tunes as melodic as that and lyrics as literate as the one Johnny Mercer attached to it to be hits in America; the great American song tradition had not yet been fully effaced by rock-and-roll. He seemed wary. Or perhaps he was merely baffled by his sudden fame. If he was suspicious, it was no doubt because he had been under assault from elements of the east coast jazz critical establishment because of *Peter Gunn*.

His detractors were so busy deploring what Mancini had done with jazz that they overlooked what he was doing for it. Until that time, film-scoring was almost entirely derived from European symphonic composition. Mancini changed that. More than any other man, he Americanized film-scoring, and in time even European film composers followed in his path.

Although others had used elements of jazz in film underscore before him, Mancini was the man who opened the way for the full use of this music in drama. Mancini proved that the vocabulary of jazz could be used to express tenderness, romanticism, fear, laughter, pensiveness.

But his purpose was not to write jazz, any more than it was to write symphonies: it was to underscore drama. "Everything I have ever written comes from the picture," he repeatedly asserted. Mancini was the principal figure in developing what could be called the song score. Whereas earlier composers in the field had tended to use "classical" music techniques of thematic development and non-melodic orchestral writing, Mancini began writing scores such as that of *Breakfast at Tiffany's* and *The Pink Panther* series that contained almost as many fully developed song melodies as a Broadway musical. And he used all sorts of devices of the dance bands to set these melodies off, from jazz walking bass to Caribbean dance rhythms. That he was capable of a quite different kind of writing is evident in the score for the suspense mystery *Arabesque*, which is comparatively abstract, or that of *The White Dawn*, or the stripped and austere score of the Paul Newman version of *The Glass Menagerie*.

Mancini was revealed in *Breakfast at Tiffany's* as an inventive and original writer who enormously expanded the vocabulary of modern orchestration. An awareness of "classical" orchestration was wedded to a fluency in American big-band writing, to sometimes startling effect.

The combination of these things made Mancini the first film composer to emerge from the anonymity of that profession to become a public figure with record sales in the millions, and shelves full of Grammy, Oscar, and other awards, and the conductor of concerts everywhere.

"What did being an only child do to you?" I asked him just before our plane landed.

"I had to make do, learn to do things myself. I can still make it alone. It's just having to do for yourself."

There was no welcoming committee when we landed at the Pittsburgh airport; he hadn't asked for it. Mancini never had a retinue around him. He traveled with only his road manager. A key group of musicians – the rhythm section, the lead trumpet, and a saxophonist, Al Cobine, who was also his contractor – would meet him at the job. He called them "my guys" and they were a close-knit group who had been with him for years.

We were driven to the newly built Vista Hotel where we checked into our rooms. The first rehearsal was set for the following day.

The four nights of concerts he was about to conduct with the Pittsburgh Symphony were already sold out. The repertoire for these concerts included his *Overture to a Pops Concert*, a commission by the Boston Pops Orchestra for its hundredth anniversary, a slapstick Stan and Ollie theme from *A Fine Mess*, three of his television themes (*Hotel, Newhart*, and *Remington Steele*), three movie songs ("Life in a Looking Glass" from *That's Life*, "Crazy World" from *Victor/Victoria*, and "It's Easy to Say" from *10*), music from *The Thorn Birds, Charade*, themes from *Lifeforce, The Great Mouse Detective, The Glass Menagerie*, and part of his *Beaver Valley '37 Suite*, a memoir of his childhood originally written for the Philadelphia Orchestra; and finally, of course, the requisite "Pink Panther", "Peter Gunn," "Two for the Road," "Mr. Lucky," "Dear Heart," "Days of Wine and Roses," and "Moon River." The last-named song has been recorded more than 1,000 times.

The next morning a driver took us to Heinz Hall, named for the famous food family, home of the Pittsburgh Symphony.

The concert was to last two hours: and the rehearsal was scheduled for two-and-a-half hours. Hank was one of the few people in the world who could prepare a two-hour concert in two-and-a-half hours. One reason was that his musicians would communicate to the orchestra and lead its phrasing. Hank said that a good many film composers who had done pop concerts with symphony orchestras presented them with extremely difficult scores. The composer who did that chewed up rehearsal time on hard passages, leaving an orchestra to scramble. And Hank was deliberately easy on orchestras, which was one reason they liked him.

They also liked the music. A woodwind player in the Pittsburgh told me, "You wouldn't believe all the crap we have to play in the pop concerts. This orchestra feels this is the best, that's the reason they like to see Hank come in. It's an easy gig, but this is music, and we recognize it and like it."

And so Hank would complete a rehearsal with a good orchestra in ten minutes under two hours, and with a less professional regional orchestra in ten minutes over two hours.

And this one came in almost exactly ten minutes under the two hours. "See?" Al Cobine said, as if he'd won a bet.

The orchestra's players were making their crowded way down a corridor to the dressing rooms. A tall violinist said to a petite girl walking beside him, "The thing I like about him is that he doesn't throw his fame at you." The backstage mood was good.

"He has a great deal of reserve about him," said saxophonist Al Cobine, who contracted the orchestras with which Hank worked on the road, "at least until you get past it. I find it in his reticence to talk freely. He's a storehouse of knowledge if you can get him to talk. We've all observed for years how complex he can be. For example, he always seems to know who wrote the lyrics to songs. We started talking about some very early characters in jazz, and he knew all about them and what they did. And he remembers faces and names in all the orchestras. He'll ask about them, he has a deep memory.

"Another thing is that he is very patient with people. He can be cutting at times, but he'll say it, and it's over and forgotten."

Ginny, Hank's wife, said that he always told her, "When something goes wrong, lay out four bars before you do anything."

At the concert's intermission, his dressing room was crowded. His expression would light up when he recognized faces from long ago, and he would ask after this old friend or that, after someone's brother, or a musician he had worked with in the early days when the Sons of Italy band played on a bandstand in a vacant lot in West Aliquippa.

I noticed a tiny but vigorous woman among the well-wishers. She was less than five feet tall, and I was astonished to learn that she was 82. She looked about 65. Hank brought her to meet me, grinning and with a solicitous loving air. "This," he said, "is Madeleine Paoline." I knew who she was: she was his godmother, and she had been his teacher in Grade Five. She sat down on a sofa in the dressing room, a little prim in manner, and formally erect.

She remembered that the conductor of the Sons of Italy band was Carlo d'Atri, an immigrant. Madeleine's husband played valve trombone in the band, which in the band's hierarchy made him second to the baritone horn, and her brother was the first clarinetist. They rehearsed every Sunday morning after church, and crowned their labors each year with performances on the festa of St. Anthony and that of Santa Magno.

What was Henry like in the fifth grade?

"He wasn't a candidate for a Rhodes scholarship," she said. "But he was an alert boy, an average student. He was impish and with a subtle humor. He liked sports, which he was allowed to play until the time his mother or father would yell, 'Henry, time to practice.' He loved to eat. He doesn't look a bit different now than he did then.

"His father was so proud of Henry, it's a wonder he had any buttons left on his shirt. He would send clippings about Henry home to us from California."

This image of the father was at sharp variance with the one I was to gain from Hank.

Hank was handsome, and elegantly urbane. His tailoring was always impeccable. He was a connoisseur of wines and a gourmet. No one ever looked more as if he were to the manor born. He spoke beautifully. In the first years I knew him, we never talked of books, and I was surprised, later, to discover how much he read; indeed how much he knew about many things. He simply didn't parade it.

Small wonder, then, that I had trouble reconciling the sophisticated and enormously successful man I'd known for nearly 30 years with the little Italian ragamuffin he says he was as a boy, growing up in West Aliquippa. On Sunday afternoon, we were going to drive out there to look at it.

Or what was left of it.

The first concert was held on 13 November 1987. The audience devoured it. Afterwards there was a reception given by the Rotary Club in a large room in the basement of Heinz Hall. From the head of the staircase, you could see them sipping from wine glasses, talking, laughing. As Hank descended the broad stairs, ladies pressed programs upon him for autographs, all the faces in the room turned suddenly upward to watch him. One person and then another would say some variant on, "Henry, do you remember me? I used to . . . " And he always did remember.

He stayed for a time, signing autographs, chatting with strangers and old acquaintances alike, and then with a conspiratorial smile and a lift of the eyebrows suggested it was time we left. It was obvious that when he is traveling, the company he prefers is that of his "guys," and some of them were waiting.

Al Cobine said the symphony musicians sometimes ask, puzzled, "Why does he do this? Obviously he doesn't have to, he doesn't need the money."

"Because he likes it," Cobine would tell them. Hank always told his guys to live well on the road. As we left with one or two of them, laughing about something or other, I suddenly realized what Henry Mancini, in his heart of hearts, really was.

Henry Mancini was an old road musician.

The next day, about noon, 14 November 1987, the Musengos arrived – Helen, the cousin Hank had said was like a sister, and Ralph, her husband. They had driven down from Cleveland on the freeway. The trip is perhaps 100 miles. When Quinto Mancini, Hank's father, made it here in his old Chevrolet about 1930, tires were poor and roads were narrow, and it is not recorded how long the journey took. It was probably an ordeal. Henry was 6 then.

Henry Mancini was born in Cleveland on 16 April 1924 (the year Puccini died), but in the late 1920s his father moved to West Aliquippa, this little town twenty miles northwest of Pittsburgh on the bank of the Ohio where it flows through Beaver Valley on its way to become part of the Mississippi. He'd heard they were hiring men at the Jones and Laughlin Steel Company. Hank would always consider West Aliquippa his home town.

Hank's relationship with his father was always strained; he adored his mother, a plump woman less than five feet tall. One day in 1935 his father drove him to Pittsburgh. His father, who was from Abruzzi, often cursed him in the dialect of that region, calling him a little *cafano*, which means hick, or an *animalo*, animal, or *porco Madonna*. *Porco* means pig, and *Madonna* refers to the Virgin Mary.

His father took him to Loew's Penn Theater that day. Hank told me: "We entered this luxurious cavern with a gold-and-white ornate ceiling that seemed as far away as the sky. We settled into red velvet seats, the lights went down, and the big screen lit up with the name of the movie. It was Cecil B. DeMille's *The Crusades*. I still remember the huge black-and-white images of knights in armor, Arab warriors in flowing robes, horses and tents and sand and gigantic faces that opened their mouths and talked. I had never seen a talking picture, only the silent comedies. What I remember most of all from that day is the music, the sound of a big orchestra: I had never heard anything like it. I'd never heard anything much but the Sons of Italy Band in which I played flute and piccolo. We played such things as the *Zampa* overture and 'Morning, Noon and Night in Vienna.' I had the flute solo on *The*

William Tell Overture. My father started me on the flute when I was 8. He played flute and piccolo, and he was determined that I would learn them. Very determined. He took the wooden perch out of a birdcage, and if I'd play a wrong note when I was practicing, he'd hit me on the head or the back with it.

"He told me that the reason we were seeing this movie was that he wanted me to have a sense of history. But why?

"When the picture was over, I followed him to the car. I was still fascinated by the movie and the music in it. I thought that there was a big orchestra behind the screen, but he said that this just showed you what an ignorant little *cafone* I was. He told me the sound of that orchestra was actually *in* the movie.

"We headed north in the valley along the riverbank toward home. My Dad told me I would study hard, go to university, get a degree, become a teacher, and escape the steel mills. But I had already made up my mind I was never going to be a teacher. I didn't tell him then or for a long time after, but I knew what I was going to do when I grew up.

"I was going to write music for the movies."

Quinto Mancini – Quinto means *fifth* in Italian – was born in Scanno, a small town in Abruzzi. Quinto Mancini's grandfather was a farmer who owned a house. So he was a man of some property, not a sharecropper. Quinto disliked his cousins, and with cause. When Quinto's grandfather died, the property was deeded to Quinto's father and his brother. The uncle cheated Quinto's father out of the property in some Machiavellian maneuver, and Quinto and his siblings were thrown off the land.

About 1910 or 1911, at the age of 12 or 13, Quinto Mancini made up his mind to emigrate to the United States. He made his way to Naples, where he boarded a ship, then Boston, where he worked in a shoe factory, then Cleveland, and finally to West Aliquippa. He played the flute.

"Wherever there were communities of Italians in the small towns of America," Hank said, "and especially in western Pennsylvania, they were like modules, cocoons, of the old country." Hank said he might as well have been growing up in Italy, so Italian was the West Aliquippa community. Surprisingly, he never learned to speak Italian; but he did put olive oil on his hair which, his mother said, would make it strong and healthy. Comparatively early in life, Hank's forehead receded and eventually he was pretty much bald on top.

Ralph Musengo described Anna Pece Mancini as "a really nice woman. She and Helen's father came from a family of contentment and joy."

"I think Quinto was a sentimental man," she said. "He cried when Ralph and I got married and when our first child was born. Quint always talked about Henry and the great pride that both he and Annie had in him."

Quinto was making fifteen dollars a week, Helen said. She remembered that Anna once forswore a winter coat so that Henry could have his arranging lessons.

I said, "Hank told me that he doesn't remember his father ever showing one sign of affection to either him or his mother."

Helen said, "I think it was the era. Parents of that generation were not as outgoing as they are today. I think Ralph will agree with me. We thought Quint was very loving toward Henry."

She said Henry looked like his father.

Ralph said, "In about '41 or '42, we made a trip to visit Annie and Quint in West Aliquippa. It was a very meager home, meager surroundings. You could tell that there wasn't much money in the family."

Helen said, "But she was happy, made the best of everything."

Ralph said, "She was always happy. It shows how much she loved Quint. And I'm sure it was reciprocated."

Hank never forgot the soot and smoke from the mills. Sometimes in Pittsburgh, street lights would be turned on in the day. The mills, Hank said, stained the night skies orange, and "the soot and fly ash murdered the air we breathed . . .

"The first snowfall always seemed magical. It was lovely when it first came down, putting caps on roofs and clinging to the branches of the trees . . . but it soon became what is called black snow . . . " One of the titles in his *Beaver Valley* orchestral suite is "Black Snow."

On the hills above Aliquippa lived the white-collar workers and supervisors of Jones and Laughlin, looking down – literally – on the homes of the mill hands. In high school, he tried to make friends, but was soon reminded by the Cake Eaters, as the minorities of the town called those who lived above them, that he was Italian. It didn't help that the lunches his mother packed always contained a salami sandwich, in a time when salami was really greasy. It would soak through the brown-paper bag, leaving a grease stain in his desk. He was very sensitive about this.

But by now, he was a moderately accomplished flautist, and he played in the Sons of Italy marching band as well as small regional dance bands.

The family's house was about 100 yards from the Ohio riverbank. Offshore were Hog Island and Crow Island, connected to the shore by two barges that functioned as a pontoon bridge. Families who worked at Jones and Laughlin were allowed to garden there. His mother had a vegetable plot, where she would grow tomatoes from which she would make paste or set out to dry in the sun.

From time to time a paddlewheel steamer would pull in at Crow Island, and Hank, with others from the community, would go on excursions to an amusement park downstream in West Virginia.

When he was about 14, he heard a dance band on one of these excursions. Its personnel included a rhythm section, three trumpets, two trombones, and five saxophones. The musicians were black. The band was in what he would later recognize as the Fletcher Henderson–Count Basie style. He was exalted by their music. And by that time he was trying to learn to arrange, slowing the family gramophone and laboriously writing out arrangements by the Artie Shaw band and others. He never knew the name of that band. But the experience, he said, was metaphysical. "At such times you know you're in the presence of something extraordinary."

Whatever the strain in their relations, Hank's father sent him to Pittsburgh for piano lessons. He studied arranging with Max Adkins, who led the pit band at the Stanley Theater. Adkins trained a number of major musicians, including Jerry Fielding who, like Hank, would become an important film composer, and Billy Strayhorn, with whom Hank became friendly at that time. Adkins not only taught Hank to write, he taught him to dress, how to give tips, how to behave generally. Hank always considered him one of the most significant figures in his life.

Hank graduated from high school at 17. Adkins recommended him to Benny Goodman when the latter played an engagement in Pittsburgh. Goodman assigned him to write an arrangement. Hank sent it to Goodman. Goodman wrote back, "Come to New York."

By then Hank had applied for admission to the Juilliard School of Music. He left for Juilliard on a scholarship in 1942. Goodman was playing the Paramount Theater. He assigned Hank to write an arrangement on the song "Idaho," and Hank met the band's pianist and arranger Mel Powell, scarcely older than Hank. Goodman didn't like the arrangement and never played it.

Hank played gigs around New York, with Johnny Long and Vincent Lopez, among other bands. His father sent him a little money every month. Hank was studying the music of Bartok, Mozart, and particularly Debussy and Ravel. He turned 18, was drafted, assigned to the Army Air Corps, and sent to Atlantic City for basic training. There he met some of the members of the Glenn Miller air corps band. They urged him to apply for the band and arranged a meeting with Miller.

He remembers Miller sitting at a table, looking at him through his rimless glasses and saying, "I hear you're an arranger. Do you write well?"

Hank said, "Well enough, for what I've done. I also play flute and piccolo and piano."

Miller said, "Okay," and took Hank's serial number.

When he finished basic training, Hank expected to be sent to gunnery school. To his surprise, and on Miller's recommendation, he was assigned to the 528th Air Force band under Master Sergeant Norman Leyden, an arranger and conductor with a degree in music from Yale. Hank considered the encounter with Miller one of the incidents of luck in his life. Without it, he thought, he might have died as a gunner on a B-17.

At the time of the Battle of the Bulge, many air force band musicians were reassigned to the infantry, and Hank was sent on a troop ship to Le Havre, where he was assigned to an engineering brigade. But when he was on the way to the front, he was reassigned yet again – as organist for the company chaplain. Hank played hymns on a small pump organ.

That chaplain, who had a small trailer behind the jeep Hank was assigned to drive, would load it with champagne which he would sell to soldiers at the front. And as they passed through the many villages, the chaplain would enter empty churches and remove their stained-glass windows, some of them hundreds of years old, which he would have crated by the engineers and shipped back to the United States, where he could sell them after the war. Hank retained contempt for that chaplain all his life.

Hank reached Linz, Austria, in early May 1945. His company was sent on an assignment. "We weren't told where we were going," Hank said. "I was with the chaplain, driving the jeep. We proceeded east for about fifteen miles and went through a small village. Making a final turn leaving the town, we came upon an expansive meadow of lovely green grass reaching to the top of a nearby hill. Perched on it was a huge gray stone structure: it was the Mauthausen concentration camp. We went in.

"The scene was unreal, dreamlike. Under American supervision, surviving prisoners, in their striped uniforms and carrying rifles, were escorting squads of SS troopers in full uniform. The SS men were carrying shovels, and with the rifles of the prisoners on them, they were using the shovels to give decent burial to the dead, many of whom were simply lying there naked in the dirt. The smell of quick-lime was everywhere. The cremation ovens were still warm, with traces of smoke rising from the chimneys.

"At the end of the day we left. As we drove back to our camp, I saw the villagers through different eyes than I had a few hours before. Within a mile of them, unspeakable horror had occurred; here life went on as usual. Some of them must have known. No one could convince me otherwise.

"The war in Europe was over by 8 May."

By another stroke of luck, Hank was able to get assigned to a band that soon was posted to Nice. "It was one of the best periods of my life, ever," Hank said.

His cousin Helen had married Ralph Musengo, who had been working in the Counter Intelligence Corps with Italian partisans behind the German lines. Ralph spoke fluent Italian. Now Ralph was stationed at Nice.

Ralph said, "You know, I remember two Italian boys that came to the villa near Nice with Hank just at the end of the war. We had a hell of a lot of fun.

One of those boys said, 'Some day this guy's gonna be a big star. You wanna put some money on it.'"

Hank was discharged on 30 March 1946, at Fort Dix, New Jersey. His old Master Sergeant, Norman Leyden, was now chief arranger for the postwar Glenn Miller band, led by Tex Beneke, who was just out of the navy. Its personnel included Conrad Gozzo, Pete Candoli, Paul Tanner, Rolly Bundock, and Jack Sperling. Hank would some day use them on the *Peter Gunn* music. But first Hank went home to see his mother and father and his old teacher, Max Adkins. Hank's father wanted him to go back to Juilliard, so that he could become a teacher, but Hank had by now gained valuable writing experience and wanted to go directly into the business. Adkins was supportive, Hank returned to New York and, on Norman Leyden's recommendation, was hired without audition by Tex Beneke as arranger and pianist. He was paid 125 dollars a week.

"So I went with the band and didn't go back to school," Hank said. "I felt this was an opportunity I couldn't miss. I could speculate as to what might have been. I might have been further ahead in certain ways as far as education goes, because my musical education is a patchwork. I've had some great teachers, like Castelnuovo-Tedesco and Krenek, I've done a lot of study, but I have not had that formalized thing where you go through this which leads to that. But I don't think I'd trade it now.

"The big thing about the Beneke band was that I was there, I would write something, we'd rehearse it, and I'd hear it played."

Another arranger for that band was Marion Evans, fresh out of the US Marines and the war in the South Pacific.

The Beneke-Miller band carried a string section. I said, "How in the hell did you balance thirteen strings against all that brass?"

Hank laughed. "We usually didn't. In an up jazz arrangement, there is no way to do it, unless you're recording. I think they had only one mike on the strings. The bands in those days did not have many mikes, they were hardly miked at all. It was on the ballad arrangements that I really learned a great deal about balances. Thirteen isn't a lot. In fact, I remember after I was married, Jerry Fielding called me one day and said, 'I'm going to have to write for strings here, and I don't know what to do.' He came out to see me. We spent a whole day just talking about strings, and here I was, the expert – who had probably done about fifteen charts for strings!"

I said, "But you'd studied the books, the Berlioz, the Rimsky-Korsakov, the Reginald Forsythe."

"Sure. But I hadn't had much actual experience with strings."

With the Beneke band, "we played the Glen Island Casino, the Meadow-brook, Coney Island in Cincinnati, and all the theaters," he said. "Sometimes we would stay in a location for a week or two at a time. In theaters we would play four shows a day. It was an exciting time. Nobody had even a remote idea that the age of the big bands was ending. The public still idolized band-leaders like Benny Goodman, Artie Shaw, Duke Ellington, Count Basie, Woody Herman.

"When you were on the road with a band, you lived in a capsule, a cocoon. There was no other world but the band, because you were always leaving behind the people you met along the way. The only continuity you had was with the band itself. You breathed and talked the life of the band. You could almost complete everybody else's sentences. You knew everything about everybody. You were always on that bus, and you settled into a groove. Everything came down to two things: where do we eat, and what time does the job start? I was by now more than slightly interested in girls, but even they didn't enter into it that much: you were always waving good-bye to them through the bus window.

"I cannot remember ever finding a restaurant that was any good, nor can I figure out how we got our pressing done. You did your socks and under-wear yourself in the hotel-room sink, but how we got pressing done is still a big mystery to me."

The band took on a vocal group from Los Angeles, the Mello-Larks. A member of that group was Ginny O'Connor. Hank was skeptical of Holly-wood people and, he said, reflexively looked down his nose at her. Ginny was half Irish, half Mexican, and spoke Spanish before she spoke English. Her father had driven trucks at MGM, and Ginny knew the movie business.

Ginny told me she was taken by him from the very beginning. The musi-cians in the band knew it. They would see to it, on boarding the band bus, that all the seats on the bus were occupied except the one by Hank, which they'd left for her. Hank said, "I think Ginny saw something in me as a musi-cian that I didn't see myself," which is a serious understatement. Ginny said that because of the way she was always looking at him, the musicians called her Dopey. But soon they were dating, and without a formal proposal assumed they would be married.

Ginny hated life with that band. She was a California girl, and she loathed the cold. She was making 90 dollars a week; Hank by then was earning 300 dollars. When the band played Cleveland, Hank took her to West Aliquippa to meet his parents. Ginny's mother – who had played piano professionally – disapproved of the relationship. She didn't want Ginny to marry a musi-cian. She said that if she did, she'd starve.

Ginny by now knew Hank's dreams. She said that if he really wanted to write music for movies, he should make the move now. She gave Tex her notice and returned to Los Angeles. Hank too gave his notice, telling Tex he was going to be married. Tex gave his blessing, saying that even if he couldn't travel with the band, he'd like Hank to keep writing for it. Ginny's mother, despite her reservations about musicians, set up a room for him in their home, and he lived there until they were married and took an apartment in Burbank. Hank's best man was Jerry Gray, born Graziano, who had been Glenn Miller's arranger and composer of the Miller hit "A String of Pearls." Gray and composer David Rose got Hank some of his early assignments in writing for drama, in those days radio drama. With Ginny singing in the studios – she was a first-rate sight reader – they eked out a living, doing without furniture in their living room.

Hank told me, "My mother and father came out to visit both summers after Ginny and I were married, driving all the way across the country. They liked it, and then in 1949, when my father got his Social Security, they wrapped up everything in Pennsylvania and moved out here. I realized when he arrived that year that my dad had it in his mind that he was going to live with us, as is the custom with families in Italy. We didn't even have a house yet, only our apartment.

"I was not working very much, and things were very difficult for Ginny and me. With what little money I did have I helped my parents buy a house in Bell, southeast of Los Angeles. It was a little cracker box of a place, but comfortable.

"My relationship with my father grew more strained, and eventually turned a little nasty. He went back to work, in a shoe factory, doing, I suppose, whatever he had done in that shoe factory in Boston.

"Then my mother had the first of eight heart attacks. We found her the best of nursing care around the clock. She had a telephone by her bedside, and the anticipation of hearing our phone ring at odd hours of the night was a nightmare for us. She was visibly deteriorating.

"My dad became even more difficult to deal with. He felt he was being punished for something and he blamed everyone. He was even angry at my mother for being sick. He wouldn't give her the time of day, and she just remained sweet and quiet. I don't think his attitude did much to make her want to get well.

"I would try to talk with my parents every day. We would drive the two hours there and back at least once a week. He became very sullen and more difficult to communicate with, and I came to feel guilty about the situation. He was always civil to Ginny but he really took his anger out on me.

"And he never let me forget that I hadn't gotten a degree in music. He pounded me with it. When I would get a nice little job, and turn in a piece of work I was proud of, and try to tell him about it, he'd say 'Well, if you had your degree you'd be teaching school.'

"I have felt an overwhelming sadness, the kind of pain you can't control, emotion that overwhelms you to the point that you break down and sob, once in my life. It was after we received the call that my mother was dying. We drove to Bell, and I cried in the car. A priest was there. We were at her bedside when she released the death rattle. It's a sound you don't forget."

Hank by then was writing for the Buddy Rich band.

If Hank always wondered what would have happened to him had he not needed a haircut that day, I have wondered what would have happened to him had he not met and married Ginny O'Connor. She had grown up in comparative poverty during the Depression. By the time she was 12 she was dancing professionally to add to the family's meager income. She would save pennies all week to accumulate enough money to go to the movies on Saturday and forget, in their flickering fantasies, the difficulties of her daily life.

She learned to sing early and she was doing it professionally before she was out of her teens. Her friends were the young Hollywood crowd, including Donald O'Connor, Peggy Ryan, Judy Garland, Mel Tormé, Sammy Davis Jr., and Blake Edwards, whose father and grandfather had been in the movie business. She knew the ways of the industry, and indeed she got Hank his first movie assignment: writing an arrangement for a short subject featuring the Jimmy Dorsey band at Universal in which she and the Mello-Larks were appearing. The studio was about to make several musicals and Joseph Gershenson, head of the music department, liked Hank's work and gave him another assignment, writing music for one scene in an Abbott and Costello film called *Lost in Alaska*. The job paid 225 dollars a week and was supposed to last two weeks. Hank stayed on staff at Universal for six years, writing music for all sorts of pictures, thoroughly learning his craft. He rarely did a complete score, writing only a few scenes here and there in association with other staff composers.

By now Hank and Ginny had three children, Christopher, born 2 July 1950, and twin girls, Monica and Felice, born 4 May 1952. The girls looked so much alike that, later, they could fool their father about which of them he was talking to; even in their adult years, they could deceive him on the telephone.

Better pictures, and pictures with bigger budgets, came Hank's way. He wrote the underscores for both *The Glenn Miller Story* and *The Benny Goodman Story*. The former included a melody that gave one of the first hints that Hank was a formidable melodist. With lyrics by Don Raye, it took on a life of its own as the song "Too Little Time." And then Hank got a more important break: he was assigned the score of the 1958 Orson Welles film, now viewed as something of a classic despite butchery in the editing room by the studio brass, called *Touch of Evil*. And it is here that we first hear a distinctly Mancini-esque score, with jazz brass used to contribute to the dark mood of the picture. He used such musicians as Conrad Gozzo and Shelly Manne in the band. It was a genuine departure in film-scoring, though little noticed as such at the time.

Hank never claimed to be a jazz musician or composer, and he had enormous respect for those such as Billy May whom he did put in that category. But he had roots in jazz and, more particularly, the big-band era that was coming to an end when he was with Beneke. And as soon as he had the stature, the authority, and the opportunities to draw on that background, he did so.

Hank always retained one horrific memory of his days at Universal.

One of his closest friends was the actor Jeff Chandler, an aspiring lyricist who also liked to sing, although, Hank said, despite a rich and beautiful voice, he had pitch problems. Hank wrote act music for him when he played Las Vegas. They wrote a song for the Ross Hunter movie *All I Desire*. Then Tony Curtis made a movie called *Six Bridges to Cross*, which Hank was to score. It needed a song to be used during the closing credits: he and Jeff Chandler wrote one. Hank knew Sammy Davis Jr. quite well; Ginny had known him since they were very young. And in his autobiography, *Yes I Can*, Sammy said that Jeff Chandler was like an older brother to him. Chandler called Sammy, who was playing the Last Frontier in Las Vegas with the Will Mastin Trio, and said that he and Hank wanted him to sing the song for the film. Sammy's career was on the verge of major success.

Davis told Chandler, "Well, man, I'm here for the next month. I'll tell you what, I'll come down for the day and record for you and then come back to Vegas."

Sammy finished work at midnight and left in his new Cadillac convertible for Los Angeles with his valet Charley. Charley drove for a time, then Sammy took over and Charley slept in the back seat. He heard his hit record of "Hey There" on the radio. Then, at sunrise, a car passed him. Then its driver tried to make a U-turn on the highway. Sammy swerved to miss the car, lost control, and hit the other car's rear fender. The police arrived. Charley groaned in the back seat, unable to speak because of blood in his throat. He pointed at Sammy's face. Sammy put his hand up and found one eye dangling by a thread of nerves on his cheek. He tried to stuff it back into the socket, falling to his knees and saying, "Don't let me go blind. Please, God, don't take it all away!" And in the ambulance he thought, "I'm never going to be a star. They're going to hate me again."

Jeff Chandler, Hank, and the orchestra were assembled in the studio at Universal by 9 a.m. When Sammy didn't show up, they were surprised, and as time wore on, they grew increasingly uneasy. Hank rehearsed the orchestra, then at noon dismissed them for lunch. Chandler, on a dark hunch, called the sheriff's department and learned that Sammy was in a hospital in San Bernardino. He had lost an eye.

Always the professional conscious of his obligations, Davis asked Chandler to sub for him at the Last Frontier, and Chandler flew to Las Vegas with the act music Hank had written for him. As soon as he was out of the hospital, Davis recorded the song for the picture.

Chandler, born Ira Grossel in Brooklyn on 15 December 1918, died on 17 June 1961: he was 43. The official cause of death was given as blood poisoning sustained during back surgery. Hank and others of his friends said he died of medical bungling. They were heartbroken and furious.

Sammy acquired a glass eye and became the star he had always wanted to be. He remained close friends with Hank and Ginny until his death on 16 May 1990.

Touch of Evil was one of the last scores Hank would do at Universal; he always considered it one of the best he'd ever written. The old studio system was breaking down, with more and more movies being made by outside production companies. And that is when Universal got rid of all its staff composers; and the day Hank needed that haircut.

Johnny Mandel and others with jazz background were getting into film scoring. Indeed, Johnny had composed a jazz score for the 1958 Susan Hayward movie *I Want to Live*. But Johnny is the first to tell you that it was Mancini who made jazz widely acceptable in film-scoring.

"The idea of using jazz in the *Gunn* score was never even discussed," Hank told me. "It was implicit in the story. Peter Gunn hangs out in a jazz roadhouse called Mother's – the name was Blake's way of tweaking the nose of the censors – where there is a five-piece jazz group.

"It was the time of so-called cool West Coast jazz. And that was the sound that came to me, the walking bass and drums. The *Peter Gunn* title theme actually derives more from rock-and-roll than from jazz. I used guitar and piano in unison, playing an ostinato. It was sustained throughout the piece, giving it a sinister effect, with some frightened saxophone sounds and some shouting brass."

In those days, it was unusual for the scores to movies to be released on records, and unprecedented for TV scores. But Ray Anthony had had a hit record with the *Dragnet* theme and he had another with his recording of the *Gunn* theme, which Hank arranged for him.

Shorty Rogers was by now a big jazz star, and his LPs for RCA Victor automatically sold 80,000 copies or more, a lot of albums in those days. An RCA executive thought Shorty should record the *Gunn* music. Hank had lunch with Shorty, who said, "Hank, I have no reason to record this. It has no connection with me. *You* wrote it, *you* arranged it, and *you* should record it. This music is *yours*."

Hank said, "But Shorty, I'm not a recording artist. I'm just a film-writer. Nobody knows who I am. You have a name."

Shorty was immovable. He told Hank, "It's your baby, and you should do it." RCA agreed to let Hank record his *Gunn* music.

Peter Gunn hit the television screens of America in September 1958. RCA had pressed only 8,000 copies of the album. The 8,000 were gone in a week and, as Hank put it, "All hell broke loose. They were running around like madmen at RCA, trying to keep up with the demand."

The album went to the Number One position in the *Billboard* charts and stayed there for ten weeks, and when it fell from that position it didn't fall far. It remained in the charts for more than two years, ultimately selling more than a million copies, an unprecedented sale for a jazz record.

And it made Henry Mancini a huge name with the public. Later, Hank would wonder not only about that haircut but what would have become of him if Shorty Rogers had decided to record that music himself instead of pressing Hank to do it.

The success of *Peter Gunn* led to a new opportunity for Blake Edwards and thus for Hank. Prior to Gunn, Hank had worked on three pictures with Edwards. One of them was *Mister Cory*, a film about a professional gambler starring Tony Curtis. This was the source of the idea for Edwards' next television series, *Mr. Lucky*. Hank wanted to come up with something different for a main theme, and he found it: a gorgeous melody played by strings with Buddy Cole on Hammond organ punching out accents, like a brass section. Since the film was about a suave character who runs a gambling ship off the California coast, religious fundamentalists put pressure on CBS, and Blake Edwards was forced to turn his protagonist into a restaurateur. The ratings of the series began to slip, but not before Hank had another top-ten album with *Music from "Mr. Lucky"*. After a year, Edwards told Hank he could no longer lend his name to this compromise, and he closed the show down.

His television days were ending, in any event. He was about to move on to directing solely for the big screen. The first picture he was to do was *Breakfast at Tiffany's* for Paramount and he asked Hank to do the score.

The score required a song for Audrey Hepburn to sing on a fire escape. The producers of the picture thought they should hire a Broadway composer to write that song. Mancini had no track record as a writer of melodies, but he begged Blake Edwards for the chance to do the song as well as the score. Edwards took up Hank's cause with the producers and they decided to let him have a try at it.

But given the chance, Hank couldn't think of anything. Finally, at home one night after dinner, seated at the piano, he came up with a simple three-note fragment in the key of C. It took him only minutes to write the tune; it had taken him six weeks to get the idea for it. He called Johnny Mercer to ask if he would write a lyric.

Johnny was at a low point in his career. Rock-and-roll had taken over the music business, and he felt that his own career was probably finished. He listened to Mancini's new tune and made one of the most inaccurate predictions in music history. He said, "Hank, who's going to record a waltz? We'll do it for the picture, but after that it hasn't any future commercially." Hank gave him a tape of the tune and Johnny went home and began to write.

Hank was to conduct the orchestra for a benefit at the Beverly Wilshire Hotel. Johnny arranged to meet him there to show him what he had written. Hank played the melody on the piano in the deserted ballroom. Johnny showed Hank three lyrics. One was "Moon River," and Hank said that the moment he heard it, it gave him chills.

The lyric was perfect for the picture, evoking the wistful yearning of the somewhat lost girl of the story. Johnny was very much in touch with his southern roots, and the song has a folk quality about it. Blake Edwards and the producers loved it. As for Mercer's prediction that the song had no future, it proved remarkably inaccurate. The song was a huge hit for Andy Williams, who became ever afterwards identified with it.

In view of the propensity of many producers and directors for meddling in the scoring process, the relationship between Blake Edwards and Hank was amazing. Edwards allowed him complete freedom. He wouldn't ask to hear the music while it was being written, not even the title theme. His first knowledge of what Hank was doing would come at the recording date.

And this went on in 28 pictures, among them *Days of Wine and Roses*; *Victor/Victoria*; *What Did You Do in the War, Daddy? The Party*, and *S.O.B.*

Hank had received his first Academy Award nomination in 1954 for *The Glenn Miller Story*. But in 1961, he received three nominations, one for the score of *Breakfast at Tiffany's*, another for the song, and a third for the song "Bachelor in Paradise," with a lyric by Mack David. He won for the score of *Breakfast at Tiffany's* and for the song "Moon River." He had already won a Grammy for the *Peter Gunn* album.

Hank soon was working on *Hatari!*, a 1962 film with an African setting directed by Howard Hawks. One scene in the picture was purely fortuitous. Three baby elephants took a great affection to actress Elsa Martinelli and started following her. Hawks simply shot footage of it, without knowing whether he even wanted to use it in the final picture. Hank looked at it, at Hawks' request, and remembered a Will Bradley boogie-woogie hit record, "Down the Road A-piece." He used it as a model, and the boogie-woogie piece he wrote, played on a calliope, "Baby Elephant Walk," became yet another hit.

That very same year, 1962, Hank scored another film for Blake Edwards, *Days of Wine and Roses*, with Jack Lemmon and the late Lee Remick. It is a poignant tale about alcoholism. Edwards thought it needed a song, and that its title was a promising seed for one. It derives from a poem by Marlowe ("The days of wine and roses, they are not long . . . ") to whom Johnny Mercer, who wrote the lyric, always gave grateful credit. Hank wrote the melody in about half an hour; he played it over the telephone to Mercer, who called back in a few days to say he had the lyric. Hank was thrilled by it, and arranged for Blake Edwards and Jack Lemmon to hear it. He and Johnny performed the song for them in an old sound stage at Warner Brothers.

"I was sitting with my shoulder toward Blake and Jack," Hank said. "Johnny, of course, was facing them. When we were through, there was a long, long, heavy, terrible silence. It probably lasted ten seconds, but it seemed like ten minutes. Finally I couldn't stand it, and I shifted myself around to look at Blake and Jack. And there was Jack with a tear rolling down his cheek, and Blake was misty-eyed. We didn't have to ask them if they liked the song." In 1962, it won Hank and Johnny another Academy Award.

But it was not just that Mancini was *only* an outstanding melody writer. Hank, from at least the days when he scored *Touch of Evil*, had a distinct and instantly identifiable style of orchestration. It was often imitated, never equalled. One of its components was the way he used French horns playing the top of chords over trombones, sustained pads against which he would set melodies. Another factor was his use of flutes. As a flute and piccolo player himself, he knew what these instruments could do. He would, for example, use high piccolos in unison with the lead line on string passages. It would give the strings an icy sound. And he virtually invented the use of bass flutes. When he started using them in film scores, there were few of the instruments available; but he insisted on them. Bulky and awkward looking with their twists of pipe, they can produce a gloomy and ominous sound, and Hank used them to great effect in dramatic passages. And of course his string-writing was always clean, and clear, and elegant. That he was as good at suspense stories as he was at romantic tales and comedies was amply demonstrated, if *Touch of Evil* had not already established this, in the 1962 picture for Blake Edwards called *Experiment in Terror*.

A year later he did a film that Blake Edwards wrote but didn't direct, *Soldier in the Rain*. Of all Hank's themes, this and the theme for *Two for the Road* were his own favorites. The latter is my own favorite of all his themes.

Hank by now had so much prestige that he could demand, and often get, the publishing rights to his own music: this was unheard of. Movie companies extorted from composers the rights to publish the music they wrote for the picture. This meant that on any subsequent use of the music, in recordings or radio or television performances, the movie companies' music-publishing subsidiaries got half the royalties. Hank, again, broke precedent. And the reason, again, was the generosity of Blake Edwards.

Johnny Mandel is of the opinion that Hank had a good business head. He thinks Hank liked and enjoyed the business part of the profession. Whatever the reason, Hank made astute moves. He asked Edwards, as an independent producer, if he would let him retain the full rights to the *Peter Gunn* music, and Edwards quite casually consented to this. Later, Hank would ask for publishing rights before signing a contract to score a movie. He wouldn't always get it, and he didn't turn down attractive assignments if he couldn't. But sometimes he would get what he wanted, and sometimes he would get half the publishing.

He always thought he was an unlikely person for all this to be happening to. Major singers were recording his songs. Almost every film score he wrote was immediately issued in an album by RCA, and would usually make the best-seller lists. It was at this point that Jerry Perenchio, who was in the concert-booking division of Music Corporation of America, approached Hank about doing concerts. The first experimental concert, putting Hank on a bill with Johnny Mathis, took place at the Seattle World's Fair.

After a somewhat unsuccessful group of concerts with pick-up orchestras, Hank conducted the Cleveland Orchestra, one of the best in the world.

"By then I had done a concert album," Hank said. "Instead of second-string pick-up orchestras, I started to think in terms of the true symphony orchestras around the country. I began to get offers from them. Then one came in from the Cleveland Orchestra. Since I was born in Cleveland, I figured if I couldn't make it there, I couldn't make it anywhere.

"That engagement, in the fall of 1963, was very successful. After that I began to make regular appearances with symphony orchestras, both major ones and local ones like the San Fernando Symphony Orchestra, in high-school auditoriums or even in parking lots. In 1965, I did a concert at the Greek Theater in Hollywood, and in 1968, in a program with the Fifth Dimension, the first of many at the Hollywood Bowl.

"If I'd shown any tendency to a swelled head, my father took care of it. I remember that he came to one of the concerts. It was a great thrill for me. I thought I conducted well, and the audience gave me a standing ovation.

"After the concert I was walking out through the parking lot with my dad. He gave me one of his I-want-to-say-something-but-I-don't-know-how looks. Finally he said, 'You know, Henry, you should take conducting lessons.'"

In 1963, Hank went to London to score Stanley Donen's romantic thriller *Charade*. The resulting main-title theme, with a lyric by Mercer, was nominated for an Academy Award, but lost out to *Call Me Irresponsible*. The song illustrates Mercer's remarkable ability to turn almost any title or idea into a lyric.

By now, Hank was an international celebrity. In the winter of 1967–68, he and Andy Williams did the first of several tours of Japan, and then played the Royal Albert Hall in London, selling it out for three concerts.

Of all the comedies Hank scored for Blake Edwards, the best known are the *Pink Panther* movies, featuring the clumsy Parisian detective Inspector Clouseau, played with brilliant invention by Peter Sellers.

Sellers and Edwards did not get along well. Hank often found himself, given his perpetual apparent equanimity, acting as the mediator between them. But Edwards and Sellers had great mutual respect, and the symbiosis of their relationship was fruitful.

The saxophonist in *The Pink Panther* was Plas Johnson. This reveals one of the characteristics of Hank's writing: his jazz background. He always wrote with the style of specific instrumentalists in his mind's ear, and this theme was written for Plas Johnson's big, solid tone, as the *Mr. Lucky* theme was written specifically with Buddy Cole in mind. There are several gorgeous ballads in *The Pink Panther*, one of them, titled "Piano and Strings," that features another of the great jazz musicians, pianist Jimmy Rowles.

Blake Edwards decided to use an animated cartoon of a pink panther under the opening credits of the film, and the theme became irrevocably associated with that little character. A series of cartoons has been built around it, and it is seen now on television around the world.

"None of us," Hank said, "really foresaw what was going to happen in the years ahead to the Pink Panther, Blake, Peter, and me. This was, as far as we knew, a one-shot project, which we were very happy about – on a high, really, because the script was so good and the performances excellent. I don't believe that there were even the problems on the set that you so often run into in pictures.

"It was during the making of *The Pink Panther* that Ginny and I visited the town where my father was born. When we arrived in Rome, I hired a driver – I had no intention of driving those roads the way they were in those days. We traveled over a rocky, dangerous road through terrible terrain. It looked like a moonscape. I had never seen such rough country, rocky, bleak, jagged, and almost devoid of trees.

"I kept looking out the window and I said to Ginny, 'My God, how did my Dad make this trip? How did he get down to Rome and then to the port at Naples?' When he made that journey, there not only were no cars, there were no roads. I could envision him walking most of the way, perhaps hitching a ride now and then on a horse cart. The trip took us four hours: it must have taken him two or three weeks. I tried to put myself in that position, making that trip on foot, with very little money, knowing only that you had an appointment to leave on a boat, because he had arranged for a cousin who lived in Detroit, and whose name I do not know, to meet him at Ellis Island. It was mind-boggling that a boy could make that trip alone. Why did he do it? Why was he so determined? I couldn't begin to re-create that trip in my mind.

"At last we got to Scanno in Abruzzi. It was a typical mountain town with stone houses and cobbled streets. It probably hadn't changed in a century or more. The women still wore black and carried baskets of bread and various other things on their heads. There was an Italian wedding going on in a restaurant near the church. We went to the church, but we couldn't find any records, and as far as I knew I had no relatives there now. Or, if I did, my father never had spoken of them. There was no reason to stay. Ginny and I looked around, then had the driver take us back to Rome, over those awful roads.

"Now a freeway connects Scanno to Rome. There is good snow-pack in those mountains, and the terrain is scattered with resorts. The international crowd hasn't discovered it yet; it's where the Italians go to ski."

The Pink Panther produced yet another Mercer–Mancini song, "It Had Better Be Tonight." And so did *The Great Race*, a Tony Curtis comedy about an automobile race from New York to Paris. For this, Hank and Johnny wrote "The Sweetheart Tree."

Hank's style was so distinctive that you can tune in during a movie on television and recognize his sound instantly. And yet it was amazingly versatile, whether he was scoring comedies like *The Great Race* and *A Shot in the Dark* (one of the Pink Panther films) or serious dramas such as *The Molly Maguires*, the suspense thriller *Experiment in Terror*, or *The White Dawn*, a picture about three Boston whale-hunters stranded around Baffin Bay and discovered by Eskimos on an ice floe. Hank researched what little Eskimo music there is and developed a theme based on a simple rising two-note theme played on a recorder. *The White Dawn* is one of his most interesting scores.

If film-score albums became a fashion in the record industry, Hank certainly was the most influential figure in establishing the pattern; and no one else ever had the sheer number of such albums released.

From 1958 on, Hank averaged three film-scores a year. Given his income from the constant showing of these films on television, the number of recordings of his songs, and the income from his concerts, he became no doubt the wealthiest movie composer in history, and certainly the most popular.

The money would roll in almost relentlessly. For Hank did not write for the transitory pop-song market: he wrote for film. At any given moment, many of his films are being presented on television, and royalties are paid on the music in these (and all other) films by the broadcasting company. This meant that all his life, Hank received royalties not just on the famous pictures such as *Breakfast at Tiffany's* and *The Pink Panther*, but on earlier work such as his contributions to *Abbott and Costello Go to Mars, The Creature from the Black Lagoon, Ma and Pa Kettle at Home, Tarantula, Francis in the Haunted House*, and one of the first rock musicals, *Rock, Pretty Baby*. These royalties will be paid for 50 years after his death, which means that not only his grandchildren will receive them, his great-grandchildren will do so as well. As he put it, "Movies are for ever."

I once asked Ginny what had been the greatest shock when she and Hank passed quite suddenly from being a young couple struggling to make ends meet to being genuinely rich. "The need to be on guard," she said. "I didn't like that at all."

She continued to work as a singer long after it became unnecessary. Indeed, she was Hank's vocal contractor, assembling the choral groups heard on his albums and film scores, and sang with them. She always retained contact with her old friends among the studio singers. Some of them, and even some big stars such as Betty Hutton, Ella Mae Morse, and Helen Forrest, had fallen on hard times. Ginny became the founding president of the Society of Singers, an organization specifically set up to help them and others in similar situations.

At the organization's initiation, Ginny threw a party at their huge Holmby Hills house. Just about everyone you could think of from that world of singers was there in the huge living room under a beamed high-vaulted ceiling. They gathered around the piano and suddenly started to sing – a grand chorus improvising the harmony parts on some standard song. They finished it and laughed and started another one. There must have been twenty of them, falling into their parts as naturally as breathing. It was remarkable, and Hank said, affecting indignation, "Do you hear that? Do you hear what they're doing? Do you know how long it would take me to get a sound like that on a record date? Do you know how much it would cost me?"

Ginny eventually quit the business. It happened on one of Hank's own record dates. She and the singers she had hired arrived to find no musicians in the studio. Where were they?

Hank explained that the singers would overdub the voices on rhythm tracks that had already been recorded; full orchestra would be added later. "That's the way we do it now," Hank said.

"Not me," Ginny said. "When the fun's gone, I want no part of it." She said the warmth and camaraderie had gone out of recording, and besides there were other singers who needed the money, and she didn't. After that session, she quit.

Hank's relations with his father continued to be difficult. Hank said, "One thing that helped in raising the children was that Ginny and I held a united front. I can't ever remember speaking a word of anger in front of the kids. Chris has said that he has never seen me lose my temper. I don't know if that's good or bad. But Ginny bore the burden of the problems with the kids, and she came out the other end with her sense of humor and our marriage still intact. The credit is all hers."

Hank won at least twenty Grammy Awards and four Academy Awards and at least eighteen nominations. He scored more than 80 movies and a number of TV films as well, including *The Thorn Birds*. He composed themes for something close to twenty TV shows, and recorded more than 80 albums. He performed (if this means anything to you; it means nothing to me, although I think Hank, with the Cake Eaters and the greasy salami sandwiches in his school desk never far from memory, was proud of it) four times at the White House and three times for the British Royal Family.

Hank's was an astonishingly fertile life work, characterized by a supreme elegance. Of all the things I have heard said in praise of it, one stands out in my mind more than any other. A woman said it to me: "His music makes you feel beautiful."

Before the concert that evening in Pittsburgh, there was a glorious Italian dinner at a restaurant, with Hank in an elated mood and ordering the wines with the grand satisfaction of some great signore entertaining his friends. "This is what life on the road is all about, man," he said.

The next morning, 15 November 1987, in front of the hotel, Hank and I got into the Lincoln he had rented. We drove out along the Allegheny River, with its countless bridges, into the point of land where the Monongahela meets it, creating that prow point of downtown Pittsburgh called the Golden Triangle. We crossed a bridge heading north and found ourselves in a tangle of small streets in an area of small industries. "Hey, I remembered!" Hank said triumphantly as he made a turn into one of the streets.

"What, are you afraid senility is setting in?" I chided.

"No, man," he said, "it's just that it's been so long." We picked up a street on the northeast bank of the Ohio called, logically enough, Ohio River Boulevard. The day was clear, and exceptionally warm for November. The road ran along the shoulder of the high riverbank. Bare trees stood like black lace on slopes made brown by fallen leaves. The car drifted smoothly along to Ambridge, a community whose name is contracted from that of the American Bridge Company. We crossed the river on a long bridge, then swung north. We were now, Hank told me, in Aliquippa. Aliquippa at this point consisted of a tree-clad slope above us on the left and a long expanse of abandoned factory on the right. I had heard about this, read about it, seen it on television, but all of it together had not prepared me for the vision of a dead industry. What had been the Jones and Laughlin Steel Company, stretched for miles northward along the riverbank, was a deserted dead thing, with smokestacks like the fingers of supplicant hands against the sky. All the prayers in the world wouldn't help: the massive mismanagement of the economy had done its work, and American capital had fueled the steel mills of Korea.

We passed long stretches of chain-link fence protecting properties whose furnaces would never be warm again. And a few miles to the south, in West Virginia, towns such as Davy were dying because Pittsburgh no longer bought their coal. In a strange bleak way, this vista of ruined industry was impressive. One thinks of America as young, and growing, and vital; not depleted and moribund. The terrible reality we were seeing was heartbreaking and awesome.

At last he turned off the highway. "Well, this is it," he said. "West Aliquippa." Hank swung the Lincoln into shabby streets of a tiny town. They were paved with brick cobbles; the town had never even got to asphalt. Grass grew between the bricks. "Now at one time we lived . . . " Hank said, turning a corner. "It's gone!" We looked at an empty lot between two crumbling and deserted frame houses. "Wait a minute," he said. He was disoriented. He drove on. Nobody lived in these houses. This town wasn't dying, it was dead. "Now, this is one of the places we lived," he said. "This is 401 Beaver Avenue."

We got out of the car and looked around. Hank walked up the short sidewalk to the house. The house was painted a hideous green, and it was in an advanced state of deterioration. I turned 360 degrees, surveying the decay of the community. I thought about the condition that the wiring of these places must be in, the crumbling foundations, the dry rot and wet rot of the wood, all the ravages of neglect. There was nothing you could do for this town but put it out of its misery: burn it to the ground and let nature reclaim this devastated terrain.

I tried to imagine the boy Hank had been, playing stickball in the streets. I listened for the cries and laughter of children. I heard nothing, not even wind. I turned and looked at 401 Beaver Avenue. Hank was sitting on the steps to its porch. He was wearing an exquisite black windbreaker of thin glove leather, and a black Greek sailor's cap, purchased perhaps in Athens. Then, just for a second, I almost saw the boy who used to practice flute in this house.

We got back in the Lincoln. Ahead of us a cat crossed the cobbled street. We drove around the town a bit: it comprises no more than ten square blocks. Hog and Crow Islands, where Hank's mother once tended her vegetable plot, were gone: landfill had joined them to the shore, and on it stood a large steel plant. It appeared to be fairly new, but it was deserted.

We passed a building whose windows and doors had been bricked in. Why preserve it? It would never be used again. "That was the Sons of Italy hall," Hank said. One house we passed had a well-tended little vegetable plot in the backyard. An old man was standing looking at it. Somebody still lived here. I wondered what he thought of the Lincoln passing by. "We lived here for a while, upstairs," Hank said. It was a two-storey building of flats. "There was a fire, and I remember my father carrying me down the steps." But the steps were gone, and the sagging balcony would fall in a year or two. "Over here was the Serbian hall, and that empty lot, that's where the band-stand was, where we played in the Sons of Italy band."

We left West Aliquippa, and not far away turned into the main street of Aliquippa proper. Hank said it was named for some ancient Indian queen. Its main street lies in the length of a wooded ravine cut eons ago by some feeder of the Ohio. It was a much larger community, not yet as dead as West Aliquippa. A few people were to be seen on the street, though they seemed to be going nowhere in particular. Storefronts were boarded up, there was trash and broken glass in the gutters and on sidewalks, and weeds grew in cracks in the cement. "How do you feel, seeing this?" I said.

"Empty. Hollow," Hank said. "Just hollow."

He headed the car up a slope of the river bluff. "This was my high school," he said. It was an extensive brick plant on the brow of the hill. We got out. "I want to see if I can find the band room," Hank said. We entered a door and looked around. Hank walked ahead of me. A small stern woman in her 60s emerged from an office and said to me severely, "Can I help you gentlemen?" Hank was too far ahead of me to hear her.

"My friend," I said, "used to go to this school, and he wanted to look around."

"And who is your friend?" she said. Maybe she thought we were dope pushers.

"Henry Mancini," I said.

"Henry!" she cried, her face lighting. "I graduated with you!"

And she rushed toward him. I thought she was going to embrace him. She told him about her family, and Hank remembered them. Hank said he was looking for the band room. She led the way, and they talked about old friends.

We climbed a flight of stairs, and in a dusty cluttered office the woman introduced us to the band director. This is how the world has changed: the band director's name was Victoria Eppinger, and she told us she had gradu-ated from the University of Illinois. She was in her late 20s or early 30s.

"I've found a lot of clippings about you," she told Hank, and dug them out. "I've only been here this year, and I'm still going through old files." She showed us the newspaper clippings, most of them about his occasional returns to Beaver County, to play benefits for one cause or another. "Henry Mancini Returns to Help," one headline proclaimed.

She even had his high-school year book. The entry on Hank said that he wanted to be an arranger and hoped some day to have his own band.

We went into the band room. Two boys were sitting on folding chairs, looking at music stands. "Hey, that's the same piano!" Hank said, looking at a scarred old brown spinet standing against the wall by a blackboard. The keyboard cover was secured by a padlock. Hank said, "I think that's the same goddamn padlock! I used to play this piano!"

We went to the school's main office. The lady who had greeted us so severely introduced Hank to two women on the staff. One of them asked Hank if he remembered So-and-So, her cousin. He did. At last we left. We were standing in front of the school's pillared portico when a black man in his 40s with a compact, neat, muscular body came up to us and said, "Aren't you Henry Mancini?"

"Yes," Hank said.

"You went to this school."

"Yeah," Hank said.

"I work here," the man said. He had a bright, warm, accepting smile, which Hank reciprocated. In photos Hank has a rather stiff smile, not unlike the uncomfortable smile of Glenn Miller, but in person it is ready and easy. "Man, what a pleasure to meet you," the man said, pumping Hank's hand.

In 1946, Pittsburgh instituted a grand reclamation project. Blighted areas were razed and laws were put in place requiring the steel and coke industries to put scrubbers on their stacks and cease their pollution of the air. Today the rivers of smoke are gone and Pittsburgh is one of the cleanest cities in America. Further, its dead industries are being replaced by computer and communications companies and it is becoming a major medical and educational community. It is a great city, rated by surveys and studies as probably the best in America in which to live. And that orchestra is superb.

I had become curious about the two theaters that had played such an important role in Hank's youth – the Stanley and Loew's Penn. He'd told me as we were on route to Pittsburgh that they were both gone now, victims of progress. But since our arrival, he'd learned that the Stanley hadn't been torn down: on the contrary, it had been refurbished at a cost of millions and now was named the Benedum Center. Its stage had been enlarged and now it was a home for opera and musical theater. Hank had arranged to go through it when we got back from Aliquippa.

We stood in the wing stage left. "I used to stand here and watch the bands," Hank said. "You know that mist they use on movie sets for effect? Well, they didn't need that: the air looked like that on this stage in those days. You could always smell the coke ovens. I remember watching the Ellington band here. You see that first balcony out there? Well in the 1937 flood, the water was right up to there."

Hank asked someone on the Benedum staff about the basement of the place, where he'd studied with Max Adkins. But the whole basement had been restructured and that office was gone. Hank asked when the old Loew's Penn had been torn down. He was told that it had never been torn down: on the contrary, it had been restored on a grant from the H. J. Heinz people, and it was now Heinz Hall, home of the Pittsburgh Symphony.

It hit us both at the same time. I said, "That's where you're standing to conduct. Just in front of the proscenium! Right where the screen was on which you saw *The Crusades*."

On 17 November 1987, Hank and I returned to California.

Hank was one of those fortunate souls able to sleep on airplanes. I envied him this ability. After a while he awakened.

I felt I had come to understand something about the Peces and Mancinis. Most of the immigrants to America came from deep poverty, from a desperate peasantry. The Pece family had money. And so, until his father was cheated of the house and the lands around it, did the Mancinis. Possibly – we'll never know now – this was the reason for Quinto Mancini's silence: a bitterness that he, he of that family in Abruzzi, had to work in a steel mill. There was probably a knot of anger in his stomach. James Joyce's short story *Counterparts* describes a man's frustrations during his working day which, at its end, he takes out on his kid. Maybe that's what Quinto Mancini did. But he made sure Henry had his music lessons, and Henry never went to the steel mills. Who wrote, "We are all the victims of the victims"? I told Hank what Ralph Musengo had recalled of the family history, the theft of the house.

"I never knew that," Hank said, and fell silent.

"Helen," I said, "gave me an impression of a warm and affectionate man."

"Yeah," Hank said. "Well, that's what he showed to the world. It's not what he showed me."

After a time, Hank opened the handbag he carried in travels, took out Pat Conroy's novel *The Prince of Tides*, and began to read. Something gave him pause, and he sat pensively for a time. Then he handed me the book, tapping his finger on the final paragraph of an early chapter. "Read that," he said, and I did:

When parents disapprove of their children and are truly deceitful about that disapproval, there will never dawn a new day in which you know your own value. Nothing can fix a damaged childhood. The most you can hope for is to make the sucker float.

In October of 1994, my wife and I went on a jazz cruise of the Caribbean on the SS *Norway*. Hank and Ginny booked themselves aboard the ship, brought their friends, the great comedy writer Larry Gelbart and his wife, and asked to be seated at our table. The week was incredible fun, and Larry brought out the funny, relaxed side of Hank. It would be the last time I would ever see Hank. It occurs to me that I saw Gerry Mulligan for the last time aboard the *Norway*. Within weeks of our return to California, I learned that Hank had cancer.

Hank knew it was terminal, and he handled it with surprising calm, if not serenity. Al Cobine told me that Hank wrote two letters to what he called "my guys." In the first of them he urged them all to take care of their health, saying, "In three months I'll be out of here." The second letter was a simple good-bye.

I have long since learned *not* to avoid contact with friends who are in the late days of their lives. I guess there is a great loneliness in dying, and it must be some consolation to know you did not pass through here without someone paying attention. I called him and we talked for perhaps twenty minutes. He said, "I've had a very good life." He asked me to call again, and I did, several times.

Henry Mancini died on 14 June 1994. He was three months short of 70 years old.

11

Bright laughter: Billy May

Paul Weston used to say that Billy May would be writing the third chart for a record date while the first one was being recorded.

"That's kind of an exaggeration," Billy said. There is a bubble of irreverent laughter in almost everything he says. "No. I would time it so that if the date started at 4 o'clock in the afternoon, I would finish about five minutes to 4 on the last tune and give it to the copyist. Paul overstated it a little bit. Or sometimes I would leave it there in the capable hands of Heinie Beau or Harold Mooney, or someone like that who used to help me out."

Further legend has it that he wrote his arrangement of Ray Noble's "Cherokee" right on the Charlie Barnet record date that made it famous. Is *that* story true?

"More or less," he said. "I wrote most of it at home and part of it on the way down to the date. I finished it up on the date. Then after that I wrote "Pompton Turnpike" and a bunch of stuff like that for Charlie."

A bunch of stuff indeed. Billy May wrote much of the book of the Charlie Barnet band when it was at its peak; and made not inconsiderable contributions to the Glenn Miller library as well.

E. William May was born in Pittsburgh, Pennsylvania, on 10 November 1916. The bassist and painter John Heard, also a Pittsburgh native, remarked, "What makes Pittsburgh unique is that they never got rid of their coal miner's mentality, people like the Mellons, Carnegie, Frick, Heinz. These people wanted to bring culture *in*. Thanks to Carnegie, Pittsburgh had the first public library."

Because of the huge endowments left by these industrialists (Andrew Carnegie tried to give away all his money before he died, and failed), Pittsburgh, John says, has always been culturally rich, with young people given exposure to it under excellent conditions: he remembers attending all sorts of free public events as a boy. With unabashed civic pride, he is quick to name the jazz musicians born or at least raised there: Billy May, Ahmad Jamal, Kenny Clarke, Mary Lou Williams, Erroll Garner, the Turrentine brothers,

Henry Mancini, Earl Hines, Ray Brown, Paul Chambers, George Benson, Joe Pass, Sonny Clarke, Dodo Marmarosa, Jerry Fielding, Ron Anthony, Paul Humphreys – and, he adds, even Oscar Levant. Gertrude Stein was born in Pittsburgh. So was Gene Kelly, who once told me, "I danced in every joint up and down the river valley."

"Some of the money must have trickled down," Billy said. "I first learned music in public school. They taught me, when I was in the second or third grade, solfeggio. I learned to sight-read. And I had some piano lessons, but I didn't practice. Then when I got into high school, I had a study period and I learned the intermediate band was rehearsing. So I went around. The teacher said, 'Do you want to try something? Come after school.' One of the kids showed me a tuba. By the next semester I was good enough to play in the intermediate band. I just went on from there."

He went on to become one of the most admired arrangers in jazz and popular music. He also wrote miles and miles of television music, the royalties from which keep him and his wife Doris comfortable in a large home high on a hill overlooking the Pacific Ocean at San Clemente, California.

"I did a bunch of music for Jack Webb at Warner Bros," Billy said. "I did a cop show for him, and I did a fire department show. You know how they pay composers for television through ASCAP and BMI – by the minute. You get young producers who are insecure. And they've got a fireman hanging off the building. There's nothing happening, the people are down in the street hollering, and they want you to keep some music going. And it's counting up.

"Somebody just bought a whole bunch of it in Germany. I got a nice fat check about two weeks ago."

Billy's background is substantially German. "My father's father was from the Ruhr Valley and worked in steel mills," he said. "My grandmother was a farm girl from eastern Germany. My mother's people were English and Scotch–Irish. Of all the people in the world, they were all good but the Catholics. That was her attitude.

"My father was in the building trade. He was a drunk, too. I inherited, with my daughter, the same thing. It's passed on from generation to generation. All three of us are sober. My dad was sober for twenty years before he died."

Henry Mancini, Jerry Fielding, and Billy Strayhorn all studied with Max Adkins, who conducted the pit band at the Stanley theater – one of the major stops for bands in the swing era – in Pittsburgh. "I didn't study with him," Billy said. "I met him. But I was too busy making a living. I didn't know Mancini until after the war, when he was writing for Tex Beneke.

"I met Strayhorn in Pittsburgh. Strayhorn understood about classical music. I've never lost my interest in classical music. Strayhorn had the verse of *Lush Life* in Pittsburgh. He used to play it for us. He said, 'I can't think what to do afterwards.' I knew Erroll Garner in Pittsburgh too. Erroll and Billy were friends.

"In high school I fooled around and watched the other guys in the band and I got interested in why they did what they did. I figured out that the valves worked the same, whether it was a tuba or a trumpet. Then I had a pal who was a clarinet player, and I looked at that. Then I took bassoon one year and I ended up playing second bassoon in the high-school orchestra, and that was good training. And I had a couple of semesters on string bass.

"One of the kids hipped me up to Casa Loma, and Billy Rausch used to hit a high F every night. It impressed the hell out of me: still does! They had wonderful arrangements. Gene Gifford wrote most of them. By the time I got out of high school in 1935, I was writing arrangements, trying to copy Casa Loma. But it was a very stiff band, reminded me of Glenn's band." He sang the kind of rigid phrasing one heard in Casa Loma's up-tempo work. "'Maniac's Ball' and all that. They were too labored. Tonight we're going to be hot! New Year's Eve hot.

"But swing music should be *relaxed*."

By the time he graduated high school, Billy had played something from almost every family of instruments.

"By then I was writing for little bands. In 1935, like now they have rock groups, they had little dance bands. Some of the mothers wanted their sons to become another Rudy Vallee. There were always bands around. The Depression was on, and I was working three or four nights a week, making three bucks a night, playing the trombone.

"Pittsburgh was where Blue Barron got started. Lawrence Welk too, and Sammy Kaye. I got a job with Barron Elliott. Barron Elliott was Pittsburgh's answer to Guy Lombardo. It was a good-paying job – I bought myself a new Chevrolet, 900 dollars, that was 1937 – but it was a shitty job. I was playing trombone, and I had it down so while the guy was singing the vocal, I could write an arrangement. We tried to do some of the hot things. Benny Goodman was making records then, so we had to do things like that. The two trumpet players were great playing Lebert Lombardo . . . " He imitated the ricky-tick phrasing. "But they couldn't play shit for chords. 'Gimme a G chord!' So I started doubling trumpet. And that's how come I became a trumpet player, 'cause I could belt it for them. When you're young, you've got good chops. So I slowly diminished my trombone playing and increased the trumpet playing.

"I figured out a long time ago that to be a successful arranger, you had to be a decent player to get recognized. But that's all I used it for. I played enough to be established, so I could write.

"And then Barnet came through Pittsburgh. I heard them on the radio, and I thought, 'Oh boy, what a great band.' He had six brass, four saxes, the rhythm section, and himself. They were playing a tune called 'Lazy Bug.' I don't know who the hell ever wrote it. So I went out and asked him one night if I could write an arrangement for him. He said, 'Yeah, we're gonna rehearse tomorrow, if you can get it ready.' So I stayed up all night and made it and took it out to him and he liked it and bought it and hired me for six or seven more. So I wrote them and sent them in, but he got married then and broke up the band.

"That was in June or July of '38. Then he put the band back together, and I heard him on the air from the Famous Door just before New Year's Eve. I wrote him a letter and asked for my money. So he called me and offered me a job to come to New York and write four arrangements a week for 70 dollars. I took it: it was better than playing for Barron Elliott.

"I checked into the Park Central Hotel with him. I was there for about three weeks. I brought my horns. He said to me one day, 'Do you think you can help me out? One of the trumpet players is sick. Can you work the show?' So I went down to the Paramount Theater and played first trumpet for the shows that day, and that cemented my job with him for ever. I knew the book. I was able to sit in and play it. I went back to just writing.

"But then Charlie always had it in mind that he wanted four trumpets. Basie came in to New York and played the Famous Door, and he had four trumpets. Barnet came back one night and told me, 'We're going to have four trumpets. Get a coat. Get down to the tailor and have one made like the guys.' We made a new deal for the money, and I said, 'What am I going to do for a book? The book's written for three trumpets.' He said, 'Well you wrote the son of a bitch, you can make up a part.' And I did, I just made it up as we went along.

"That was about August. We were playing the Playland Ballroom in Rye, and that's where we did 'Cherokee' and all those things. Right after that we went into the Meadowbrook, and that's where I broke in on fourth trumpet. After that we did one-nighters all the way out to the Palomar in Los Angeles.

"We went into the Palomar. The war had started in Europe on 1 September. A couple of nights, Phil Stevens, the bass player, ran over to the curtains with a pitcher of water: the curtain had caught fire from the heat of the lights. The management never did anything about it.

"The night of 1 October, a Sunday night, we were doing a remote broadcast. A fire started, we were off the stand, and there was no one there to throw the water on the curtains, and the whole friggin' ballroom burned down. So it was a good thing I didn't write too many fourth parts, because I had to write the whole library again. Skippy Martin was in the band, playing saxophone. So he and I rewrote the whole goddamn library."

Barnet took the fire philosophically, saying, "Hell, it's better than being in

Poland with bombs dropping on your head." He recorded a tune called "Are We Burnt Up."

"After the fire, it took us about six weeks to get the band back together. Everybody lost their horns. We got back on the road and did one-nighters all the way back from California. We played in Boston. That was in November 1939. That was the first time we went in the Apollo theater with Charlie. I think we were the first white band to play the Apollo. We played 'Cherokee' and they loved us. We did a bunch of Duke's things. We played the Lincoln Hotel, and did one-nighters."

Barnet was famous among musicians for his wild behavior. Nor did he discourage it in his musicians. That was, by all accounts, the craziest band in the business, and one of the best. Barnet was born to considerable wealth, defied his family's wishes that he become a lawyer, led a band on an ocean liner when he was only 16 – according to Leonard Feather, he made 22 Atlantic crossings. By 1932, he was leading a band at the Paramount Hotel in New York City. Eventually he became one of the most famous of big-band leaders. He was also one of the handsomest, which helped him indulge his taste for women. Estimates of the number of his marriages run from six to eleven, but six is probably the accurate number.

His sexual escapades were legend. "He liked the dames," Billy said. "We played some one-nighters somewhere around Youngstown, then a one-nighter in Erie, Pennsylvania. The promoter came up and said, 'Now we're gonna have a jitterbug dance.' The contest was going to be between Mrs. So-and-so, the wife of the promoter, and Mrs. Charlie Barnet. We thought, 'Who the hell is Mrs. Charlie Barnet?' And up comes this sleek-looking chick, some broad he got out of a house of ill repute in Youngstown the night before. So she's sitting up there on the stand. She was with the band four or five days. We were working all around those coalfields in Pennsylvania, Middleport, Johnstown, and we ended up in Buffalo, New York. We played a battle of music with Andy Kirk.

"We get off the stand, and we're standing around and Andy Kirk's band's playing, and suddenly I notice there's a whole bunch of guys in overcoats standing around us, they've got us surrounded. And one of them says, 'Which one is *Bahnet*?' So we said, 'There, right there.' So they surrounded Barnet. That was the last we saw of the lady. She was a whore, she was a good money-maker for them. That's one of his adventures. With Charlie it was New Year's Eve every night."

Barnet acquired the nickname the Mad Mab. Its origin is obscure, but it was so widely used that even the trade magazines used it; Barnet seemed not to object.

Then Billy got an offer from Glenn Miller. This custom of raiding each other's bands for personnel was endemic to the era; Woody Herman ripped

Barnet off for quite a number of musicians, including Ralph Burns. There was apparently no resentment, and Woody and Barnet remained friends.

Billy said, "From what I was told, Glenn got wondering about who was doing the writing for Charlie.

"Barnet worked Atlantic City. We were back in New York, then we went to Boston. Miles Rinker was an associate of the Shribman brothers." Cy and Charlie Shribman, based in Boston, booked bands, and backed a good many of them, including Glenn Miller's. Rinker was a brother of Al Rinker, who sang with Bing Crosby in the Rhythm Boys, and Mildred Bailey. "Miles came to me and said, 'When you get to New York, go into Hurley's bar on Sunday night. Glenn Miller wants to talk to you. And don't talk to anyone about it.'"

Hurley's was at the northeast corner of Sixth Avenue and 49th Street. Its history is interesting. It was a true New York Irish bar whose owner refused to sell it when the Rockefellers wanted to build Rockefeller Center. They were able to buy all the land they needed, except this one small rectangle. All their legal coercions failed, and they had to revise the plans for Rockefeller Center. They built it around Hurley's. It still stands there, an architectural anomaly, and NBC personnel make it their hangout.

"So I went into Hurley's bar," Billy said, "and I met Glenn and his wife Helen, and he offered me the job. I tried to work it out, saying, 'Well I'll let you know.' I was going to go to Charlie and ask him if he would match it. But Glenn said, 'No, you gotta let me know right now.' I gave Charlie my two weeks and joined Miller the night Roosevelt was elected in 1940, for the third term.

"Helen was a real nice lady, though she had that little iron hand in there. I liked her very much. I got to know her pretty well after Glenn was gone. I had my band by then and was playing the Palladium and she came in to hear the band. I thought that was very nice of her.

"Actually, there are two versions of the story. Glenn wanted to hire a trumpet player. He was unhappy and he needed a guy in the section. One version is that he wanted Bernie Privin, who was in Charlie's band at the time. Or he wanted me. And he wanted me to screw up his arrangements. So he hired me. Ray Anthony and I joined the band at the same time – November 1940.

"John O'Leary made sure we were on the train and all that. He was the road manager, and a good one too. John was a good Catholic. He was an old man. We'd be riding on the bus, doing the one-nighters up in New England, and Sunday you'd wake up at 6 o'clock, 7 o'clock in the morning, and the bus would be stopped. A nice bright sunny day in New England. And you're outside a Catholic church. And the bus driver was there, with his hat down over his face. He said, 'John O'Leary just went in for Mass. We'll be going in a minute.'

"Miller was a good arranger. And he was a number one fixer. You'd get at the rehearsal, and the tunes were running too long, or somebody's key didn't fit, he was a demon at fixing things like that. He wouldn't transpose it, but he'd be able to patch it together so that it was presentable for a program. I learned an awful lot from him when we did those fifteen-minute Chesterfield shows. 'Cause he was always adjusting them, or cutting them down, or putting them in medleys – you know, he had a lot of hit records – and he'd make them fit the program, and he'd get as many tunes in as he could. And the pluggers were busy in those days; I'm talking 1940 or '41 now. He'd get all the plugs in he could for the guys, and things like that. He was a demon at cutting here, and putting in a bell note there, and then maybe he'd write a little thing for the saxes – dictate it to them – and it would be ready. He really knew how to run a rehearsal.

"But with Glenn, everything was always the same. You'd come to work, you didn't wear the red socks, Jesus Christ, there'd be a big scene. I learned to live with the routine; I was newly married. We were making good money – 1940, '41, I was making 150 dollars a week guaranteed, but some weeks we'd make four or five hundred, because we were doing the Chesterfield show, and working in New York doing the Paramount Theater, and stuff like that. I bought my first house out here with that. Then I made the two pictures with Glenn, *Sun Valley Serenade* and *Orchestra Wives*."

The two films often run on television. If you look closely, you can see a young – he was 25 – and chubby Billy May back in the trumpet section.

"After the second picture," he said, "we were supposed to have some time off. Instead, all of a sudden, we take the train back to Chicago. And that was a surprise. We were going back to work. We were working out of the College Inn at the Sherman Hotel. We were doing the Chesterfield show on network radio three nights a week. And every weekend, we'd go out somewhere, working an army or navy base somewhere. And it soon became apparent that Glenn was scouting around for something. Meanwhile, I had some friends who were publishers. I let it be known that I didn't want to play that much any more, I'd rather be writing. And I got a deal with Alvino Rey and the King Sisters.

"The Miller band had a couple of weeks off. I went down to Philadelphia, did two or three charts for Alvino, and I got a good deal with them. They gave me 150 bucks a week to write two charts. I went back with Miller. We were playing in Youngstown, Ohio. I went in and told him, I said, 'I've got a chance to stay in New York writing and I won't have to travel any more, so I'd like to leave the band.' He said, 'It's no surprise. I'm going into the service, that's why we've been working all these places. I'm expecting a commission to come through any time. I'd like you to stick it out just until the end. Because I don't want people to think the rats are leaving the ship.' That's the term he used.

"So I said, 'Okay,' because he'd been pretty good to me over all. He was a pain in the ass to work for, but the deal was okay. He said, 'I'm going to come out of this war as some kind of a hero, you wait and see.' It came out a little different than he planned.

"I think Glenn was an alcoholic. I think he was a dry drunk. He kept it inside of him. I saw him get drunk a couple of times, and he went completely off his rocker. Just for a couple of days.

"Chummy MacGregor was playing piano in the band. He was the first guy that told me about DTs. Chummy would wake up in the morning and there was nothing there to drink, so he'd have to get down to Plunkett's speakeasy. That was the only place you could get it. He'd run down and get a cab. And when he tried to get in, the back seat would be full of lions and tigers, and he would have to run down on the street. Chummy had been dry for six or seven years when Glenn started the band. Chummy was his friend from way back.

"And I know a couple of times Glenn was drunk when we were working a theater somewhere. And he was staggering, emceeing a show, and Chummy didn't let him up. Every time he'd come near Chummy, Chummy would say, 'Whatsa matter, someone hit you with the bar rag, for Chris'sake?'

"'Dry drunk' is an expression in AA – when a person stays sober but hates it. He wants to let all that stuff out, but he doesn't know how to do it unless he gets drunk.

"He was a *terrible* drunk. But when he'd go on the wagon, he'd be one of those stiff people. He never learned to be a decent, sober man. He needed a couple of good AA meetings.

"I know other people with the same personality. I knew when I drank and I'd stop, I'd grit my teeth, and say, 'I'll stay sober, god damn it!' And then when you'd let go, you went crazy. And AA showed me the way to get over that.

"The rest of the time Glenn was kind of mad at the world. He was bitter about everything. Kind of a down kind of guy. Putting things down all the time." Billy affected a grousing snarl: "'Ah for Chris'sake, Dorsey did that.'

"He used to like some of the stuff I wrote. But then he'd get around to Duke: 'Bunch of sloppy bastards.' True, but it was also good.

"When he got the power of being a leader, and got his own publishing company, he got to be a power maniac. He had control of Thornhill, and Spivak, and he controlled Woody, I think. And he controlled Hal McIntyre. He had a piece of Charlie Spivak and a piece of Thornhill.

"I was in the band about two weeks when I got to know Willie Schwartz, who was playing clarinet.

"I've got to tell you a story. After the war, Willie worked a one-nighter with Tex Beneke at the Palladium. It was a Miller memorial. When the band was off the stand, a guy came up to Willie with a shoe box. He opened it. He had some straw or dirt or something in there. He said, 'Do you know what this is?' Willie said, 'No.' The guy said, 'That's the last piece of dirt that Glenn Miller stepped on.' He asked Willie what he thought he should do with it. Willie said, 'Why don't you smoke it?'

"The one guy who had Miller buffaloed was Moe Purtill. As a drummer, his playing wasn't that good, but we liked him as a guy. He was a good guy, and he didn't take any shit from Miller.

"Miller was cruel to Bill Finegan, he really was. He messed with everybody's charts, but especially Bill's. 'That introduction, take that out. Start down here.' Merciless. The intro would be *beautiful*. 'Take that out.'

"I got that treatment too, but on a smaller scale, 'cause I didn't write that much for him." Billy played solos on "Song of the Volga Boatmen" and "American Patrol," and he arranged "Ida," "Delilah," "Long Tall Mama," "Always in My Heart," "Soldier Let Me Read Your Letter," and "Take the A Train." He was co-arranger with Finegan of "Serenade in Blue" and "At Last." By far the bulk of that book was written by Finegan, including major hits such as "Little Brown Jug" and "American Patrol," with Jerry Gray making large contributions, including "A String of Pearls," when he came over from the band of Artie Shaw.

"I stuck it out until the end," Billy said. "By the time the band broke up, in Passaic, New Jersey, the NBC band in New York was short trumpet players, and they made a deal of Mickey McMickle and me and somebody else who had an 802 card. So I stayed in New York, working at NBC and sending charts to Alvino.

"I played in the NBC house band. I played on *The Chamber Music Society of Lower Basin Street* with Paul Lavalle. I was working there with a wonderful trumpet player named Charlie Margulis. Charlie was a don't-take-any-crap-from-anybody kind of guy. We were playing along and rehearsing in studio 8-H, and Paul Lavalle was rehearsing the band. He stopped the band because there was a trumpet unison passage. He said, 'Play it alone, trumpets.' So we played it alone. He said, 'Try it once more.' So we played it again. He said, 'Try it one more time, please.' And Charlie Margulis says, '*Why!?*' Like that. And Paul Lavalle says, 'It isn't together.' And Charlie Margulis says, 'It's together back here.' And Paul says, 'Well it's not together up here.' And Charlie says, 'Well clean the shit out of your ears!'

"What Charlie didn't realize is that up above us is the glass where the twenty-five-cent tours are going through, and they can hear it. That was the last time Charlie worked there.

"Alvino was working around out here. My first wife was a Los Angeles girl, and I thought, 'Well, I'm gonna have to go in the army.' John Best and those guys were already in the service. John went to the South Pacific with Conrad Gozzo and all those guys, in the Artie Shaw navy band. So I came out to California. I was jobbing here. I put my card in for local 47. When I got my draft notice, they found out I'd had asthma when I was a kid, and they never called me again.

"I worked for Woody in the Palladium. That was '43. He wanted me to go with him. We really got drunk together in the Garden of Allah. I think two or three nights in a row. Woody left. Bing Crosby was going down to San Diego to work at hospitals. They were taking some singers and some dancers and a little Dixieland band to fake everything. Bobby Goodrich was playing trumpet, and Bobby got drafted. They called me to fake on that show, and I did.

"I guess they liked the way I played. I couldn't play Bing's radio show, because I still had some time to wait on my local 47 card. John Scott Trotter, who knew my work, asked me to do a couple of charts. So I wrote for him. I worked some one-nighters with Bob Crosby and Alvino Rey. I finally got my card, and kept on working. I started doing some work for Ozzie Nelson.

"It was a good band. They had a roving baritone saxophone against a cornet, and they used that as a counterline against the whole band. I asked Ozzie who thought that up, and he couldn't remember. Some arranger had figured that out. When they were doing *The Joe Penner Show* – "Nelson played that show from 1933 to 1935 " – they were using that even then. And I was always interested in the arranging. The band had really good writing."

I pointed out to Billy that Gerry Mulligan liked that band for just that reason. And I liked it for charts such as "Swinging on the Golden Gate," which I remember from childhood.

"I enjoyed working for Ozzie," Billy said. "He was a stickler, but he wasn't a bad guy about it, like Miller was. He was a guitar player, and a bad one. He just said, 'That's no good, change it.' He was an attorney. But he knew what he was doing. I ended up playing trumpet for him, then writing for him, and finally conducting for him. I wrote the cues and bridges on the Ozzie and Harriet show on network radio when his kids were so small he had actors playing their parts.

"Meanwhile, I knew the King Sisters, and they were working for Capitol, and some of their husbands were working for Capitol, so I got in there. I knew Paul Weston, and he was music director of Capitol. I did the Capitol children's things, 'Bozo the Clown' and all that.

"Then Capitol needed some foxtrots for an Arthur Murray package, so I wrote four or five instrumentals. They liked them so well they put them out. And that's when I started using the sliding saxophones.

"With the sliding saxophone effect, they attack the note out of tune and slide into it with the lip. And certain pitches work better than others, so you've gotta know that. An E on the alto will work as well as an E on the tenor, but they're different pitches. And I always had good saxophone players. I had Willie Schwartz and Skeets Herfurt and Ted Nash and guys like that. They knew what they were doing and they knew what I wanted.

"I did a bunch of those albums, *Sorta May*, then *Sorta Dixie*. They were expensive in those days, but they made it into the black."

"And I got in the band business," Billy said. "My first marriage was falling apart, and my drinking was getting to the point where it started to get pretty glamorous. So I made an alcoholic decision and I took the band out on the road.

"Eddie Sauter and Bill Finegan had a good band. I liked their band. We played a battle of music in Canobie Lake, New Hampshire. My band and the Sauter–Finegan band. When we got there, I remembered a while before that with Glenn when we played there. That was in 1942. And John O'Leary, the road manager, introduced Glenn to the guy who managed the ballroom. Mr. Sullivan, I think. 'Mr. Sullivan owns the park and the lumber yard and everything all around.' Glenn said, 'How do you do?' And the guy said, 'It's ten minutes to nine, you'd better get up to get ready to start.'

"So when I played there with Finegan, I thought, 'Jesus, that son of a bitch, I'd better watch out for him.' We got up and played and the Sauter–Finegan band got up and played, and some kid came up to me and says, 'Hey, Billy, you're off for a while. Come on back into the office.' I went back in the office, and I looked around, and I said, 'Where's Mr. Sullivan?' And the kid said, 'Oh he died about four years ago. He left this place to his kids, and I'm one of them. Have a drink, you don't have to get on the bandstand again.' It was the greatest party we ever had.

"I was out on the road about two years, and I realized it was a losing cause. I don't like to be a bandleader, stand up there. I used to use it in my AA pitch. I said I didn't want to be a bandleader because you had to stand up there and do 'Happy Birthday to Myrtle.' If somebody asked me to play 'Happy Birthday to Myrtle,' I'd tell them where they could shove it. And that ain't the way Lawrence Welk does it.

"I ended up selling the band to Ray Anthony – the name, the personal appearance rights. I didn't want to stay in the band business, I wanted to get the hell out. The agencies and everybody were on my back, 'Go on out, you can do great.' And I did. I grossed $400,000 one year. But where did it all go? To get out of that, I sold it to Ray.

"In 1963, booze had started to create some pretty good problems. I was married for the second time. I was working, I was handling everything, and the finances were okay. But I started to feel bad. One day I got chest pains, and I was lying on the bed, smoking, and I had a drink. This was November of '63. My stepdaughter worked in a doctor's office. She said, 'Do you mind if I talk to the doctor about your chest pains?' I said, 'Okay.' The next thing I know I hear a siren. And here come two paramedics. They said, 'Put your cigarette out, you're having a heart attack.' They took me down to St. John's. This was in the days before they had bypasses. I had to lie in the hospital for two weeks. While I was there, I figured I'd try to stop smoking. I was smoking two or three packs a day. I was able to stop smoking during that period. When I got out, I got to thinking, 'How noble can I get? The least I can do now is drink.' And about four months later I called Dave Barbour, who was a good friend of mine. He was in AA. I couldn't reach him; but I knew a lady he had helped.

"So through her I arranged to go to a meeting. I had a few inches in the bottom of a vodka bottle, and I figured there's no use in wasting it. So I drank it, and they tell me I really enjoyed that first meeting." He laughed. "The first meeting I went to I met Red Norvo, and a saxophone player I used to get drunk with in New York, Larry Binyon. Good all-round clarinet player. Larry kind of took me over. The guys all called me the next day: that was in July. I didn't actually stop drinking until later.

"The last time I got drunk was at Charlie Barnet's party. Charlie threw a party for his fiftieth birthday, and he hired Duke Ellington's band. It was the night of all nights. It was at the country club in Palm Springs. I remember drinking some Martinis before we went. Seeing Duke and everything. When I woke up the next day, I was lying on the floor in my house in Cathedral City. I knew what I had to do. I had to get to a meeting, and I did. That was it. I haven't had a drink since October 1964."

Some of the finest charts Billy wrote at Capitol were for Frank Sinatra, seven albums in all. "I started working for him, and I started working for Peggy Lee.

"Sinatra was good to me. I got along with him. The reason is I never got too close to him. I went in and did my job and got the hell out of there. My wife Doris and I have been guests of his. He invited us to go to the symphony with him and Barbara. He was very knowledgeable. I was surprised to find he knew a lot about Scriabin. He was a much better musician than people realize."

The Sinatra albums included *Come Fly with Me*, *Come Dance with Me*, *Come Swing with Me*, and four more. Billy worked with George Shearing on *Burnished Brass* and had hit singles with Nat Cole, including "Walkin' My Baby Back Home."

"Pretty soon," he said, "television came around. The first show I did, or the first you ever heard of, was *Naked City*. I did that for two or three years. Then I went to work for Lionel Newman, and I wrote a bunch of *Batman* sequences. Neal Hefti wrote the theme, and on the cue sheet Lionel listed it as 'Words and music by Neal Hefti.' Lionel was a good cat. I wrote a bunch of *Mod Squad* episodes. Then when John Williams went to Boston, he asked me to do some charts for the Boston Pops Orchestra, probably 25 or 30 for them.

"I lived up in Cambria for three or four years." Cambria is a beautiful ocean-side community up the coast from Los Angeles; in those days it would have seemed quite remote. "I wrote the *Time-Life* series, for Capitol Records. They remade the swing era. It was a good gig for me, because they gave me the tapes on Tuesday. I'd take them up and write next week's show, send them in to the copyist, come down and record them on Monday night. They said, 'Would you do a couple of dates for us?' It ended we did one record date a week, and sometimes two, for over three years. They've repackaged them. That was from '69 through '72. It counted on the musicians' pension fund for the guys and for me.

"I did some work for Jack Elliott and Allyn Ferguson when they were writing for television together and had that office on Coldwater Canyon at Ventura Boulevard. I ran into Lou Busch – Joe 'Fingers' Carr – and told him I was in AA. He'd quit drinking some time before. I said, 'What's new?'

"And he said, 'I'm getting married again.'

"I said, 'Oh? Anybody I know?'

"He said, 'No, I finally kicked the girl-singer habit too.'

"I told that to Jack and Allyn at their office. Dave Grusin was there. He said, 'Where do those guys hold *their* meetings?'"

I first met Billy in that office. I was in slight awe: after all, he had been one of the heroes of my adolescence. Jack and Allyn were in the process of founding what is now called the American Jazz Philharmonic to play scores that partook of both jazz and classical music. A score had been submitted by Frank Zappa. Billy was sitting in an armchair, reading it.

He said, "Look at all the percussion it calls for." And he read the list aloud, culminating in "two garbage cans."

Billy paused a moment and said, "Twenty or thirty gallons?" and I about rolled out of my chair with laughter.

"I'm not doing any writing now," Billy said. "I quit. The last thing I did was a year and a half ago, Stan Freberg's *The United States of America Volume 2*.

"The last couple of things I did were so different from the way I like to record. Everybody's out in different rooms. The drums are out in the men's room. Who needs that? I did a thing for Keely Smith. The only reason I did it was because they offered me a ridiculous amount of money. We did it at Capitol, and everybody's out in different rooms. I said, 'How can the guys hear?' They said, 'They can listen on their headphones.'

"Screw that. And I don't like the CD sounds at all. I think they're terrible.

It sounds to me like all the mixers are young and their idea of a good balance is the Beatles. It's the same thing in symphony; you hear too much pounding."

Billy has had a wispy gray beard for some years now. He has dieted away some weight. He has a sharp sense of life's incongruity, and humor has always infused his writing, whether his compositions or his arrangements, though his ballad writing is always beautiful and sensitive. (The chart on Sinatra's *Autumn in New York* is his.) This bright laughter is perhaps the reason he has not been given the credit that is his due.

Except of course among musicians, particularly arrangers, none of whom will be pleased to learn he has retired.

As an old expression has it: the cats always know.

12

The worlds of Mel Powell

Much was made of the fact that Mel Powell was 17 years old when he joined the Benny Goodman band as pianist and arranger. Given the the long history of prodigies – Mendelssohn wrote his *Overture to a Midsummer Night's Dream* at 16 – perhaps too much. Certainly too much was made of the fact that he had an extensive "classical" training in both piano and composition, as if he were the first of his breed to enter jazz. Almost all the better jazz pianists had solid academic training, whether formal or self-imposed.

What is more remarkable is that Mel Powell should have cast so long a shadow in the jazz world when his career in the idiom was comparatively brief. He worked with Goodman in 1941 and 1942, and, bored with playing the same material night after night, left the band in the late summer of 1942, not yet 20. His compositions for the Goodman band, not to mention his charts – the arrangements of "Jersey Bounce" and "A String of Pearls" are his – are part of the legacy of the big-band era, along with his dazzling piano solos in both the big band and the Goodman chamber subgroups.

Powell eventually became head of the composition department of the school of music of the California Institute of the Arts, called CalArts. When he was in his 60s, he contracted a neurological disorder that caused him to move about on an electric tricycle. When he struggled to his feet and supported himself with canes, he was still a little over six feet. His hair was plentiful, but faded from the blond of his youth to a silky white.

"Very often in the class," he said in a cultivated, sonorous teacher's voice, "we'll be talking something technical, say, Renaissance, and I'll point out certain syncopations, and then I will say, 'That's very much like what happens in jazz.' And at the end of the lesson, a student will say, 'Mr. Powell, how come you know that much about jazz?' I'll come back and say, 'The *right* question is, "How come I know so much about the Renaissance?"' Then I tell them about my past.

"And they are *stunned*."

Mel's concerto for two pianos was performed by the Los Angeles Philharmonic and won the Pulitzer Prize. Soon thereafter his malady, inclusionary polymyocitis, caused him to take a fall, cracking his head so severely that he was hospitalized in a coma. For a long period of his recovery he was unable to speak, and when the ability was restored to him, he quipped to Peggy Lee, still his friend nearly 50 years after their service in the Goodman band, "It's a good thing I didn't win the Nobel Prize!"

He was born Melvin Epstein in the Bronx on 12 February 1923, which, being Lincoln's birthdate as well, meant that he never had to go to school on that day.

His father, Milton Epstein, and mother, nee Mildred Mark, were both from Russia. His maternal grandfather, who lived with the family, was a Talmudic scholar. Mel's father spent a period of his youth as a professional boxer, but abandoned boxing for the jewelry business and, with the advent of the Depression, became a traveling salesman. Then Mel's parents were divorced, which was very unusual in Jewish families. Mel was the youngest of three children. He had a sister, Elinor, and a brother, Lloyd, four years his senior.

I mentioned to Mel that Glenn Gould never practiced: "He told me that if a piece presented some particular digital problem, he might go to the piano to work out the fingering in that passage. But otherwise, he thought the music through, and then just went and did it. A friend of mine said that if you build your technique early, it stays with you, but if you build it later, you have to work hard to keep it."

"That sounds reasonable," Mel said. "I've always thought I was fortunate in having begun so early."

"How early?"

"Four, five, with piano lessons. With a very stern German lady named Sara Barg, who'd slap you and all that. But I appreciated that later. And then, so far as my work in composition is concerned, I was delighted that she spoke sometimes like a theorist, rather than a piano teacher. She would say things like, 'No, no, no! Be sure to show the sub-dominant!' That was nice. Learning by rote can ruin you."

Mel grew up in a building on 161st Street in the Bronx, so situated that from its roof one could look down into Yankee Stadium. People would gather there for a free view of games, and Mel showed a brief entrepeneurial spirit by selling them peanuts.

Mel won a third prize in a city-wide contest for young pianists and was advised by Walter Damrosch to go to Germany to study. But his brother Lloyd had already turned him on to jazz. The family had moved, when Mel was about 11, south to West End Avenue at 102nd Street. Lloyd and Mel would listen to remote broadcasts of the bands during the time when

Mel was going to De Witt Clinton High School. Later he went to City College of New York, where he majored in French.

When Mel was 13, Lloyd got him to go to the Paramount theater to see the Benny Goodman band. Mel was mesmerized by its polish and precision and the playing of Lionel Hampton and Teddy Wilson. Soon he was listening on records to Art Hodes, Jess Stacy, Bix Beiderbecke, Fats Waller, and, most significantly, Earl Hines. A friend took him to Nick's in Greenwich Village, where he heard Sidney Bechet, Bobby Hackett, and Zutty Singleton. One night he asked, with precocious courage, to sit in. A man sitting near the piano told him, "You're going to be a real one." It was Art Tatum. Soon Mel had a job at Nick's, working with Brad Gowans, Pee Wee Russell, and Eddie Condon.

One night Dorothy Parker and John Steinbeck, both jazz devotees, came into Nick's. She had already had a good deal to drink. A man approached their table, sat down, and began talking. She stared at him through fog until he felt the chill. He said, somewhat testily, "I guess you don't remember me."

"My memory," she said, "is so bad that I don't remember asking you to sit down."

Mel added: "That's not a story. I was *there*."

At one point he worked opposite a young pianist from Chicago, two or three years his senior, with whom he became friends: Nat Cole. "I think we were both influenced by the same people," Mel said. The primary influence was Earl Hines, the dominant force in jazz piano and the influence in turn on Tatum and Wilson.

"What in your view was the value of Hines?" I asked. "He was obviously your major hero."

"Yeah," Mel said, nodding. "Well, he was damn good! Well. Let's start with what everyone knows. It's a little bit fictitious, a myth by now: the business of the octaves sounding like trumpet, which is a far cry from ragtime and stride. That would come to some degree because of his association with Louis Armstrong, I would think. He also played trumpet when he was a kid.

"That seemed to me very important. Why, specifically, I thought so much of him is that he was just this side of irresponsible. Of all the pianists, none lived so close to the edge of terrible risk. When he went for what we all go for – octaves, runs, whatever – it was always just a little more dangerous, from perhaps even the technical point of view, than it needed to be. Many of us found a haven in doing things that were very effective, but we knew we'd come out winners."

A short, one-beat chuckle: "Ha! I would never want to bet the ranch with Earl! And yet he would always be phenomenal. It was a temperament, that very disquieted and disquieting temperament, that I found absolutely irresistible: compared, for example, to others I admired very much.

"Fats Waller. Fats had an enormous sense of humor, had a *gorgeous* bounce in the stride that he would play. If you didn't smile at *that*, then you ought not to listen to music altogether. Or Teddy Wilson, with that gorgeous civility. Teddy coming from Earl, I think. But none of them, except Tatum . . . I think Tatum had the kind of temperament that Earl had. I think that's true. Although it's a totally different creature. That kind of temperament was not around, except with Earl Hines and Art Tatum.

"And once a young pianist like myself confronted that, it was quite clear what the Olympian heights were, and what a steep incline to get near there. The more specific answer has to do with choice of notes, things of that sort, and sounds to me more trivial than what I was trying to say. Earl added to the risk of improvisation this technical peril that would make you want to duck. He'd wade right into it. And so, again, with Tatum as well, there was this ability to – how should I say it? – embrace ecstasy. Earl Hines could do that. Transporting the listener . . . and probably himself as well. I don't think I ever heard him do anything safe."

Mel played a few years at Nick's. One can imagine that he startled the customers, the lanky kid with his glasses and fair hair and serious respectable mien. Writer George Simon eventually arranged for him to audition for Goodman, who hired him for the enormous (for the time) salary of 500 dollars a week, and Mel found himself in the fast company of Sid Catlett, Cootie Williams, and Goodman.

His compositions for the band included "The Earl," written in tribute to Hines, "Mission to Moscow," and "Clarinade." In "The Earl," his own solo work revealed how much of Hines he had absorbed, including the fluent running octaves and a startling dexterity. These works were the foreshadow of his later career.

I said, "When I was a kid, classical music and jazz were looked on as two separate musics, and when some of the guys went to conservatories, why, jazz was being corrupted. But I have become more and more aware that a lot of the early people, such as James P. Johnson and Willie the Lion Smith, had good training. You can hear the roots of stride in Chopin and that set of variations Schumann wrote on his wife's maiden name. The left-hand pattern. Even the trumpet players had good brass training. The myth of separate, competitive musics doesn't make sense."

"Of course," Mel said. "I never took the separatism seriously. I thought it was merely a way of making bad use of bad categories. I remember there was a guitarist, I wish I could remember his name, a jazz player, he was the first one I ever heard play excerpts of *Wozzeck*."

"On guitar?"

"Yes! I was *stunned*. This was in the '30s."

"That he even knew *Wozzeck* . . . "

"There wasn't a player in the New York Philharmonic who knew it, I can guarantee you. The fact is that not only the eighteenth and nineteenth century had been exploited and explored by a lot of early jazz players – I'm talking about Fats Waller and so on, not today's kids who are in the atmosphere of college. You're exactly right. Jazz and classical music were looked on as very different because of the sociological, not the musical, environment.

"When I think of Bix and "In a Mist" and so on, I want to say that the jazz player could be counted on to respond more intelligently to the more interesting advanced, serious music, than any of the so-called classical players. I loathe the term 'classical', it's a misnomer, but you know what I mean."

"Yes, but we're stuck with it, as we're stuck with the term 'jazz.'"

"Yes. But the jazz player, unquestionably, even if he only said, 'My God, dig those changes!', was responding in a far more profound sense to everything advanced than the classical players."

"Did Earl know the legit repertoire?"

Emphatically: "Yes!" Then: "It was a narrow range, by which I mean he knew some Beethoven, some Brahms. He certainly knew some Scarlatti and some Bach. Then at that point in his life he got busy with Detroit, Chicago. I heard him play some Chopin. You don't have the technique that Earl had out of the gutter, don't kid yourself. He was a startling player."

I said, "Don Redman was a schooled musician, Lunceford was a schooled musician. Bix was listening to Stravinsky."

"No question," Mel said. "You can note it from his piano pieces."

"Now, all of those guys were becoming aware of the movements in modern music in the 1920s. William Grant Still was studying with Varèse by 1927. The harmony in dance bands became more adventurous through the 1930s until you got Boyd Raeburn in the '40s, and Bob Graettinger's 'City of Glass' for Kenton, which sounded radical to me at the time but no longer does. I can't believe that the arrangers were not aware of all that was going on with the extension of harmony in European music. Bill Challis was starting to use some of that stuff when he was writing for Goldkette. Is there an answer to this question: were the writers waiting for the public to catch up?"

"I think I'll surprise you," Mel said. "They were waiting for the bandleaders to catch up. The bandleaders were much more aware of what a negotiable commodity was." He chuckled. "When an arrangement would be brought in and rejected because 'That's too fancy,' that was a signal that I was no longer welcome. So I meant exactly what I said. If the arrangers were waiting for anything, they were waiting for the bandleaders."

"Okay. Given Benny Goodman's inherent conservatism, I am surprised that he welcomed what you wrote. Because some of it was very radical. 'Mission to Moscow' is radical for the period."

"Yeah. It gets close to peril," he said. "Now, why would Benny respond very favorably to that? And also, by the way, to Eddie Sauter. I don't think we did this out of slyness. The clarinet music was very interesting. And it was great fun for Benny to play. Yes. 'Mission to Moscow,' he had this duet with the piano. So he would put up with these quasi-innovations. I thought that Eddie Sauter brought in some of the most inventive, imaginative things. Eddie was really devoted less to composition than he was to arranging, in the best, deepest sense of 'ranging'. He was really given over to that. I can recall rehearsals when Eddie Sauter would bring music to us, and it would be rejected. A lot was lost. On some pieces that we do know – for example his arrangement for 'You Stepped Out of a Dream,' which I always regarded as a really advanced, marvelous kind of thing – Benny would *thin it out*. And sometimes get the credit for it being a hit, getting it past the a&r men. I don't think the thinning out was an improvement. Quite the contrary. I think that Eddie, and I to a lesser degree, were exploring harmonic worlds that ought to have been encouraged, rather than set aside."

Powell loved the job, the travel, the glamour of the moment when the band rose out of the pit at the Paramount, the attention. Goodman's notorious quirks, peculiar moods, absent-mindedness, and even downright rudeness never fazed him.

"Benny and I got along very well," Mel said. "We remained friends to the end of his life. He always used to make me laugh a lot. I had my own bargain-basement psychology involved. Benny seemed to think that I had a lot of money. I don't know why." He laughed. "It must have been the way I behaved. And therefore he thought I didn't need the job. But he always made me laugh.

"He expected us to fight over who was picking up the tab. And he was making all that money. And then marrying a Vanderbilt!"

Mel met Peggy Lee when she joined the band in Chicago, "this gorgeous blonde Scandinavian from the deep midwest," Mel remembered. Benny was as cool to her as he was to most new members of the band. Peggy had to sing everything in keys set for Helen Forrest, who had just left the band. She has said that Benny gave her no rehearsal, and that her saviour was Mel Powell, who patiently rehearsed her in whatever little time they had.

"Sid Catlett was in the band when you were," I said.

"I used to really love Sidney Catlett," Mel said. "Whitney Balliett, who I think was a drummer when he was younger, absolutely adored Sid. So did Buddy Rich. So did Louis Bellson. So did Gene Krupa. And there was good reason.

"Teddy Wilson had a marvelous band at Barney Josephson's Cafe Society Uptown in which Big Sid was the drummer. Often I'd go in. Teddy and I were very good friends. Teddy would ask me to play. And I loved to play.

I thought I was imitating him all the time. And playing with Big Sid! It was enchantment to play with that drummer. The taste, the touch. I can't even imagine what would have happened if he'd had the kind of equipment that later drummers had. He had a bass drum, a snare drum, a couple of cymbals, and that's it.

"Sid had an ear for pitch, indefinite or indeterminate pitch. You'd marvel at the way he'd pick spots on the snare drum. And then when he went on the cymbal and started pushing the band! In fact, he was the only one who ever got me to take my hands off the piano. I was taken by the force. I'm sitting here, he's sitting up there. I'm doing whatever I'm supposed to be doing. This was in Chicago in the Sherman Hotel. Sidney was sitting up, third level, with the trumpets. Band's playing, wow! 'One O'Clock Jump.' Marvelous! And I'm looking at him. A kind of wink, a smile. It was there, it was actually happening. And he was gritting his teeth, he had the greatest control of that kind of tempo. It *seemed* as if it was loud, but it wasn't. You know what I mean?"

"Sure. When drummers get forceful, they tend to get loud. The drummer who can play forcefully without getting loud is one of God's gifts to music."

"Buddy Rich," Mel said. "That's one of the things Louis Bellson certainly learned from Big Sid. Big Sid was doing this, and I was so stunned that believe it or not, unbeknownst to me, my hands just fell. I was just in the audience. And then the piano solo came. It took me a couple of beats. Happily, thank heaven, it wasn't the *Emperor Concerto* or something. I was so taken by that guy's playing."

"Supposedly Benny fired Catlett during a record date. Why?"

"I've never known really what was what," Mel said. "We made 'The Earl' on that session."

"Is that why there are no drums on it?"

"Exactly. I am almost certain it was in Liederkrantz Hall in New York. Right then and there, as we were recording. I have been asked a hundred times what happened between Sid and Benny. I will never know."

As much as he liked working with Goodman and the superb musicians Goodman hired, including Charlie Christian, Mel would within a year begin to tire of the band.

He said, "When I to some degree lost interest and went on to do some other things instead, it was largely because formulas were replacing improvisation in a certain sense. It was still improvised: but very predictable. I don't really want to make anyone sound like a culprit. But the demands of the profession – I think it was a wonderful band – nevertheless, every night the same pieces . . .

"I preferred the small band. I think Benny played better when I was the leader than when he was. He was able to loosen up and forget about it."

"I think the best I ever heard him play," I said, "was on your Commodore record of 'The World Is Waiting for the Sunrise.'"

"I'm not kidding," Mel said. "I do think it was his best."

"Cannonball Adderley came to hate his own hits because he had to play them every night."

"Sure. It's very difficult to stay at the perilous stage. It's very difficult to do that when you know everything that's coming. The whole point is not to know almost anything that's coming.

"I think jazz is the ideal performer's music. Spontaneity is *it*. Make it up as you go. I think it *has* to be that. I think Benny tried hard. There's a great difference between pianists. Certain of them, you hear them, and it sounds like they improvised that. The catch, however, is that every time you hear them, they play exactly that. That's a different business than we're talking about."

I said, "There are some records of Teddy Wilson, different takes of the same tune, where what he plays is pretty set. There's some variation, but a lot of it is set. Certain patterns at certain places."

"Pretty set, yes," Mel said. "No one admired him more than I did. Nevertheless, I'll be audacious enough to say that despite the fact that I took much from him – as I did from others, from Earl, from Fats too, I think, from Tatum – the fact is that at any cost, I was improvising. I would be willing to be bad, but I was going to improvise. Teddy would not do that. He always sounded *marvelous*, of course. But that didn't seem to me to be what was necessary.

"Even Louis of all people played as though it were a set piece. But Earl didn't. Again, the peril, the risk. You had no idea what was going to happen when Hines started to play. And I don't think he did."

After leaving Goodman, Mel did some freelance studio work in New York but then got his draft notice and was shipped to Fort Dix. "I encountered a southern sergeant who had a genuine hatred of Jews, and when he saw the name on my papers, he assigned me immediately to latrine duty. I changed it legally. An uncle had done it before me, taking the name Powell from Poljanowsky."

He would not have stayed on latrine duty in any event: hardly was he accustomed to the feel of his uniform than Glenn Miller commandeered him to play in the latter's Army Air Force band. His bandmates included Ray McKinley, Carmen Mastren, Zeke Zarchy, and Peanuts Hucko. The band had a string section, and Powell was able to write string trios for some of its players. And it began rehearsing at Yale University. Mel had no way of knowing that Yale would become his home in a few years.

Almost everyone in the band was under 30. Miller was 38. Probably the youngest member was a trombonist from Brooklyn named Nat Peck who, at 18, was not long out of high school. A Swing Sextet was organized within the

Miller band, with Mel as its director. Long afterwards, Peck said that "Mel took a liking to me for some odd reason and I was chosen to do it . . . The reason I was picked, I think, was that I was the only one in that trombone section who had any sort of experience in playing jazz . . . Mind you, at the time I was very nervous about it – I didn't know Mel that well. Mel was a very distant sort of a personality – not that he was unkind, or anything like that, but he was already very big-time . . . and I used to sit in (the) band a little worried about things and he misinterpreted my attitude. He thought that I was putting him down, or being critical about what was going on in the band, when, to tell you the truth, I was more scared than anything else. He discovered that, though, soon enough and we ended up really very, very good friends."

Peck made these comments to a British writer, Geoffrey Butcher. They are quoted in Butcher's book *Next to a Letter from Home* (Sphere Books, London, England, 1987), a chronicle of the sojourn in England and France of the wartime Miller band. That Miller thought as highly of Powell as Goodman before him is evident in Peck's comment: "Mel had a completely free hand. The only time Miller ever turned up was on the first rehearsal . . . Probably it wasn't from lack of interest, but he listened to the broadcasts and he found them eminently satisfactory and decided not to intervene in any way and Mel was free to do as he wanted."

Paris was liberated on 24 August 1944. Mel, by then a sergeant, allowed considerable liberty by Miller, managed to slip over from England two or three days later, when the city's mad partying was still in progress.

"I went to the Bibliotheque Nationale," Mel said. "At the time my French was reasonably fluent, which was gratefully acknowledged by the music librarian. As a matter of fact, everybody was out drinking and running around, and here I came in with the eyeglasses and speaking French. The place was absolutely empty. And I asked if I could see some of the early work of Debussy.

"He said, 'Sure.' This was before Xerox, of course. This was the original stuff. Perhaps they had microfiche by then, I'm not sure. There were some photographs, certainly. I have *The Golliwog's Cakewalk* in the autograph. I was shown work he did at the age of 11 or 12, work that nobody knows. This was the grandest discovery I made. The most remarkable thing was that there was the stuff, the parallel fifths marked as mistakes by the teacher. The harmony was poor. But the counterpoint was incredibly good. Twelve to sixteen part stuff! This kid at 12 or whatever he was at the Conservatoire." (Debussy entered the Conservatoire at 10.)

"It was exactly the opposite of what you would think," Mel said. "You'd think the harmony would be excellent, the counterpoint perfunctory. Un-unh: the exact opposite."

Miller prepared to move the band to France by Christmas. On 15 December he took off in an 8th Air Force Norseman aircraft piloted by Flight Officer John R. S. Morgan. Their flight was lost over the Channel. Ray McKinley, the one member of the band who was an experienced bandleader, took over the direction of the Miller crew. On Christmas Eve they made a broadcast from the Olympia theater in Paris, on the same program with Robert Farnon and George Melachrino.

With the fall of Germany in May of 1945, the Miller band was shipped home to the United States. It was being readied to go to the South Pacific under Ray McKinley's direction when the bombs fell on Hiroshima and Nagasaki, and suddenly it was over.

Mustered out of service, Mel returned for a time to Goodman. He was offered a job on the composition staff of MGM, probably on the recommendation of his friends Lennie Hayton and André Previn, who were already there. He took the job and hated it, but it was during this period that he met Martha Scott, who unsentimentally describes herself as "an old actress from Kansas." But, she quickly points out, she grew up in Kansas City when the Basie band was forming there and, later, when Charlie Parker was flexing his wings. She was a jazz-lover, and the affinity of Mel and Martha was immediate. She and Mel were married in 1946, eventually had two daughters, and remained devoted to each other.

As his duties at MGM palled on him, Mel applied for admission to Yale, submitting a composition to Paul Hindemith, head of the composition department.

By the end of the 1920s, Hindemith, then 25, was esteemed as the outstanding German composer of his generation. Like Mel Powell, he was considered something of a prodigy: conductor of the Frankfurt Opera Orchestra by the age of 20, and then an outstanding viola player. He was an outspoken opponent of the serialism pioneered and expounded by Arnold Schoenberg, and argued that all music was inherently tonal. (Schoenberg himself objected to the term "atonal.")

In 1934 Hindemith was publicly denounced by Josef Goebbels as "a spiritual non-Aryan" and a "cultural Bolshevist" and although he was not, as Arnold Schoenberg was, Jewish, he joined a large migration of German artists, Schoenberg and Thomas Mann among them, and more from other countries, including Stravinsky, Milhaud, and Bartok, to the safety of the United States.

Hindemith was an outstanding educator. He had taught in Berlin and Ankara, and continued his work at Yale University. His prestige at the time Powell applied to study with him was enormous.

"Now," I said to Mel, "the last jazz records of yours I had were in the early days of the LP, the ten-inch LP. You did some sessions for John Hammond on Vanguard, things like 'Russian Lullaby' with Ruby Braff and Edmond Hall and a wonderful rhythm guitar player named Steve Jordan."

"Yes."

"Why did you keep going back to jazz and working with Goodman if that was not going to be your direction? For money?"

"Yes. Money."

"And how were you funding your studies?"

"The GI bill. And don't forget, by then I was married. I had a wife who was a working actress. We could not have lived as well as we did had it not been for Martha's income." A chuckle. "I hope I've made it up to her."

"You wrote a *Sonatina* that you recorded in one of those albums. And I realized a change was in the works."

"That was serious."

"Then I heard a piece you wrote for the Louisville Orchestra."

"Really?"

"Yeah. For three years I covered that program. Elliott Carter, Ginastera, Orrega Sallas, all of those new works. I reviewed all that stuff. But that's when I heard one of your orchestral pieces. And then you just ceased to play jazz?"

"Yes. Except when we got a little bagged, Hindemith and I. He was to deliver the Norton Lectures at Harvard, *A Composer's World.* I had written a paper on Alban Berg. Apparently I was the most literate of the group that interested him. So he invited me to his house to touch up his lectures.

"Which I did. You know, André Previn is a phenomenon for his command of English, when you consider he didn't speak it until he was 14. André used to howl when I told him about this: how I would say to Hindemith, 'No, we don't say, "now to my house going." We don't do that in English. I would change it and he would always fight. He would say, 'My words! You're changing my meaning!' I'd say, 'Maestro, no. Take my word for it.' And we'd get loaded. Liebfraumilch was his big drink.

"Sure enough, he had two pianos upstairs. He'd get a little bit bagged and we'd go up, and we would do two things. We would play Verdi opera. Or we would play his jazz of the 1920s. He had played it in bad bands in Germany. Very few people know that. I was amazed. He would sit there and play the most atrocious stuff."

Hindemith was unimpressed by Mel's facility and subjected him to severe compositional disciplines. Mel says that Hindemith had the greatest pedagogical mind he ever encountered.

"He would look at something of mine and say, 'Po-vell.' Being German he couldn't pronounce Powell. He'd say, 'Po-vell, why have you written this?' I would say, 'I feel that –' And he would say, 'I don't care how you feel. That is for your doctor. Why did you write it?'"

Mel survived, earning his master's degree and becoming Hindemith's teaching assistant. People in the jazz world would hear of him occasionally, but he seemed like a fading wraith. When Hindemith left Yale to return to Europe (where he died in 1963), Mel succeeded him, becoming a full professor and head of the composition department.

I said, "When you withdrew from jazz, the air in the press was like you had deserted this music for classical music. There was that view of jazz as gutter music and your move being an aspiration to respectability."

"Yes. To this day, I will come upon old friends from the jazz world, who will, in fun and good spirits, call me a traitor. It always seemed absurd to me, since what passes for my own philosophical outlook is that we ought to do *everything* – when we can.

"Oddly enough, I am still known, I think – well, this generation doesn't know anything – as a decent jazz pianist, despite the fact that I spent comparatively little time in jazz, which must mean I came to the attention of people when jazz was the most attractive, the most illustrious, the most public and the most famous kind of popular music. It was just extraordinary. I've often thought it was much like late nineteenth-century Italy, where the best music of the time was by coincidence also the most popular."

I said, "It was a very short period. If you date the era from Whiteman and Ellington and Goldkette, it lasted about twenty years, but its big period was from the time Benny broke through until 1946, when so many bands folded, which makes it about ten years. Rock-and-roll has been with us for nearly 40."

"Isn't that amazing?" Mel said. "I assume I've missed something very important in not knowing about rock-and-roll."

"I assume I haven't. Someone is always telling me there are nuggets there if only you have the patience to search. I say that Bach is nothing but nuggets. The lode is infinitely richer, and how much time does each of us have to explore it?"

"Yes," Mel said, laughing hard, "but I deal with young kids every day."

"That music has no harmonic interest to me."

"None whatsoever."

"I find it rhythmically stiff."

"Rhythmically, it's terrible," he said, "and melodically, it's absurd. And the lyrics, whenever I can understand the declamation, which isn't frequently . . . Well, I do understand the word 'baby.'"

"The other one is 'girl,'" I said. "As in, 'Hey, girl.' They throw 'girl' in a lot."

"Much beyond that, I don't hear. Perhaps the lyrics are interesting, though I think not.

"You know, I think the inability to admire contributed greatly to the growth of rock-and-roll. When you and I first heard music, we began right off the bat saying, 'That's marvelous! I can't do that!' I don't care whether it was Jascha Heifetz or Fats Waller. When I first heard Tatum, my inclination was to say, 'I can't do that!' But the kids hearing rock-and-roll say, 'I can do that.' And I think that that kind of narcissism came into the world . . ."

"Adlai Stevenson came up with the phrase. He said, 'We have lost our regard for excellence.' It was in everything, every field."

"In everything. It also got confused with what was politically perhaps very attractive, and that was the disrespect for authority. That's fine. But I think it got mixed up with that."

I said, "Well, there was a PR campaign by the entertainment industry to the effect that any respect for excellence was elitism, and that this was somehow anti-democratic. That's more of the nonsense that helped wreck this culture, which is in pretty bad shape."

"Bad shape," Mel concurred with a sigh. "You're talking to someone who tomorrow morning meets with young people in their 20s. And I have to bear in mind that it's something like 33 years since Humphrey Bogart died. So I have to be careful. Some of my references are useless. I'm talking about so-called classical music."

"You mean, young classical musicians, who don't know the tradition?"

"Don't know it. My contribution has been to argue that, ironically, composers like Elliott Carter, Milton Babbitt, and myself, are in fact Eurocentric. It's ironic since, certainly in my own case, and in Milton's, jazz played a big part in our development."

"Yeah, Milton Babbitt played jazz clarinet, I believe."

"Yes. There's no reason to know that. What I was going to say is that our form of composition tends to be Eurocentric. It derives from Stravinsky and Schoenberg, two different worlds merging, more or less. Schoenberg has won out for the waning years of our century.

"But the kids coming up today are *not* Eurocentric. One day I was talking about Mahler, and I made a reference to *The Magic Mountain*. I got those glazed eyes. And then I realized they were thinking of the playland Magic Mountain, and they wanted to know what Mahler had to do with a roller coaster. We no longer have a common referential framework.

"I was talking to Susan Sontag. She was bitching that she had done two weeks' teaching in Salt Lake City or someplace. I said, 'Two weeks? I've been teaching for 40 years. What chutzpah to say that.' I told her about the Magic Mountain business. She said, 'You were looking for kids to know Thomas Mann?' I said, 'Yes, I was.' She said, 'I just spent two weeks in Utah looking for anyone who had heard of Mussolini!'

"That broke me up."

"The question of accessibility in music has troubled me for years," I said. "Schoenberg is still considered avant garde art. And it's getting on toward being a century later. So are Joyce and Picasso. You were talking about the period when the best music of Europe was also the most popular. What is the responsibility of the composer to the public? You strike me as a fascinating dichotomy, because of your ability to make tremendously accessible music such as 'Mission to Moscow,' and then to go in this other direction."

"The answer is direct," Mel said. "I don't feel any particular responsibility toward anyone other than the severest critic, whom I identify as myself. It's not elitism I'm talking about."

"Well, I'm an elitist in the sense that I certainly prefer Jerome Kern to Lennon and McCartney."

"There you go," Mel said. "Exactly. So do I, by the way. Not only that. I happen to think of Rodgers and Hart as men of genius. Really. I'm absolutely bowled over by them. But from my work, you'd say, 'Did Powell really say that?'"

I said, "Well the question that has been hanging over us for a long time is: is the tonal system obsolete?"

"Oh, I see. Well. Actually, we're making a bad mistake in talking in terms of tonal or non-tonal – I call it non-tonal – music. Out of deference to Schoenberg, I call it non-tonal. It's a mistake on Schoenberg's part, on all our parts, to talk in terms of pitch, which is what the tonal or non-tonal system focuses on. The truth is that the fundamental element, fundamental dimension, of the art is time, and the way time is used is *far more* strategic, more mystifying, and more important than the way pitch is used.

"It's easy enough to say that Schoenberg is obsolete, Berg is obsolete. Eurocentric is obsolete, if you hear John Adams. You'd think there had been a most remarkable regression, with the Beatles coming after Duke Ellington. Chronologically, there is something wrong in terms of sophistication, complexity, and so on. And here is John Adams, a young guy of 38 or 39 or so, writing operas and so on. It's simply music on a loop. It goes around and around and around. Like Philip Glass or Steve Reich. Just over and over again. What we would in jazz call two-, three-, four-bar riffs. They just keep going for twenty minutes, and then another riff.

"Non-tonality is extraordinary in what is implicit in it. But what is far more significant and extraordinary is the nature of the usage of time. That's where revolutions are made, you see. For that reason I think that Claude Debussy is perhaps the most revolutionary of all twentieth-century composers. He changed our view of time. There's been a mistake all these years to be looking at his thirteenth chords and whole-tone scales. Forget that. The extraordinary thing that Debussy did, and only *l'esprit Gallique* could do it, was to flatten out the difference between an up beat and a down beat.

"Here would be dominantic harmony, and *here* would be dominantic harmony. Unthinkable from the German point of view. So he began to equalize, and in doing that he touched on what I think is one of the essentials in the new music and the more interesting music."

"That's a startling thought," I said. "I have always viewed him for the harmonic factor."

"Let us grant that. But all that stuff was there in Cesar Franck. All that stuff was there in Wagner, all that stuff was there in Richard Strauss. Really.

"I think our teaching and learning have become so subordinate to the needs of institutions – I'm sounding awful, saying this – that we tend to emphasize the more teachable. Pitch happens to be very teachable.

"I could, in three days, show you the entirety of Schoenberg, Berg, Webern. I could show you how the pitch operates. And it's original and interesting. But I could show you the systematics.

"But I'd have a hell of a time telling you what Webern was up to with respect to *time*. And how he *prevented you* from sensing it. So when you looked at the score, you would say, 'My God, was that four-four? Where was the down beat? Was there a structural down beat?' Etcetera.

"*That*'s where the mysteries reside. And Debussy was the first. Where I bet the ranch is *L'après-midi d'un faune*. I always tell the students, 'Please, when the flute begins that piece, don't look at the conductor. Because Debussy has done everything possible to keep you from knowing what the hell is going on with . . .'" And he sang the opening flute line of the piece. "Weird. Where is one? He's done everything possible to conceal it. Don't watch the fool doing this . . . " And he waved his hand slowly, like a conductor. "Which gives you beats that aren't there. They aren't sonic, they aren't acoustic.

"No, I can't rave enough about the incredible invention by Debussy of a new usage of time, and I think that our century at its best is about that. It's one of the reasons why I think jazz is so important, and why I think rock-and-roll is not. Rock-and-roll is not only not a new use of time – for the most part – it is a very dull, old use. It would be like somebody writing in the so-called classical world like Clementi.

"So. Yes. The use of time. I speak, possibly for only aesthetic purposes, of temporal structure – I am tired of the word 'rhythm.' Most of the analysis that I teach now – driving the kids nuts – is indeed to show how uninteresting (this is a terrible thing to say!) most eighteenth- and nineteenth-century European music is. Terrible. I should bite my tongue.

"I'm speaking only of the rhythmic dimension, of course. Not textural. Bach, I think, is the greatest composer who ever lived. Or the *incredible* brain work of Brahms that's not widely known. He was very much a twentieth-century kind of thinker. The music, disguised as pretty lyricism, has a lot of terribly serious, inventive kinds of things. There is an irony in that we thought Wagner was the *zukunstwerke*, the music of the future, artwork of the future, and Brahms was the old shoe of the Romantic era.

"It's turned out quite differently. Brahms' way of putting music together turns out to be much closer to what interests post-Schoenbergians. Even though Boulez doesn't play him.

"After studying with Hindemith, I wrote quite like him, and quite like most Hindemith students. And I strongly recommend that people do that. I think it's foolish to study with, let's say, Bartok, in order to write like Schoenberg or Berg. If you are fortunate enough, as I was, to study with a world master such as Hindemith, the very best thing to do is write quite like him."

"That makes complete sense to me," I said. "In the Renaissance, students were made to copy the works of the masters. If you want to find out about his brush strokes, his texture, if you want to get the feel of the paint on the brush and give of the canvas, copy him until you get it right."

"Well," Mel said, "that's almost essentially what I did with Hindemith. Including the Louisville piece you heard. It's an analogue of a piece of Hindemith's. How else can you really come to terms with a master? You go deeply, deeply into what he knows."

"That's why I get annoyed when I hear critics saying some young jazz player is 'derivative' of somebody."

"My goodness, yes. Now, when you do that, copy a master, there comes a moment that is miraculous. Not necessarily happy. There comes the moment when you now have full grasp of the technique and craft of a great master in his terms, and you are aware of the fact that it ain't . . . your . . . cup of tea. It is not with lack of respect or even reverence for it. *Et après*, as the French say. You're going to write another Hindemith piece? We don't need another Hindemith piece.

"You know, Hindemith taught negatively. He rarely gave a compliment. Eventually I gave him a piece, and he said, 'That's pretty good, Po-vell. I could have written it.' And he laughed and said, 'I think I did.'

"Now that takes a couple of years, to get that command of another man's usage. When it happens – it was for me, in any case; and others I've talked to: Pierre Boulez, they've all experienced it – it was one of the most strategic crises I've gone through. It came to me that now I could do *anything*, I had the technique to do anything compositionally, I could now sit down and plot out my life. I'll write ten symphonies, in order to get one past Beethoven. I'll do three operas, I'll do fourteen piano concertos, etcetera etcetera. But it would have to be in that language, because that's where the technique is.

"That was a terrible moment. I dropped the pen, at least metaphorically. I said, 'We *have* Hindemith. And we don't really require me to do anything, unless perhaps I should just teach, since I understand it so deeply.

"I realized it could not work for me, because the rhythm was square, and that I had been forcing myself in the early Hindemith pieces into, uh, corny rhythmic sequences in order to let the system work. It *demanded* that.

"A real style finds every one of its dimensions analogous. If Mozart ends a phrase melodically, he does so harmonically as well. He does so in terms of orchestral color – the winds have just come in. Or just gone out. He does so in terms of pitch. Everything ends simultaneously. It may be only measure eight. Wagner does not. It's Romanticism. The dimensions are arguing with one another.

"When I say that every dimension in a real, real classic style – in the other sense – really works, all you have to do is imagine Debussy orchestrating Bruckner or Mahler. It would be absurd. Or vice versa. All the dimensions have to be aligned. Think of the vagueness in Debussy. There's no possibility that it would work, if he orchestrated Mahler.

"When it came to me that what I had been doing deliberately with the fundamental element, time, was making it very Germanic, very straightforward, because it was the only way that that language Hindemith had taught, and invented for his artistic purposes, would work, that was a dismal day. I had to go crawling around elsewhere. What I could now do very well was not what I cared to do.

"On the one hand I had learned what I wanted to know about the craft. But no, this somehow would not serve my needs. And of course at the same time I ran into some other composers, Webern etcetera. Most important was that in order for Hindemith's language or any so-called neo-classic writing to work, it was necessary to have a pulse, or striated time." He tapped a steady beat on his desk. "The harmony would not work without it, the melodies would make no sense, indeed even the coloring – although that begins to get complicated – would make no sense.

"I once, in a class, speaking of timbre or color, showed – maybe being a little too smart; I was a young professor then – that Mozart with the simplest of orchestras manifested the most impeccable correlation of structure and color. For example, a move from X to Y, usually from tonic to dominant, would be marked. For it was there, when the dominant was reached, that the woodwinds came in. He's only got woodwinds and strings in his orchestra; the horns and the trumpets play long notes. In short, all the dimensions have to stack up and agree, to make any sense. So, facing all these things really caused me a good deal of discontent. That was a rather dark night.

"It's easier for me now to look at that comparatively young fellow who was meandering about. I was heading for or had arrived at 30. So here I was, equipped as I had wished to be, and yet couldn't use the stuff. The only analogue I can think of is that it was as if somebody had bought you a baseball bat, a catcher's mitt, and a mask, and now you wanted to play football.

"I had to start all over again, within the domain of so-called serious music.

And I began, to speak in the simplest terms, to veer from neo-classicism, which entails many things, not just tonality, which is the most notable perhaps or at least the most discussed. What should be equivalently obvious is the formal structures of classicism, sonata allegros, scherzos and trios."

"Debussy had little attraction to those forms."

"Well," Mel said, "Debussy is *so sly*. What he does is so underground."

"Now," he said, "I am going to give you one thought that is going to be repugnant to you as a lyricist. I now tell my students that if they are interested in writing art songs, that the ideal thing for them to do – and I give them some formulas and things – is write melismatically. Why? The very thing you as a lyricist dislike."

"Not if it's total," I said. "If you're going to use the voice as a wordless instrument, that's another thing. But if you're going to use words . . . "

"Ah but there's a deeper reason," Mel said. "They always get the point, and it saves five lectures. I tell them, if you try to compete with the great American pop songs, you're going to be knocked out in the first innings. Because of the match of tone and words. I tell them, don't compete. Go over somewhere else."

I said, "I am always conscious of intervals in speech and even in birds, all sorts of recognizable intervals. Once, in a Chinese restaurant I heard the owner and his wife arguing in the kitchen. I kept catching inversions of the major triad. And emotion was being conveyed. Entire communications can be made by speech inflections and pitch alone."

"That goes into training for actors, by the way," Mel said.

"Pitch to me has distinct communication value."

"No question," Mel said, and sang, "Johnny," a falling minor third, as if calling a child. Specifically, he hit A-flat and F.

"The first inversion of the major triad has a very playful sound," I said.

"Sure."

"Kern is an utterly distinctive melodist working within a system that is now centuries old."

"Yes."

"And you say 'Don't compete with the likes of Kern.'"

"Or Oscar Hammerstein or Lorenz Hart," Mel said. "My God. I actually pushed and taught the melisma because they ain't never gonna do 'Night and day, you are the one . . . ' So in a certain sense, I've given them the easy way out. Now, on the other hand, abstractly, the melisma can be expressive of whatever you want to be expressive of. However, non-tonality restricts the expressive domain, the terrain. There are restraints. I could make you giggle by saying, 'Imagine Schoenberg writing a comic opera.'

"It ain't there. Forget it. The only thing that will make you laugh is the idea of such a thing happening. It's not going to happen with Webern, it's not going to happen with Alban Berg. Non-tonality, or atonality as some like to call it, is restricted in its expressive power. Well, that's the price you pay. Most languages *are* restrictive in their expressive power."

"Sure. You can say and think things in French you can't say in English, and vice versa. The French have no word for upstairs. Or home."

"Exactly. You don't say, 'Thou shithead.' I mean, please. One or the other. I can handle either language. Similarly in music. I point out that, after all, opera was alive and well in Bach's time. Bach didn't touch it. Bach wrote philosophic disquisitions. The fugue is not a form, the fugue is a process, a thinking process. Whereas Verdi, more than a century later, would simply write a so-called Italian sixth chord with two clarinets and two bassoons in *Rigoletto* and scare the hell out of you. You look at the page and say, 'What *is* that? It's just a chord there.' Yeah, well, it's the *right* chord at the *right* moment for Italian opera. Bach didn't touch it. His language *also* had constraints.

"So. I make that quite clear. I say, 'Don't try for "the corn is as high as an elephant's eye." You ain't gonna get it, unless you've got Oscar Hammerstein as your collaborator.'"

"But we're getting," I said, "at what is dichotomous with you. I have been on a collision course with this thought for years: what is music for? Why do we do it? What is its specific function? I've always said it's a mysterious language. We don't know why and how music affects the emotions."

Mel said, "One of my pet theories is that at some point, someone yelled, 'Help!' And that would have meant hysteria. And he or she in a moment of serenity when he or she had escaped recalled that peculiar effect of the heightened inflection, and did it again, only this time without the panic."

I said, "This is the theory of music as abstracted speech. But I have become convinced that speech is abstracted music. To me, the idea of music as symbolic speech must be inherently incorrect, because there was music before there was speech, if only in the cries of birds. So I suspect that speech *arises out of* music. We're never going to know."

"Oh, I'm sure we will," Mel said. "Some day we'll do it with confidence. The only way we can handle this is when we close in on, first, what we mean by emotion, and second, what is the bridge that creates the linkage between emotion and the expression thereof. Words are there, of course. But music is there, so much more powerfully in so many ways. We organize the world into space and time. Fine. It seems to correspond to our senses. But that's the way we see the world. So do we see the world as: this is intellect, this is intuition, etcetera. Although I can never do that seriously.

"One day I walked down the street in New Haven with a young colleague of mine, who was a professor of biochemstry. At the time I was practicing scientism. That is, my lectures eliminated all adjectives, etcetera etcetera. This guy, on the other hand, said, 'Are you familiar with the binomial theorem?' I said, 'Yeah.' He said, 'Beautiful, isn't it?'

"I was stunned to hear the word 'beautiful.' And he meant beautiful in the sense *we* mean beautiful. And I thought, 'This guy is over there in the bio-chemistry hence science department. I am talking about registral invariance, which is a very complex way of saying a certain tessitura is predominant. I'm talking like a brain surgeon or something, and this guy is talking like a jazz fan.' It was like, 'Dig these changes!' or something. He meant *beautiful*. So therefore let us assume that it's only convenient for us to say, 'Thus and so is intellectual, thus and so is intuition.' Now you've got that wonderful Stravinsky expression: 'Intuition never misleads you. When it does, it's not intuition.' That's nice, that's cute.

"But that's the best we can do in organizing things. You read Einstein, as far as you can, which is not terribly far in my case. I can read ideas and opinions, I can read those books that he wrote. And if that isn't 'warm' and if that isn't almost vibrato on the cello!

"So I am willing to accept the modes of organization with a reservation underneath. When you come to the question of what is music *for*, we're touching on that kind of fundamental thing. You know, Verdi fell to the floor the first time he heard a big C-major chord in church, in the little Italian village where his mother took him to church. He fell into a dead faint. You can imagine this resounding, great huge organ playing a big C-major chord with all the stops out, two feet, four feet, sixteen feet, everything. And the kid went plop! Fainted dead away. I don't think there was any word or any combination of words that could have affected him that way.

"Maybe at that moment – we can only guess – all these things were integrated, what we call the intellect, the intuition, the emotions, all the things we have names for. Maybe music can do that."

I said, "It's been a mystery all my life, how music does this, causes tears, causes laughter. I've heard jazz solos that made me laugh, laugh out loud at something somebody played, and I can't even tell you what was funny. It just was."

"Absolutely," Mel said. "Wit. Caprice. Bunny Berigan playing 'I Can't Get Started,' if you happen to like that, which I do. Music can do that. Music can integrate. I always must say this apologetically: I know very few writers of words who can even approach this. Music can make you fully aware of the inadequacy of the verbal language."

"I call music the language beyond language. Music can express, and evoke, the emotions for which there are no words. Bill Evans could play shades of emotion you didn't know you had. Bill played emotions that were so private that I have never even *tried* to express them."

"Sort of as if he looked over to see is anybody watching?" Mel said. "This is *my* business."

"Given that this capacity is there," I said, "what do you expect people – I am asking not the you you, but a whole range of people, including Milton Babbitt."

"Elliott Carter," Mel added, knowing where my question was leading.

"What do you expect the audience to bring to this experience?"

"The ability to say 'Wow!' That's all."

"How do they get to this if the language is strange to them?"

"By giving up the attempt to understand anything, and marveling at imagination. Wow!"

"I got some moments of that out of your Pulitzer concerto, which I haven't yet listened to enough. I get moments of it out of Penderecki and Ligeti. But not for long. I can't take an hour of it."

Mel said, "Well, I have these egomaniacal aspirations. I hope that the 32 minutes or so that the piece takes, the concerto, doesn't seem long. I've heard ten-minute pieces that sounded longer! At least to me."

"I didn't realize it was that long," I said. "I was going to tell you it seems rather short."

"Good! That's good. I'm happy about that. I think . . . This is dangerous to say, because God knows the younger people today don't need any authorization for stupidity. They seem to have all the stupidity they need. But you can take virtually any piece of music – you might even be able to do this with prose – and show relationships that are so involuted, so strategic, clever, crucial, yet were never known to the composer. You can only do it backwards. Here's the piece that one writes. And now the analysis."

"Sure. And if you were consciously aware of all these things while working, you couldn't do it in the first place. Technique must be unconscious. If you have to think about the clutch and the gearshift and the brake, you aren't ready to drive the car. Unless the mechanics of the craft have sunk to that level, you're not even in business."

"Yes," Mel said. "*That* then is what I meant.

"If you approach the task of musical analysis as though you are decoding some cryptic message, you're wrong to start with. It's not what it's about. You will see and hear in the work of a gifted and competent craftsman many things that are craftsmanlike, just as you will with any writer. You will see them playing with words like wizards on the stage. Sometimes I'll read a sentence or two of Loren Eiseley, say, who was very careful about words. He's using one- or at maximum two-syllable words. But there probably are certain things that a writer would see, patterns of vowels, rhythm, long sentences, short sentences, the building of paragraphs. All those things should be known after you have learned the craft. But I can show you much more complex, profound relationships after the fact: did the composer know that?"

"Well," I said, "it's always coming up: if you work hard enough, God will be nice to you."

"Yes!" Mel said, chuckling. "If you work hard enough, God will drop something in your pocket. Eventually the *geist* will be there. That's one of the reasons why going to your desk, at whatever you do, on a quite steady basis, is crucial. You have to, as the gamblers say, be able to cut your losses. But you have to be there where the action is. And sooner or later, I think God will be nice to you if you work hard enough."

Mel made the move from Connecticut to California in the mid-1960s, when Aaron Copland recommended him to head the music department at CalArts, an institution set up partly with money from Walt Disney and designed as a place where artists from the various disciplines could meet and talk and affect each other. Kingman Brewster, president of Yale, urged Mel not to make the move to California, saying, "All they have out there is carnivals," but the idea of an interdisciplinary institution was attractive to Powell, and he took the job. He was provost of CalArts from 1972 to 1976, but he hated the job and resigned to devote himself strictly to teaching, which he loved, for all his wry humor about the limitations and lack of cultural education of young music students.

Mel was a dedicated tennis player until one day he was on his way to a match when his legs gave way and he fell on a sidewalk. He got up, went on to his game, and didn't think much about it, but it happened again, and he consulted his doctor. Eventually his disorder was diagnosed as inclusionary polymyocitis. The disease had affected the quadriceps, making it difficult for him to lift his legs. He is a man remarkably devoid of self-pity, although he admitted to missing tennis. He said, "My reaction wasn't: why me? It was: why not me? And I felt how lucky I had been not to have had anything wrong with me before."

Mel wrote in a study off the kitchen of the one-storey house in which he and Martha had lived for many years, down a step that was now covered by a ramp. He would tell you to stand back as he came down the ramp on his electric cart, saying that the gadget, which he maneuvered with great skill, had been known to misbehave. "A regular Barney Oldfield," he said. The studio contained a baby grand piano, some sort of electronic keyboard, a desk, a writing table, and the inevitable messy clutter of books and scores and manuscripts. A few floppy disks on the table reminded you of the electronic music which is one of his interests.

Martha became part of a cabal to get him back to playing some of his beloved jazz. Also involved in the conspiracy were Hank O'Neal and Shelly Shier, who ran the jazz cruises on the SS *Norway*. Finally they persuaded him to take part in the 1987 cruise. I'd heard that Mel practiced for six months to get ready for that cruise. Was it true?

"Yes! That probably sounds a little more ferocious than it actually was. But there is no question that for *at least* six months, I'd get up in the morning, and I'd go to the keyboard like a good boy, and I'd do what I had not done in a long, long time, which is essentially practicing."

"How did it feel, to be back out there sitting in a rhythm section, banging away?"

"I was just grinning for two weeks. At the time, since it was considerably before some of the affliction took hold, I had a drink of Irish whiskey, got up on the bandstand . . . and there were old friends like Joe Williams. It was wonderful! Wonderful to see Joe again, and Dizzy! And Louis Bellson. You don't know how good these guys are until you've been a long time away from them. *Then.* The way Louis played! I mean, the way he wasn't there and was there, you know? Oooh! I was stunned. I was just stunned at that kind of support. And Milt Hinton! And Major Holley. A young kid named Howard Alden on guitar, very good. Buddy and I and Dizzy playing some stuff. God, the way these guys play!"

Mel Powell embodied what for me is the aesthetic dichotomy of our time. He not only did not resolve my bemusement over it, he deepened it.

The question of accessibility in art is a vexed one for which there is no simple answer, perhaps no answer at all. Popularity is no proof of excellence. Having reached this obvious conclusion, one must be cautious, for neither is the lack of it. One of the problems of jazz has always been that a certain kind of admirer prefers that it be considered arcane, in order that his or her taste for it can be self-seen as informed, exceptional, and superior. This attitude is pilloried in Dave Frishberg's lyric "I'm Hip." It is probably not as common as it once was, but one encounters it.

I have believed since my earliest years that if the artist wishes to communicate, the onus is on him to be clear. But clear to whom? An imbecile? Or to the sophisticated, informed member of the audience, capable of detecting every echo and inversion and retrograde presentation of a piece of thematic material and all its implications of rhythmic and harmonic and orchestrational texture? Should one listen to the "serious" composer for the purpose of solving his puzzles? Mel said not. So much for a possible theory of contemporary composition as an exercise in acrostic decipherment. But what can make us say "Wow" if we do not understand? Somone might write an emotional poem, but if it's in Urdu, it cannot make us say "Wow."

I take consolation in something Mel's friend André Previn wrote about him. André said that Mel's music became "more and more complicated and private, and some of his work taxed any musical mind severely, unless it had been schooled by the likes of Elliott Carter." André described it as being "as easily assimilated as the Dead Sea scrolls but . . . quite marvelous."

I went back in time to the *Sonatina* (1953), first recorded by Mel on Vanguard and recorded again in 1989 by a pianist named Delores Stevens.

I was surprised at how accurately I remembered it. It is an exquisite piece of music, strangely serene. It is from the time of Mel's studies with Hindemith, but I cannot see it as neo-classical except in the constant discretion of its choices and in the same sense that Ravel was Mozartean. It puts me in mind not of the classical period so much as the "modern" French, while in its American quality, it faintly evokes Charles Tomlinson Griffes, or perhaps what Griffes might have done and been had he lived longer. It is more severe than Griffes, more mature, less sentimental.

And so back to the Goodman band, and the charts Mel wrote, many of them available again through the CD reissues on CBS. They are wonderful. They remain as fresh as when they were written. And he was apparently churning the stuff out then, utterly prolific. His playing is exuberant, exultant, laughing, and inventive. Then comes the diminuendo of the late 1940s and early 1950s, the Vanguard records, and at last tacet, at least from *that* Mel Powell.

And then the 1987 burst-out, the cruise on the *Norway*, some of which is to be heard on the Chiaroscuro album *The Return of Mel Powell*. This too is delightful stuff, his interplays with Benny Carter, Howard Alden, Milt Hinton, and Louis Bellson. It's loose, it's unrehearsed, and happy.

It is as if sometime around 1959, Mel Powell shoved his ship into warp drive and accelerated past the red shift and vanished, leaving on the retina a faint after-image of stardust, the memory of years gone by. "The Earl," "Mission to Moscow," "The World Is Waiting for the Sunrise." Then, suddenly, in 1987, he reappears, playing those lines in octaves, trying for long ski-slope runs and bringing them off, embracing ecstasy and laughing all the way. The music hasn't aged. Einstein was right.

I make my usual mistake. I long for a perfect world.

On 31 October 1990, there was a performance of his works in tribute to Mel Powell in the Terrace Theater of the Kennedy Center in Washington. Mel was in the audience.

I try to step back and look at all the worlds of Mel Powell, peanut salesman, baseball buff, jazz musician, composer, teacher, raconteur, wit, the kid reading Debussy manuscripts, the white-haired wise professor.

Wow.

Mel Powell died on 24 April 1998. He was 75.

13

The man that got away:
Marion Evans

Once upon a time in Baghdad-on-the-Hudson, as O. Henry called it, on 49th Street between Sixth and Seventh Avenues, there was an apartment with at least eight rooms, including an enormous living room; and in Midtown Manhattan, that was a lot of space.

Among its distinctions, it had been the famous whorehouse run by Polly Adler. That era of its history ended during World War II when the authorities, with that sudden moral fervor in minor matters that apocalyptic horror always seems to induce in Those in Charge, closed it down in a predictably fruitless effort to discourage in servicemen that activity for which our species has long shown an impetuous proclivity. They had done something similar in World War I when they effectively closed down Storyville in New Orleans, thereby casting to the winds the spores of jazz, which took vigorous hold in other cities.

Eventually this capacious pad came to the attention of a lady who was engaged to the superb arranger Don Costa, and he rented it. When they married, Costa turned it over to another arranger, his close friend and sometime business partner Marion Evans. Marion set up his bachelor abode there in 1957, and the place became legendary because of all the arrangers who studied there with him, among them J. J. Johnson, Jimmy Jones, Torrie Zito, and Patrick Williams.

Patrick Williams – he was known as Pat in those days, but then his record company presented him with a bouquet of flowers and he retired the name – turned up at Jim and Andy's bar when he was 23, seeking to establish himself as an arranger. He did this remarkably quickly, then moved to Los Angeles and became one of the most respected of film composers, a position he holds today. He still returns to arranging. He wrote the Sinatra *Duets* albums.

"I had many late nights in Marion's infamous apartment," Pat said. "He introduced me to the music of David Raksin, Alfred Newman, Hugo Friedhofer, and of course Robert Farnon. I think it was not so much about the technique of writing music that Marion taught me.

"Actually, I think I was a lousy student. For me he was an arrow to what was quality in music and what was not."

Marion never charged for his seminars on arranging – the pain of which was often soothed by substantial nocturnal libation – but he had two strict rules for his students: they had to listen diligently and analytically to all the orchestral albums of Robert Farnon; and they had to do the exercises in the several books on composition by Percy Goetschius. Marion even turned me on to the Goetschius books, and I dove into *The Homophonic Forms of Musical Composition*. It requires intense, patient dedication.

I said, "That's dry, tough stuff."

"Well," Marion said, "the only person I ever knew, except myself, who went through all of the Goetschius books and really did the work was Torrie Zito."

It is in part because of Marion's work that Robert Farnon has had his inestimable influence on the art of arranging and orchestration in America, and for that matter around the world.

Marion said, "Don Costa and Jerry Bruno had that apartment. Jerry was the bass player with Vaughan Monroe – Vomit Roe, we used to say. He and Bucky Pizzarelli and Don Costa were all on Vaughan Monroe's band. I took it over because I was doing a summer television show with Helen O'Connell at NBC, which was right up the street at Sixth Avenue. It was a great place because I could play the piano all night and the hi-fi as loud as I wanted to, and stay up until the sun came up. And besides that, it wasn't far from Jim and Andy's, so I could go and eat.

"The apartment had lots of room and everybody could fall over and rehearse.

"And of course you know what happens at 3 or 4 o'clock in the morning: the bars close. The doorbell would ring, and here comes whoever, hadn't had the last drink yet.

"One night Sarah Vaughan came by with her accompanist, Jimmy Jones. He was a long-time student, and an old friend. That's when I discovered she could really play the piano. She and Jimmy would come by at 4 in the morning, and there'd be some stride piano going on. Both of them loved stride piano. She could sure play.

"Jim and Andy's closed at 4, and I was one block north. In fact you could walk right through the parking lot. So we'd get a lot of musicians between 3 and 6 in the morning."

I said, "Remember how Jimmy Koulouvaris used to clap his hands and yell, 'All right, everybody out!'"

"Oh yeah."

Jim and Andy's was one of four taverns in Midtown that catered to musicians; and it was by far the favorite. Owned by a Greek former Seabee named Jim Koulavaris, it was home to a lot of us.

The 1960s were heady days in the music world of New York. The big-band era had ended, but there was an enormous amount of recording going on that employed the musicians left over from that era, plus all kinds of symphony musicians. Famous jazz musicians worked studio jobs, recording excellent arrangements for singers by such gifted writers as Peter Matz, Claus Ogerman, Patrick Williams, Marty Manning, Don Costa and, high on that totem pole, Marion Evans. The singers included such excellent people as Marilyn Maye, Steve Lawrence and Eydie Gormé, Ethel Ennis, Marge Dodson, Fran Jeffries, Vic Damone, Lena Horne, Billy Eckstine, Tommy Leonetti, David Allyn, Johnny Hartman, Sarah Vaughan, Ella Fitzgerald, Tony Bennett, and more. The roster of singers and musicians and arrangers in Los Angeles was equally awesome. Further, the big television variety shows had their own orchestras. The level of the musicianship was incredible.

Marion wrote all or parts of albums by Tony Bennett, Jane Froman, Judy Garland, Urbie Green, Merv Griffin, Dick Haymes, Lurlean Hunter, Howard Keel, Julius LaRosa, Felicia Sanders, Steve Lawrence, Burt Bacharach, Gordon McRae, Helen O'Connell, Jaye P. Morgan, Lillian Roth, Doc Severinsen, Julie Wilson, and a lot more.

"I've written well in excess of 100 albums," Marion said. "However, I refuse to admit to any association with the vast majority of them. If there is a deaf singer, dead or alive, I've worked with them. How about six albums for Kate Smith? Wow! As someone once said, 'It's amazing how Kate Smith retained her figure all those years.'"

The bands and orchestras he wrote for include Tommy Dorsey, Benny Goodman, Vaughan Monroe, Percy Faith, and the Boston Pops. In television he worked on the shows of Steve Allen, Red Buttons, Perry Como, Johnny Carson, Arthur Godfrey, Jackie Gleason, Jack Parr, Ed Sullivan, and more.

Marion said, "I remember when I was going to the Conservatory in Birmingham, Alabama, having great conversations about: 'Be careful you don't write this sort of thing.' I remember specifically a whole thing about the cello, things you don't want to do. I come to New York and I was doing a session with Costa. I saw this almost perfect example of what you're not supposed to do for the cello. I watched this cello player as we went through the record date. He could hardly take time from reading the *Wall Street Journal* to play the part, and it was, like, nothing. Sure, if you're in Birmingham, Alabama, don't write that for the cello. If you're in New York and you've got any number of people I could name, they don't even know that that's hard to play. In fact, many of the hard things, they've spent more time practicing than they did anything else, and it becomes easy. Especially the clarinet. You tell Walt Levinsky, 'Hey, Walt, I'm sorry I wrote this,' and you get 'Oh no, that's great, that's the easiest part to play.'"

The cavalier attitude of string players on sessions was notorious. Charles Munch, in his book *I Am a Conductor*, offered a piece of advice to younger conductors. He cautioned them to remember that members of the other sections knew in their student days that they would play in orchestras, but violinists aspired to be famous virtuosi, and, remaindered into orchestras, were all disappointed men. He counseled conductors to be kind to them.

On recording dates with singers, or jazz musicians, they seemed to feel they had sunk to the lowest levels of their careers, and their indifference, even hostility, was conspicuous, the excellent money they were making notwithstanding. One would see them doing just what Marion said: reading the *Wall Street Journal*, cigar in mouth, between takes.

There were certain key string contractors, the most important being David Nadien, Harry Lookofsky, and Gene Orloff. And if one of these was on the date, you could be sure the others were not.

Marion said, "When I could put together the string section I wanted, I'd sit the ones who hated each other side by side."

"Why?" I said.

"Because they wouldn't talk," he said. "It really worked."

One of Marion's friends was (and still is) the phenomenal pianist Dave McKenna. At some point McKenna was bunking in with Marion in that big old pad on 49th Street.

Dave in his past has been a serious drinker; he doesn't drink at all now. Gentle when sober, he could be sullen when loaded. Dave is held in immense affection by everyone who has ever known him. The stories about him are simply funny, that's all.

"Dave was staying with me," Marion said. "He came home late. I was studying Farnon's arrangement of 'Two Cigarettes in the Dark.' In the middle, I heard something and said, 'Isn't that beautiful? I've got to take that off the record and see what he's doing there.' About that time, McKenna comes floating in. He listened to it, and said, 'There's an F-sharp or whatever it was in there.' And of course he was right, as it turned out. He went to bed. Next afternoon, when he was able to pull himself up and everything, he went over to the piano and played the whole arrangement. By memory. Everybody has had experiences with Dave doing things like that. He's incredible. I would put him, as a musician, on a level with Bob Farnon in terms of just raw talent.

"One Hallowe'en the doorbell rang and I opened the door. There were two characters there with masks on. It was Bob Farnon and Red Ginzler." (Ginzler, another arranger, was a close friend of Farnon.) "I started to play a Dave McKenna album, one of his first, maybe *the* first. I didn't get past eight bars and Bob said, 'Who is he and where is he?' I said he was working down in the Village. Bob said, 'Let's go see him.' We went out looking for him, but I don't think we ever found him that night. Bob immediately recognized what he was listening to.

"When Dave had his sixtieth birthday, I was living temporarily in an apartment hotel in White Plains. There was a very nice Italian restaurant downstairs. On the weekend they had a guy who played really very nice piano. He was a professor at Pace University. I invited Dave and his wife, Frankie, to come for the weekend. We had a birthday party for him. The weekend before they came I was talking to the guy who played the piano and I said, 'I have a very close friend who's a wonderful piano player. He's coming next weekend.' He said, 'That's great.' I said, 'I'd like for you to meet him. We'll have a drink.' The guy said, 'What's his name?'

"I said, 'His name is Dave McKenna.'

"He stopped playing the piano in the middle of the chorus. He said, 'Dave McKenna's gonna be here next Friday night?'

"I said, 'Yeah. Come and join us.'

"He said, 'I won't be here.'

"And he wasn't. The guy quit. I never saw him again."

Marion was as noted among musicians for his dry southern wit as he was for the quality of his writing. I used to delight in his company in Jim and Andy's. I remember one occasion when, as we were having lunch, a strange woman – and a stranger to Jim and Andy's; you could always spot the strangers, they just *looked* as if they didn't belong there – wearing a large floppy sun hat and a white dress with huge black polka dots, came over to our table. She said, "Are you fellows musicians?"

Marion looked up at her and said, "Well you might say that."

She showed us a piece of sheet music. She pointed to a note in the second space up in the bass clef, and said, "What's this note?"

Marion said, "Do you know 'All Cows Eat Grass?'"

She said, "Yes, but what's this note?"

Without a flicker of expression, Marion repeated: "All Cows Eat Grass."

"I know that," she said, "but what's this note?"

I said, "It's a cow," and Marion almost strangled on his drink.

We finally told her it was a C and she left. As she walked back to her booth, Marion crossed his arms at the wrists, flapped his hands like the wings of a bird, and whistled a rising tremolo. I put my face on my forearms on the table and laughed till I wept. I have ever since then used this for the odd people one encounters as one trudges one's road through this vale of tears.

Marion's evaluations of singers are always interesting. Of Frank Sinatra he said, "He has the best intonation relative to the musical surroundings of any singer I've ever heard.

"Steve Lawrence has a fantastic voice. He's an excellent singer. I remember once we did one take, and it was excellent, and I said, 'Play it back.' Then I said, 'Let's go to the next number.' Steve looked at me and said, 'Why aren't we going to do another take?'

"I said, 'If you stay here till Christmas, it won't get any better or worse. You did it just as good the first time as you would the fiftieth.'

"Tony Bennett is completely different. He blows the first few takes, and you're going along and all of a sudden it's like magic in the room. Even the musicians know it. Tony has risen to the occasion. I listened for one thing. As soon as you got through with a take that was really great, there would be five seconds or so of silence, and the whole band would get up and go to hear the playback. They knew that was the take. When he's cooking on all cylinders, he's got incredible instinct."

Of Dick Haymes: "The story went around for years that Dick never paid people to write music. It just wasn't something he believed in." That's one of those Marion Evans understatements; you have to watch for them.

"I was doing a session for him. George Green, who used to copy for me, told me, 'Are you sure we're gonna get paid?' I said, 'Well at least we'll get paid from the record company.'"

When arrangements are used on a record date and then as road charts, the arrangers and copyists by union rule are supposed to be paid a second fee.

"After the session," Marion said, "I noticed that while everybody was hearing the playback in the booth, Dick was picking up the music and putting it into his briefcase. He was gonna take it to Las Vegas with him. And I knew we'd never get paid.

"As we left, we were standing on the corner, waiting for a cab. He was living at that time on York Avenue. I suddenly said, 'Dick, you're going to Vegas tomorrow, and you're gonna be rehearsing. I don't know how to tell you this, but you're taking this music with you, and some of the people who copy the music have had bad experiences with singers who never paid them for it. The only reason I mention this to you – I don't really care – is that all this music has been copied in 24-hour ink. You're probably going to be right in the middle of rehearsal tomorrow, because this was copied this afternoon, and the notes are just going to disappear off the page.'

"He said, 'How could that happen?'

"I said, 'It's copied in 24-hour ink.'

"He said, 'What can I do about it?'

"I said, 'Well fortunately the copyists had this chemist develop this, and they've got a spray that can fix it. If they get to it before the notes disappear, and they spray the parts, it'll never disappear.'

"He said, 'Can you get that done?'

"I said, 'Yeah, sure.'

"We got a cab and he said, 'Come on up to my house, I'll give you a check.'

"I said, 'They won't take a check, Dick. You're gonna have to get the cash.'

"He said, 'Where am I going to get cash tonight?'

"I said, 'I don't know, but if you don't, you're gonna have blank manuscript paper tomorrow. I'll tell you what. Why don't you give me all the parts, and I'll take them over and get them sprayed, 'cause it's gonna take some time for them to dry. And I'll call you up, and if you've found the money I'll come by and we'll exchange downstairs, I won't even bother to come up.'

"So I went over to George Green's, and we watched a TV show, and then I called Dick up and said, 'Okay, we've sprayed the parts, and they're all dried.'

"He said, 'Well I've got the money.'

"I said, 'I'll meet you downstairs.'

"He came out with a brown bag and I gave him the music and that was the end of it."

Marion was at the peak of his musical career when, seemingly abruptly, toward the end of the 1960s, he walked away from the business, leaving his friends startled. Even more startling was the fact that he became a financial consultant. I remember saying to someone or other at the time, "Any guy who can think voice leading the way Marion can shouldn't find the stock market all that difficult." I didn't know it but Marion had not two but three professions.

"I was born," Marion said, "on 1 May 1926, in Goodwater, Alabama, which is south of Birmingham. My father was in two businesses, lumber and banking. My Uncle Will was president of the bank, and he was the one who got me interested in finance.

"Not that I was interested at that time. But it is the vocabulary that you pick up. Long-term interest rates and amortization and accrued interest and things like that. I knew that about the same time I knew the C-minor chord. It's an acquired language, and I really intended to go into finances. I never intended to be a musician.

"But I had a very intense musical education because of my mother. I worked the harmony exercises and started the violin and fought my way back from the violin teacher every Saturday afternoon."

"How old were you when you *started* to study harmony?"

"I have no recollection of not doing it: it was just something that I did. When I got out of high school, I went to Auburn to study engineering. The reason I went there was that they had a wonderful band and I wanted to play trumpet with it. It's a very big university now, but at that time they didn't even have a music department. That's the band Urbie Green came from.

Later Toni Tennille sang with the band. Toni Tennille's father played drums with the band in 1930.

"They have a very good music school there now. In fact the guy who basically endowed the college had once been a member of the college dance band. He left huge amounts of money to the school but with the provision: it's okay to play the cello, it's okay to be an opera singer, but you gotta have a quarter in Glenn Miller, a quarter in Benny Goodman, a quarter in Tommy Dorsey. In other words: I don't care what you major in, but you've got to study a little bit on the history of jazz, or commercial music, or whatever you want to call it.

"That band is so over-endowed that they have asked people not to make any more donations. When we were there, we had our own house, which we called the Cat House. We worked usually on Fridays and Saturdays.

"Today, if you want to go there, and they're looking for a new trombone and you can make it, you do the rehearsals, you don't have to be a music major. You can study law or whatever you want, but if you can get into that band, you have your full tuition, everything, paid for. The competition is ferocious, but you have your entire college education paid for.

"I studied engineering until I got drafted. And that changes your whole life. After I had been in the Navy about ten minutes, they assigned me to the Marine Corps, and I wound up in the Seabees. I went overseas with the 19th Construction Battalion, the First Marine Division, and spent a year and a half on Okinawa.

"One of the first people I met was Sam Donahue. He had the Navy band that Artie Shaw had had. Obie Massingil was in the band. Osie Johnson was the drummer. I first saw that band on a place called Mog Mog Island in the Ulitha Group, about a day's travel from the Philippines.

"I met these guys from New York, who had played with this band and that band, and the initial attraction after I got home was to show business. I had to come to New York and see all that stuff when I got out of service in 1945.

"I went to the Conservatory in Birmingham because there was one man that I wanted to study with who at that time was getting his PhD in composition at the Royal Conservatory in Toronto. His name was G. Ackley Brower. He was Percy Goetschius's assistant at what later became Juilliard. At the turn of the century, it was the Institute of Musical Arts, and Walter Damrosch was the president. Even as late as 1946 or '47, they did not offer a PhD in composition anywhere in the United States. But the Royal Conservatory offered it, and every summer G. Ackley Brower went up and wrote a symphony and all of that, and got his PhD. And I wanted to study composition with him."

"Did you get a bachelor's?"

"Yeah." He laughed. "I haven't seen it since I graduated. Nobody ever asked me for it.

"I came up to New York in the summer – probably 1947 – and studied three months at Juilliard. I still wasn't sure I was going to be an engineer. What are you sure of at that age? I didn't get a degree at Juilliard, but I studied there until I went to work.

"A friend of mine from the band in Auburn played lead alto in the Tex Beneke/Glenn Miller band. One weekend Tex and the band came through Auburn. I wasn't able to go to the concert because that weekend my grandfather died. When I came back the following Monday, my friend told me he'd given Tex some arrangements I had written for the Auburn band. I was ready to kill him. I was just hanging out with the band. I was trying to decide to go into engineering.

"About six weeks later, I got a beautiful letter from Tex. By then I figured they'd burned the arrangements. He said, 'As you know, we don't rehearse when we're on the road. We didn't get around to playing the arrangements until we got to the Palladium.' He offered me a job. I showed up 24 hours later in New York. Tex is a very nice man.

"I started writing for him. Henry Mancini was still there. I sort of replaced him, writing, when he went to California.

"This was approximately 1950. There was a man named John O'Leary who had been with the original Miller band. He was sort of the road manager. Dick Gabbe was the agent for the band. They had an office on the second floor in the old Piccadilly Hotel. And they had all the old Miller records there, all the air checks, all the old arrangements.

"John said he had to have a plywood thing built on the wall to hold these huge platters, fifteen-minute broadcasts. Miller would play them once or twice, to try to figure out how to make the broadcasts better. John labelled them and put them back, and they were perfect.

"I called RCA. I think it was Eli Oberstein. I told him what I'd found. He said, 'Lock the door and stay there. A Brinks truck will be there within an hour.' They transferred them to tape. They released a lot of them.

"I saw a lot of scores by Jerry Gray, who wrote tons of things for the band. And Bill Finegan, who was an idol of mine. Bill wrote some wonderful arrangements for the band, but Jerry Gray wrote it by the pound, y'know. Glenn would redo it with a pencil on the top of the saxophones or at the top of the score. He would make very detailed rhythmic notation, for the phrasing. And I thought, 'What the hell was he doing?' And it dawned on me after a while that he was having the band play the implied lyrics of the song. You could tell from the lyrics, if you knew them.

"All these things were very systematic. The format was clear. From a short introduction, which was basically meaningless, the band would play eight bars in the Miller style with the doo-wahs and the brass and the clarinet lead and all that. If Miller didn't like it, he'd change it. And then there would be a modulation into a vocal. And the rhythm section, while they kept going in time, wasn't playing just straight four, they'd play backbeats on two and four, and Glenn would come out and announce. And he would look at the band and say, 'Here is so-and-so to sing "I Love You."' The band would go doo-doo-doo, a big button. And then they'd go into straight four again. The audience would turn and look. They were sort of cued. I watched them many times. The guy'd have the arm around the girl, and they'd look up. And then the band would hit straight four. At the end of the song, sometimes the band would be ritarded.

"One of the things he did on almost every arrangement was a cut-off on the fourth beat, whereas most people end on the third. Ritard, turn around, and big ending, and everybody applauded. It was a one-act play. It was very successful and they didn't deviate much from it."

Beneke's name had grown increasingly prominent, but he still was only a salaried employee of the Miller estate. Beneke wanted more credit, and Don Haynes (who had been Miller's prewar manager and executive officer during the war) and he had a parting of the ways. Haynes ordered the Miller arrangements picked up by court order, which was a little silly in that arrangements could not be copyrighted. The charts were seized at the Palladium in Hollywood. Marion said that Tex chatted pleasantly with the sheriff, who apologized profusely for taking the arrangements. And Tex said, 'Well, it's been nice chatting with you, but we've got to go back to work.' And they went up and ... " Marion sang the opening lick of "In the Mood." He said the band played the book from memory.

Beneke told me they'd known for weeks that the situation was coming to a head, and so he'd had copies of the music made. There were no photocopy machines in those days, and this had to be done by hand. Trombonists Jimmy Priddy and Paul Tanner did some of the work.

Marion said, "But by that time the band really could play those charts by ear. I did record copies of 'Juke Box Saturday Night,' and some more. I'm not sure I'm the first to ever say it, but I've been blamed many times for saying, 'It's too bad Glenn didn't live and his music had died.' That's been around a long time."

The version attributed to Jake Hanna is: "Don't you wish Glenn Miller had lived and his music had died?"

Marion said, "Did you see that thing that went around all the fax machines in the music business, *Help Stamp Out* 'In the Mood'?"

"Oh sure. *To qualify, play this lick ten thousand times.*" At one point I sent it to Rob McConnell. He sent it back with the inscription "I *have* played it ten thousand times."

I asked Marion: "Did you study with Schillinger?" Miller of course had done so.

"No, but I studied with Ted Royal, who taught at Juilliard, which is how I got into the Broadway show thing." Marion orchestrated a lot of Broadway shows, starting with Lerner and Loewe's *Paint Your Wagon* which, he agrees with me, is a really bad show; and the movie is worse. On Broadway, he worked on *Almost Crazy*, *The Boy Friend* (with Julie Andrews), *House of Flowers* (with Pearl Bailey and Diahann Carroll), *Mr. Wonderful* (with Sammy Davis Jr.), and *What Makes Sammy Run* (with Steve Lawrence), and more.

"The Broadway show thing was a factory approach to writing," Marion said. "Horrible. Horrible music. Ted Royal taught the Schillinger system. I sort of took to it. I think one reason was my background in engineering. It was something I sort of identified with. Nothing that I used too much one way or the other. All you have to do is tell a bunch of musicians that they're studying something mathematical and you've got a riot on your hands.

"One of the most famous examples that Schillinger used came to me from Lyle Dowling, who I also studied with. Suppose you had a piano that had only four white notes on it, C, D, E and F. How many different melodic thoughts can you write, using just those four notes? It's an exact mathematical amount. It's called the factorial of four. Four times three times two times one. It comes to 24. There are immediately 24 possible combinations, without any rhythmic variations or octave changes, or anything like that.

"Immediately, instead of beating your head, you know there are 24. So listen to them, depending on your background, your inclination, your character, your training. At least you begin more to work with these. For all we know, Beethoven might never have thought of more than nineteen or twenty of them – we don't know that.

"A lot of famous people studied with Schillinger. Lynn Murray studied with him. Glenn Miller. George Gershwin studied with him four and a half years.

"I was recently looking at *Porgy and Bess*, and it's just full of Schillinger. I can see all the techniques. But of course, with a George Gershwin, it doesn't matter who he studied with, he's going to write great music.

"People do Schillinger a certain amount of disservice. The basic problem is that he was not nearly as good a musician as he was a mathematician. His book was lousy, from a musical point of view. If you're a musician, and you play one of those exercises, it'll turn you right off. But if you're in mathematics, you wonder how he came up with that. I think there's some good thoughts and some bad thoughts in that book.

"I'm pretty much a Percy Goetschius product. Goetschius wrote basically all the great books on classical composition. In the 1880s he was a professor of composition at Stuttgart. I don't think very much has improved on those books since."

"There are five volumes of the Goetschius books?"

"At least. I don't remember how many volumes, but there are a lot of them."

"And you still give them that high status?"

"Oh absolutely. I mean it's not tone row. It's not Igor Stravinsky. But if you want to know Beethoven, you want to know Bach, you want to know the entire tradition, that's it. The guy I studied from, D. Ackley Brower, is the one who translated all those books from German to English. He also translated Sergei Tanief's book on convertible counterpoint. He taught in Russia a hundred years ago. Mr. Brower left all those books to me, and they have never been published. I have all the original manuscripts. Sergei Tanief was the boss on convertible counterpoint.

"As far as I know, I have the only English copy of his work. Mr. Brower had been the chief editor at Carl Fischer and Company. He was not the world's greatest musician, but he knew which side of a B-flat a stem went on, and that was more important to him than what it sounded like. But, y'know, there's a place for that too."

"So you used as teaching tools Farnon records and the Goetschius books."

"Absolutely. The very first time I ever heard of Bob Farnon, I was driving in a car with Tony Tamburello. We were in New Jersey somewhere. I was driving. Tony had the radio on. We heard an arrangement of 'Donkey Serenade.' I just about drove off the road. I had to pull over to the side and listen. When I came to a phone, I called William B. Williams at WNEW, and said, 'Who is this?' and so forth. And that's when I found out that Tony knew him. Bob had been living in New Jersey for a while. He had come down here from Canada."

"Yeah. He came down briefly after the war, and didn't like it, and went back to England."

"Right. I wrote him a fan letter. He came over. I had an album that had just been released. I think it was *Two Cigarettes in the Dark*. I had an all-night party for him, and every arranger in the world I could think of showed up. I still have pictures of them. Whichever album it was, a week later there were a lot of broken pencils around."

"Quincy Jones," I said, "said that if you'd fired a bomb in that apartment that night, there wouldn't have been another note of music written in New York for at least five years."

Marion said, "Anybody who wrote notes was there. Irv Kostal, Frank Hunter, Al Cohn, Eddie Sauter, Red Ginzler, Manny Albam, Earle Hagen. Everybody. Don Costa called in the middle of the party because he couldn't be there, but he wanted to meet Bob on the phone." Also present were Jimmy Dorsey, Urbie Green, and Milton Hinton.

"Milt Hinton, who had been on the road with Dizzy with Cab's band, had known Farnon from Toronto before the war. Dizzy was working at Birdland. Quincy went over and got Dizzy and brought him to the party about two o'clock in the morning. It was sort of philosophical time. So, Dizzy, being the clown that he was, started kidding Bob, knowing he used to play the trumpet. He said, 'Ah, you never could play the trumpet. You were a lousy trumpet player.' Bob said, 'Well, you know, the first time I heard you play, with Cab's band, I just couldn't believe it. I went home and I made a lamp out of my trumpet.'

"On that note, Milton Hinton said to Dizzy, 'That's the greatest contribution you ever made to music.'"

"Okay, Marion," I said, "that's cute and funny, but the story's dubious. In fact they jammed together all night. And of course that session started their friendship, up to and including the concerto Bob wrote for Dizzy that never got recorded, and indeed the friendship lasted until Dizzy's death."

"Well, you know music stories and war stories," Marion said. "After 40 or 50 years, they get better with the telling. But that's a cute comment by Milton."

"How did you get to be known as such an arranger for singers?"

"Oh God, I don't know. I think I went through about twenty years of being totally impervious to my surroundings. I was busy all the time. I never thought about the entertainment business. It was just notes by the pound, busy busy busy all the time."

"Tell me about your partnership with Don Costa."

"Well, when I was writing for Tex, Don was writing for Vaughan Monroe. And it turned out that both bands had the same copying service, a guy named George Green. When I was going to Juilliard, there was a man in the class with me studying Schillinger: his name was Harry Miller. Harry was quite a bit older than me. And Harry had been a vaudeville comedian, interested in music, wrote a few songs but didn't have much background. We became good friends. I'd help him with his harmony exercises and so forth. Harry told me they had this crazy guitar player who wrote music for the show, named Don Costa. Some years later, I was up at George Green's having a score copied. George introduced me to Costa. I remember the first thing I said to him was, 'Oh you're that crazy guitar player.'

"We went back to Don's house. He got an album out, Dave Raksin's music for *Forever Amber*. Don played those old 78 records. I said, 'God, I've worn out two sets of those. That's my favorite movie score of all times.' So we started playing it on the piano, and we became fast friends.

"Over a period of time, we had to write so many things. I'd help him when he'd get hung up and he'd help me, and next thing you know we were working together. We had an office at 1595 Broadway, a block up from the

Brill Building. It later became sort of a rock-and-roll building. We would do record dates, whatever it was. Sometimes I'd start at the beginning and write half-way and he'd write the end, or the other way around."

"You told me once you couldn't remember who wrote what."

"That's right."

"It must have been something like the Spencer–Hagen partnership."

"That's right, it was. Herb Spencer and Earle Hagen. What a musician Herb Spencer was. Well, when you're writing it by the pound, the thing is to get it to the record date. Costa and I had sort of complementary backgrounds. We came at the music business from the most 180-degrees diverse backgrounds that two people ever had. I came from a very strong academic background, and Don's was, like, if it doesn't sound good, he won't play it. He was such a wonderful natural musician, and did not have a lot of technique. But the music was so musical. At record dates, I'd see him run the orchestra down, and every time he'd play it, it would sound better and better and better. He would go 'way in the booth, and somebody else would conduct. The band would figure out where to cut the notes off and how to phrase it, and fix a note here, and next thing you know, they're *into* it much more deeply than they would be with someone like me. His music would just get better."

"You mean his notation was careless?"

"Yeah, to a great extent. But he was a very fast writer, and that was great too. It wasn't laborious. It was right off the top, it was very natural-sounding. The last thing he thought about was whether or not it should have an eighth note tied over. That was wonderful at the session. First time you'd run the arrangement down, every hand in the band would go up. And everybody's in conversation. And Costa would go into the booth. He'd come back twenty minutes later and the band would have it figured it out, what they were gonna do. And they were *into* it. If they weren't into it, it wasn't going to happen."

"You mean they *liked* the writing."

"Oh! They understood what he was trying to do. You should have seen one of those parts after the record dates. The pencil marks on it looked like chicken scratchings. But they *really* got into the music, strong into it, and their sense of what he was trying to do got better. If he stayed away 30 minutes, it would get still better. It was an interesting thing. I came more from an engineering approach. I would play something down, and it wouldn't sound much better if I stayed there three weeks. Don and I learned to complement each other.

"I learned *a lot* from him, just in his basic musicality. And then of course Bob Farnon comes along, and that blew the whole thing out.

"Bob's talent is always superior to his intellectual knowledge. You can get anybody with reasonable intelligence, if they want to do the work and learn. But when you get somebody with Bob's ability, he would have done it without it. Don Costa was a perfect example of someone who achieved wonderful results with very little training. If Don Costa had had a formal education and studied a great deal, like Bob, I don't know what he would have achieved. It was amazing what he could do. Bob has a lot more structured outlook on what he does than you might think. It sounds so easy; but of course that's what it's supposed to sound like.

"People like that with marvelous ability naturally, most time they're far ahead of their intellectual learning, and they do things that nobody told them they couldn't. Bob is an exception to anything.

"Bob messed up everything for everybody. Once you heard him, that sort of ended it. I was a big Victor Young fan until I heard Bob Farnon, and that ended Victor Young. Not that I didn't like Victor Young: it just took care of it. I didn't play any more Victor Young. I didn't play any other records except Bob Farnon: how to write for orchestra, that was it, end of story. And still is."

"And what is it about his writing?"

"It's indefinable. Well, I can define it up to a point. Here is a person with infinite talent who also has a very strong academic background. I mean: he *understands* what he's doing. That takes it up to a certain level, but past that, there's no conversation about it. He's got it all. He has a certain Mozartish quality about him, in the sense that Mozart would write some of the worst music you ever wanted to hear, because he didn't labor over it. But that very quality also puts you in the position to write some of the greatest music in the history of the world, because it's a spontaneous combustion kind of thing. I think Ravel once said that his greatest problem was that he wrote masterpieces. And it's true. He wrote perfect things. Bob can put something down, and it's nothing; but for the most part, when he wrote something that was sensational, there was nothing like it."

"You said to me once that he had formidable orchestral technique, and his talent exceeded his technique."

"That's right."

"Which is to say that it isn't merely mechanical."

"Oh absolutely not. Because orchestration, in the ultimate, is an extension of the compositional process. It isn't something that you just arbitrarily say, 'Well, I'll have the oboe play that rather than the violin.' It's all part of the conceptual process in the hands of a Farnon. Also, Bob was one of the few arrangers who actually *composed* an arrangement for the orchestra. It wasn't just an arrangement; it had a huge compositional element about it. And I think the most outstanding part about him is how easy it all sounds, how effortless. It all came together for him. It had nothing to do with him; he didn't have anything to do with the genetic structure of Bob Farnon. He's a guy who happened to be in the right place and had the right education and woke up one day and he was the greatest arranger the world has ever known."

"Bob told me he started by writing parts, not scores."

"I did too. Neal Hefti and a lot of people did that. Many people would gravitate to putting four pieces of paper one on top of the other, and writing four parts, but as you graduate into more experienced composition, you create scores to express that."

"Marion, how well did you know Billy Byers?"

"Few people knew Billy as well as I did. We had the same birthday, on 1 May. I was a year older than Billy. Billy was the first musician I ever met when I left home. I was in Hollywood: he was with a youth band that played Hollywood during World War II. Billy played trombone with them.

"In later years I worked with him a lot: he was an amazing musician. I think most people in the business knew that. Back when you'd go in and do four sides in three hours, I always thought, 'I want Billy Byers on this session.' And if you had a hot band you'd get Al Cohn with the saxophones, because if you'd get into trouble on the session for reasons you can't antici- pate – crazy singers who want to do it up a third; or wrong copying on the parts – all you needed was Billy Byers and Al Cohn. You're running around trying to keep the singer from committing suicide. You'd go and talk to them for ten minutes, and Byers or Al Cohn would have it all fixed when you came back. You didn't have to tell 'em to do it. I often wondered why arrangers never did lean on musicians like that.

"I used to love to do orchestra sessions with Corky Hale, because there's nothing she can't do in any key, on harp, piano, sing it, tap-dance it, what- ever. I had a session once with Tony Bennett. Tony comes in and wants to do the verse without the orchestra. Fine: maybe his is the correct judgement. I said, 'Corky, play the verse.' 'Okay.' She plays it better than you could begin to write it.

"You've got to have people like that when you're under pressure, or else you'd flip out. I didn't know why arrangers didn't take advantage of people like that. Not only could Byers write, but he could play the trombone as well as anybody. You could have four other trombone players, and not as good as Byers, and none of them had a musical background like his. He just took care of everything. It was wonderful.

"We were real good friends."

"When did you really chuck the music business? God knows you were suc- cessful enough. And more importantly, why? The rise of rock-and-roll?"

"Well, you look around, and there was one band in town, the *Tonight* show. And they were about to go to Hollywood. What was gonna replace it?

Nothing. And I always thought the stupidest thing you can do in the world was to go to a rock-and-roll session with a toupee.

"At that time, if I'd had three kids and a mortgage and a house in the country, I'd have been doing whatever you have to do. I wasn't gonna starve. But I didn't have any obligations. And I like finance, so the hell with it. I made plans to get out of the music business a couple of years before I did."

"When you were doing all those record dates, I presume you were making investments."

"Always. Did that all my life. It's like anything else, it can be a vocation or avocation."

"I suspect that it's something you can't *get* interested in. You either are interested or you aren't."

"Unfortunately, you look around today, and most people have *gotten* interested in it. The neighbor next door bought something that doubled his money. And you see huge amounts of money going into it, and you've got to stand back and look. The same thing is happening here that happened to the music business. Jim and Andy's wasn't going to go on for ever: and neither is this bull market. I look at these poor guys from the *Tonight* show and everything and they're over in New Jersey selling accordions and guitars or something. They're not doing what they want to do."

"What did you do? Did you just look around one day and decide to quit?"

"It's more complicated than that. It was an emotional thing. I suddenly realized that I was becoming emotionally very difficult to deal with, which is not a nice attribute. I always thought that if it got to the point where I didn't like the business, I should get out.

"Barbra Streisand's manager called me to do an album with her . . ."

"You're talking about Marty Ehrlichman."

"Yeah. I just didn't want to do the album. And I couldn't get him off the phone. He kept saying, 'How come you don't want to do an album with her?'

"So, stupidly, I said, 'Well, I just don't like the way she sings.' Now if you're in the music business, you don't do that. If you want to do an album, who else are you going to do it with? Barbra Streisand, Tony Bennett, Frank Sinatra, people like that, that's who you want to do it with.

"A couple of days after that, I said, 'What the hell am I doing, turning down an album with Barbra Streisand? That's stupid. I gotta get out of it. 'Cause I'm gonna *get myself out of it* if I keep doing that.'"

There is more to that Marty Ehrlichman story than Marion apparently remembers; I remember it because I laughed so hard over it at the time.

Marion can sound like a real country cracker when he wants to. Given Marion's brilliance, Johnny Mandel – who's been a friend of his since they were young guys getting established as arrangers in New York in the late 1940s – thinks he does it to let people think he's a little slow. Indeed, that may be a trick of Southerners; I've encountered it before. Marion has a weird way, as one speaks, of listening with what seems like a blank and uncomprehending stare. Anyone dumb enough to think that Marion doesn't get it is in for a rude awakening. As Mandel put it, "If he arrived to fix your plumbing, you'd have serious reservations about his competence. And all the while that mind is working . . . "

Marty Ehrlichman wanted that Streisand album written in only a few days. He told Marion that Barbra could give him an hour of her time on Tuesday or some such and they wanted to record the following Monday. And Marion told him, "Well, Marty, that presents a bit of a problem. Y'see, the machine I use to write all mah music is broke, and ah have to write all them notes by hand."

Marion used to claim that at Columbia Records, engineers were hired and promoted by seniority, not ability. If the company posted a notice that a position was opening up in engineering, the janitor with the greatest seniority would get the job. Once, Marion told me, he wrote an album for Steve Lawrence and Eydie Gormé. He took the tape home to listen to and next day went into the Columbia offices at 799 Seventh Avenue, just up the street from his apartment, and played it for the chief engineer, saying, no doubt in his deceptively unruffled way, "How many men do you hear on this?"

Marion said, "You could hear the wheels turnin' in his head. He knew it was more'n ten and less'n a hundred. Finally he said, 'I hear about fifteen.'

"I said, 'You're right. That's what I hear too. And I used 35 men on that date. Now I have an interest in financial matters, and I calculate that Columbia Records is losing three million dollars a year on musicians who never get heard.'

"In fact, I remember the day I finally made up my mind that I would get out of the music business. I was doing an album with Steve and Eydie. We had a big orchestra. Frank Laico, the chief engineer – who did everything with Tony Bennett – couldn't be there. They sent a guy in who edited records up on Seventh Avenue. He'd never done a session before. They've set up the orchestra and we're about to start. We run the music down. I look over and I see the boom in front of the violins. The mike is lying on the floor. I figure somebody's going to come out and fix it. We get ready to make a take, and nobody had done anything.

"I get down on my knees and crawled across the floor and started tapping on the microphone. Is anybody here? And I hear, 'No no! You're not supposed to tap on the microphone. Don't do that!'

"I said, 'I'm glad to know the mike is on, even though it's in the wrong place.'

"'Oh? Where should it be?'

"I said, 'Well, how 'bout we raise it up?'

"The sound was so bad, that I finally said, 'This is it.' I don't think I ever did another session after that.

"Psychologically, you reach sort of a crescendo. I figured that for most people in the pop music business, you've got a period of about ten or fifteen years, a window, and you identify with it. And music passes by and you no longer identify with it. One of the primary reasons for being in music originally is because you love it and enjoy it. And if you don't like it, you should get out of it.

"I went into the institutional money management business, managing other people's money."

"How did you break in, how did you have the credibility?"

"Oh I knew more people in the investment business than I ever did in the music business. I was already doing it. I just quit the music business and kept doing what I was doing.

"I was in the money management business all through the '70s and early '80s. I had a great deal of money under management. One institutional account was four billion dollars. I had another account that was multi-billion, the Avon Foundation. It's a foundation from the original founders of Avon, with a strong bias toward medical research. They give about 50 million dollars a year to Columbia Presbyterian Hospital and places like that. And I used to manage the foundation's money.

"I always knew how it worked. The problem was that the back-office operations got extremely complicated.

"At that time, Wang Laboratories had the first really great mini-computer. I bought the thing and brought it home, and then I called them up and said, 'Where's the program that does the back office?'

"They said, 'What are you talking about?'

"I said, 'Well, I just paid $55,000 for a mini-computer and it runs like a Model T.' They didn't have a back-office program.

"So I wrote a program to do my back-office accounting. Over a period of time, friends would come by and say, 'Oh, you've got a computer system. Boy, we need that.' So I gave it to a few friends and the next thing I know, I was in the computer business. And it got to be a bigger business than my money management business, so I sold the money management business and I set up a company called Maximum Data.

"We had the first international portfolio management system. This was a thing called pooled industry knowledge. When I first went into the computer business, I got a guy at Oppenheimer Company to do a study for me. I said, 'I want to know why most computer software firms go out of business.' I found out it was because they customized everything. Each client has a slightly different system. So I never customized it.

"I went to some of my clients, each one of them noted for some particular thing. For example, Deutschebank is the world's foremost authority on accounting in Germany. If Deutschebank does it *wrong*, it's okay. Merrill Lynch, who was my first client in asset management, Salomon Brothers, Shearson-Lehman, Bank of Tokyo, Nomura, Mitsubishi, I had a deal with each one of them where they would keep me advised on what was necessary to keep the system up to date. And each one of these was an expert on some particular thing.

"One of the partners of Keystone Investment Management Company called me up one day and said, 'We just got a billion-dollar account from Canada, and one of the requirements is that we have to report all of their holdings, no matter where they are, in Canadian dollars. And we have to diversify globally, we've got to buy Japanese securities, everything, and we have to report it in Canadian dollars. What will it take to change your system, because we've never managed anything but US dollars before.'

"I said, 'You don't have to do anything. It's sitting right there.' I said, 'Press this button over there, enter a trade.' And all of a sudden he saw a different screen.

"He said, 'Where'd that come from?'

"I said, 'It's been there for seven years, you've just never used it. Deutschebank designed that portion of it.'

"I took the point of view that nobody knows enough about the business to do it all. You've got to have help from all these people as a daily thing.

"This got to be a hot item. International investing began to come in. And I had the only software that would handle international investments. It's a very complicated area. That's why I made deals with all these people to advise me on this.

"This thing grew and grew and got out of hand, so I moved out of New York up to Purchase, and then I got tired of that too. I recently sold that business."

"So now you're retired?"

"No, just tired."

"You told me you just wrote a chart for a band."

"Yeah, a bunch of guys. The Geritol age, over in Jersey."

"Was it fun?"

"Yeah."

"Do you want to do more writing?"

"No."

"None at all?"

"Well, I may write my mother a letter or something. I don't have any desire to go write a hot arrangement for eight brass and five saxes. Not that it might not be fun, but I have other things I'd rather do."

He sang a commonplace big-band lick. "How many of those things can you write?

"I see those people wearing toupees playing 'In the Mood'."

And then came an afterthought about the complex computer program he had developed: "And you know something? All of that put together is nowhere near as complex as the development section of the Beethoven Fifth Symphony." Pause. "There are millions of computer programmers. There's only one Beethoven."

During our Jim and Andy's days, I thought Marion was probably a permanent bachelor. He would turn up now and then with some good-looking singer, but I always suspected them of wanting his charts. Then, to my surprise, in 1990, at the age of 63, Marion got married.

Teresa Rinaldi is an opera singer, a strikingly beautiful woman who now teaches voice at New York University. She is Italian by blood, and her father too was an opera singer who eventually settled in the South. She's an incredibly good singer: I've heard her on tapes and seen her on a video Marion played me, over her objections. Her father is dead now, and her mother lives with Marion and Terri in their large and beautiful home in Connecticut. Marion is a gourmet cook and a lover of good restaurants. A few months back I drove out from New York to visit them, and ended up staying with them for a few days. Terri has never had the recognition that I think she deserves. The reason, I suspect, is a basic shyness, and a lack of arrogance about her abilities.

"I met Terri in 1965," Marion said. "I was living in New York. She's also from Alabama. She's from Birmingham. She had been Miss Alabama. When she went to Atlantic City for the Miss America contest, she was a trained opera singer. All ten of the girls that year were opera singers, but she won the talent contest and got a full scholarship to Juilliard. We had a lot of mutual friends back in Alabama.

"She was in California for many years. She sang with Nelson Riddle's band on the road. She did a lot of studio work, she did roles in a lot of Broadway shows, *How to Succeed in Business*, she sang in Vegas. She's got an extensive background. She's a very talented musician."

In other words, she and Marion had known each other 25 years when they got married. Not exactly a matter of impetuous haste.

They talk occasionally of giving up their house in Connecticut and moving back to Alabama.

Those days in New York came to an end as rock-and-roll gained ascendancy. One of the first arrangers to drop out and go to Hollywood was Henry Mancini.

Claus Ogerman, saying he had grown tired of "writing string roofs for rock groups," gave it all up, went home to Germany, and dedicated himself entirely to composing orchestral music. He now lives in Munich, writing things like his *Sarabande-Fantasie, Preludio and Chant,* and *Concerto Lirico.* In 1969, one of Marion's star "students", Patrick Williams, after a career writing for singers as well as his own albums, moved out to Los Angeles. Since then he has written more than 200 film scores, as well as an enormous number of television scores and themes. Now and then Pat returns to his first love, arranging. He wrote both the Sinatra *Duets* albums, and an album by singer Monica Mancini of her father's music, and his own instrumental album (on EMI-Capitol) titled *Sinatraland.* Mandel, whose superb film scores include *The Americanization of Emily, The Sandpiper,* and *Harper,* also has returned to arranging from time to time, writing albums for Natalie Cole, Shirley Horn, and Diana Krall. But such assignments are rare.

And even film-scoring work has largely dried up for composers, with producers who grew up on rock using records for sound-track or electronic "scores". Benny Golson and J. J. Johnson went back to playing jazz; J. J. made an album in England with charts by Bob Farnon, one of his idols.

And so, as much as I would like to hear Marion's writing again, I hold my tongue. Urge him to return to the music business? What music business? The days of musicians criss-crossing New York in taxis, on the way to countless studio dates? They're gone, like the snows of yesteryear.

And Marion is the man that got away.

14

Soaring:
Roger Kellaway

One can speculate on the reasons for it. We embody the suspicion in the expression "Jack of all trades and master of none," though it has been discredited by artists throughout history, spectacularly by Leonardo da Vinci. Studies have shown that those with artistic proclivities in one field usually manifest them in several. In most careers, the artist eventually is forced by the constraints of time to concentrate more on one of his abilities than the others.

A tendency to patronize or be skeptical of wide-ranging talent is pronounced in America, where it has flourished along with a supposed antithesis between jazz and classical music. This is part of the mythology of jazz, although from the very beginning, as witness the career of Will Marion Cook, a thorough knowledge of and interest in classical music has been commonplace in jazz musicians and composers: Earl Hines, Don Redman, James P. Johnson, Fletcher Henderson, Bix Beiderbecke, Artie Shaw, Joe Venuti, and many more. Hank Jones was, like virtually all jazz pianists, trained in classical music and might have become a concert pianist had that world not been closed to blacks. So too Milton Hinton, originally a violinist. And on the other side of it, Itzhak Perlman, an Art Tatum fan, recorded an album with Oscar Peterson. Shelly Manne told me once that at home he listened only to classical music, and many jazz musicians would say the same. Charlie Parker wanted to study with Edgard Varèse, and William Grant Still did. Hale Smith is a classical composer, trained (along with Jim Hall) at the Cleveland Institute of Music; he is also a very good jazz pianist. Keith Jarrett has recorded an outstanding album of Bach's *Goldberg Variations*.

Gil Evans and Eddie Sauter were in love with the Russian composers, including Prokofiev. Allen Eager's great love was Prokofiev. Stravinsky has been a powerful inspiration to jazz musicians. The entire Woody Herman band of the *Caldonia* period was in love with his work, among them Neal Hefti and Ralph Burns. It is probable that Stravinsky wrote his *Ebony Concerto* for the Herman band because he had heard Ralph's *Bijou*. Ralph told me a few months ago, "It sounded like Stravinsky: it had his sound. Not a copy of any notes, or anything. It was what Stravinsky did that nobody else did. All the grunts and cheeps and everything. *Rites of Spring, Petrouchka*."

A problem in earlier days was that many of the people who wrote about jazz, such as Ralph Gleason and George Hoefer, knew nothing of classical music, and thought jazz musicians had invented what they had merely adapted. Yet the first serious evaluation of jazz came in the 1920s from two men, Carl Engel and R. D. Darrell, who were trained in classical composition.

The idea that jazz and classical music are separate and unrelated musics has been persistent, and has damaged some careers. When André Previn was principal conductor of the London Symphony Orchestra, so often did British writers refer to him as "former jazz musician" that he quipped, "Is there a statute of limitations on this?"

No one, however, has suffered as much from the propensity to pigeonhole art and artists as Roger Kellaway. Kellaway has all his life refused to be placed in categories. To make things harder on himself, he often mixes the idioms. If his jazz playing reflects his knowledge of twentieth-century composers from Stravinsky and Ravel to Lutoslawski and Cage, the inflections of jazz are heard in his classical music.

These works include *Songs of Ascent*, written for and performed by the New York Philharmonic and tuba virtuoso Warren Deck; *Portraits of Time* for jazz quartet and orchestra, performed by the group Free Flight with the Los Angeles Philharmonic; *David Street Blues* for jazz quintet and orchestra, performed by the National Symphony Orchestra; *PAMTTG*, a ballet commissioned by the late Georges Ballanchine and performed by the New York City Ballet; *Memos from Paradise* for clarinet, string quartet and jazz quartet and recorded on the GRP label by Eddie Daniels; *Fantasy Absolut*, performed by the New York Pops Orchestra; *Two Moods of Blues* for cello and jazz trio, which he played at Carnegie Hall with cellist Yo-Yo Ma; and *The Morning Song*, for F tuba and piano, commissioned by yet another tuba virtuoso, Roger Bobo of the Los Angeles Philharmonic.

Kellaway has written a considerable body of works for tuba, and there are classical tuba players all over the world who play them without knowing that he is also a jazz pianist, composer, and arranger.

But none of his recordings has caused as much bemusement as his Cello Quartet albums. Merchandisers just don't know what to make of them.

In 1964, two Russian jazz musicians, alto saxophonist Boris Midney and bassist Igor Berukshtis, defected to the west, and since the US State Department was always enthralled by such defections for their propaganda value, the two were given a red-carpet treatment that American jazz musicians never get from their government. But having got them here, State didn't know what to do with them. I suggested that Helen Keane, Bill Evans' manager, should take over direction of their careers, if any, in America, and she in turn set up a record date on the Impulse label, appointing Roger as music director and pianist. The album was released as the Russian Jazz Quartet.

Boris Midney married Tanya Armour of the Armour meat family, began to dress beautifully, and disappeared from the jazz world. Igor Barukshtis became a teacher and also disappeared from jazz.

But the album allowed Kellaway the chance to do something he had long had in mind: use a cello in a jazz context. A bass player himself, he had an affinity and sympathy for the cello. And on two tracks of that album, he used cellist George Ricci, brother of the violinist Ruggiero Ricci. Ricci could phrase jazz, so long as it was written for him.

A few years later, Herb Alpert crossed Roger's path. Having, with his Tijuana Brass records, made a fortune for himself and the label, of which he was a co-owner, he wanted to indulge his love of jazz.

"In 1969, I wrote some music for cello and piano," Roger said. "I wanted to do something more for cello, but my way. Edgar Lustgarten would come by my house and we would play through it. The piece 'Seventide,' in seven-four, which was recorded in *Come to the Meadow*, was one of the first pieces I wrote for him. Also 'Jorjana Number 2.' That was the birth of the Cello Quartet.

"With the addition of bass and marimba, the group would include only instruments made of wood. The only cymbal I let Emil Richards play was a little tiny seven-inch splash cymbal. At the time, I still had my other quartet, with Chuck Domanico, John Guerin, and Tom Scott. There were two piles of music: one pile of music was called the sax quartet, the other pile the cello quartet. And that's where the name came from."

The group with Tom Scott made an album in 1967 called *Spirit Feel* for the Pacific Jazz label. With Paul Beaver adding taped *musique concrète* effects, it is one of the earliest examples of the use of electronic sounds in jazz, and since they were added randomly, reflected Kellaway's interest in John Cage and the aleatory. Most striking to me at the time were the title tune, Milt Jackson's blues "Spirit Feel," and the ballad "Comme Ci Comme Ça." The former demonstrated that Kellaway, then 28, was one of the most powerfully swinging and inventive pianists in jazz, the latter that he was a ballad pianist of uncommon lyricism and sensitivity. In "Comme Ci Comme Ça," I discovered his flawless time. He takes the tune at one of those ballad tempi dear to Carmen McRae. If you listen to it a few times, you discover that the rubato is completely centered. What he steals here, he replaces there, and you may find yourself tapping your foot very, very slowly.

Then: "Herb Alpert and I would run into each other in the studio," Roger said. "He was interested in my music. I proposed five projects. He asked me which one I most wanted to do and I said, 'The Cello Quartet.' And he supported that all the way through to a 38-piece orchestra on three tracks. I even have a letter announcing how proud they were to have the Cello Quartet as part of the label."

"We did the album and the next letter I got said, 'We don't know what to do with this. Would you mind doing, for your next part of our agreement, an album more like what we're used to promoting?' Steve Goldman was my producer, and we did anything from Luciano Berio to Spike Jones for the next album."

The resulting LP, *Center of the Circle*, using a big orchestra, is very funny, weirdly so. It satirizes what record companies were at that time trying to sell, including rock-and-roll.

"I did it to appease them," Roger said. "For $70,000 we did seventeen completed masters. I know exactly what I want when I go into the studio. I'm not trained to go in with a monstrous budget and guess all the time, as in the theory of an infinite number of monkeys. The people who don't have very much talent somehow always get that opportunity. But the people who have been trained to understand what the sound is from the beginning don't get that chance.

"So we did *Center of the Circle*. It sold about five copies. Then we went back and did the second Cello Quartet album, *Come to the Meadow*."

The personnel on the Cello Quartet albums comprised: Kellaway, piano; Emil Richards, marimba; Chuck Domanico, bass; and Edgar Lustgarten, cello.

Ed Lustgarten was one of the world's great cellists and a major teacher of the instrument. When he was very young, he played under Toscanini and later worked extensively in the movie studios. Again disproving the myth of separation, Ed, like Itzhak Perlman, had a great love of jazz. And, like George Ricci, he would phrase it, so long as it was written for him. Had Roger not found Ed, that group probably never would have existed.

The Cello Quartet was recorded again in an album with the Singers Unlimited titled *Just in Time* for the MPS level. Then, with Joe Porcaro added on drums, it made a fourth album called *The Nostalgia Suite* for the Denon label. (It is available in CD format on the Voss label.) For one track of that album, Roger transcribed a Serge Chaloff solo he had always admired. Edgar studied the original record and played the solo with Chaloff's phrasing. The album was done direct-to-disc, each side made without interruption and no possibility of splicing.

It was fascinating to watch the group record, particularly under that kind of pressure. Ed, incapable of improvisation, would go into an inner panic when Roger would take off into some of his wilder fantasies, afraid he would not come back in at the right place. But he never missed. How he loved that group. He said to me that day, "I call Roger the bottomless pit of melody."

Roger Kellaway was born in Waban, Massachusetts, a suburb of Boston, on 1 November 1939, one of three children. He has two sisters. The family background ultimately is Scottish; the name Calway was Anglicized to Kellaway, and the actor Cecil Kellaway was a distant cousin.

His father was a painting contractor. Both of his parents played piano. "It was my father's playing of 'The Bells of St. Mary' that led to my taking piano lessons," Roger said. "I had learned to play it on my own." He started formal study at 7. At 12, already listening equally to jazz and classical music, he decided that he wanted to spend his life in music. He attended Newton High School, at that time ranked the number three high school in the United States, studying college-level music theory and playing double bass and percussion in the school orchestra, performing works by Mozart, Beethoven, and Bach, and playing bass in an extra-curricular big band. At one point, he and a fellow student had a Jackie and Roy kind of vocal duo. The girl was Meredith d'Ambrosio, now a successful singer and the wife of pianist Eddie Higgins. Another schoolmate was cornetist and future journalist and jazz historian Richard Sudhalter, who would co-author a major biography of Bix Beiderbecke.

Sudhalter vividly remembers those days. "Roger was gawky, angular, with a brush cut that wouldn't quite behave and an enthusiasm that wouldn't quit," he said. "He was a year behind me at Newton High, class of '57 to my '56. He lived up in Waban, a generally quite well-to-do part of the city. My only memory of my few visits to his home is of an utter absence – can I be wrong about this? – of musical environment. I'd been used to a family that lived and breathed music. Besides my father, my brother played the saxophone, my sister the flute, and we all played the piano.

"We had a big band that met after hours at the high school, usually playing Basie, Goodman, and Glenn Miller stocks. More memorable was a sextet, which took on the name The King's Men when we played dances. Me on cornet, Dave Shrier on tenor, Don Quinn on clarinet (when we couldn't get young Frank Nizzari, a prodigy from nearby Needham), Fred Giordano on piano, Anthony 'Bud' Farrington on drums, and Roger on bass.

"Of course we knew he played piano, and inevitably every evening he'd play a few solo numbers. Roger, we said, was too 'modern', though, ironically, the pianist at some of the frequent jam sessions held in my basement was Steve Kuhn, a year ahead of me at Newton. Looking back, and listening to tapes of some of our efforts, I think a more accurate explanation is that he was too busy. He'd not yet learned how to feed soloists, how to leave room for others to breathe. The impression, heard now, is that he needed to fill every available hole, play every clever alteration and substitution.

"Giordano, though perhaps half the pianist Roger was, played very spare, rhythmic stuff, and basic harmonies, leaving maximum latitude for the soloist. Even Shrier, who loved Prez and Wardell Gray, Hank Mobley and Sonny Rollins and other contemporary guys, found Roger crowded him by saturating the background and leading him too much harmonically. It was mostly because of that, I suspect, that Roger wound up playing bass most of the time.

"On several occasions we played at the Friday afternoon 'Teen Age Jazz Club' sessions run by George Wein and Father Norman O'Connor at Storyville, in the Copley Square Hotel. Opposite us would be whatever major jazz attraction was being featured at the moment, either there or downstairs at Mahogany Hall.

"One session stands out. After our warm-up set, the Clifford Brown–Max Roach Quintet and the Herb Pomeroy–Boots Mussulli–Serge Chaloff sextet did a set apiece; then Serge and Clifford did one with Richie Powell and Max.

"Our Dave Shrier, never short on *chutzpah*, asked to join them. He lasted, I think, about four choruses of a Mach-two *Indiana*, then withdrew from the field and let Serge and Clifford get on with it. An extraordinary day."

Roger said: "I remember that session. Steve Kuhn and I both sat in for a bit. I wanted a piece of that."

"Roger in those years was an omnivore, open to everything," Dick said. "The older styles interested him as much as the new stuff, as evidenced by the ease with which he later took to associations with a wide range of musicians. His capacity for absorption was limitless – procedurally, a little like Dick Hyman's, in that he'd figure out how a style worked, how a sound was produced, then just add it to his arsenal of skills. Small wonder that those two guys have gotten along so well through the years."

(Roger and Hyman like to play two-piano duets, and have recorded in that format.)

Sudhalter continued: "I always felt that the amount of time Roger spent around me had much to do with the fact that I was steeped – nay, submerged – in one general period and set of musicians. He was determined to find out everything he could about it, and to become adept at whatever it had to offer.

"One time Bud Farrington (later to become a top-ranking USAF strategic officer) went off for a fortnight's vacation, leaving his drums in my basement. Roger and I were at them every day after school, taking turns at playing along with records. He later became quite skilled as a drummer, and to this day could doubtless swing a rhythm section."

This bit of information startled me. Dick had undoubtedly given me the clue to the astonishing rhythmic – no, polyrhythmic – independence of Roger's two hands. He can play the most complex rhythms of any pianist I've ever heard.

"In general," Dick said, "Roger spent a lot of time at our house. Though my father, Al Sudhalter, had been out of professional music for nearly twenty years at that point, he remained a respected figure, one of the finest saxophonists to come out of Boston in the late '20s, long-time friend of Hackett, Kaminsky, Gowans, Pee Wee Russell, and the rest. Toots Mondello credited him with having inspired him to play alto.

"Roger caught the attention of my father, who immediately pronounced him 'a real talent'. My father was still playing wonderfully, working now and then, whenever the urge took him. During our basement sessions, if he was at home, he'd await his moment, then saunter down the stairs and ask with studied nonchalance, 'You fellas mind if I join in for a number or two?' The answer was always yes, and of course he always blew us away."

Roger said, "Those were very fond times for me, very impressionable times. Dick was introducing me to Bix and Dixieland music while Dave Shrier was pushing me in the modern direction.

"I also can remember listening to George Shearing's 'I'll Remember April,' and Billy Taylor's 'A Bientot,' and the whole series of 'Oscar Peterson Plays.' I wore out the songbook albums on Verve, Duke, Gershwin, all those trio records. And! André Previn was part of my listening too.

"One of the most important times of my life was being with Dick Wetmore and Sam Parkins, playing Dixieland, but leading to doing jazz and poetry with twelve-tone rows. Dick was teaching me who Django Reinhardt was. Meanwhile I was still listening to Schoenberg and Berg and Spike Jones. I was teaching myself how to play percussion. I almost played percussion in the Massachusetts All State Symphony. I did play fourth bass in the All State Symphony.

"I enjoyed piano music, but I listened mostly to orchestral music. The Budapest String Quartet playing the Ravel String Quartet was one of my favorite albums. I had a timer on my phonograph and I'd wake up in the morning to *Le Sacre du Printemps* followed by Woody Herman and the Third Herd. Or maybe Schoenberg followed by the Boston Blowup with Herb Pomeroy, Serge Chaloff, Boots Mussulli, and Ray Santisi, that Boston bunch."

From high school Roger went to the New England Conservatory, where he studied piano with Roland Nadeau, bass with Georges Molleux (principal bassist with the Boston Symphony), composition with Judd Cooke, and chorus with Lorna DeVaron, performing the works of such composers as Stravinsky, Honegger, and Hovhannes, as well as the more traditional reper- toire. As a member of the New England Conservatory Chorus, he sang bass- baritone with the Boston Symphony under Charles Munch.

One of Roger's teachers at the New England Conservatory made his stu- dents improvise in two keys simultaneously. This became second nature to Roger, and one of the characteristics of his playing is a tendency to slip into passages of bi-tonality, which no doubt is disconcerting to those who want their jazz conventional. He has a sharp sense of how long to stretch these excursions, returning to simplicity just when you think he might snap the thread and lose the concentration of the audience.

After two years at the conservatory, he went – playing bass – with cornetist Jimmy McPartland.

"The most interesting bass players to play for," said Roger, as a pianist looking on bassists, "are those who play *the bass*. A lot of the younger players remind me of the Barney Kessel line to a bass player after a duo gig: he said, 'Hey man, you and I need a bass player.'

"While I was with McPartland, I was starting to play like Scotty LaFaro. Jimmy was drinking in those days, and he was loaded. He turned around to me on the bandstand and said, 'Play the bass.' I knew that he wanted me to play the lower register, but it took me a long time to realize that what he wanted me to do was play the *function* of the bass.

"A lot of young players want the amplification to be the energy. When I played bass, there were no amps, you had to put the energy into the instrument."

"After Jimmy McPartland, I went with Ralph Marterie's band. When I got my night – and everybody got one – Marterie said, 'Hey, kid, you've got a small combo sound.' I got that from him all night."

"Was he rough to work for?"

"Oh yeah."

I said, "Don Thompson, being both a bassist and a pianist, said to me that he thought that a lot of young bass players had picked up on Scott LaFaro's techniques without understanding what he was doing and why. Ray Brown said to me once, 'Scott LaFaro can walk when he wants to.'"

"Actually, he could," Roger said. "There seems to be a renaissance going on, a return to acoustic bass and the tradition of what the bass is about. I enjoy this, when I come across those players. Neal Swainson in Toronto is one of the greatest bass players I've heard in my life. He can play the upper register any time he wants, but he never leaves the whole bass behind. And he always plays interesting, meaty solos.

"I am so thrilled to have had the chance to play bass in a big band. A big band is a real experience. A band doesn't sound like a band without the bass. You can take the drums out. Drums are not the focal point of the rhythm section. It's the bass. It's a thrill to play bass in a big band – I think more so than the piano, when it's really swinging. It's one of the great forces of all time.

"Joe Farrell was in that band with me. The gig lasted about six months. Six months with Jimmy McPartland, six with Marterie, then on to New York."

Roger began freelancing on piano and never really played the bass again. By the age of 22 he was one of the busiest – and respected – pianists in the city, playing record dates and working with singers such as Lena Horne.

In 1962, he became a member of the Clark Terry–Bob Brookmeyer Quintet. He recorded two albums with that group and his first album as a leader. He played piano on many albums during that period, including Sonny Rollins' *Alfie*, Oliver Nelson's *More Blues and the Abstract Truth*, and Wes Montgomery's *Bumpin'*.

It was at this time that I met Roger. The first singer ever to record a lyric of mine was Mark Murphy, to whom I had been introduced by his manager, Helen Keane, later Bill Evans' manager and producer. She showed Mark the tune, which had music by Warren Bernhardt and heavily reflected the bossa nova influence to which we had both been exposed on a recent trip to South America. Roger played piano on that date.

Though I immediately respected his playing, he struck me as being sullen, withdrawn, and isolated. He hardly spoke to anyone, and though he did his work beautifully, he did it with what one might call a bad grace.

I asked Roger recently, "Why were you so closed in on yourself when I first knew you? It was like a locked door."

"Yeah," Roger said. "Nobody could get in."

"You were awful young. That was 1962."

"I was 22. I'd already been with Patty for a couple of years." Patty Hale was his first wife.

"I was that way probably until 1971. It took Jorjana" – his second wife – "six or seven years to pry open all this stuff. I started to become happy at that point.

"I was attacked a lot in that first marriage. And in defense, rather than attack back, I withdrew. I withdrew to protect my music with my personal being. It was at that time that I began to separate the two. My feeling was, 'Okay, you're going to attack me, and you can get me, but you're never going to get my music.'

"At that time I became much more interested in avant garde music. And the more I played it, the more Patty hated it."

"She was Zoot Sims' cousin, as I recall."

"Yeah. The Sims family still think of me as part of the family."

Zoot's brothers included trombonist Ray, trumpeter Bobby, and guitarist Gene.

All of them could sing, and Ray was prominently featured as a vocalist with Les Brown. They were from a family of vaudevillians. It is then unsurprising that Patty Hale was a singer.

"Being only 19 when I got married, I didn't know how to deal with the personal assault. It was like playing emotional chess with someone and realizing that six moves down the line, you'll still lose. But I still felt that it was a situation that I should tolerate because I should be able to find a solution. This is what my personal make-up was about, and that's why people couldn't get in, 'cause I was extremely protective. It took Jorjana a long time to get me to understand that I couldn't have the musical part of me without the personal part of me. It took her that long to get me back to understanding that it was the same being.

"I wasn't really able to cope with my personal life in those early years. But musically, it was another matter. Around that time, I spent a whole summer with Bobby Hackett. I'd look at his little chord sheets that would say C sixth, and I'd listen to Hackett play four notes and make so much music it was unbelievable. The lessons of simplicity that I was getting! I would really understand it twenty years past that. I was really getting a lot of wonderful lessons."

Years later, in a solo piano album, Roger played Louis Armstrong's "Lazy 'Sippi Steamer Going Home." He told me it was a little tribute to Bobby Hackett who had made him understand the beauty that could be achieved with triads.

"Maybe a year after that, I was with Bob Brookmeyer and Clark Terry. Brookmeyer never had the 30-second note chops that a lot of the players had. He'd play quarter notes. Maybe to some people that was negative, but to me it was, Yeah! Quarter notes! Up-tempos, quarter notes! Yeah! A whole new world of time opened up, where you didn't have to do eighth notes or sixteenth notes. Oh, it had been: you have to do sixteenth notes, you're young! You have to show all this speed and versatility!"

Roger told me on one occasion that Brookmeyer was a major influence in another way: the compositional nature of his solos. And Roger's solos do indeed have a compositional logic about them.

"The Mulligan Quartet was another major influence on me," Roger said. "The pianoless groups. Listening without any harmony to two horns blend and making harmonic implications." Later, Roger would work with Mulligan; he is the pianist on Mulligan's *The Age of Steam* album.

"Another major influence was the Jimmy Giuffre Three with Jim Hall and Ralph Peña. I saw them in Storyville as a kid, maybe 17. I couldn't believe it. Because Giuffre was beginning to experiment with folk forms. As a matter of fact, that was probably the single most important influence on the Cello Quartet – to changing my thinking about what jazz was about and where I wanted to go in composition. The Jimmy Giuffre Three blew me *away*. Then there was the woodwind album he did on Atlantic where on one track the playing is just clarinet and foot-tapping. I freaked over that, I loved it so much. It was *so* simple."

Patty Hale and Roger were divorced in 1965.

In 1968, Lucia Davidova, a dancer friend of Georges Ballanchine, director of the New York City Ballet, who'd gone to Condon's to hear Dave McKenna, heard Roger instead. She bought a trio album he had recorded for Prestige four years earlier. She played the record for Ballanchine, who, on the strength of it, commissioned Roger to write a work for his company. It was an amazing development.

Roger said, "He gave me almost no instructions or restrictions. The assignment was: 'Write me 22 minutes. I'd like to hear some blues. And I'd like to hear the Pan Am radio theme at least once, "Pan Am makes the going great."' No story line. Just images of airports.

"It was a thrilling experience. I feel honored that I had that opportunity, and I'd like to work more with dancers and in the classical field. It's a different kind of . . . well, putting your ass on the line. That's the only way I know how to put it. I don't have all the chops and all the knowledge that a lot of these people have. But I've got a different kind of feeling, something that comes from my jazz background that's inherently American. It's something I can bring to this fusion that could get as much respect as somebody else who can do millions of notes perhaps with no feeling. And there's plenty of that around."

Roger worked on the ballet at Steve Goldman's ranch in Callabasas. One of California's devastating fires broke out, and he and Goldman were not allowed to go into the property. Fire crews told them that everything had burned anyway. Roger assumed that he had lost the sketches for the ballet and the hundreds of symphony and other scores he had been accumulating since his adolescence.

He said, "We're possessive beings, we like having *things*, we're collectors. And suddenly I had to release all that, and go on. And I achieved the release. A few days later they allowed us back in to the ranch, and lo and behold, the house had not burned down. Every blade of grass on 180 acres had burned, but the house was still there. My room was still there, and there was the ballet. I was caught between being thrilled and, having released all of this, accepting the fact that I still had it. Amazing. It was a difficult process.

"The ballet premiered on a Thursday night. On Saturday, the third night, Robert Irving, the conductor of the orchestra, decided he wanted to go to Chicago. And I was told to conduct the ballet. But I overslept that day. When I got to the rehearsal I had time for only one run-through, and that was it, on with the tuxedo, Saturday night, orchestra pit, New York City Ballet. Man, it was like home base! Unbelievable. There are a lot of places where the dancers have to make ready for downbeats. The middle movement was the blues, and that was completely comfortable for me.

"But I was using Ballanchine's copy of the score, and in the last movement, there were two pages missing! And it was in 11/8. My memory just clicked in. It was so much fun! My hands weren't even sweating."

(Years later, the New American Orchestra, as it is now called, did a rehearsal performance of Roger's music from *PAMTGG*. I surreptitiously taped it for him, and afterwards we sat in his car listening to it. At the end of the music, he said softly, "Well, I guess I have *some* talent.")

In 1968, Roger wrote the music for *The Paper Lion*, the first of his 22 film scores. The closing theme for *All in the Family*, titled "Remembering You," which he wrote in 1970, is still being heard on television around the globe. The problem *it* created is that there are people in this world who think of him as a player of honky-tonk piano.

During this period, Roger was also Bobby Darin's musical director.

Every pianist I have known who is a sensitive and sympathetic accompanist to singers also sings, if only a little. Roger is no exception: he could have made a living as a singer. It is this sympathy to the voice that has led him to write for and accompany an astonishing range of singers, from Melanie, for whom he wrote four hit albums, to Joni Mitchell, Carmen McRae, Mark Murphy, Helen Merrill (with whom he toured Japan), and Darin. He wrote the arrangements and conducted Darin's *Dr. Dolittle* album. Roger was very close to Darin.

I met Darin in 1959 or 1960, while I was with *Down Beat*. The publisher wanted to do a cover story on him. I was reluctant. About all I had heard of him was his silly song "Splish Splash." But keeping an open mind, I flew down from Chicago to St. Louis to spend four or five days with Darin and his rhythm section (Ronnie Zito was the drummer) during their engagement at a prominent hotel. I hung out with them in the daytime, went to the gig at night. And I acquired great respect for Walden Robert Cassotto, born in the Bronx on 14 May 1936. Why he chose such an obviously generic show-biz handle as Bobby Darin I do not know. Paul Emil Breitenfeld said he got Desmond out of a phone book, but the origin of Darin is unknown.

Bobby's show surprised me. He sang his pop successes because he had to: the audience, or at least part of it, expected them. But it became apparent that his venture into trash was a calculated career chess move. He had good time, good intonation, good phrasing, and sang good songs with good charts. He moved on stage with a dancer's grace and eccentric humor and that indefinable quality one can only call energy. That he had a certain cockiness was undeniable, but it didn't bother me: modesty is not part of the job description for a career in show business. Indeed, maniacal self-absorption may well be an asset.

But what made Bobby tick? In later years, Bobby Scott and Roger, both of whom had worked as his music director, told me that Bobby had had rheumatic fever as a child, lived with a damaged heart, knew his life would not be long, and intended to cram as much into it as he could. That is now part of the legend; but it's true. Bobby felt he didn't have time for polite subterfuge, the affectation of an ah-gee-whiz humility. That he was a talent was obvious to me by the end of my stay in St. Louis, and I wrote an article in his praise.

These memories came back to me as I listened to a reissue CD of an album Darin made 32 years ago – the music from Leslie Bricusse's score for *Dr. Dolittle*. In spite of mediocre lyrics, it is an outstanding album, arranged by Roger, who was 27 at the time. That he was even then one of the finest arrangers in the business is obvious in the *Dolittle* album.

Curiously, I had never heard it, although Roger had mentioned it over the years. The reason is simple.

Darin's record company, Atlantic, was less than enthusiastic about the project, and his producer, Arif Mardin, advised him not to do it. They wanted their nice little profitable Bobby Darin of "Splish Splash" and "Queen of the Hop" and "Mack the Knife" with its godawful chart. The film's producer, Arthur C. Jacobs, apparently didn't think Darin could do the *Dolittle* music justice; if he'd been in St. Louis with me, he would have been under no such impression. Atlantic nonetheless indulged Bobby to the extent of letting him and Roger do it. The album was recorded in July 1967 in Los Angeles and released almost in secret. Bobby got the shaft and Sammy Davis got the hit on *Talk to the Animals*.

And thus it was that I never heard the album until its release on CD. Roger had been trying to get it re-released for years. He gave me a copy. I put it on the stereo, and was blown away, both by Roger's charts and by Darin.

But the CD saddens me in a way. I think of the guy I got to like in those days and nights in St. Louis. I think about the fine acting job he did in *Captain Newman MD*. I listen to his beautiful time and intonation and enunciation and phrasing, his musicality. Walden Robert Cassotto was a giant talent, still unfolding.

Maybe he didn't get to do it all: but he came close.

He had open-heart surgery and died on the operating table on 20 December 1973. He was 36.

Oh could he sing.

Roger said, "I learned everything I know about stage presence, pacing, timing, all of that, from Bobby; well, from Bobby and Jack E. Leonard." Roger was also Leonard's accompanist for a year, working a lot in Las Vegas. Roger adored Leonard who, for all his bluster and insult comedy, was a gentle and considerate man in private. He was always, Roger said, concerned for the welfare of the musicians he worked with.

It was the time of the Maharishi Mahesh Yogi and Transcendal Meditation, made famous by the Beatles. Flautist and saxophonist Paul Horn had become deeply interested in it, then became a meditation teacher in the movement. "He was my initiator," Roger said. Roger began to study meditation. In 1969, while touring Britain with Darin, he made a side trip to Bangor, Wales, to meet the Maharishi. Fad of the moment or not, the movement's effects were to be far-reaching, and indeed, some of its results are paralleled in biofeedback techniques and a growing medical appreciation (if not much comprehension) of the complex interaction of the mind and body – not to mention Christian Science, which anticipated biofeedback by 100 years.

Roger still practices meditation every morning. For a time he took EST training. Whatever one thinks of these practices, they have contributed to the most remarkable example of inner development I have ever seen in a human being.

The first Cello Quartet album was made in 1971. It was a milestone not only in Roger's life but in mine as well. I had come out to Los Angeles from Toronto to write lyrics for a movie score or other with Lalo Schifrin. One night, afflicted by depression, I was visiting a friend who also was a friend of Roger, singer and vocal arranger Morgan Ames. She asked if I had heard the Roger Kellaway Cello Quartet album. I had not. She played it for me. Hours later, I was still listening to it, struck by its pure beauty. I had seen contradictions between someone's music and personality before, spectacularly so in the case of Stan Getz. But something else was happening here. I sensed that Roger Kellaway had an inner musical life that had nothing to do with the man I thought I knew. One of these two impressions had to be untrue.

I called him the next day. He and Jorjana then lived in Thousand Oaks, a bedroom community of Los Angeles, a hilly, bleak little town of sun-bleached beige grasses and big spiky agaves and dusty palms whose desiccated whiskers rattled in the occasional wind and cowboy-booted rednecks and pickup trucks with bumper stickers bearing such maxims as *America – Love It or Leave It* and beer bars in which Tammy Wynette, or somebody like her, whined from juke boxes about road-house love. It since then has become a city of substance, with malls and department stores, Cadillac and Lincoln dealerships to serve an accrual of refugees from Los Angeles, a Bob's Big Boy, and a not-bad Japanese restaurant.

I drove out to see him and did an interview for my *High Fidelity* magazine column. He had converted his garage into a studio, which housed a magnificent seven-foot black Blüthner piano, his bass, which lay on its side under the Blüthner, shelves of music scores, piles of paper, a spinet piano that he had "treated" to produce peculiar pitches, some odd percussion instruments, a tabla, and something I found extremely significant. On the front of the drawer of a filing cabinet was a small card saying *Projects uncompleted due to lack of talent*. I still found him guarded and suspicious, as if he were thinking, 'Why should this guy be doing anything for me and my music?'

I did the interview, finding that he had one of the most interesting musical minds I had ever encountered. He was an eccentric, to be sure, but a brilliant one.

I left, and wrote the column about him. I certainly did not foresee the countless hours Roger and I would spend working together in that cluttered converted garage.

I next encountered Roger in Toronto in early 1974, when he was on tour with Joni Mitchell. The company played Massey Hall, long the home of the Toronto Symphony, and site of a famous Charlie Parker–Charles Mingus–Max Roach concert.

Roger recalled "I did 55 concerts with Joni Mitchell and the LA Express – Tom Scott, John Guerin, Robben Ford, Max Bennett.

"I used to wear weird clothes. The Fender Rhodes was set up on the edge of the stage. So however big the audience was, there was nothing hidden about where I was. I started to learn how to use that, to start to dress. I dressed more rock-and-rolly. Joni's manager would say, 'The way you dress, do more of that.' I bought some over-the-knee musketeer boots. I used to play glissandos in some of my solos. Tom Scott's wife at the time used to call me Chicken Lee Lewis.

"That was an experience! Eleven days learning a complete show, learning a different kind of music. But learning a music that was so musical! And working with someone who didn't have the musical knowledge but hired an entire band that did! And it worked perfectly. We all respected one another. She is a very consistent performer.

"And the endlessness of her songs is so far superior to the work of most of the so-called songwriters. You can't even call them songwriters nowadays. There's an innate sophistication about the way Joni writes that's just different. It was thrilling to deal with."

A few months after that Massey Hall encounter, I was again in Los Angeles. I called Roger. One of us suggested that we should try writing some songs. We spent a lot of time together during those weeks, and gradually I came to feel we were becoming friends. He was changing, almost before my eyes. It was about then that I made the decision to move to Los Angeles.

I called Roger and told him I was making the move in December. I packed my car, and my wife and I left for California. I drove through bitter winter weather in Texas, then sleet and snow in the passes of the mountains in California. It was the most miserable journey of my life, filled with a sense of foreboding and failure. On the last night, peering past the windshield wipers into the driving wet snow, I kept thinking, "Oh God, if only I can get to Roger's!"

We stayed with Roger and Jorjana at the house in Thousand Oaks for a few days, then took an apartment in Woodland Hills, a San Fernando Valley community that is part of Los Angeles. Roger and I soon determined that it took twenty minutes to travel between our two places. I did some magazine freelancing and drew an advance on my song royalties to keep going.

Then Roger came under consideration to write the score for a children's animated cartoon feature based on Russell Hoban's wonderful symbolic novel *The Mouse and his Child*, about a little mechanical mouse and his child exiled for ever from the toy store where we first encounter them. Roger proposed to the company, Murakami Wolf – an important animation house, working in television commercials – that it be a song score, with lyrics contributing to the narrative. He must have done quite a sales job on my behalf: the company's principals asked to meet me. We talked to them at their office in Hollywood and we got the job.

As elated as children, we got into his car, a gray Mercedes Benz sedan, and instead of taking the freeway we drove up to Mulholland Drive and followed it along the crest of the mountains, looking down at the Los Angeles basin on the left and the San Fernando Valley on the right. It was like flying, in every sense of the word.

We went to work on the score immediately. Roger wrote a main title theme and played it for me. I had grown very tired of composers' egos. I thought, 'This relationship is going to live or die in the next few seconds, because I'm going to tell him the truth.'

"It's excellent and it's wrong," I said.

"Why?" he said, a little defensively.

"This picture is about a child. And that's be-bop. It's too sophisticated."

Pause. "You're right," he said, and in the next half-hour wrote one of the most glorious melodies I have ever heard. To be sure, it was a three-two samba, but it *seemed* naïve and gentle and simple. I called it "Tell Me My Name," and wrote lyrics for both the main title and the closing credits. From that moment on, Roger and I would never hesitate to criticize each other's work.

Fred Wolf and Charles Swensen came out to Roger's house. We performed the song. I kept trying to see Fred Wolf's face, to divine whether he liked it or not. A husky, bearded, powerful, impressive man, Fred came from a family of New York policemen. He had even been a cop, but he hated the work and went back to his first love, art. At this time, however, I had no idea of his sensitivity. He kept turning away from me, and my heart sank: I thought he hated the song.

When it ended, he turned on me and said with attempted ferocity, "What the hell are you looking at?"

There were tears streaming down his face.

We went to work on the full score, with Roger composing in the studio and me sitting by the swimming pool, with a tape recorder, working on the lyrics. One scene in the film shows rat characters in a city dump, symbolizing hell, I suppose, listening to an old record on a wind-up phonograph. Roger wondered what kind of music we should use, since this was a "source cue". I suggested we listen to Bing Crosby and the Rhythm Boys with Paul Whiteman, which we did. Roger came up with a Dixieland tune, but I couldn't think of a lyric to suit it. He even came up with a title: "Skat Rat."

I stayed overnight. Just before I went to bed, Roger gave me a book of John Cage's prose. I found myself enjoying it, as odd as it was. I began thinking about Laurence Stern's *Tristram Shandy*, Lewis Carroll's *Jabberwocky*, and Joyce's *Finnegan's Wake*. I went to sleep, awoke in the night, and wrote a lyric that at first made sense. Then I began transposing syllables so that it didn't, yet seemed to. It had an odd, surreal, allusive effect. I left it on the kitchen table and went back to sleep. When I got up in the morning, Roger had already read it and was ecstatic about it.

And I knew I had made a step into freedom.

Roger and I loved working with Wolf and Swensen. We completed the songs, Roger orchestrated the score, and it was recorded with some superb musicians in the band, including Chuck Domanico on bass and Gene Cipriano on tenor. The film was completed and released, but never got the attention it deserved. You can get it on videotape in Europe.

The money from that score saved my life.

Roger and I wrote together through the rest of the 1970s. In 1977, he was signed to write the underscore for Barbra Streisand's *A Star Is Born*. As it progressed, he realized that for two source cues (music that comes from a source actually in the film, such as a radio or a juke box) he needed lyrics. They had to be rock songs. He asked me to do them and I did: both are satires on rock lyrics, but nobody noticed. For his work on that picture he received an Academy Award nomination.

But there were problems. Not that my own character is beyond reproach; hardly. But when he had been drinking (and we consumed huge quantities of Johnnie Walker's Black Label in those days) he could unpredictably turn angry, sarcastic and unpleasant, not just to me but to others as well. It seemed that whenever he began to feel free in a relationship, he would test it, to see whether the person could be easily alienated.

Then came a crisis, a step beyond that moment when I'd told him the main title was wrong. We'd been working on one project or another and went for a late lunch. We were sitting at an outdoor table in a cafe by a lake in bright sunlight. He was doing martinis, and began to turn hostile. I ignored it with a patience that is not normally an element of my nature, then fixed him with a stare and said, "Look, you can keep on testing all you want, *but you can't alienate me. I've heard your music and I know who you are.*"

Something changed in our relationship. Neither of us ever, after that, distrusted it, and we never turned back. And I watched Roger grow constantly more at ease with himself, happier, more open, and funny.

He got an assignment to write the score for a television movie called *Sharon: Portrait of a Mistress* for Paramount. Its cast included Trish Van Devere, Patrick O'Neil, and Sam Groom. Roger wanted to use lyrics in some sequences, and got approval. We wrote a main-title song called "The Days Have No Names," and, luxury of luxuries, got Sarah Vaughan for our vocalist. The band included Lew Tabackin, Shelly Manne, and Bob Brookmeyer, among others. The movie is numbingly banal, one of the worst pieces of soap opera ever put on film, and it still turns up on television. Avoid it if you can, unless you are willing to tolerate the corn to get to some good fragments of jazz in the underscore, including a remarkable performance by Sarah Vaughan.

By now I'd bought a house in Tarzana, a town absorbed into Los Angeles, whose terrain was once the ranch of novelist Edgar Rice Burroughs, who named it after the "jungle lord" who'd made him a millionaire. At the back of the property was a large separate building that I used as a studio.

Then, to my astonishment, Roger and Jorjana broke up. He asked if he could store his equipment, including his piano, in that studio. I agreed of course, and Roger and all his records and scores moved in. He occupied a small room off the garage when he was there, but much of the time during that period he lived in London, where he had taken a flat.

One day Chuck Domanico called to tell me that Edgar Lustgarten had died of a heart attack and asked if I knew where Roger was. At that moment, he was in London. I called him. Roger was having a party; there was laughter in the background. I told him about Ed.

"I remember that call," Roger said. "I was completely devastated by it."

It seemed the Cello Quartet was dead.

Roger lived in London for a year, staying at my house in Tarzana during his trips back to California.

We had good friends, a lot of them, including Thumbs Carllile. Thumbs was one of the greatest of all country-and-western guitarists. He played with the instrument resting flat across his lap, like a dobro, pressing down on it with his left hand and picking the notes with his right. His use of both thumbs in his playing was the reason for his nickname. He once retuned my guitar so that he could play it and when, later, I picked it up, I found that the open strings constituted a kind of E-flat major chord. Thumbs could play voicings available to no other guitarist. Furthermore, he was also a superb jazz musician, although he was always a little in awe of jazz. Still, it was strange to hear him in a country-and-western band, blowing out lines in the style of Charlie Parker. He played completely by ear and, like Wes Montgomery, couldn't read a note of music or explain to you what he was doing.

In 1980, my wife and I decided to move to Ojai. Roger returned from London and prepared to take a house in the Hollywood Hills area. By fortuitous coincidence, every neighbor on all four sides of that half-acre property, which was walled, was a jazz fan. We decided to throw the loudest party we could possibly arrange before leaving there, and invited all the neighbors. We prepared immense quantities of chile and rice and green salad and awaited the revellers.

Everyone came. As we had foreseen and indeed planned, a jam session broke out. There were a lot of pianists there, Mike Lang being one of them. Chuck Domanico played bass. Oscar Castro-Neves and Thumbs Carllile played guitar. John Guerin hadn't brought drums, but Thumbs' daughter Cathy had a set of student drums in the car, and we pressed them into service. Dick Nash, self-effacing as always and insisting that he wasn't really a jazz player, played some of the hottest jazz trombone anyone ever heard.

The party went on late into the night. As dawn broke, there were warm bodies sleeping on the carpet in the studio. And that period of our lives was over.

For a time Roger lived in a little house on the beach at Malibu. Then he and Jorjana reconciled and, eventually, moved to New York, where I'd see him whenever I was there.

Abruptly, in 1984, he quit drinking. Completely and permanently, and on his own.

Whenever I had to go to Los Angeles airport, I'd pass the little house in Malibu where we'd had some good times and written some good songs, and I would always feel a twinge.

Yet we continued to work together, by telephone when necessary.

It fell to me to tell Roger of the loss of yet another friend. Thumbs Carllile died, like Ed Lustgarten, of a heart attack: a unique musician and a great loss.

The respect in which Roger is held by jazz musicians can be perceived in a remark Cedar Walton made about him: "He can do with either hand what I can only do with one." Meaning, of course, the right hand. Since Cedar Walton is a formidable pianist, the compliment is not to be taken lightly.

Oscar Peterson esteems Kellaway just as highly. Kellaway's name came up in an interview I was doing with Oscar. He said, "I love Roger Kellaway!" Oscar is severe in his judgements of pianists, and so I said, "Why?"

Oscar gave a remarkably apt summation of Kellaway's playing: "He knows the tradition and he's not afraid."

At the time, they had never met. Knowing that Oscar had been one of Roger's early idols, I excerpted Oscar's comment and sent a taped copy to Roger, who was thrilled by it.

Kellaway's attitude to Peterson reveals much about his own playing, which is consistently, unfailingly powerful. And, like Oscar, he can swing at very slow tempos.

On 8 April 1984, Roger and I found ourselves in Milan. Oscar was to play a concert that night. I'd seen him earlier in the day and he'd asked me to bring Roger by the hotel to meet him. We were crossing the Piazza del Duomo, the magnificent paved square in front of the famous Milan cathedral when I asked Roger what it was about Oscar's playing that had appealed to him.

"It was the whole trio," he said. "It was the will to swing. It wasn't just Oscar. It was Oscar, Ray Brown, and Herb Ellis. I was listening to the *Stratford Shakespearean Festival* album the other day, and I got to reacquaint myself with an awesome trio and pianist. It certainly could have defeated me when I was young, because it was so brilliant. But it was the will to swing that I picked up from them, basically. I remember going into Storyville in Boston in the early 1950s to hear Oscar, with the intent of sitting in. And I never sat in. And that evening I did feel defeated."

Oscar, I pointed out, had been similarly intimidated the first time he heard Art Tatum.

"Understandably," Roger said. "I think Oscar comes as close as anybody could to Art Tatum. But I couldn't compare Art Tatum with anyone. Or Oscar either, for that matter. Oscar is his own person. The dexterity and the cleanliness of the sound are just impeccable, always. The will to swing. To get on the stand and pull it all together and have that kind of energy has always been to me the most astounding thing. One of the reasons I revere Oscar is that he plays the *piano*. He is a total musician. And in his relationship to the instrument, he plays what I call two-handed piano. All the things that differentiate the men from the boys. It's a mind-blower. He's absolutely complete as a pianist. It's a kind of tradition that I feel is my responsibility too, now.

"You know, the artist rarely has the opportunity to be acknowledged by one of his heroes, and that's already happened because of the tape you gave me, where he said, 'I love Roger Kellaway.' I still have it. That was a milestone in my life already. And now to meet him, at a hotel, and in Italy, to boot. It feels like life on the road."

We reached the hotel, I introduced him to Oscar, and that night we attended Oscar's concert. They have been friends ever since. And I used Roger's phrase as the title of my biography of Oscar: *The Will to Swing*.

A year after that, in 1985, Dizzy Gillespie took Roger on tour to Israel in a group that included Ray Brown, Mel Lewis, and Frank Foster.

"I was curious about being in Jerusalem," Roger said, "since you have three of the world's great religions there. It was interesting being with Mel Lewis, since he was Jewish, and I was developing an interest in the Jewish aspect of being there. It was the only time in my entire relationship with Mel that I actually hung out with him and let him tell me everything he had to tell me. Most of the time, when you started a conversation with him, you were kind of looking for the bailout point.

"I got back and a dancer friend of ours said, 'If you're interested in Judaism, read a book called *Studies in Prayer and Symbolism* by Abraham Heschel. And that's what did it for me. From there I started going toward the mysticism, and that's how I now spend every day of my life. There are some wonderful values that I appreciate.

"I wrote a piano trio dedicated to Jerusalem, of which the movement *David Street Blues* was orchestrated for the National Symphony Orchestra for the fortieth anniversary of Israel. David Amram conducted. It was a beautiful experience.

"One night, Dizzy started to give this incredible build-up to the audience, talking about a musician he wanted them to hear. It went on and on, and I began to look around to see who was in the wings. And it turned out to be for me. I couldn't believe it.

"I just loved working for Dizzy. I have found playing accompaniment to be rewarding: most of the time, that is!

"I've always been looking for whatever the lesson is in playing with everyone. Clark Terry is different than Bob Brookmeyer. I love to work with Eddie Daniels because he can do absolutely anything.

"Sonny Rollins is different from Gerry Mulligan. Working for Sonny Rollins was a wonderful time of my life.

"I was a big fan of Sonny's. I thought he in fact was *the* giant tenor player. It was never Coltrane for me. Even to this day, I am much more sympathetic with players who come out of Sonny than out of Coltrane. Most of the Coltrane devotees come out of the *My Favorite Things* aspect of his life. So many people who have adopted that way of playing have no sense of editing whatsoever, and they're such a bore to play for. Fortunately, being a pianist, I can lay out a lot of the time – just let them foam at the mouth for twenty or thirty minutes and then I can come back in. But I'd much rather play for somebody influenced by Sonny.

"I liked playing with Mulligan, Jimmy McPartland, Yank Lawson, Cliff Leeman. There are ways to play with people who play drums. Mel Lewis. There are just lessons you can learn by being a rhythm section player and being co-operative, looking for what the whole experience is.

"And I just loved working with Benny Carter. It was fabulous: it was like going to school. He's one of the most interesting musicians I've ever worked with. Out of all the players I've played with, he's in the top of the list. He's imaginative. He's never let his curiosity dwindle. It's absolutely fascinating, the lines he comes up with. Maybe it has to do with the fact that I'm only partially familiar with his upbringing, in terms of his coming up through the 1920s. All that staccato kind of stuff in the saxes in that period, and the way he weaves that into the phrases he plays, causes you to learn something different about music, because you can't comp for him in the same way. So in order to get the lesson, you have to go to a new space.

"All the great players do that to you. It's not only the notes that the person plays but the sound that they play with. You would not play the same way behind Ruby Braff that you would play for Clark Terry or Joe Newman. They're completely different styles, and *deserve* to be accompanied in a different way. And if you in fact look for the right way to accompany them, there's a lesson in how music goes together.

"The main thing for me is that I want music to win. When I criticize the way somebody plays now, it's not like the way I criticized someone twenty years ago in wanting to justify the fact that I knew more about music than they did, or at least that's what I assumed from the way they played or wrote. It's not a matter now of being right or wrong. It's a judgement on what the potential of music is and how far someone goes with it. If I feel that they have the potential to go farther and they don't even take the chance to try to do that, music loses: and that hurts me. It's a different kind of judging. And I'd like to remove judging completely."

I can testify to Roger's sympathy and flexibility as an accompanist, since I've sung with him a great deal. We spent most of the weekends of one pleasant summer singing and playing at the Montecito Inn in Montecito, a suburb of Santa Barbara. Roger had a nine-foot Yamaha at his disposal and the gig was thoroughly enjoyable. In the afternoons we could walk by the sea, and talk, usually about music. We did an evening at Green Street in New York, and a week at the Chateau Laurier in Ottawa. We recorded an album of our songs (plus two by Dave Frishberg) for Gerry Macdonald's Choice label. In the summer of 1999, we did a concert with l'Orchestre Populaire de Montréal, conducted by Marc Fortier.

Among the songs I sang was "Our Love Is Here to Stay." To do it in Montreal, where I once botched it, was important to me. A little thing, maybe. But had I not made a small error in that song, I might have joined Kenny Wheeler in England, and my life would have been completely different.

When Roger was a young bassist, his idol was Red Mitchell, the immensity of whose talent, the depth of whose intellect, and the length of whose shadow tend to be underchronicled in jazz. Since Scott LaFaro was one of his protégés, and LaFaro's influence is enormous, that alone qualifies him for a higher rank in the history books.

In the late 1980s, Roger began a close professional and personal association with Mitchell. It took him repeatedly to Scandinavia. They recorded eight CDs, five of them in Stockholm, where Red was living. They made an album in Norway with singer Magni Wentzel, and another in the United States with Helen Merrill. They played together in clubs, including Bradley's in New York. Their rapport was conspicuous and immense, for Red was a bassist who had been a pianist and Roger was a pianist who had been a bassist.

"For the last six years of his life," Roger said, "we were partners. I once told him, 'We should sound good together – you trained me.'

"I wish Red had played with the bow. I wish he had been more interested in experiment. But I was able to give him the space he demanded, and he gave me a lot in return, especially the bass tuned in fifths."

When Red died in October 1992, it came Roger's turn to call me and tell me about the death of one of our friends.

In 1990, Roger was assigned by WDR – West Deutsche Rundfunk, the major German broadcasting network – to write a show on the music of Kurt Weill.

WDR maintains three full-time orchestras, a magnificent jazz band many of whose members are Americans, a full symphony orchestra, and an orchestra devoted to what the British call light music. Knowing that I had made a fairly deep study of Weill in the process of writing a biography of Lerner and Loewe, Roger asked me on the phone for advice. Following some of my suggestions, he researched the music and wrote the score. The singer with whom he worked was Caterina Valente. They were to become good friends.

"You know," he said, "until I did that show in Cologne, and wrote for the WDR band, I never thought I was a big-band writer. But I sure did after that show. I loved that! And to study Kurt Weill's music. To do all that reviewing that you and I did, and talking about it. That was a high point of my life, just as the ballet for Ballanchine was a high point. The commission from the LA Philharmonic, the commission from the New York Philharmonic.

"If I were to think about what my goals really are, I certainly want to write a great symphonic piece of music. I'm trying to figure out what it is I want to do stylistically as a writer, because I've done so many different kinds of things. What I have to be wary of is not to write the way I think I *should* write. You can get intimidated by the European concept, which has affected a lot of American contemporary writers.

"There's such a sense of craft in the classical music world. If the craft isn't there, you're dismissed. I want to go in ten directions. I have no less a definition of myself than anyone else. It's just that I like to include the twentieth century's classical music along with Berio and George Crumb and the rest. George Crumb is probably the most imaginative of all the contemporary American composers. Crumb is fascinating. Imagination is one of the things that interest me. I admire the path someone takes that's simple. Let's say all they want to be is a great symphony composer: I want to be that too. But along with that I have to put out what it is I know about the piano, how much I love to play the piano, how much I love to improvise.

"It takes me back to the time when I used to listen to Erroll Garner and Oscar Peterson and identify them in a second. But I couldn't identify myself. That bothered me for maybe twenty years, until I realized there are just more spokes to the wheel, if you want to think of each person as a single soul that's metaphorically like a wheel. I choose to express myself in more different ways, so it's even harder for myself to identify myself. But I arrived at that point finally."

"I don't know," I said, "from day one, I found your playing identifiably distinctive."

"Yeah, well *you* did. *I* didn't. Being diversified has made my life extremely interesting, but difficult for people who are trying to market me, for they keep looking for the ultimate category I'm in, and I'm not in one. They're trying to put me into Urban Something, or New Age, or Jazz or Classical. They're trying to find the overall bin, because that's the way society is going: towards the compartmentalized mind. And it's not where I'm at. And if you want to talk esoterically about The Oneness, that's too abstract for the industry."

"André Previn suffered from it too," I said.

"One of the greats of music," Roger said. "And Leonard Bernstein too. My favorites. I've been a fan of André Previn since I was probably 13. But when he became the conductor, the composer, and all of this, I admired him even more, because he's done so many things."

In 1991, Roger was again commissioned to write a work for the WDR Big Band, as it's called. The producer, Wolfgang Hirschmann, wanted him to create a musical portrait of New York City, again utilizing Caterina Valente for at least part of it. Roger didn't want to assemble the usual songs about New York, and had asked Hirschmann to let me work on the project with him. Hirschmann had agreed.

Roger was trying to find a thematic approach to the piece. I suggested he think about the Doppler effect of one of the express trains of the New York subway when it roars through a local station. An imitation of that effect became the key motif of the music. Meanwhile, I wrote a long, very free poetic reflection on the nature of the city itself.

To find an idea, I peered, as writers usually do, into my own past. I remembered going out to Orly Airport in Paris. There on a bench, all alone, sat Erroll Garner. "Erroll!" I said, and his face lighted. He too was going home. We found we were on the same flight. We managed to get seats together and crossed the Atlantic in the night. In the pre-dawn darkness, we decided to share a cab into town. When the driver asked where he was going, he said, "Seventy-first and West End Avenue." I laughed. I was going to the same corner.

We got out of the cab at early light. Erroll lived in a glassy modern apartment building on the north side of 70th between West End and the West Side Highway. So did Roger Kellaway. Erroll and I shook hands and parted. I lit a cigarette and sat down on the stone steps of the brownstone in which I had a basement apartment and watched the day arrive, inhaling the smells of New York. I tried to capture that moment in the lyric. Roger and I called the song "New York Night." It takes a weary and realistic look at the city.

My poem, if that's what it is, was translated into German for the narrator, but Caterina sang "New York Night" in English. This work was performed in three concerts in Cologne and nearby cities in the summer of 1991, then recorded for broadcast on the WDR network. The band is superb; the drummer is Dennis Makrell.

Roger still couldn't get the Cello Quartet out of his mind.

"The next experience I had with that music was five years later in New York," he said. "I had a cellist come by my apartment and play the music

Edgar had played. I was still drinking in those days. I just got bombed after-wards.

"The next thing that happened was through Yo-Yo Ma, when I wrote 'Two Moods of Blues' for him for Stephane Grappelli's eightieth-birthday celebra-tion at Carnegie Hall. Something different happened with Yo-Yo because his sound is not close to Edgar's, it's a different way of playing. It was a different time for me, and I was more open to the experience perhaps and could look at the cello in a different way and reacquaint myself with my love of the instru-ment. So I started writing a bit for him. That takes me on to the formation of the new group with Fred Seykora."

Fred Seykora, a great cellist who had been a friend and professional asso-ciate of Edgar's, had often sat in the next chair to Ed's in the recording studios. He had substituted for Ed in the original Cello Quartet during Ed's periods of illness. Seykora has similar musical qualities, including a facility with jazz phrasing written for him, and a gorgeous tone.

When Angel Records approached Roger about doing an album for them, the group came back to life, now as a sextet, with Emil Richards on marimba, Joe Porcaro and Robert Zimmitty on percussion, and Fred Seykora on cello. It was issued under the title *Windows* and, as I have for a number of Roger's albums, I wrote the notes for it.

And then came another Kellaway surprise. Growing tired of the pressures in New York, he and Jorjana were considering moving permanently back to California, where she was born. They came up to Ojai to visit. They came back again, increasingly struck by the beauty and the quiet of the valley, with its surrounding protective mountains, eleven miles inland from the sea. And they announced that they'd decided to move here.

They found a house and moved in. After all these years, we now live about two miles apart, and I see him constantly, unless he is out of town or I am.

We were engaged to do a joint lecture at the Music Academy of the West in late July. The title I had given it was *First Cousins: Jazz and Classical Music*. We met for lunch at an outdoor restaurant whose balcony overlooks a golf course and the green mountains, to discuss it.

Roger said, "Jazz and classical music were once closer than they are now. There were improvisatory elements in it. I think classical musicians think more about aligning their improvisation to the composition than the jazz musician does. The jazz musician improvises more off the *feeling* of a tune. By and large it's been society that has told us that they're different. The people who define legitimacy and seriousness in such a tight way, in these little boxes, they don't have any variables to include something like jazz, which is improvisation and perhaps to them a completely out-of-control medium. How could you possibly be serious? You're improvising!"

I said, "Glenn Gould explained something to me once, something I had not understood before. He said that the reason for the clichéd nature of the continuo played by keyboard players in Bach is that Bach wrote figured bass for those things. He didn't fill the parts in because he was going to play them himself. He was like a jazz musician writing chord symbols, and he knew what he was going to do. Glenn said the clichés became fixed over time."

Roger said, "We know that the figured bass is the precursor to the lead sheet. But don't ever give *me* one! It's a state of mind to read a figured bass. I'd rather read A-minor seven flat five."

"John Mehegan tried to introduced figured bass into jazz and it didn't catch on."

"Too heavy."

"Yeah," I said, "but you know the Roman numeral chord names in all keys. You know what is the five chord of A-flat and the three chord of D-natural. All the guys do, except they may be a little hesitant in some of the sharp keys. So in that sense your mind does work in figured bass, without the inversions specified."

"Yes, that's true, and just a little more complicated than that, we had to learn the dominant of the dominant."

"Secondary dominants, I was taught to call them."

"Now that's classical," Roger said. "I learned that at the New England Conservatory. We're talking about a terminology that you learn in classical music that crosses over into jazz, where we can both talk about the same thing. Mehegan came up with a system that wouldn't permit that, and a lot of people rejected it because of that. Incidentally, the oddest phenomenon about this is that Nashville is the place that uses the Roman numerals. All the guitar players work by I, IV, V, VI, III. That way they're able to instantly transpose to anything."

"When you think of all the studio work we've been involved in, and you have A minor, and they ask you to put that up a minor third, some guys have to think about it a bit. Those guys in Nashville don't. They say, 'Okay,' and bang, they do it. I'm a big fan of a lot of those people. They've got transposition completely covered."

I said, "They're not adding sevenths in most cases either, unless you were Hank Garland or Jerry Reed. If you did, Thumbs Carllile said, they'd give you a funny what-the-hell-was-that look. Remember what Thumbs used to say about it?"

"No," Roger said.

"Well, he said their attitude was:
Don't play me no sevenths,
No ninths or elevenths,
Just let that E-chord ring!"

"That's lovely," Roger said. "Wow." And after a pause, during which, I daresay, he was thinking of our vanished friend, as I was, he said, "I realize that inherent in my terminology is that I find Nashville music simplistic. That's not so. The truth is I have a great deal of respect for it, and in fact, looking at the last twenty or so years of songwriting, and the abomination of craft reduced to nothing more than style and for the most part not even singing anymore, Nashville is one of the few places in the world that still produces songs. They actually have melody and lyrics."

"And sometimes very good ones," I said.

"So," Roger said, "I'm looking forward to doing something about that, not necessarily playing country music, but hanging out more with these people. They may be the last people left on the planet who know what a song is! So, where are we going? We have to go to Nashville. You and I have spent part of our life teaching people what songwriting is. But you'd like to hang out with some people who already know. And let's be clear about it, instead of abstract: a song is an entity with harmonic and melodic and lyric elements, and you can take them apart."

"If they're good."

"Each lives on its own. The music lives on its own, the lyric on its own. And when you put them together you have a wonderful marriage."

I said, "The lyric is less able to stand on its own than the music. A poet once said song lyrics, as opposed to poetry, are like water weeds. They have to be sustained by the music. That's generally, but not universally, true. Lots of Mercer's lyrics stand on their own. Howard Dietz's stuff. By the way, there's a terminology that's crept into jazz that I don't like. It's the misuse of the word 'song.' A song is a total unit of melody with words. An instrumental composition is not a song. It may be a tune, but it's not a song. That's why Mendelssohn called the piece *Songs Without Words*."

Roger said, "Everything's a song. I can't remember the last time somebody came up to me and said, 'I'm a songwriter,' and I wanted to hear what they wrote. I'm sorry, I don't mean to shut people off, but in most cases I'd have to go into a dissertation on: 'What do you think a song is in the first place?'"

"I don't blame you," I said. "When I meet people, I don't tell them I'm a songwriter. Because it seems like everybody is an aspiring songwriter. Elevator operators, dental assistants, cab drivers. If I say, 'I'm a songwriter,' they'll say, 'So am I! Would you look at some of my songs?' Or, worse yet, 'I just wrote one that would be perfect for Tony Bennett or Jack Jones or whomever. Would you show it to him for me?' And the answer is a fast, 'No!' So I just say I'm a journalist, and let it go at that. It avoids awkward situations."

Roger said, "I've had people write lyrics on things of mine and send them to me. Generally they pick some orchestral melody that's at least two octaves in range, but they love it, and they write a lyric, and it's very difficult to tell them it can't even be sung."

"Oh, I get the opposite," I said. "One musician brought me a tune, wanting lyrics, and I immediately looked at the range. It was a tone over two octaves. I said, 'Nobody can sing it, it's got too much range.'

And he immediately said, quite defensively, 'Sarah Vaughan could sing it!'"

"Or Yma Sumac!" Roger said. "And she isn't around anymore either."

"And sometimes," I said, "it isn't just a matter of range. It's the character of the melody. That thing I wrote with Bill Evans, 'Turn Out the Stars,' the range is only a tenth, but the character of the melody makes it difficult. I've heard some good singers come to grief on that song. It's a great piece for piano, but not for voice. What is a song? A short story set to music. To me, singing is composed partially of the actor's art and partially the musician's. And when singers dispense with the actor's art and want to be horn players with lyrics, they lose me.

"The only singer to me who has ever been able to alter melodies and intervals and if anything deepen the emotional effect of the lyric is Carmen McRae. She's astounding. You wrote an album for her that I liked a lot."

"I had a wonderful experience with Carmen," Roger said. "We got along."

I said, "You're one of the few people I've known who have worked consciously on their own evolution."

"I want to go faster," Roger said. "I want to know more. I want to be purer, I want to have purer thoughts. I want to totally understand that my reality is created by my thoughts. I want to project healthful things for humanity."

I said, "After we pass 50, we all know that the numbers are getting smaller. At 20, you can't even conceive of being 50 or 60, and life seems to stretch endlessly in front of you. Artie Shaw once said to me, 'Look, I can do the arithmetic as well as you can.'"

"Yes. As you know, in my current record company I'm dealing with somebody who's 28. I'm now the old guard."

I told him about an incident in my life. "On an afternoon in 1958, I was in Nadia Boulanger's apartment in Paris. She had some friends in and she was reminiscing about her career and talking about her age." Boulanger, who quit composing in 1918 after the death of her composer sister Lili, spent the rest of her life teaching. Her influence on American music is inestimable, since she taught so many American "classical" composers, including Roy Harris, Walter Piston, Roger Sessions, Aaron Copland, and Virgil Thompson, and since Leonard Bernstein studied under Piston, the influence is passed on through him. And since she also taught Darius Milhaud, and Milhaud taught Dave Brubeck, her influence was further extended in the United States. But she also taught American composers in jazz and other fields, such as film composition, including Allyn Ferguson.

Boulanger was in her early 70s when I met her, slim and beautiful even then. But she was feeling the weight of time. "And," I told Roger, "since she had opened the subject, I asked her how it felt, trying to foresee, to imagine, the experience of age."

"Well," she said, "it's very strange. I still feel like a young woman. I simply cannot understand how I got into this old body."

"And," Roger said, "we know exactly what she meant by that."

One of the things about music that astonishes me, I told Roger, is how long chops remain at a peak when other forms of neuromuscular decline have already begun. Vladimir Horowitz was playing well in his 90s, and Benny Carter, apparently impervious to time, is playing superbly into his 90s.

Roger said, "Getting older myself, I'm putting out this spiritual vibration that I want in my life, and I'm beginning to meet more people all the time who are of like mind, who are concerned about the planet, about humanity, who are interested in what one might call the wake-up call.

"The earth has supported the human race for a long, long time, and the information we get about catastrophe on this earth is nature telling us, 'Come on!' The planet needs to have more love and attention to it. It's our home, and we trash it. Living out here in nature, seeing the mountains all the time, I'm thrilled and thankful when I wake up and see the beauty of my back yard. I have a completely different relationship, a new respect for the earth.

"I have a lot to be thankful for."

I find it hard to picture Roger in high school with, as Dick Sudhalter said, a brush cut. When I met him he had a full head of dark hair and a beard. The hair still is dark but is progressing toward invisibility on top, and the beard, which he started in high school, has white in it.

Where is that sullen kid I met on that record date?

Gone. Long gone. I guess he was busy in those days, giving birth to himself.

One of Roger's loveliest solo piano albums is titled *Soaring*. I think that describes his whole life. And there is an exquisite album he did with his friend from long ago, Dick Sudhalter, on cornet. I am often fascinated by how many relationships in music go back to the high-school years.

One day early in 1999, Roger called. He said, "I'm going to England to write incidental music for a play. I'm thinking of recording a CD of the music with an all-star British group. I'd like to have Kenny Wheeler on it. Do you have his phone number?"

"Hang on," I said, "I'll get it for you."